From Modern to Contemporary

D0209343

James E. B. Breslin

From Modern to Contemporary

American Poetry, 1945–1965

The University of Chicago Press · Chicago and London

James E. B. Breslin is professor of English at the
University of California, Berkeley. He is the author of
William Carlos Williams: An American Artist.

The University of Chicago Press, Chicago 60637
The University of Chicago Press, Ltd., London

© 1983, 1984 by The University of Chicago
All rights reserved. Published 1984
Printed in the United States of America
93 92 91 90 89 88 87 86 85   5 4 3 2

Library of Congress Cataloging in Publication Data

Breslin, James E. B., 1935–
  From modern to contemporary.

  Includes index.
  1. American poetry—20th Century—History and
criticism. I. Title.
PS323.5.B7 1984   811'.54'09   83-17869
ISBN 0-226-07408-0

For Ramsay, Jennifer, and Susannah

CONTENTS

ACKNOWLEDGMENTS

I am indebted to the National Endowment for the Humanities and to the Regents of the University of California for generous grants that gave me the time I needed to work on this book. Thanks are also due to the editors of the *American Poetry Review* for permission to reprint sections of my Wright and O'Hara chapters which originally appeared in their journal.

Many friends and colleagues have contributed to this book, often in ways that neither they nor I were aware of. I continue to be grateful to J. C. Levenson, with whom I began my reading of American poetry. Marjorie Perloff and Michael Davidson read the completed manuscript and provided an ideal combination of encouragement, criticism, and constructive suggestion; thanks to them I added my conclusion. Frederick Crews, Robert Hass, Robert Pinsky, Carolyn Porter, and Alex Zwerdling read parts of the manuscript and offered substantive help. Two of my friends—Andrew Griffin and Michael Rogin—have, in addition to their detailed readings of my manuscript, given stimulation, support, and lots of specific suggestions. Most of all, I am grateful to my wife, Ramsay, for reading the manuscript, for listening to me talk about it, for her criticism, for her ideas, and for her support and love.

Permission to quote from the following sources is gratefully acknowledged.

Allen Ginsberg, *Empty Mirror*. Two untitled poems. © 1961 by Allen Ginsberg. Published by Totem Press/Corinth Books.

Denise Levertov, *O Taste and See*. Copyright © 1964 by Denise Levertov Goodman. Reprinted by permission of New Directions Publishing Corporation.

James Wright, *The Branch Will Not Break*. "Spring Images." Copyright © 1960 by James Wright. This poem first appeared in *The Sixties*. "Beginning." Copyright © 1963 by James Wright. "A Blessing." Copyright © 1961 by James Wright. This poem first appeared in *Poetry*. "Two Hangovers" (#2). Copyright © 1961 by James Wright. This poem first appeared in *The New York Times*. Reprinted from *The Branch Will Not Break* by permission of Wesleyan University Press.

Frank O'Hara, *The Collected Poems of Frank O'Hara*. "A Step Away from Them." Copyright © 1968 by Maureen Granville-Smith, Administratrix of the Estate of Frank O'Hara. "Why I Am Not a Painter." Copyright © 1958 by Maureen Granville-Smith, Administratrix of the Estate of Frank O'Hara. "Personal Poem." Copyright © 1960 by Maureen Granville-Smith, Administratrix of the Estate of Frank O'Hara. "Essay on Style." Copyright © 1961 by Maureen Granville-Smith, Administratrix of the Estate of Frank O'Hara. "Meditations in an Emergency." Copyright 1954 by Maureen Granville-Smith, Administratrix of the Estate of Frank O'Hara. "On Seeing Larry Rivers' *Washington Crossing the Delaware* at the Museum of Modern Art." Copyright © 1956 by Maureen Granville-Smith, Administratrix of the Estate of Frank O'Hara. Reprinted from *The Collected Poems of Frank O'Hara*, by permission of Alfred A. Knopf, Inc.

John Ashbery, *Self-Portrait in a Convex Mirror*. "A Man of Words." Copyright © 1972, 1973, 1974, 1975 by John Ashbery. Reprinted by permission of Viking Penguin, Inc.

Allen Ginsberg Papers, by permission of the Rare Book and Manuscript Library, Columbia University.

William Carlos Williams Papers, by permission of the Collection of American Literature, the Beinecke Rare Book and Manuscript Library, Yale University.

Robert Lowell Papers, by permission of Houghton Library, Harvard University, and the estate of Robert Lowell.

PREFACE

In 1959 I lived in a one-room apartment in southeast Minneapolis. Outside there was a low, black sky, 19° below zero temperatures, and snow that fell in October but did not melt until April. Across the street was a railroad yard, a grain elevator, and a feed mill which filled the brutally cold dry air with a stench exceeded only by that of Addie Bundren's rotting corpse. All night long railroad cars were coupled, uncoupled, recoupled, each time producing a jolt that reverberated slowly down the endless trains. On one side of me lived my landlady—seventyish, Methodist, mother of one Benjy and (inevitably) owner of a parakeet; once, just after the start of the hunting season, she offered me a "deerburger." On the other side of me lived a Turk, a graduate student who was probably the world's leading admirer of the music of John Philip Sousa and Minneapolis' leading seducer of young women: each night would end with the strutting rhythms of Sousa and lusty shrieks. Inside my apartment there were seven doors: two opened for a Murphy bed to descend, two more to reveal a kitchen, one led to a closet, another to a bathroom, and the last was (thank God!) out. There were two windows, which I was not permitted to open during the winter months, so that to take a deep breath of the heavy, almost solid air was to re-experience my last several meals.

In such a place as this—amid the railroad cars, the parakeet, the Turk, John Philip Sousa—I, a graduate student in English, slightly overserious, having been assigned to write a "thematic analysis" of a recent American poem, opened the pages of a two-year-old copy of the *Evergreen Review* and found the following poem:

A Step Away from Them

It's my lunch hour, so I go
for a walk among the hum-colored
cabs. First, down the sidewalk
where laborers feed their dirty
glistening torsos sandwiches
and Coca-Cola, with yellow helmets
on. They protect them from falling
bricks, I guess. Then onto the
avenue where skirts are flipping
above heels and blow up over
grates. The sun is hot, but the
cabs stir up the air. I look
at bargains in wristwatches. There
are cats playing in sawdust.

                          On
to Times Square, where the sign
blows smoke over my head, and higher
the waterfall pours lightly. A
Negro stands in a doorway with a
toothpick, languorously agitating.
A blond chorus girl clicks: he
smiles and rubs his chin. Everything
suddenly honks: it is 12:40 of
a Thursday.

                Neon in daylight is a
great pleasure, as Edwin Denby would
write, as are light bulbs in daylight.
I stop for a cheeseburger at JULIET'S
CORNER. Giulietta Masina, wife of
Frederico Fellini, *e bell' attrice*.
And chocolate malted. A lady in
foxes on such a day puts her poodle
in a cab.

             There are several Puerto
Ricans on the avenue today, which
makes it beautiful and warm. First
Bunny died, then John Latouche,
then Jackson Pollock. But is the
earth as full as life was full, of them?
And one has eaten and one walks,
past the magazines with nudes

and the posters for BULLFIGHT and
the Manhattan Storage Warehouse,
which they'll soon tear down. I
used to think they had the Armory
Show there.

        A glass of papaya juice
and back to work. My heart is in my
pocket, it is Poems by Pierre Reverdy.

I wish I could say that all seven doors suddenly flung open. But they did not. In fact, I immediately dismissed the poem as a bit of charming triviality—and turned to the weightier pages of Robert Lowell's *Lord Weary's Castle*. And why not? After all, mythical resonance, literary allusion, paradox, irony, tension, buried metaphoric systems, authorial distancing—all the certain certainties of critical discourse in the fifties—were missing. And what was worse, the absence of any meter, rhyme or any obvious assonance or alliteration left "A Step Away from Them" without most of the features that conventionally mark a piece of writing as a poem; the only such marker that remained, the breaking of the writing into lines of verse, struck me as purely arbitrary. All of this, plus the poem's way of proceeding as an indiscriminate catalog of mundane thoughts and observations, convinced me that the primary selecting, controlling, formalizing characteristics of art had been airily dispensed with. It was not that "A Step Away from Them" was a *bad* poem; it was *no* poem.

When O'Hara strolled out of the Museum of Modern Art that noon, he had also, it seemed, stepped outside of Literature. In retrospect, however, we can see that in the fifties the only way to renovate literature was by annihilating it—the prototypical avant-garde gesture. This book began, really, with the fact that O'Hara's poem stuck in my mind; it *was* a poem; and in what follows I try to come to terms with O'Hara's generation, with the constricted set of expectations that dictated their audience's and their own early sense of what could count as valuable in poetry (or even count as poetry at all), and with their individual and collective challenges to those expectations.

The history of American poetry forms not a "continuity," as Roy Harvey Pearce has argued, but a series of discontinuities, eruptions of creative energy that suddenly alienate poetry from what had come to seem its essential and permanent nature.[1] One of these surges of activity—the subject of this book—occurred in the late 1950s, announced most dramatically by Ginsberg's "Howl" (1956), Robert Lowell's *Life Studies* (1959), and Donald Allen's *The New American Poetry* (1960). In these years the paradigms for poetry were transformed in ways that affected and still affect a whole generation of American poets. If now, some twenty years later, the insurgents of 1960 are comfortably occupying the literary armchairs and if their poetic procedures are beginning to look a little too easy, stiff, and predictable to younger poets, then the time may be right to go back and take an historical look at this originating moment in contemporary poetry. My own belief is that this moment saw the emergence of an antiformalist revolt which can best be understood by an historically informed formalist criticism—that is, one concerned with the changing theories and practices of poetic form.

In the ten years following the Second World War, literary modernism, like an aging evangelical religion, had rigidified into orthodoxy. In fact, with the publication of the widely used second edition of *Understanding Poetry* (1950), modernism had been codified into a textbook. The most conspicuous feature of the writing produced by younger poets—Robert Lowell, James Merrill, W. S. Merwin, Richard Wilbur, for instance—was their revival of the very traditional forms that modernist poets had sought to dismantle; the predominant mode became the well-made symbolist poem. Yet in the modern era, the very existence of an identifiable mode, much less its perfection, is self-discrediting, so that during the fifties the predominant mode came increasingly to feel limited, excluding, impoverished. Robert Lowell, among many others, perceived a literary crisis.

> Poets of my generation and particularly younger ones have gotten terribly proficient at these [set] forms. They write a very musical, difficult poem with tremendous skill, perhaps there's never been such skill. Yet the writing seems divorced from culture somehow. It's become too much something specialized that can't handle much experience. It's become a craft, purely a craft, and there must be some breakthrough back into life.[2]

1. All of its major historians agree that American poetry forms a continuity, though that appears to be one of their few points of agreement. In *The Continuity of American Poetry* (Princeton, 1961), Pearce locates it in the dialectical relation between "Adamic" and "mythic" poets, while in his *American Poets: From the Puritans to the Present* (Boston, 1968), Hyatt Waggoner finds it in the persistent influence of Emerson, as does Harold Bloom in *A Map of Misreading* (New York, 1975), pp. 160–206. Bernard Duffey's *Poetry in America: Expression and Its Values in the Times of Bryant, Whitman, and Pound* (Durham, 1978) appears to stress historical *dis*continuity, but for an argument against this claim see my review of the book in *Georgia Review* 33 (Spring 1979): 227–30.

2. "The Art of Poetry: Robert Lowell," in *Robert Lowell: A Collection of Critical Essays,* ed. Thomas Parkinson (Englewood Cliffs, 1968), p. 19.

At this moment of crisis, poetry once again became disruptive—critical of its culture, of its immediate past, of itself; by way of repudiating orthodox modernism, American poetry once again became modern, "of the present."

The 1950s, then, were by no means a static, homogeneous "period"— the clichéd "tranquilized fifties"—that informs the mythologizings of a book like Morris Dickstein's *Gates of Eden*.[3] If the decade experienced what Allen Ginsberg called "the syndrome of shutdown," it also included Ginsberg's eloquent resistance in "Howl."[4] During this time, in fact, the Beat poets, the Confessional poets, the Black Mountain, New York, and Deep Image groups proposed a range of alternatives to the established mode, and they provided the leading sources of the new paradigms for poetry that became visible in the late fifties and early sixties. These clusters of poets differed from each other in fundamental ways and in some instances were mutually antagonistic; but they agreed in their renunciation of the well-made symbolist poem and in their search for poetic forms that could capture temporal immediacy, for the language of a "breakthrough back into life."

My study of this radical transformation of poetic theory and practice begins with two chapters that set an historical context for contemporary poetry. In "The End of the Line" I view the younger poets of the fifties in their uneasy relations with the two poetic generations preceding them, especially with the powerful presences of the still-living modernists. "The New Rear Guard" examines more specifically the traditionalist poetics of the fifties, while "The Opening of the Field" unfolds both the possibilities and the problems entailed by the counterpoetics, especially as it was articulated by Olson. In subsequent chapters I select one figure from each of the major clusters of poets that emerged in the late fifties: Ginsberg from the Beats, Lowell from the Confessional poets, Levertov from the Black Mountain group, Wright from the Deep Image, and O'Hara from the New York school. Since both these particular selections and the principles behind them are likely to be questioned by many of my readers, I want to justify them as fully as possible. In the first place I decided that, while I wanted to argue an historical thesis, I would not try to demonstrate it by a broad survey. Admittedly, my more selective method has disadvantages; it rules out from the start certain writers—Ammons, Dickey, Kinnell, Merwin—not closely connected with the movements I am concentrating on, and it has kept me from writing about some poets—Ashbery, Duncan, Plath, the later Rich—whose work I admire. Choosing to end in 1965 has also excluded two crucial events in contemporary poetry—the

3. *The Gates of Eden* (New York, 1977).
4. Quoted in Jane Kramer, *Allen Ginsberg in America* (New York, 1970), p. 119.

war in Vietnam and the feminist movement—from consideration. But comprehensive coverage is obviously an illusion in any period, the more so in contemporary poetry, with the field rapidly expanding even as the critic tries to map it; and the danger of breadth is superficiality. Instead, I have aimed at particularity and depth by detailed study of a relatively few figures, while also suggesting the variety and scope in contemporary poetry by choosing poets to represent the five major innovating movements of the late fifties. In further deciding, say, which Black Mountain or New York poet to write about, I have allowed the absence of any stable canon in contemporary poetry to free me to follow my own preferences. At the same time I do not think my selections are crankish or idiosyncratic; Ginsberg, Lowell, Levertov, Wright, and O'Hara are all standard figures in the anthologies of contemporary poetry, and my experience in writing my last five chapters has been that these poets have rewarded the attention I have given them. By following these principles I have attempted to write a literary history that would be literary, historical, and a testament to some personal enthusiasms.

ONE

The End of the Line

Immediately after Eliot and Pound, and Hart Crane and Stevens and William Carlos Williams, to mention only a handful, it was difficult to be taken seriously as a new American poet. For the title to the new poetry was in possession of a dynasty of extraordinary gifts and powers, not the least of which was its stubborn capacity for survival. These poets would never consent to die. It is amazing—their longevity.[1]
—Stanley Kunitz

I think it was rather an advantage not having any living poets in England or America in whom one took any particular interest. I don't know what it would be like but I think it would be a rather troublesome distraction to have such a lot of dominating presences, as you call them, about. Fortunately we weren't bothered by each other.[2]
—T. S. Eliot

When the third generation of twentieth-century American poets—writers such as Allen Ginsberg, Robert Creeley, Gary Snyder, W. S. Merwin, Robert Bly, Adrienne Rich, Louis Simpson—began to write in the 1950s, they were faced with a dilemma which the first generation of modern poets had not had to confront.[3] The problem for the new generation was, in fact, the existence of the first, their perverse refusal (in any sense) to die. In an essay weighing Pound's early impact on him, Eliot declared that when he tried to recall the literary scene in America in the early 1900s, his mind became "a complete blank."[4] Denied the support of any vital tradition, modern poets were thrust, often unwillingly, into rebellion, even if it was often one made in the name of tradition. But when a young contemporary writer recalls, say, the ten years between the end of the Second World War and the mid-fifties, he or she is much more apt to

1. "An Evening with Ted Roethke," *Michigan Quarterly Review* 6 (Fall 1967): 234.
2. Donald Hall, "The Art of Poetry I: T. S. Eliot," *Paris Review* 21 (1962): 50.
3. As someone who has sat before a long list of twentieth-century poets and their birth-dates, I am well aware of the arbitrariness of the conception of poetic generations. Yet such fictions seem to me to have real value, especially when (as here) they accord with the self-conscious awareness of the writers under discussion. For consistency, I have placed anyone born before 1900 in the first generation, those born between 1900 and 1920 in the second, and those born after 1920 in the third.
4. T. S. Eliot, "Ezra Pound," in *Ezra Pound: A Collection of Critical Essays*, ed. Walter Sutton (Englewood Cliffs, 1963), p. 17. The essay originally appeared in *Poetry* 68 (September 1946): 326–38.

imagine a crowded and stultifying space, one filled with the most suffo-
cating presences of all—canonized revolutionaries.[5]

For Paul Carroll, poet, critic, editor of *Big Table,* the literary scene of
the postwar period was hemmed in by the remote "dominating presences"
of early modernism.

> To a young poet the scene in American verse in the late 1940s and
> early 1950s seemed much like walking down 59th Street in New York
> for the first time. Elegant and sturdy hotels and apartment buildings
> stand in the enveloping dusk, mysterious in their power, sophistica-
> tion, wealth and inaccessibility. One of the most magnificent houses
> Eliot, his heirs and their sons; other tall, graceful buildings contain
> e.e. cummings, Marianne Moore, Ezra Pound, Wallace Stevens, Wil-
> liam Carlos Williams.[6]

To Richard Howard, these poets seemed more than an intimidating landscape; they were actively threatening, comparable to "certain enormous
creatures like dinosaurs that crawl around on the earth's surface": "you
try to keep out of their way."[7] Perhaps Carroll and Howard were only
discovering the limitations of their own talents; but even a major figure
such as Robert Lowell recalls asking, "Were we the uncomfortable epigoni
of Frost, Pound, Eliot, Marianne Moore, etc? This bitter possibility came
to us at the moment of our *arrival.*"[8] And a very different poet from
Lowell, James Dickey, confesses that he "never had great hopes for the
poets of [his] time," anticipating they would create "a kind of Georgian
era that would be annihilated by some new revolution of the word, much
as Pound and Eliot blew the literary world apart around 1912."[9]

The moderns were haunting figures, at once inaccessibly distant and
omnipresent; and they had preempted the revolutionary possibilities of
their successors. "When I was a young poet in the 1940's I felt chronologically deprived, and so did my friends," Hayden Carruth recalls.

> We had been born too late, that was our trouble. The great epoch of
> "modern poetry" was in the past; its works, which we desperately
> admired, *The Waste Land, Lustra, Harmonium, Spring and All* and

---

5. My argument in this essay is, of course, indebted both to Harold Bloom's *The Anxiety
of Influence* (New York, 1973) and Walter Jackson Bate's *The Burden of the Past and the
English Poet* (New York, 1972). Of the two I find Professor Bate's assumptions the more
congenial. Bloom's categories, as provocative as they are, are universal and *ahistorical,*
while Bate holds that the feeling that there is nothing left to do "can become more acute
under some conditions than others" (p. 4); it seems to me to have become especially acute
in the poetry written in America in the ten years after the Second World War.

6. *The Poem in Its Skin* (Chicago and New York, 1968), p. 204.

7. "Made Things: An Interview with Richard Howard," *Ohio Review* 16 (Fall 1974): 44.

8. *New York Review of Books,* 6 March 1972, p. 3.

9. *The Suspect in Poetry* (Madison, Minn., 1964), p. 65.

so many others, had been written long ago and had exhausted the poetic impulse. Nothing was left for us to do.[10]

Carroll agrees: "All of the major poetic discoveries and innovations had been accomplished—or so it seemed."[11] In fact, as early as 1942, Randall Jarrell had plaintively asked: "How can poems be written that are more violent, more disorganized, more obscure, more—supply your own adjective—than those that have already been written?"

The answer, Jarrell proposed, was that they can't: "Modernism As We Know It—the most successful and influential body of poetry of this century—is dead."[12] Yet it has been amazing—its longevity. Jarrell's is one of the first of many announcements of the end of modernism, but like the rest it has the air of a wish for its passing rather than of a lament for what has already gone. "To the artists of my generation," W. D. Snodgrass wrote some thirty-five years after the Jarrell essay,

> that originally revolutionary movement had become something fixed, domineering and oppressive. We had come to have a tradition of academic experiment, experiments using thoroughly predictable materials and reaching thoroughly predictable answers.[13]

But even to Snodgrass, the accomplishments of the first generation still seemed "definitive." Like some character invented by Beckett, modernism might become enervated, its limbs might stiffen, or even fall off, yet no one could say for sure whether it was dead or alive.

Moreover, if the "dominating presences" and "definitive" works of the early modern poets created one set of problems, another set derived from the apparent defeat—the absence—of the middle generation of poets, including such figures as John Berryman, Elizabeth Bishop, Randall Jarrell, Stanley Kunitz, Charles Olson, Theodore Roethke, Muriel Rukeyser, Delmore Schwartz, Karl Shapiro, and Louis Zukofsky. In Delmore Schwartz's *Shenandoah,* the main character, with his childhood self in his arms, invokes the presences of Eliot, Pound, and Yeats, "the great men" "who will obsess this child when he can read";[14] the scene is archetypal for members of the middle generation, who seem to have been born listening to the voices of their immediate predecessors and later became obsessed with the ideals of achievement and success that these

10. "Foreword," *The Voice That Is Great within Us: American Poetry of the Twentieth Century* (New York, 1970), p. xix.

11. *The Poem in Its Skin,* p. 206.

12. "The End of the Line," in *Literary Opinion in America,* ed. Morton D. Zabel (New York, 1951), p. 747. This essay originally appeared in *The Nation,* 21 February 1942, pp. 222–28.

13. "A Poem's Becoming," *In Radical Pursuit* (New York, 1975), p. 47.

14. *Shenandoah* (Norfolk, Conn., 1941), p. 20.

great men set for them. Certain of these poets—Bishop, Kunitz, Rukeyser, and Zukofsky—worked steadily and independently, but the cost was isolation and critical neglect. Others made a more direct assault on the status accorded their predecessors. Schwartz, Jarrell, Shapiro, Berryman all started quickly, establishing themselves as brilliant young critics and poets at an age when many of the first generation were still awaiting their first publication. In many ways, their position seemed chronologically advantaged—with an audience already created for their work as well as prestigious literary journals to convey their work to that audience. When Schwartz published his first book, *In Dreams Begin Responsibilities* (1939), it was widely acclaimed; the title story had already appeared as the first item in the first issue of *Partisan Review* that also contained Wallace Stevens, Pablo Picasso, Edmund Wilson, Lionel Trilling, James Agee. The story "almost overnight" earned Schwartz "a reputation for precocious brilliance."[15] In 1940 he published a translation of Rimbaud's *A Season in Hell;* in 1941 he did a verse play, *Shenandoah,* and in 1942 a long poem, *Genesis, Book I.* Meanwhile, in 1940 he began to teach at Harvard, and he soon became an editor, later an associate editor, for *Partisan Review.* "Everyone said that Delmore Schwartz was brilliant," Louis Simpson recalls, "and he was praised by T. S. Eliot, which was like being canonized by an archbishop."[16] During the forties Schwartz was mythologized into the best mind of his generation, a legend perpetuated by Bellow's recent novel *Humboldt's Gift,* and even in the fifties, when his literary achievements seemed less than his reputation, he was still celebrated for his incandescent presence and brilliant conversation. Dwight MacDonald has said that if Schwartz "were English he would have been knighted for his conversation."[17] When Schwartz died in 1966, however, he was living in a seedy hotel near Times Square, believed that he was being pursued by the Rockefellers, who were damaging his brain with rays sent out from the Empire State Building, and had alienated himself from practically all of his former friends and admirers. Such disasters are ultimately personal, but the frequency of such events in this generation suggests that historical pressures worked to exacerbate private conflicts. As early as 1948, John Berryman, surveying the work of this "middle generation," concluded that "it has gone to pieces"—a statement that seems even truer now, given the high incidence of alcoholism, mental breakdown, and suicide among its members.[18]

15. According to Donald A. Dike and David H. Zucker, eds., *Selected Essays of Delmore Schwartz* (Chicago, 1970), p. ix.

16. "The Ghost of Delmore Schwartz," *New York Times Magazine,* 7 December 1975, p. 38. Archbishops, of course, don't have the power to canonize.

17. "Delmore Schwartz, 1913–1966," in *Selected Essays of Delmore Schwartz,* p. xv.

18. "Waiting for the End, Boys," *PR* 15 (February 1948): 256.

For this was the generation of poets who, as Kunitz put it, were "born in the shadow of the great names" of modernism.[19] "A poet is judged, in part, by the influences he resists," Roethke wrote in a notebook, a truth that came with particular urgency to his generation, which often seemed to others and to itself to be overshadowed by those awesome presences that came just before them, figures one might yield to or strive to defy, but whose achievement and fame it became imperative to equal.[20] "When we look back at the generation that began to publish around the time of World War II, we see that they had no sense of community, only an image of fame," Louis Simpson observed.[21] It was an image to which many felt called, but few were chosen. Karl Shapiro's jaunty, ironic, formal representations of American middle-class life in *Person, Place and Thing* (1942) and *V-Letter* (1944) reveal a strong debt to Auden and won Shapiro a Pulitzer Prize in 1945 at the age of thirty-two. To his credit, Shapiro decided to strike out on his own, but the only route he found was to make a career out of polemic attacks on the very poets who had most influenced his early verse. Even the titles of his later books—*In Defense of Ignorance* (1960) and *The Bourgeois Poet* (1964)—reveal the only way Shapiro can identify himself: in opposition to the alienated cosmopolitanism of modernist poetry.

A very different poet, Charles Olson, impressed many young writers in the early fifties as perhaps *the* second-generation poet that had successfully broken with the first. As we shall see, Olson was an important catalyst, but his own relation to his predecessors remained highly ambivalent, and it can be questioned whether Olson ever did establish an independent literary identity, though he certainly established a following. Referring to his own worries about resisting the influence of the early moderns, Olson wrote in a 1948 notebook of "the pathetic struggle to keep my own ego above their water."[22] A few years before, Olson had published a commentary on the Pound trial in the form of an imaginary address by W. B. Yeats. Olson has Yeats conclude the piece by warning younger poets away from "passive" acceptance of his own generation: "It is the use, the use you make of us" that is the key question, Yeats declares.[23] Like Shapiro, Olson correctly saw the problem but proposed a different solution, no less problematical. At first, Olson's strategy—one to be em-

19. Michael Ryan, "An Interview with Stanley Kunitz," *Iowa Review* 5 (Spring 1974): 83.

20. *Straw for the Fire: From the Notebooks of Theodore Roethke, 1943–63*, ed. David Wagoner (Garden City, 1972), p. 176.

21. "Ghost of Delmore Schwartz," p. 41.

22. Quoted in Introduction to *Charles Olson & Ezra Pound: An Encounter at St. Elizabeth's*, by Charles Olson, ed. Catherine Seelye (New York, 1975), p. xxiv.

23. "This is Yeats Speaking," in *Charles Olson & Ezra Pound*, p. 30.

ployed by many poets of the third generation—was to identify with neglected figures like Williams and (especially) Pound, then to deploy their views in an attack on their more established contemporaries. "The word / is image, and the reverent reverse is / Eliot // Pound / is verse," Olson wrote in "ABCs."[24] Pound is the "one / true / immediate / predecessor."[25] It is not surprising, therefore, that Olson became an early and frequent visitor of Pound at St. Elizabeth's Hospital. Often Olson found the older poet gracious, civilized, penetrating, "his eyes no longer hooded with hate," but eager and animated, sometimes touchingly shy.[26] Olson, an ardent New Dealer, was eager to steer their talk away from political matters that would confront him with Pound's less gracious side. But on one visit Olson was told that the virulent right-wing journalist Westbrook Pegler was one of the "best minds" around "and with that, for the first time, the full shock of what a fascist s.o.b. Pound is caught up with me."[27] Nevertheless, Olson, reluctant to resist the influence of Pound, continued the visits for two and a half years, beginning in January of 1945. In 1948, however, just before he terminated the visits, he asserted in a notebook that "I would rather be less than I dream myself to be & to be myself than any longer strive to be something each of these men [Eliot, Yeats, Pound] would admire."[28] Subsequently, Olson made public gestures at repudiating Pound, gestures that sometimes ended up by implicating him even further. "I, Mencius, Pupil of the Master" attacks the rhymed, ballad stanza of Pound's translations of Confucius. "That the Master / should now be embraced by the demon / he drove off," Olson laments, and resolves "We'll to these woods / no more, where we were used / to get so much."[29] Yet, as Donald Davie has acutely observed, this poem rejects the Pound of the *Confucian Odes* in a style that is derived from the *Cantos*.[30] "Write as the fathers to be the father," Olson directed himself in a 1945 notebook.[31] It was a dream of himself he found hard to give up, even when he was consciously striving to topple the father.

"In any quest for identity today—or any day," Theodore Roethke believed, "we run up inevitably against this problem: both the literal or blood, and the spiritual ancestors. Both, as we know, can overwhelm us. The devouring mother, the furious papa. And if we're trying to write, the

24. *The Distances* (New York, 1960), p. 13.
25. Ibid., p. 28.
26. *Charles Olson & Ezra Pound*, p. 36.
27. Ibid., p. 43.
28. Ibid., p. xxiv.
29. *Distances*, p. 63.
30. *Ezra Pound: Poet as Sculptor* (New York, 1964), p. 251.
31. *Charles Olson & Ezra Pound*, p. xvii.

Supreme Masters.''[32] Roethke himself provides a striking instance of a middle generation poet who resisted the pull of the ''Supreme Masters'' preceding him—but only for a short time. In fact, his development, moving from skillful imitations to original experiment to participation in the New Formalism of the early fifties, reenacts the history of a half-century of American poetry. A slow starter, Roethke did not publish a book until he was thirty-three, and while the title poem of that book, *Open House* (1941), proclaims ''My heart keeps open house,'' the poems guardedly imitate such fashionable models as Auden, Donne, Marvell, and Emily Dickinson in a language tersely fitted to strict, rhymed forms.[33] ''You dread / The menace of ancestral eyes,'' Roethke wrote in ''Feud''; but ''this ancient feud / Is seldom won. The spirit starves / Until the dead have been subdued.''[34] But with the freer, autobiographical and more truly open poems of the ''Lost Son'' sequence, Roethke, not so much triumphing in his battle with the dead as transcending it, broke through to a more energetic language, one uniquely his own:

> Where do the roots go?
>   Look down under the leaves.
> Who put the moss there?
>   These stones have been here too long.
> Who stunned the dirt into noise?
>   Ask the mole, he knows.
> I feel the slime of a wet nest.
>   Beware Mother Mildew.
> Nibble again, fish nerves.[35]

''The coarse short-hand of the subliminal depths,'' Roethke called this style,[36] and with it he sought to make poems that would have ''the shape of the psyche itself.''[37] Yet Roethke aptly described these poems as ''a kind of tensed-up'' version of *The Prelude,* a *Prelude* without the discursive sections—suggesting that Roethke had trouble launching any poetic project without some model in front of him.[38] Moreover, he found it hard not to view his own literary achievements as weapons in a war against his immediate predecessors—which is perhaps why he worked most successfully when his model was an historically distant one, like Wordsworth,

---

32. ''On 'Identity,' '' in *On the Poet and His Craft: Selected Prose of Theodore Roethke,* ed. Ralph J. Mills, Jr. (Seattle, 1965), p. 23.
33. *The Collected Poems of Theodore Roethke* (Garden City, 1975), p. 23.
34. Ibid., p. 4.
35. Ibid., p. 52.
36. ''Meditations of an Old Woman,'' *Collected Poems of Theodore Roethke,* p. 164.
37. *Straw for the Fire,* p. 178.
38. *Selected Letters of Theodore Roethke,* ed. Ralph J. Mills, Jr. (Seattle, 1968), p. 148.

Blake, or Whitman. As he was making a selection from his own work for John Ciardi's *Mid-Century American Poetry,* he wrote Ciardi that he had become excited with the possibility that the anthology of younger poets "will do something, as you say, for this generation of poets. The boys of the '20's have taken too many bows."[39] Just a few months earlier in 1949 he was even more grandiose in his ambitions and more direct in expressing his feelings of rivalry toward that writer of the twenties that he liked to refer to in his letters as "Tiresome Tom, the Cautious Cardinal."[40] "I think I've got hold of a really big theme," he told Kenneth Burke, whom Roethke addressed as "pa":

> it's got everything, involves just about every neurosis, obsession, fundamental itch or what have you. I wish I could sit down and talk to you a little about it. It may take me five years or longer; but when I get done, Eliot will be nothing: a mere *littérateur.* He ain't much more, anyway.[41]

But by the middle fifties Roethke, though no candidate for cardinal, was clearly getting cautious. The "Lost Son" poems, he wrote in a note-book, "came out of a special and terrifying experience" of mental break-down. "I took chances on my life to write them, and I was a fool for doing so."[42] In his new love poems, his "Four for Sir John Davies" and "The Dying Man" sequence, Roethke, embarking on what W. D. Snod-grass called a "flight from his own experimental drive,"[43] returned to strict forms, elegant language and conscious imitation, notably of Yeats: "I take this cadence from a man named Yeats."[44] Even in his most im-pressive later work, "Meditations of an Old Woman" and "North Amer-ican Sequence," Roethke often seems to be repeating himself—and others; in particular the presence of the Eliot of the *Four Quartets,* sometimes ironically echoed, sometimes imitated, always seems to be hovering over the writer's shoulder. All of this means not that Roethke's feelings of rivalry with the established moderns had been resolved, but only that they had taken a different (and for him less productive) form. In an essay called "How to Write Like Somebody Else" (1959), Roethke is undoubt-edly speaking autobiographically when he remarks that when a young poet

39. Ibid., p. 159.
40. Ibid., p. 154.
41. Ibid., p. 150.
42. *Straw for the Fire,* p. 229.
43. " 'That Anguish of Concreteness'—Theodore Roethke's Career," in *Theodore Roethke: Essays on the Poetry,* ed. Arnold Stein (Seattle, 1965), p. 78.
44. "Four for Sir John Davies," *Collected Poems of Theodore Roethke,* p. 101.

takes pen in hand the great models of the past may seem far away
and even absurd, and the big names of his own time awesome, overwhelming. Particularly if he is a provincial far from a good library, or
from any practicing poet, the immediately preceding literary generation, or the more precocious around his own age—and not always
the best of these—may exercise a powerful attraction.[45]

Roethke confesses to his own imitations and defends them with the reasonable argument that poets should not be so uncertain of their individuality that they refuse to submit themselves to the discipline of another
writer's language. The essay makes someone like Shapiro or Olson seem
a little too nervously insistent in the determination to "be himself." Yet
imitation could not finally be a disinterested, neutral act for Roethke, or
any member of his generation: "true 'imitation' takes a certain courage,"
Roethke insists. "One dares to stand up to a great style, to compete with
papa," as if the energies and resources of the master could somehow be
appropriated and turned against him—hardly a stance of self-reliant independence.[46] In fact, it seems more likely that the later Roethke sought,
by invoking the styles of established masters, to participate in their
greatness.

The all-too-living figures of the first generation did obsess the members
of the second, whose dilemma can be summed up in some lines from a
late poem by Berryman: "I didn't want my next poem to be *exactly* like
Yeats / or exactly like Auden / since in that case where the hell was *I*? /
but what instead *did* I want it to sound like?"[47] The poets of this middle
generation seemed to have been haunted alternately by grandiose expectations and by the fear that in the end they were mere epigoni. Critics
have been as affected by both the high expectations and the doubts as
the poets themselves, and the result has been that the real achievements
of these poets have often been underestimated. Nevertheless, in the fifties
young poets felt a special sense of generational discontinuity. If a member
of the third generation looked up, nobody was there—except the awesome, now idealized poets of the first generation. Eventually, this gap
helped to create a space in which many poets could work more freely,
on their own, but at first it was perceived as another piece of chronological
deprivation. When Louis Simpson published his first book, *The Arrivestes,*
in 1949, poets like Schwartz and Shapiro "were imitating their elders and
had no theories about what they were doing." Consequently, Simpson
complains, "those who came after them were wandering about in a desert

45. *On the Poet and His Craft*, p. 63.
46. Ibid., p. 70.
47. "Two Organs," in *Love and Fame*, rev. ed. (New York, 1972), p. 16.

in which there were no sign posts."[48] Hence, when the poets of the third generation started their careers, they began with no literary fathers—but with a formidable set of grandfathers.

"It is necessary to be absolutely modern," Rimbaud proclaimed at the close of *A Season in Hell.* "Nothing is good save the new," Williams declared, and Pound demanded that writers "Make It New." Among literary movements modernism is unique in defining itself not so much as a new world view ("romanticism") or as the revival of an ancient one ("neoclassicism") but as an absolute break with the past, including its own past. The motives for such a renovation run deeper than the expectation of originality which has burdened poets for the last hundred and eighty years, and they run deeper than a mere desire for novelty and experimentation for their own sakes. The modernist thrust in all the arts derived from a shared sense of cultural crisis, the collapse of all systematic explanations of the world and the consequent questioning of all established ways of "forming" experience. As we shall see, the ensuing effort to make poetry "modern," of the "present," is an extremely problematic one. A "modern poetry" is certainly a poetry that has grounded itself on a very slippery piece of territory; yet it is this very elusiveness and evanescence of the moment that creates the historical dynamic of modernism. "Modernity," Octavio Paz writes in *Children of the Mire,* "is a polemical tradition which displaces the tradition of the moment, whatever it happens to be, but an instant later yields its place to still another tradition which in turn is a momentary manifestation of modernity. Modernity is never itself; it is always *the* other."[49] In other words, modernity can only be true to itself by continually denying itself; modernity is a radical enterprise, a perpetual crisis. So, when in the postwar period we begin to encounter titles like *The Tradition of the New* and *The Modern Tradition* or a critical phrase like "the stabilization of the avantgarde," we can conclude that the dynamic of modernity has been temporarily stalled.[50]

In "The Present State of Poetry" (1958), Delmore Schwartz observed that "what was once a battlefield has become a peaceful public park on a pleasant summer Sunday afternoon."[51] Modernism had been domesticated. Certainly, many of the bold innovators of the twenties were by

48. *Air with Armed Men* (London, 1972), p. 158.

49. *Children of the Mire* (Cambridge and London, 1974), p. 1.

50. Clement Greenberg speaks of "the stabilization of the avantgarde" in "The State of American Writing," *PR* 15 (August 1948): 876. See Harold Rosenberg's *The Tradition of the New* (New York, 1959) and Charles Feidelson and Richard Ellmann, *The Modern Tradition* (New York, 1965).

51. *Selected Essays of Delmore Schwartz,* p. 44. "The Present State of Poetry" originally appeared, along with essays by John Crowe Ransom and John Hall Wheelock, in *American Poetry at Mid-Century* (Washington, D.C., 1958).

mid-century comfortably established figures, making their own contribution to the period's sense of peaceful exhaustion. According to Louis
Simpson, the older poets were no longer experienced generatively, as
"teachers," but viewed as "distant planets, each whirling in a separate
volume," though occasionally "each older poet would come out of obscurity to be given a prize and have his vogue."[52] In particular, Eliot, who
had been reviled in the twenties as a drunken bolshevik, had ascended
(or descended) to the status of a kind of grandfatherly literary institution.[53]
After the war, he was much less withdrawn and more the genial public
figure, making regular visits to the United States from 1946 on. In 1947
he was admitted to the Order of Merit (an order with only twenty-four
members) and later that year, while a visiting fellow at the Institute for
Advanced Study at Princeton, Eliot learned he had won the Nobel Prize
for literature. In January 1950 *The Cocktail Party* began a Broadway run
that was more a popular than a critical success. *Time* magazine, which
in 1923 had judged "The Waste Land" a hoax, put Eliot on the cover of
its March 6, 1950 issue. "Today at 61," *Time* declared, "Mr. Eliot is
secure and honored in his high place as one of the foremost men of English
letters."[54] At mid-century, accepted, even celebrated, by the Luce Corporation, the modernist revolution might well seem finished.

Eliot himself had issued a *Collected Poems* as early as 1936. In the
postwar period, Frost, Marianne Moore, Stevens, Williams, and Pound
all produced major collections of their work, as did John Crowe Ransom
and Allen Tate. Clearly, all these writers, no longer breaking new ground,
were consolidating their reputations. Poets like Stevens and Moore are
"remarkable," Louise Bogan conceded in a letter to Morton D. Zabel
(then editor of *Poetry*), but "THEY ARE FIXED AND FINISHED. They will
never *surprise* anyone again."[55] Moreover, in their valetudinarian mood
these literary elders, seeming to preempt attacks by anticipating them,
were often prophesying the end of what they themselves had begun. In
his answer to a 1948 *Partisan Review* symposium, The State of American
Writing, Wallace Stevens characterized the age as one no longer conducive to poetic experimentation, a view with which another contributor,
John Crowe Ransom, happily concurred.[56] But perhaps the most striking

52. *Air with Armed Men,* pp. 178–79.
53. Spender mentions the denunciation of Eliot as a "drunken bolshevik" in "The New
Orthodoxies," *The Arts at Mid-Century,* p. 11. Others mention the epithet without giving a
source; even if the story is apocryphal, it accurately evokes the public reception of "The
Waste Land."
54. *Time,* 6 March 1950, p. 26.
55. *What the Woman Lived: Selected Letters of Louise Bogan 1920–1970,* ed. Ruth Lim-
mer (New York, 1973), p. 223.
56. "The State of American Writing," pp. 855–94.

of all was T. S. Eliot's assertion in a lecture, "From Poe to Valéry," given at the library of Congress in 1948: "I believe that the art poètique of which we find the germ in Poe, and which bore fruit in the work of Valéry, has gone as far as it can go. I do not believe that this esthetic can be of any help to later poets."[57] The symbolist aesthetic, emphasizing that "the subject exists for the poem, not the poem for the subject," affected writers as different as Eliot, Crane, and Williams.[58] What Eliot was saying was that modern poetry as we know it, and as Eliot himself had written it, was dead.

Yet it was not exactly the case that the energies of the modernist movement had been exhausted. For one thing, a ground for an alternative to symbolist poetics had been cleared by Pound and Williams, both neglected until the 1950s. The publication of *Paterson* (1946–51) and even more dramatically *The Pisan Cantos* (1948) showed that some of the established poets could extend and renew their work in ways that younger poets could find instructive. Moreover, if the Black Mountain poets could move out from assumptions about poetry as speech, and form as discovery, in Pound and Williams, another group of writers including Robert Bly, James Wright, and Louis Simpson turned back to another neglected aspect of modernism, namely, surrealism. Both of these groups characterize their work as a return to the "true" principles of modernism, though of course they define these principles quite differently. In Creeley's version, the work of the twenties and thirties—"the poetry of Ransom and Tate and Bishop and that which came from the younger men such as Jarrell"—"tended to block off, not to smother but to cover, the actual tradition that was still operating" in such writers as Williams, H.D., Louis Zukofsky, and George Oppen.[59] Simpson similarly declares that "modernism in English had stopped before it had barely started" and the kind of poetry printed in Bly's magazine *The Fifties* "was a renewal of the aborted modernism of the generation of 1910."[60] Even Donald Allen in the Preface to *The New American Poetry* (1960), a book that Allen Tate once proudly announced he had thrown overboard in mid-Atlantic, speaks of his poets as "following the practice and precepts of Ezra Pound and William Carlos Williams": the new poets "are our avant-garde, the true continuers of the modern movement in American poetry."[61] Allen perceives no irony in speaking of an avant-garde that is also the continuer of an earlier movement in poetry, and he anticipates what we shall see to be one of the contradictions

57. *From Poe to Valéry* (New York, 1948), p. 31.
58. Ibid., p. 26.
59. *Contexts of Poetry: Interviews 1961–71* (Bolinas, Calif., 1973), p. 14.
60. *Air with Armed Men*, p. 213.
61. *The New American Poetry* (New York, 1960), p. xi.

of the innovative poets of the third generation: the opposition between their effort to return an authentic spirit of modernity to American poetry and their evocation of literary predecessors as authorities justifying such an effort.

Hence, the problem for a young poet in the early or mid-fifties was not simply the looming presence of that "dynasty of extraordinary gifts and powers"; nor was it exactly that all modernist assumptions about poetry had run dry. The case was, rather, that a particular phase of modernism— that identified with Eliot and the New Criticism in America—had achieved a powerful hegemony which successfully domesticated modernism. Robert Lowell recalls that he first came under the influence of the Southern Agrarians "and that was partly a continuation of Pound and Eliot and partly an attempt to make poetry much more formal than Eliot and Pound did."

> It was the period of the famous book *Understanding Poetry,* of analyzing poems to see how they're put together; there was a great emphasis on craftsmanship. Out of that, though it came later, were poetry workshops and all that sort of thing. Well, that's in my blood very much, and about 1950 it was prevailing everywhere in America.[62]

It is important to recognize that the atmosphere Lowell evokes here is a unique product of the postwar era and its literary and social conservatism. Eliot had excited younger poets and critics in the teens and twenties by urging purely æsthetic criteria in examining poetry; but in *After Strange Gods: A Primer of Modern Heresy* (1934), he had clearly shifted to grounds of a rather severe orthodoxy, a predictable change after his conversion to Christianity but one that made him seem irrelevant to a period engaged with social conflicts. In fact, in the late thirties and early forties Auden became the seminal poet, powerfully affecting the early work of such poets as Schwartz, Shapiro, Jarrell, and Berryman. In his *Essay on Rime* (1945), Shapiro correctly observed that "the man whose impress on our rhetoric / Has for a decade dominated verse / In London, Sydney and New York is Auden"; and Shapiro complained that "to open / A current magazine of rime is but / To return to Auden"—in a poem whose manner clearly derived from Auden![63] In a 1948 review of ten new books of poetry, John Berryman began by similarly observing that by 1935 "the Auden climate had set in strongly" in America, and the books under review led him to conclude that it was still running strong.[64]

62. "Robert Lowell in Conversation with A. Alvarez," in *The Modern Poet: Essays from the Review,* ed. Ian Hamilton (London, 1968), p. 191.
63. *Essay on Rime* (New York, 1945), p. 41.
64. "Waiting for the End, Boys," p. 254.

The restoration of Eliot—along with such other figures of the twenties as Fitzgerald and Faulkner—was very much a phenomenon of the postwar period; in fact, the increasing interest in Stevens, and later on Pound and Williams, partly derives from the fifties' revival of the twenties. The prestige and influence of Eliot, as reinvented by the New Critics, were enormous by the mid-fifties. According to Malcolm Cowley, twelve books and over four hundred articles had been done on Eliot by 1953, and this was only the first ripple of interest.[65] In April 1956 Eliot delivered a lecture on "The Frontiers of Criticism" to 13,523 people crowded into a gymnasium at the University of Minnesota—an audience (in more than one respect) undreamed of by, say, a Dr. Johnson or a Matthew Arnold. Signs of the restoration were already apparent in 1945. In the *Partisan Review,* Delmore Schwartz hailed Eliot as "the International Hero," the poet of the postwar age, the poet whose work, of all the moderns, had the most "direct and comprehensive concern with the essential nature of modern life." "*The Waste Land* will soon be as good as new," Schwartz correctly predicted.[66] In the same year, Shapiro wrote in the *Essay on Rime* that Eliot's "word was our poetic law"; even more significantly, the *Essay,* taken by both its author and its audience to be an attack on modernist verse, its proliferation of styles and its agonized unbelief, demanded a common style and a poetry purified of self-conscious thought—demands that derived straight out of recent essays of Eliot.[67] Just a few years later, Schwartz could accurately point to Eliot as the age's "literary dictator"— a term he did not use pejoratively—and argue that Eliot, who had revised a generation's view of literary history during the twenties, then revised his own views during the thirties and forties, had become the first literary dictator who "abdicated and immediately succeeded to his own throne."[68]

Two volumes of essays published for Eliot's sixtieth birthday in 1948 were filled with encomiums, among them William Empson's remarkable admission that "I do not know for certain how much of my own mind he invented, let alone how much of it is a reaction against him or indeed a consequence of misreading him."[69] It is likely that William Carlos Williams's well-known denunciation of Eliot in the *Autobiography*—for giving "the poem back to the academics"—reflects Eliot's position at the time the statement was made (1951) rather than the time about which the

65. *The Literary Situation,* p. 19.
66. "T. S. Eliot as the International Hero," in *Selected Essays of Delmore Schwartz,* pp. 126, 128. The essay originally appeared in *Partisan Review* 12 (Spring 1945): 199–206.
67. *Essay on Rime,* p. 60.
68. "The Literary Dictatorship of T. S. Eliot," in *Selected Essays of Delmore Schwartz,* p. 313. The essay originally appeared in *Partisan Review* 16 (February 1949): 119–38.
69. "The Style of the Master," in *T. S. Eliot: A Symposium,* ed. Richard March and Tambimuttu (London, 1948), p. 35.

statement was ostensibly made (1922).[70] It is perhaps an even more striking measure of Eliot's influence at the time that when he began "Howl," the poem that would do so much to dramatize the shift away from Eliot, Allen Ginsberg had a dream in which he appeared at a cocktail party at Eliot's London flat where his host at first naps in a farther room, but then comes forth to ask to read Ginsberg's work, and Ginsberg weeps in gratitude for the recognition.[71] One imagines that many of the best minds of Ginsberg's generation had *that* dream.

Yet the effect of Eliot went far beyond the supplying of manifest content for the dreams of younger poets. His influence was not so much specifically literary, in conveying rhythm, image, or voice, but one associated with a specific set of attitudes and values, subtly defining the expectations of many readers and editors as well as writers of poetry; and this influence was transmitted most powerfully by the New Critics. When the postwar period was not calling itself "the age of anxiety," it was calling itself (somewhat anxiously) "the age of criticism." Poetry and fiction might be floundering, but criticism flourished. In fact, while the second generation of modern poets often struggled against a sense of unrealized potentialities, the second generation of modern critics emerged as astonishingly successful. "The critic of today occupies a position of remarkable advantages, of a kind almost unknown to his ancestors," Morton D. Zabel cheerfully announced in the Introduction to the 1952 edition of *Literary Opinion in America,* one of three lengthy collections of modern criticism appearing in the early fifties. "He finds himself," Zabel continued, "in an office of wide influence and in command of almost unlimited opportunities and public attention."[72] Criticism became part of the "age of prosperity," and its position, if not quite equal to Zabel's heady claims, was significant—and not undeserved. Much of the critical work of the late forties and early fifties was brilliant and more various than is sometimes supposed. Yet it is also true that this criticism built upon premises and procedures developed by such figures as Eliot, I. A. Richards, and Empson, and that, by mid-century, criticism was less preoccupied with the uncovering of new works, as it had been in the twenties, than in elucidating a fairly limited number of texts already established as canonical. And in the criticism of poetry, the New Criticism, with its insistence on ironic tension as value and explication as method, achieved a dominance that was virtually unchallenged.

70. *The Autobiography of William Carlos Williams* (New York, 1951), p. 146.
71. Entry for 6 July 1955, in "Notebooks, 1953–56," in the Allen Ginsberg Archives, Columbia University. Material from the Ginsberg Archives quoted with the kind permission of Allen Ginsberg and Columbia University.
72. "Introduction: Criticism in America," in *Literary Opinion in America,* p. 1.

In an essay, "Criticism, Inc.," that closed *The World's Body,* John
Crowe Ransom called for a criticism that, forsaking historical, ethical,
and impressionistic approaches, would be "more scientific, or precise and
systematic," "developed by the collective and sustained effort of learned
persons—which means that its proper seat is in the universities."[73] *The
World's Body* appeared in 1938; so did the first edition of *Understanding
Poetry.* Ransom's *The New Criticism,* dealing with Richards, Empson,
Eliot, Winters, was published in 1940. As Walter Sutton points out in his
history of *Modern American Criticism,* "by the early 1940's" the New
Critics "had begun a revolution in teaching and scholarship that was
consolidated with the support of younger men in the postwar period."[74]
Ransom had founded *Kenyon* in 1939, and Tate assumed editorship of
Sewanee in 1944. In two essays that appeared in *Sewanee* in the late
forties, W. K. Wimsatt and Monroe Beardsley defined "The Intentional
Fallacy" and "The Affective Fallacy," thus making straight the way of
Ransom's "autotelic" poem.[75] When Cleanth Brooks wrote in the opening
sentence of *The Well-Wrought Urn* (1947) that "few of us are prepared
to accept the statement that the language of poetry is the language of
paradox," he was underestimating the ready-made appeal of his main
pitch.[76] In fact, with the publication in 1949 of William Elton's *A Glossary
of the New Criticism* (originally serialized in three issues of *Poetry*), the
movement achieved a precise and systematic elaboration that brought it
to self-parody. Amid extensive discussions of irony, paradox, and tension,
along with scholastic definitions of numerous critical fallacies and here-
sies, "affective" was succinctly (if redundantly) glossed as "emotive and
related to pleasure and pain, as distinguished from the volitional and
ideational aspects of consciousness."[77] So much for affect in poetry. A
few years later, one anthologist of criticism wrote that "extraordinary
advances in critical method make the inspection of a poem today by a
first-rate critic as close and careful as a chemical analysis."[78] Yet the
movement survived its own excesses partly because it was supported by
some of those very social and historical forces whose reality it denied.
During the fifties, expansion of colleges and universities in the United
States dramatically increased the size of most English departments with

73. *The World's Body* (New York, 1938), p. 329.
74. *Modern American Criticism* (Englewood Cliffs, 1963), p. 98.
75. "The Intentional Fallacy" appeared in *SR* 54 (Summer 1946): 468–88; "The Affective
Fallacy," appeared in *SR* 57 (Winter 1949): 31–35.
76. *The Well-Wrought Urn* (New York, 1947), p. 3.
77. *A Glossary of the New Criticism* (Chicago, 1949). The book's original appearance was
in *Poetry* 73 (December 1948): 153–62; (January 1949): 232–45; and (February 1949): 296–
307.
78. Quoted by Randall Jarrell, "The Age of Criticism," in *Poetry and the Age* (New York,
1955), p. 80.

the result that there were many class hours to be filled, and many books and articles to be written, by eager young professors, many of whom had very little personality to efface. Moreover, the myth of the value-free technician, working within the clearly defined limits of some specialized and self-contained area of activity, informed many professions in the fifties and helps explain the appeal of both the symbolist poem and the New Criticism. By the mid-fifties, Ransom's "Criticism, Inc." had arrived.

Yet the establishment of such a criticism, defining a prepared, receptive audience for a young poet, has distinct advantages. The New Critics, in fact, performed an important historical function: they deradicalized the modernist grandfathers and provided paternal authority at a time when beginning poets were eager to find it. Many of the features of the kind of poetry they authorized were well described by Snodgrass:

> in school, we had been taught to write a very difficult and very intel-
> lectual poem. We tried to achieve the obscure and dense texture of
> the French Symbolists (very intuitive and often deranged poets), but
> by using methods similar to those of the very intellectual and con-
> scious poets of the English Renaissance, especially the Metaphysical
> poets . . . a very strange combination.[79]

What the age demanded was a densely textured lyric, crammed with learned allusions, witty metaphors, startling changes of tone, verbal ambiguities—all packed tightly into the hermetically sealed space of the autonomous symbolist poem. It was his debt to expectations like these that led James Dickey, a student at Vanderbilt whose work was first published in *Sewanee Review,* to characterize his earliest work as "influenced stylistically not so much by individual writers as by an amalgam of writers: something called, in capital letters, MODERN POETRY."[80] "Along with many other beginners," Howard Nemerov recalls, "I learned to value irony, difficulty, erudition, and the Metaphysical style of composition after the example of John Donne" and, like both Snodgrass and Dickey, he admired William Empson, from whom he learned "to value ambiguity."[81] Both the style and the ultimate assumptions behind it are recalled by Richard Wilbur, one of its most elegant practitioners.

> Most American poets of my generation were taught to admire the
> English Metaphysical poets of the seventeenth century and such con-
> temporary masters of irony as John Crowe Ransom. We were led by
> our teachers and by the critics whom we read to feel that the most
> adequate and convincing poetry is that which accommodates mixed

---

79. *In Radical Pursuit,* p. 42.
80. *Self-Interviews,* ed. Barbara Reiss and James Reiss (Garden City, 1970), p. 46.
81. *Reflexions on Poetry and Poetics* (New Brunswick, 1972), pp. 164–65.

feelings, clashing ideas, and incongruous images. Poetry could not be honest, we thought, unless it began by acknowledging the full discordancy of modern life and consciousness.[82]

Wilbur here assumes that no single truth, no fixed position or organized system of knowledge, can fully apprehend the world and render it coherent. Such assumptions generate an apotheosis of art as the only kind of coherence available to us, an art that will be richly charged with multiple and overlapping perspectives: in fiction a self-conscious attention to the "point of view" and in poetry a language that swiftly shifts tone or attitude, thickens texture with allusion and ambiguity in an effort to examine subjects from several sides without selecting any one as final. Literary works, registering but not resolving contradictions, become self-reflexive, autonomous objects—not expressions of human emotion or criticisms of life but æsthetic objects, verbal icons, symbolist poems. Hence, what emerges from the modern collapse of belief, as we see in the early essays of Eliot, is the modernist idea of the poet as impersonal craftsman, who refuses to reduce the full complexity of human experience by thrusting his private vision upon it. It was T. S. Eliot, after all, who praised Henry James for "having a mind so fine no idea could violate it."[83]

The advantages of accepting New Critical assumptions about poetry are probably most evident in the early career of Robert Lowell, whose weak actual father made the quest for literary mentors an urgent one. In the poems of *Lord Weary's Castle* (1946), Lowell says that he tried "to write in metres but to make the metres look hard and make them hard to write";[84] in fact, not just the meters but every stylistic feature of these poems marks them as obscure, difficult—hard to write and hard to read. Consider, for example, the fifth section of "A Quaker Graveyard in Nantucket":

When the whale's viscera go and the roll
Of its corruption overruns this world
Beyond tree-swept Nantucket and Wood's Hole
And Martha's Vineyard, Sailor, will your sword
Whistle and fall and sink into the fat?
In the great ash-pit of Jehosaphat
The bones cry out for the blood of the white whale,
The fat flukes arch and whack about its ears,
The death-lance churns into the sanctuary, tears
The gun-blue swingle, heaving like a flail,

---

82. *Poets on Poetry,* ed. Howard Nemerov (New York, 1966), p. 163.
83. "Henry James," *Little Review* 4 (August 1918): 76.
84. "Robert Lowell in Conversation with A. Alvarez," p. 191.

And hacks the coiling life out: it works and drags
And rips the sperm-whale's midriff into rags,
Gobbets of blubber spill to wind and weather,
Sailor, and gulls go round the stoven timbers
Where the morning stars sing out together
And thunder shakes the white surf and dismembers
The red flag hammered in the mast-head. Hide,
Our steel, Jonas Messias, in Thy side.

Yet, in spite of what seems an almost willed difficulty, it is hard to think of a book of poems by a young poet that met with the widespread and immediate success of *Lord Weary's Castle*. The book won Lowell a Pulitzer Prize, a Guggenheim fellowship, a fellowship from the American Academy and National Institute for Arts and Letters, and an appointment as poetry consultant to the Library of Congress. And whereas in 1953 Allen Ginsberg would dream of recognition from Eliot and Roethke be enraged that Eliot would not take time out from play rehearsals to meet him, Lowell had met Eliot as early as 1946, and, in one of Eliot's rare comments on younger writers, obtained public recognition: "I must admit to a continuing respect for Robert Lowell and Richard Wilbur," Eliot confessed in the early fifties.[85] It was, in fact, Lowell who early in his career swiftly realized that "image of fame" pursued by the middle generation. Reference to the rugged force and turbulent richness of the poems is not enough to explain the book's impact, since immediate recognition of merit appears to be the exception rather than the rule in literary history. To some extent the book's success was a triumph of literary politics. Of the poems in *Lord Weary's Castle* that had earlier appeared in periodicals, thirteen had come out in *The Nation* (where Lowell's fellow student at Kenyon, Randall Jarrell, was poetry editor), nine in *Partisan* (where Lowell's Harvard classmate, Delmore Schwartz, was poetry editor), five in *Kenyon* (edited by Lowell's teacher at Kenyon, Ransom), and three in *Sewanee* (edited by Lowell's friend and mentor, Allen Tate). Major reviews, all insisting on the book's importance, appeared in all these journals: Jarrell reviewed it himself in *The Nation,* Berryman in the *Partisan,* and Richard Eberhard (Lowell's prep school teacher) in *Kenyon.* And with the awarding of the Pulitzer, Lowell became something of a public figure as well: *Time* described him as "the year's most rewarded poet" and *Life,* in a three-page story, asserted that he had "already reached the stature of a major literary figure."[86]

85. Quoted by Oscar Cargill in the *English Journal* 43 (February 1954): 64.
86. See *Time,* 19 May 1947, p. 44, and *Life,* 19 May 1947, p. 91.

Compare Lowell's reception with that of Eliot himself. At thirty Eliot had published a single volume of poetry, *Prufrock and Other Observations* (1917), only five hundred copies of which had been printed by a small press in London. Supporting himself by his job at Lloyd's Bank, dealing with the consequences of a disastrous marriage and rejected by his family for his choice of wife and literary career, Eliot had entered the period of suffering that would issue in "The Waste Land." His poems, many of which had been written for several years before they appeared in a magazine, much less a book, were known only to a small coterie. The difference is not just due to Lowell's participation in a literary mutual admiration society, whose members did no more for the book than it deserved anyway. The real reason is that while Eliot worked in opposition to the expectations of his readers, Lowell did not. To put it another way, Eliot had to create his own audience, Lowell received one ready-made—the one created (in the main) by Eliot. It is significant here that in its story on Lowell, *Life* magazine printed two sections of "Quaker Graveyard in Nantucket," probably the most obscure poem in the book, plus "Salem" and "Concord" in their entirety. *Life* was no doubt impressed by Lowell's choice of American historical materials in these poems as well as by his famous literary ancestors; pictures of James Russell Lowell and Amy Lowell were printed with the article. The reporter conceded the difficulty of the poems but far from responding with the kind of philistine scorn modernism met with in the twenties, he provided brief perceptive commentaries on the two short poems; perhaps he had done *Understanding Poetry* in a freshman English course.

Lowell, in short, had a highly sophisticated and sympathetic critical audience for his work, one that was much larger than his immediate circle of friends. *Lord Weary's Castle* could not have been written, much less intelligently received, in England, with its cult of amateurism in criticism. John Berryman correctly pointed out that the book "is the natural product of an elaborate, scrupulous, and respected literary criticism," which is to say the New Criticism.[87] "The kind of poet I am," Lowell said, "was largely determined by the fact that I grew up in the heyday of The New Criticism, with Eliot's magical scrutiny of the text as a critical example."[88] Berryman's "scrupulous" and Lowell's "magical scrutiny" are the key terms, for as a young writer Lowell seems to have sought out the most severe and scrupulous critical intelligences he could find and to wrench himself into meeting their expectations, just as he wrenched his turbulent feelings into the "hard" meters of *Lord Weary's Castle*. Hence, Lowell

87. "Waiting for the End, Boys," p. 266.
88. Stanley Kunitz, "Talk with Robert Lowell," in *Profile of Robert Lowell*, ed. Jerome Mazzaro (Columbus, Ohio, 1971), p. 54.

grew up not just in the heyday of the New Criticism—when, he says, new critical essays often "had the excitement of a new imaginative work"— he grew up with two of its most powerful proponents as his personal mentors.[89]

In 1937 Lowell left Harvard to study under Ransom at Kenyon College, where he majored in classics. "He did more than come under our official attention," Ransom quaintly recalls. "He passed beneath the lintel of my door, and lived for a year in our house"—at the same time Randall Jarrell was living there.[90] In 1937 Lowell also traveled to Tennessee to meet and stay for three months with Allen Tate, who impressed him with his courtesy—and his severity. Tate's judgments were reactionary, fierce: "turning to the moderns, he slaughtered whole Chicago droves of slipshod Untermeyer Anthology experimentalists." His pronouncements were coolly absolute, austerely purged of romanticism and doggedly New Critical: "a good poem," Tate warned, "had nothing to do with exalted feelings of being moved by the spirit. It was simply a piece of craftsmanship, an intelligible or *cognitive* object."[91] Much later, in one of the poems of *Notebook,* Lowell looks at an old photo of himself:

> I rest on a tree, and try to sharpen bromides
> to serve the great, the great God, the New Critic,
> who loves the writing better than we ourselves. . . .[92]

Serving such gods, a young poet will choose his words carefully—as if his salvation depended on it. "You think three times before you put a word down, and ten times about taking it out," Lowell told an interviewer[93]—a perfectionism evident from his continuous and extensive revisions of even the work he had already published. *Life Studies* suggests that in a very direct and personal sense Lowell had a grandfather, but no father—an absence that was at first filled by the menacing God of the early poems and the minute scrupulosity of those New Critics whom Lowell rightly imagined as his ideal audience.

"So the twentieth century is that, it is a time when everything cracks, where everything is destroyed, everything isolates itself, it is a more splendid thing than a period where everything follows itself," Gertrude Stein writes in *Picasso.*[94] The modern poets felt required to reinvent the

89. "The Art of Poetry: Robert Lowell," p. 14.
90. "A Look Backwards and a Note of Hope," *Harvard Advocate* 145 (November 1961): 22.
91. "Visiting the Tates," *SR* 67 (Autumn 1959): 558.
92. "The Literary Life, a Scrapbook," *Notebook* (London, 1970), p. 86.
93. "The Art of Poetry," p. 14.
94. *Picasso* (Boston, 1959), p. 49.

poetic medium, to make it consonant with an age where everything cracks. The result was a poetry which, while often bewildering and frustrating to read, nevertheless attains a kind of fractured splendor at its best. By the early 1950s the phase of modernism dominated by Eliot and the New Critics *had* been exhausted; and if the combination of emotional violence and formal tightening in Robert Lowell's early poetry seemed to open the possibility that these "dominating presences" of modern poetry could be beaten at their own game, Lowell himself discarded this mode after *The Mills of the Kavanaughs* (1951)—and it took Lowell eight years to accomplish the transformation of his style that we find in *Life Studies* (1959). In his contribution to a series of lectures on *American Poetry at Mid-Century* (1958), John Crowe Ransom remarked that "the chances are not so bright now for poetries which are radically new."[95] The dangers of prophecy! Ransom's pronouncement was made, ironically, just at the time when such poetries were beginning to appear—e.g., Allen Ginsberg's "Howl" (1956), Frank O'Hara's *Meditations in an Emergency* (1957), Denise Levertov's *Here and Now* (1957) as well as Lowell's *Life Studies*. Even more ironically, it was largely the New Critics like Ransom and the young formalist poets he was praising who, by reducing modernism to an orthodoxy, helped make it into a doctrine that could be assailed by the new generation of poets.

95. "New Poets and Old Muses," *American Poetry at Mid-Century,* p. 12.

TWO

The New Rear Guard

"Every poem begins, or ought to, by a disorderly retreat to defensible positions."[1]
—Richard Wilbur

"In those years formalism was part of the strategy—like asbestos gloves, it allowed me to handle materials I couldn't pick up bare-handed."[2]
—Adrienne Rich

"The neo-Flaubertian image of poetry as a 'craft' was in all the ikons I could see."[3]
—W. S. Merwin

In an essay called "The Invisible Avant-Garde," John Ashbery remembers that in 1950 "to experiment was to have the feeling that one was poised on some outermost brink."[4] Familiarity with the period confirms the accuracy of Ashbery's recollection. At the symbolic vantage point of mid-century, literary observers, among many others, were prompted to assess themselves and their profession, to measure how far they had come in the modern century. Many such self-appraisals appeared all during the fifties and it became increasingly clear that they manifested self-doubt: worried looks over the shoulder by a generation that feared that it marked the mere ebbing of an earlier creative impulse. But at first these surveys of the modern literary topography seemed made from a plateau of confidence and even complacency. In "At Mid-Century" Louise Bogan warned writers not to "insist upon a stubborn avant-gardism when no real need for a restless forward movement any longer exists." Bogan called instead "for a consolidation of resources and for a canvassing of the ground already gained."[5] Eliot had said that "old men should be explorers," but younger poets in the fifties were urged to (and did) settle into the territories already opened by their predecessors; many of them, in fact, remodeled

1. "The Bottles Become New, Too," *Quarterly Review of Literature* 7 (1954): 189.
2. "When We Dead Awaken: Writing as Re-Vision," in *Adrienne Rich's Poetry,* ed. Barbara Gelpi and Albert Gelpi (New York, 1975), pp. 94–95.
3. "Foreword," *Selected Translations, 1948–1968* (New York, 1968), p. vii.
4. "The Invisible Avant-Garde," *Avant-Garde Art,* ed. Thomas B. Hess and John Ashbery (New York, 1967), p. 183.
5. *A Poet's Alphabet* (New York, 1970), p. 12.

old structures which their predecessors had abandoned as obsolescent. In the Foreword to his *Mid-Century American Poets* anthology, John Ciardi cheerfully affirmed that the new generation was not one "of Bohemian extravagance but of self-conscious sanity in an urbane and cultivated poetry that is the antithesis of the Bohemian spirit."[6] Ciardi took particular care to show how his calm and self-assured generation had freed themselves from the unruly excesses of modernism—as if the decorums of his literary anthology were those of an academic dinner party. A cautious conservatism made these younger poets different from the rebels who had preceded them; it made them the new rear guard.

The poetry of the postwar decade was, in fact, characterized by deference to a subtly revised image of the immediate literary past along with an accommodation to the social and historical present. On both counts, this poetry effectively denied the critical spirit of modernism. By the late 1940s, the modernist movement, all the instruments seemed to agree, was exhausted. But if poets (with the notable exception of Robert Lowell) felt it impossible to create poems that were more violent, more disorganized—more *modern*—than their predecessors had, it also proved impossible for either poets or critics to construct any set of poetic propositions powerful enough to dislodge modernism. The period, skeptical of theory, produced no new ambitious theoretical formulations but instead devoted itself to a practical criticism and the cult of poetic craftsmanship, activities their proponents claimed were free of theoretical "bias." In the era that Delmore Schwartz described as like "a peaceful public park on a pleasant summer Sunday afternoon," there was remarkably little strife between poets, between generations, between poets and critics. We are "at the end of an era," Bogan announced, with a quiescence that was itself characteristic of the period; her statement and the many like it were not heady announcements of some apocalyptic end that would clear the way for a fresh start of the sort that had occurred in 1912; they were, rather, expressions of doubt, uncertainty, and drift.[7] A radical revision of poetic theory would have had the crucial advantage of permitting younger poets to be judged by standards of their own making, a situation that would have allowed them to escape the inevitable (and inevitably invidious) comparisons between themselves and the early moderns. Instead, however, the poets who began to write in the decade following the Second World War were remarkable for their avowed eagerness to meet, rather than to revise, prevailing standards; for these writers, seeking what one of them called "the reassurance of sounding like something already acclaimed" proved hard to resist.[8]

6. *Mid-Century American Poets*, ed. John Ciardi (New York, 1950), p. xxix.
7. *Achievement in American Poetry, 1900–1950* (Chicago, 1951), p. 107.
8. Winfield Townley Scott, "Dear Jeff," in *Mid-Century American Poets*, p. 107.

The past was all too little a burden for this generation, which sought to define its difference by a return to precisely those traditional verse forms which the modernists had dismantled. Robert Lowell's *Lord Weary's Castle* offered "the most decisive testimony we have had," John Berryman wrote in 1947, "of a new period, returning to the deliberate and the formal."[9] By the early fifties the "new period" was under full steam. Some of the younger poets—Wilbur, Lowell, Merrill, Viereck—were called the "New Formalists," and Wilbur politely accepted the designation. "As regards technique, a critic has called me one of the 'New Formalists,' " Wilbur said, "and I will accept the label provided it be understood that to try to revive the force of rhyme and other formal devices, by reconciling them with the experimental gains of the past several decades, is itself sufficiently experimental."[10] Here Wilbur is so sensible, so balanced, has such "complexity of attitude" on the question of form that he is left with no ground to stand on. He affirms the revival of traditional forms but, of course, he does not want to repudiate the moderns so he tips his hat in the direction of experimentalism, which he then deftly redefines as—traditionalism. His statement dramatically reveals how the poets of Wilbur's low-profile generation tried to counter strength with skill, energy with expertise; it was a stance all the more appealing in view of the dangers illustrated by the middle generation, the dangers of a rivalrous ambition that exceeded or even contaminated talent.

Nevertheless, Wilbur's stance may strike us as so self-limiting as to be at least equally dangerous. According to Roethke, "The spirit starves / Until the dead have been subdued"—not to mention some of the living;[11] but in "When Do We Inherit?" (1944) William Meredith articulates the quiet resignation of many of the third generation when he characterizes himself as "derivative, perhaps, but in modern dress"—a line that (enacting its sense) takes its cadence from a man named Prufrock.[12] But the avowedly modest stance of these writers, their willingness to sound like and to court the approval of the reigning literary authorities, should not deceive us into concluding that they were simply derivative or even fundamentally like their predecessors. The formalism of the postwar era may at first seem a point of continuity with the poetry of the early twentieth century, a poetry that was self-consciously and programmatically formalist. But when the formalism issues in the return of traditional forms,

9. "Lowell, Thomas, &c.," *PR* 14 (January–February 1947): 80.
10. Quoted in Stanley Kunitz, ed., *Twentieth Century American Authors, First Supplement* (New York, 1955), p. 1080.
11. *Collected Poems of Theodore Roethke*, p. 4.
12. *Love Letters from an Impossible Land* (New Haven, 1944), p. 16.

modernism has been annihilated. As Ronald Poggioli points out in *The Theory of the Avant-Garde,*

> Classical art, through the method of imitation and the practice of repetition, tends toward the ideal of renewing, in the sense of integration and perfection. But for modern art in general, and for avant-garde in particular, the only irremediable and absolute aesthetic error is a traditional artistic creation, an art that imitates and repeats itself.[13]

Many of the younger poets like Wilbur talked as if they were completing a revolution; what they actually accomplished was what Howard Nemerov called "a Napoleonic reversal and a Bourbon restoration."[14] In the fifties, modernism did indeed become a matter of appearance, of "dress," a fashion which had lost the life that produced it.

The period, as Wilbur said, was one of "eclectic traditionalism," more the second than the first as it turned out.[15] Stable traditional forms appealed for a variety of reasons. Poetry was no longer a crisis, a problem, but a given—with a shared, accessible discourse (rather than the Bohemian extravagances uttered at the outer brink). Even more important, inherited forms aligned beginning poets not with any specific and therefore threatening authority but with a diffused idea of authority. T. S. Eliot had related to the literary past in an openly selective and polemical way; in Walter Jackson Bate's terms, Eliot's use of Donne manages a "leap over the parental" to a more distant "ancestral" authority. As Bate writes, "the ancestral permitted one—by providing a 'purer,' more time-hallowed, more conveniently malleable example—even to disparage the parent in the name of 'tradition.' "[16] Carrying this process a step further, the starting poets of the postwar era affirmed "*the* tradition," into which they assimilated emasculated versions of at least some of the moderns; and *that* concept was used to disparage any serious idea of modernity in poetry. When, for instance, R. P. Blackmur offered his mid-century reassessment in "Lord Tennyson's Scissors" (1951), he denounced "the general prosody" of the teens and twenties as "perhaps the weakest and least conscious in English since the dead poetry of the mid-sixteenth century. It ran, under various guises and doctrines, toward a combination of absolute doggerel and absolute expressionism." At their best, Blackmur contended, Yeats, Eliot, and Pound had transcended the limits of their era by conceiving of "prosody as reason,"—a notion more exhortatory than exact, but one that allowed Blackmur to urge traditional meters as the

13. *The Theory of the Avant-Garde* (Cambridge, Mass., 1968), p. 82.
14. *Poetry and Fiction: Essays* (New Brunswick, 1963), p. 135.
15. *Responses: Prose Pieces, 1953–1976* (New York and London, 1976), p. 148.
16. *The Burden of the Past and the English Poet,* p. 22.

only way of marking poetry as the result of human control. Yeats, Eliot, and Pound are thus "central" poets in "the full tradition of literature" which at least two of them thought they had renounced.[17] The postwar period's eclecticism clearly had its limits and exclusions, as a look at its great anthology, *Understanding Poetry,* will quickly show. But by being covertly selective, poets and critics could claim a dogma-free inclusiveness, deny their own modest rebelliousness, and identify with ancestral authority.

Moreover, in the postwar era the use of traditional accentual meters was not the choice of one technical means among many; it became, as David Antin has shown, a "moral" and "symbolic" issue.[18] This was especially true for the New Critics. Although they are usually thought of as "formalist," the New Critics were primarily concerned with theme (irony, paradox, complexity of attitude) and their notions of literary form, and in particular meter, were highly mythologized. *Understanding Poetry* deals with this charged issue by pretty much suppressing it. A fifty-page chapter entitled "Metrics" mentions no alternatives to traditional versification. A nine-page "Note on Versification and Metrics" does include a single, short paragraph on "free verse," which, we read, provides a "much looser kind of organization of rhythm than there is in the ordinary accentual-syllabic verse."[19] A remark like that inhibits rather than helps critical thought: the poems that Brooks and Warren have in mind do not possess a *looser* but a different *kind* of organization from any they were prepared to recognize, much less to explain. Nor were they very eager to include "free verse" in their text, which contains only nine instances, three of them brief imagist poems. But for writers like Ransom and Tate "free verse" was not something to be ignored; it was something to be wiped out. Citing Eliot's inordinate quest for "novelty" and his rejection of "the form in which our traditionary poetry is cast," Ransom attacked "The Waste Land" in a 1923 review, declaring it "one of the most insubordinate poems in the language."[20] To the end Ransom remained uneasy about modernist experimentation, especially its breaking of meters, and his own poetic practice, derived mainly from Hardy and Robinson, proceeded as if the modernist revolution had never happened. Allen Tate had quarreled publicly with Ransom over the "Waste Land" review and he himself had early tried "free verse." But he soon returned to traditional meters and we have already seen him slaughtering "whole Chicago droves

17. *Form and Value in Modern Poetry* (Garden City, 1957), pp. 374, 381, 386.
18. "Modernism and Postmodernism: Approaching the Present in American Poetry," *Boundary 2,* 1 (Fall 1972): 117–18.
19. Cleanth Brooks and Robert Penn Warren, *Understanding Poetry* (New York, 1950), p. 702.
20. Ransom's review appeared in the *New York Evening Post,* 14 July 1923.

of slipshod Untermeyer Anthology experimentalists'' for the benefit of
the young Robert Lowell. It is Tate who most clearly perceived meter as
"an image of some moral order."[21] "Formal versification is the primary
structure of poetic order," he held, "the assurance to the reader and to
the poet himself that the poet is in control of the disorder both outside
him and within his own mind."[22] For a critic like Tate, traditional meters
defined literariness. For a young poet in the fifties, then, such forms not
only identified him with ancestral authority and with some fairly powerful
living authorities, but a "formal versification" also validated his own
literary and moral authority.

Tate was not just rejecting the notion of the poet as inspired medium
and exhorting poets to manage their experience and feelings in verse; by
identifying meter as the means to that end, as the "primary structure"
in poetry, he was saying that such control could only be achieved through
forms that were external, abstract, and timeless. Ransom, too, held that
meter was never expressive of feeling or idea, but a purely formal—
"abstractionist," he called it—element in the poem.[23] What was crucial
in the poetics of the "new period," then, was not just the return to the
"deliberate and formal"; nor was it the self-satisfied timidity which saw
nothing problematical about the revival of such set forms at the middle
of the twentieth century. Rather, it was the assumption of a *tension* between form and content. Only when we see this can we appreciate the
disruptive force of Robert Creeley's "form is never anything more than
an extension of content"—a statement that might otherwise strike us as
a rather bland revolutionary slogan.

Much of the tone and substance of this "new period" can be heard in
a symposium entitled "Experimental and Formal Verse" held at Bard
College in 1948. This meeting, with William Carlos Williams, Louise Bogan, and Richard Wilbur as the main speakers,[24] established firmly that
formal verse and not experimentalism was the prevailing thing; the symposium also presented a confrontation among three generations of American poets that was all the more dramatic because it reversed expectations:
it was not the twenty-seven-year-old Wilbur but the sixty-five-year-old
Williams who advanced the cause of innovation. The rancor with which
he espoused his position revealed, however, how out of step with the
times Williams felt—and was. Williams led off with a paper, "Some Hints

21. "Modernism and Postmodernism: Approaching the Present in American Poetry," p.
117.
22. "Poetry Modern and Unmodern," in *Essays of Four Decades* (Chicago, 1968), p. 228.
23. See, for example, Ransom's "The Inorganic Muses," *KR* 5 (Spring 1943): 278–300.
24. The Williams, Bogan, and Wilbur papers read at this symposium were subsequently
published in the *Quarterly Review of Literature* 7 (1954): 171–92. Subsequent references
are made in the text.

toward the Enjoyment of Modern Verse," that provides a characteristic statement of his version of modernist poetics. His approach is formalist in the sense that he brackets content in order to focus on "the elementary construction of the modern poem" (p. 171); but his argument is experimentalist in his unswerving repudiation of all traditional forms and his insistence on the evolution of new poetic means that are organically related to contemporary American experience. Stressed verse, in his view, is English verse, but if we "take our prosody without invention and on loan from another language," we "take the bottle with its label already applied and fill it with any rot-gut you like" (p. 172). External inherited forms are impositional; genuine poetic forms, for Williams, are evolved out of the temporal flux.

To participants in this symposium Williams, with his dogmatic, belligerent, and somewhat messianic manner, must have seemed something of an embarrassment or else an engagingly fiery old fogey. Both Wilbur and Bogan, on the other hand, must have been hard to resist; they adopt more suavely balanced—and therefore seemingly more reasonable—attitudes, which allow them to concede a certain (but limited) truth to Williams's views, before offering their own much more conservative positions. Wilbur, for example, begins by granting the dangers of inherited forms, their propensity to call up "a swarm of past uses" and to degenerate into "mere autonomous artifice" and lose touch with immediate reality (p. 187). But Wilbur's account of these risks is practical, not theoretical, the way Williams's is. Like a Wilbur poem, his essay gracefully rides the "difficult balance" between opposed extremes.[25] Poetry, of course, must continually come back to the external "reality of things" (p. 187); yet it must not surrender to physical sensation and "contemn the consciousness" (p. 188). Mere artifice and mere sensation are both to be shunned; between self and world there must be a "tension," says Wilbur, echoing New Critical poetics (p. 188). Moreover, while physical objects must always be approached, they can never finally be reached, Wilbur argues, now echoing Wallace Stevens. Hence, "the difficulty of the form is a substitute for the difficulty" of direct perception, a curious version of the theory of "imitative form," but one that allows a poet often accused of tilting too far in the direction of artifice to claim that "it is respect for reality which makes a necessity of artifice" (p. 189).

In her paper "The Pleasures of Formal Poetry," Bogan, too, defends inherited forms, but she does so by deriving iambic meter, for example, from such primitive, biological rhythms as breathing; what appears artificial to us was originally organic, she argues. Bogan appeals to the au-

25. "Love Calls Us to the Things of This World," in *The Poems of Richard Wilbur* (New York, 1963), p. 66.

thority of nature; Wilbur, to the authority of tradition. He insists upon separating the formal and the temporal; he rejects the organicist thinking in both Bogan and Williams to argue that all formal elements are "perfectly artificial and abstract": "a basic rhythm"—like iambic beat—"is as timeless and noncommittal as the triangle" (p. 190). It was this conception of poetic form as autonomous, timeless, abstract, and therefore prior to its specific occasion—a form, moreover, that very likely will call attention to itself *as form*—that established authority in the late forties and early fifties.

Richard Wilbur, in fact, may serve as one representative figure of the poetic decade following the Second World War, and we can examine his early work by concentrating on his first book, *The Beautiful Changes*. Although by no means as spectacularly successful as *Lord Weary's Castle,* this book did establish Wilbur, along with Lowell, as one of *the* two younger poets of the time—a view, as we have seen, endorsed by Eliot himself. In the young Wilbur the "anxiety of influence" burns with a very soft, emberlike flame. He does not feel he has to topple the reigning literary presences in order to begin. Instead, his derivations are openly acknowledged, as if he were deliberately linking himself with images of literary authority. He takes over poetic language and technique from Moore and Stevens; he adapts these procedures to traditional verse forms; and he works within a set of poetic assumptions derived from the New Critics. A graceful, accomplished first book like *The Beautiful Changes* thus shows once again the genuine advantages of working within an established critical framework, one that, in the middle forties, had yet to harden into the predictable operations of an orthodoxy, a critical *mold*. Wilbur's connections with the New Criticism were not as directly linked to its major figures as were Lowell's; but, Wilbur recalls, "the excitement at Amherst during my undergraduate years was about criticism. I imagine that here or there in the world, the New-Critical excitement had already broken or was yet to come, but for the Amherst I knew, it was at high tide."[26] One effect of the New Criticism on both Lowell and Wilbur was a verbal scrupulosity; their early work should be read with subtle attention to the intricacies of its verbal surface, especially ambiguity, allusion, and ironic juxtaposition. Yet the dramatic differences in the actual texture of that surface—Lowell's harsh, packed, apocalyptic language versus the elegant ease of Wilbur's ironic meditations—suggests that the two ultimately picked up on very different features of New Critical theory. Lowell was drawn toward the religious orthodoxy and literary severity of the movement and his early poems characteristically envision an absolute in which their fierce

26. "Richard Wilbur, Talking to Joan Hutton," *Transatlantic Review* 29 (Summer 1968): 58.

conflicts might be resolved. But Wilbur was most attracted by the New Criticism's poetics of tension and his secular and more playful verse sustains, rather than struggling to resolve, the contradictions of contemporary experience. Like his mentor Stevens, Wilbur really is at home in a world without absolutes.

The title of *The Beautiful Changes* contains a grammatical ambiguity that allows us to read "changes" as either a noun or a verb. Reading it both ways, we get: "the beautiful changes [alters]" *and* "changes are beautiful"—perhaps Wilbur's version of "death is the mother of beauty." In his skeptical poetry, absolutism and finality of any kind are assessed ironically, mainly because they seek to avoid or even to annihilate the beautiful changes of life in a physical world. Like the icy vision of a zealous arctic explorer or the "Bombay saint" blinded by looking too long into the sun, the Nazi in "On the Eyes of an SS Officer" goes beyond even their inhumanity by thrusting his vision of "foul purities" on innocent victims.[27] In "Water Walker" Saul's impassioned acceptance of the Christian vision makes him inhuman too ("how Saul / Cursed once the market babblers, / Righteous could watch them die!") and his dogmatism is understood as an evasion of the ambiguities of human experience, man's struggle with "the dilemma, cherished, tyrannical," of his divided nature. Many of the poems open the possibility of a kind of Platonic world of pure forms, but such images of perfection (and rest) are to be resisted since they pull us away from the "gay-pocked and potsherd world" (*PRW*, p. 196). A poem called "O" playfully concludes:

And I toss circles skyward to be undone
By actual wings, for wanting this repeal
I should go whirling a thin Euclidean reel,
No hawk or hickory to true my run.

What's "true" for Wilbur is the imperfect actual, not the "thin Euclidean" ideal. Similarly, a childhood inside the lovely "Caserta Garden" would inspire "faith that the unjustest thing / Had geometric grace past what one sees," but as soon as Wilbur arrives at this conclusion, the poem turns ironically back on itself, by invoking the mixed world beyond the garden walls that escapes "our simpler symmetries": "there is no resting where it rots and thrives."

In "Sunlight Is Imagination" Wilbur offers one of his strongest versions of this tension between real and ideal. "Each shift you make in the sunlight somewhere / Cleaves you away into dark," he begins. Once again, the

27. All quotations are from *The Poems of Richard Wilbur;* quotations from poems not identified by title will be given in the text with the abbreviation *PRW*.

beautiful changes (shifts), although the poet is not yet willing to accept either its elusiveness or its imperfect blending of light and dark. Instead, he wishes for a pure and permanent beauty, all sunlight. These transcendent longings are compared with those of Ponce de Leon, who thirsted for a fountain that would "cleanse repair / All waste" and achieve eternal perfection "where was ageless power from the first." A transcendent vision like this at first seems to bring order and direction into the temporal flux; as "Juan Ponce" neared Florida, "parrots prophesied; / Vines ciphered; to each waterside / Paths pitched in hopes to the fair and noble well." Yet, as in so many of the poems, as soon as any such sense of finality or perfection is approached, the poem turns on itself, shifts, and eludes our simpler formulations. Rather than repairing all waste, a vertical transcendence merely transforms a lush landscape *into* a waste: "makes deserts, barrens to a sign / Deckled and delicate arbors" by reducing physical objects into dead signs pointing *beyond* themselves to a center which isn't there anyway. So Wilbur resigns that transcendent "power" in order to accept an ever changing, imperfect, secular world. "All creatures are, and are undone," he writes, and rather than letting our wishes "blight / The various world," we must "welcome love in the lively wasting sun."

Much of his work, Wilbur has said, can be "understood as a public quarrel with the aesthetics of Edgar Allan Poe"—the Poe of the hypnagogic imagination, its desire for absolute beauty.[28] Yet it is wrong to conclude, as Wilbur's critics often do, that Wilbur, in refusing any disembodied beauty, simply turns to the "things of this world," because "the difficulty of direct apprehension and expression of the object" that he speaks of in the Bard symposium informs the workings of his poetry as well. The sensual world is fluid, changing, hard to grasp—especially in words. In "Praise in Summer" Wilbur begins to celebrate the season by inventing a series of metaphors; then he repudiates figurative language as the "uncreation" of physicality, only to end by disavowing metaphor in language that is itself metaphoric. His striving to push through to the thing itself is balanced against his awareness that metaphorization is inevitable. If the metaphoric turns and counterturns of "Praise in Summer" enact the difficulty of direct expression, in other poems the elusiveness of the physical world is stressed by the paradoxical language in which it is described: "the *lively wasting* sun." So the desire to reify experience, to possess objects, becomes another form of absolutism which the poems expose to ironic scrutiny. "Who wills devoutly to absorb, contain, / birds give him pain," Wilbur playfully reflects in "In a Bird Sanctuary." Like physical

28. "On My Own Work," in *Responses*, p. 125.

objects, art objects are to be valued precisely because they are "immune to us"; in "A Dutch Courtyard," based on a painting by Pieter de Hooch, Wilbur wryly mocks "Old Andrew Mellon," who, "consumed with greedy ire, . . . glowered at this Dutch / Courtyard, until it bothered him so much / He bought the thing entire." "Cigales," the first poem in *The Beautiful Changes,* confronts us with the mysterious independence of even the simplest things. The song of cicadas, a gratuitous gift of nature, provokes attempts to appropriate and contain it with meaning. Medieval "changers of miracles" perceived the song symbolically as a "simple sign"; "others made morals," but "such a plain thing / Morals could not surround." In fact, not even careful "listening"—"not 'chirr' nor 'cri-cri' "—can catch the song. But the dilemma, experienced as tyrannical by the greedy mind, can still be cherished: "this thin uncomprehended song it is / springs healing questions into binding air," as if the song's incomprehensibility, its very immunity—by stirring a self-questioning meditation—were healing.

"There is no straight / way of approaching it," Wilbur writes in "Cigales," a view that leads him to practice the poetics of "indirection" and "complexity of attitude" propounded by Brooks and Warren. In Wilbur's early poetry we feel the pull toward abstract form ("geometric grace") as well as the equally powerful pull toward "the opulent bric-a-brac earth" (*PRW,* p. 183). Each side of the opposition is entertained but each is finally resisted, with particular poems evolving from the interplay between the two. As in "Caserta Garden," "Sunlight Is Imagination," and "Praise in Summer," poetic structures gracefully fold back on and balance themselves; poetic language is similarly charged with ironic juxtaposition and paradox; and endings, often balanced antitheses like "rots and thrives" or "the lively wasting sun" sustain rather than resolve the poem's contradictions. Wilbur is like the caddis fly in "Water Walker" who knows both air and water but finally inhabits neither; he is a poet of beautiful changes, an elusive figure who can freely explore opposed perspectives because he is finally committed to neither. As Wilbur suggests in "Up, Jack," one only accomplishes a simplification of self "by pouring *all* the man into an act" (my italics). By refusing such passionate and unequivocal commitment, Wilbur frees his imagination to make the circling, playful movements of his poems.

Yet it is not as if Wilbur's poems formally enact the principle of perpetual change. Rather, in them change has been poetically appropriated and stabilized. The same oppositions that set the poems into motion provide the stability of a balanced closure; Wilbur's traditional, predetermined forms offer the reader plenty of reassurance that the poet has managed "the disorder both outside him and within his own mind." In the Bard symposium Wilbur argues that "in the best paintings of Cézanne you are aware of the tremendous mass, immediacy and entity of the world, and at the same time of the *mastery of the mind* which got that into a frame" (p. 188; my italics). For Wilbur the framing of experience—like the use of meters, for Tate—defines literariness and even humanness. "The painter who throws away the frame and rebels at composition is not a painter any more," Wilbur declares; "he thinks the world is himself, and that there is no need of a devious and delimited struggle with it. He lacks the feeling of inadequacy which must precede every genuine act of creation" (p. 189). On the one hand, framing devices offer reassurance of "mastery of the mind"; on the other hand, such mastery is "delimited," and art offers reassurance of our human, and imaginative, inadequacy. The absence of such formal reassurance means, for Wilbur, an easy narcissistic self-projection, an emotional absolutism. Significantly, the "open" poetic theories that were soon to be announced in Olson's "Projective Verse" (1950) reverse this mythology of poetic form; set forms come to signify imaginative imposition. For Wilbur, they signify a modest, delimited, and admittedly fictive control. The autotelic poem has become an elegantly made, self-balancing enclosure, in which the world's beautiful changes have been rocked into stability.

"How beauties will grow richer walled about," Wilbur writes in a kind of ars poetica line from "Caserta Garden." He is a poet more concerned with marking than with breaking boundaries, especially those between life and art. *The Beautiful Changes* is a more than somewhat precious book that is continuously preoccupied with the poetic medium, and the collection offers a dazzling display of technical mastery in a wide variety of difficult forms. In addition to several poems written in intricately rhymed and measured stanzas, Wilbur writes fourteen poems in quatrains, three in terza rima, two sonnets, and three poems in which rhyming takes place between the same lines of succeeding stanzas. Like Lowell, the young Wilbur sought the challenge of difficult forms, and while his forms are not violently thrust upon the material as Lowell's are, the effect in both cases is to draw attention to a tension between content and form, life and art. Set forms mark the work as artifice, bearing reassurance of both the poet's power and his inadequacy. In "Objects" Wilbur praises

> that devout intransitive eye
> Of Pieter de Hooch: see feinting from his plot of paint
> The trench of light on boards, the much-mended dry
>
> Courtyard wall of brick,
> And sun submerged in beer, and streaming in glasses,

The weave of a sleeve, the careful and undulant tile. A quick
Change of the eye and all this calmly passes

Into a day, into magic.

Pieter de Hooch possesses what Wilbur elsewhere calls "routine vision"—the opposite of Poe's disembodied vision—an eye that devotedly
examines the external world and seeks to render it accurately, intransi-
tively. Yet the world is not so easy to hold: "a quick / Change of the eye"
and all passes; at the end of the second quoted stanza, Wilbur seems to
conclude that the physical world eludes our grasp as the eye moves or
the world changes or as time passes. But in another of his characteristic
changes of direction, Wilbur's meditation, as it crosses the stanza break,
turns back and suggests the contrary view: that the artist, close to reality
yet transforming it as he converts it into his own medium, changes the
passing scene into "a day," into the "magic" of art. In the Bard symposium, Wilbur argues that poetry should begin with "a perception of the
hopelessness of direct combat" with the world "and a resort to the warfare
of spells, effigies, and prophecies" (p. 189). In "Objects," a phrase like
"quick change," words like "feinting," "plot," and "passes" all suggest
spells or magical deceptions. Wilbur, however, does not conceive of poetic
language as magically incarnational. Instead, the poet, an elusive figure
adept at quick changes, creates illusions; he is a magician who, all during
his virtuoso performance, winks at his audience to remind them that it
is, after all, an illusion, a feinting. A Wilbur poem, then, becomes a verbal
conjuring, a series of light, quick, beautiful changes, and its intricacy of
form becomes both part of the feat and a reminder that the poem, while
creating the illusionary presence of "mastery," remains a fictive construct.
To vary Auden's famous dictum, poetry makes nothing happen except
itself. In this way, both the poet's power and his inadequacy are inscribed
in the framed confines of art.

"Every poem begins, or ought to, by a disorderly retreat to defensible
positions," says Wilbur in the Bard symposium, locating himself at the
other end of the literary battlefield from the avant-garde. His carefully
defended and well-balanced position concedes the limitations of personal
imagination and the authority of stable traditional forms. Wilbur's refusal
to sacralize poetic language gives him a more demystified view of his
medium than many of those poets proclaimed to be "postmodernists."
Are we to look forward to a poststructuralist revival of Wilbur? Hardly;
because his works finally do enclose and reify what they also show cannot
be enclosed and reified. Similarly, his poetry and criticism both claim a
dogma-free neutrality and inclusiveness very much along New Critical

lines. But this claim of imaginative disinterestedness becomes the crack in Wilbur's defensible position, which produces a poetry based on personal removal and exclusion. In Wilbur, the beautiful changes are not experienced from inside the "field of action," as they are, say, in Olson; rather, they are witnessed through a window—beautifully and carefully framed. The window, in fact, overlooks a Caserta Garden, and there is also a view of the world beyond that "rots and thrives"; *but* "beauties will grow richer walled about." Wilbur's stance as an *observer* of change explains, I believe, why his poetry, except for a chastening of its language, has never really changed over the years, a striking phenomenon for a member of a generation with so many of the poetically "twice born." From Wilbur's poetry the urgent sense of cultural crisis that we find in modernist verse has vanished; so has the struggle to make poetry "modern," to grapple with the present. Wilbur writes like a man who is at home in a social and historical present which never enters his poetry. His poems occupy a *literary* space in which they carry on their quarrel with the symbolic figure of Poe. Yet Wilbur's critique of the hypnagogic imagination seems more like a quarrel he has with an external figure than one he has with himself. As we shall see, the young Lowell was possessed by a real thirst for the absolute; but Wilbur's movements toward such transcendence seem feinting gestures in a maneuver toward a more sensible position he has already occupied anyway. The result is a poetry that seldom challenges its readers—or itself. The violent disruptions and tensed oppositions of modernist poetry are converted into the smooth and graceful turns and counterturns of a verse retreating to "defensible positions."

In his lifelong quarrel with Poe, Wilbur was taking on the grandfather of symbolism. When Lowell renounced a symbolist poetic in *Life Studies,* he directly confronted the master, Mallarmé, in "Waking in the Blue," but Wilbur attacks symbolism at its weak, American flank—Poe. But if the young Wilbur was looking for an alternative to a symbolist poetic, his proposal of the well-made autotelic poem offers only less, not a genuine alternative. Wilbur himself, of course, did not view it this way, and his criticism provides an instructive instance of the fifties myth of modernism as aberrant and excessive. In "On My Own Work," he observes that poets of his generation are often asked "where they stand in relation to the revolution in American poetry" that took place around 1910.

> I think there truly *was* a revolution then, in poetry as in the other arts, and if one looks at poetry anthologies of the year 1900 one can see that a revolution was called for—a revolution against trivial formalism, dead rhetoric, and genteel subject matter.[29]

29. Ibid., p. 122.

In what seems like a fairly innocent historical account Wilbur here actually redefines modernism in such a way that it becomes possible for him to reject its specific character without seeming to do so. Modernism resulted from an intellectual and cultural crisis, a crisis of belief. But Wilbur's reconception of it as strictly literary, another of those perennial attempts to re-energize a worn-out poetic language, not only assimilates modernism into the tradition it repudiated; it also empties the experimental thrust of that movement of any *necessity* and thus makes straight the way of Wilbur's own return to that tradition. Granted, a revolution *did* take place, Wilbur admits, in a concession to its reality that safely distances it in the past. And from the security of his own disengaged vantage point, Wilbur can lament how poetry (like music and painting) became "entrapped in reductive theories."[30] In Wilbur, as in the fifties generally, "reductive theories" is a redundant phrase; the theories he has in mind are "reductive" in proportion as they are ambitious; and Wilbur's own more modest and nonprogrammatic stance can reduce in its own quiet ways. Here, it sounds as if he were offering a balanced critique of the excesses of a revolutionary movement, a sensible gesture that few would debate at least until they saw it applied. In fact, the theories that Wilbur does cite as reductive—the attempts to "purify poetry of all but organic rhythms," "the Imagist insistence that ideas be implicit in description," and the efforts "to abandon logical progression, and to write in quasimusical form"—were not the extreme and extravagant edges of modernism;[31] they were all serious attempts to find ways of organizing experience that were subversive of those procedures validated and established by both the culture and the literary tradition. Wilbur actually questions modernism at its core. Like his concern to reconcile "experimental gains" with traditional forms, his revisionist account of modernism, which may strike us at first as an all-too-minimal shift, actually causes a tremor along the foundations which shatters the entire modernist enterprise.

As Donald Wesling points out, the twentieth-century poet is "faced with a plurality of styles, a baffling immensity of choice." "Since Wordsworth, but especially since 1910, and more intensely since 1945, the beginning poet and the achieved master have alike been conscious that any choice of poetic form is an arbitrariness which must be justified."[32] Wesling's point can be taken one step further by saying that in this era *all* forms—inherited or invented—must *contain* their own justification. Yet for the beginning poets of the postwar period, the shaping of a poem was not regarded as a problematic activity. Invented forms were viewed as

30. Ibid., p. 123.
31. Ibid, pp. 122–23.
32. "Thoroughly Modern Measures," *Boundary 2,* 3 (Winter 1975): 455.

aberrational and read out of the canon. Set forms required no justification and were certainly not to be questioned; timeless, they possessed a privileged status and provided sturdy conventions to be adopted, perhaps refined, but used. Confronted with a stylistic abundance, these circumspect young poets constructed a garden wall and withdrew; from inside, they professed inclusiveness, eclecticism, and complexity of attitude. Yet the reality was that no period of modern literary history has been so dominated by a single idea of writing.

A more specific sense of both the extent and character of this idea of writing can be conveyed by looking at ten first books of poetry published between the mid-forties and the mid-fifties, all written by poets who have, by now, achieved established reputations: William Meredith, *Love Letter from an Impossible Land* (1944); Reed Whittemore, *Heroes and Heroines* (1946); Howard Moss, *The Wound and the Weather* (1946); Howard Nemerov, *The Image and the Law* (1947); Louis Simpson, *The Arrivistes* (1949); Peter Viereck, *Terror and Decorum* (1950); James Merrill, *First Poems* (1951); Adrienne Rich, *A Change of World* (1951); W. S. Merwin, *A Mask for Janus* (1952); and John Ashbery, *Some Trees* (1956). Stylistically, this list encompasses a range from the hard, dry satiric wit of Howard Nemerov to the elegant reveries of the young Ashbery. All of these books *are* quite different from one another—except at the level of ultimate assumption. Except for a few poems in *Some Trees,* all of the poems in all of the books are composed in metered verse and most of them make extensive use of rhyme and complicated verse forms. Pound had broken the pentameter; now, once again, it was time for carving— into stanzas. Nemerov's book, for instance, contains blank verse, couplets, quatrains, various elaborate five- and six-line patterns, terza rima, two sestinas, and it closes with the title poem in which Nemerov vows to compose "in *measured* dance, with the *whole* instrument" (my italics).

"We live in an age of sonnets," Williams grumbled in the Bard symposium, and it is tempting to dismiss this remark as the reiteration of one of Williams's favorite polemical themes. Yet the more one reads the poetry of this period, the more one is convinced that Williams might have been a little more accurate had he declared it the age of the sestina—and other such intricate forms that come to the reader marked as difficult and artificial. In his first book Merwin deals with legendary figures moving in a shadowy dream landscape, and he does so in forms that seem deliberately antique and artificial; his book includes two ballads, two sestinas, a rondel, a "half-rondel," an ode, two sonnets, three "carols," five "songs," a dramatic colloquy written in nine-line stanzas (with only two rhymes for the entire poem), and one poem in three twenty-line stanzas which uses only two rhymes for each of the first two stanzas and one for the last.

Of course, there is nothing intrinsically "wrong" with writing in set or even highly elaborate forms, though the results in this instance were something less than major work. The problem, rather, had to do with the attitude with which such forms were approached; they were not played with, explored, pushed—the way Eliot introduced new tones of feeling into the quatrain of the Sweeny poems. They were taken up seriously, dutifully, and somewhat anxiously as *foundations*. In the postwar period, poetry characteristically began as a not-too-disorderly retreat to preexisting positions. One reason for this can be found in a major theme in these ten first books: the poet's persistent representation of the self as powerless, passively suffering the burdens of a splintered, chaotic world. None of these secular poets finds any absolute principle unifying their experience; but they do not answer the violence without by a violence from within. Instead, they adopt a "mature" and unillusioned stance of accommodation, with the significant stipulation that life's disorders can be managed and even redeemed by the gentle imposition of timeless traditional forms. Order is achieved, then, only by separating art from life, and transcendence quietly reappears in the image of the well-made autotelic poem as a kind of secular eternity. In the first works of these ten poets, the imagination is valorized—by being dehistorized. They do not confront historical pressures in evolved forms that are disjunctive and heterogeneous; instead, they step back and circumscribe delimited areas of experience in stable forms. So in the fifties the poem became, as Auden pronounced, a "closed system," a sealed enclosure that was transcendent, safe, and stultifying.[33]

All of this can be seen more specifically by looking at one of these ten books, Adrienne Rich's *A Change of World*.[34] At the stylistic surface, Rich's early writing is strikingly different from that of Wilbur. The elements of verbal intricacy and display—the puns, paradoxes, clashing images, quick shifts of direction—are replaced by a plainer, more austere language, sometimes closer to actual speech. At once less lush and less playful than Wilbur's, Rich's first poems are also less preoccupied with aesthetic philosophy and the problematics of their own creation and more engaged with moral issues and psychological conflicts. In a language that is frankly discursive and openly referential, Rich shows an even stronger desire than Wilbur to find a way out of symbolist poetics, but the decorum and passivity of the poems prevent her from generating a forceful alternative. Her poems, too, approach disruptive internal and external forces

33. *The Dyer's Hand and Other Essays* (New York, 1962), p. xii.
34. *A Change of World* (New Haven, 1951). Page numbers for quotations from poems not identified by title will be given in the text with the abbreviation *ACW; Diving into the Wreck* (New York, 1973) will be cited as *DW*.

more directly than Wilbur's do, but, as Helen Vendler points out, "the danger" is always "contained, and in fact the action of containing danger" becomes "gravely obligatory, a sacred trust."[35] *The Beautiful Changes* and *A Change of World:* the titles themselves reveal the crucial differences and similarities between these two poets. Wilbur accepts, celebrates, and even enacts in the movement of his verse processes of change, from which he has distanced and exempted himself. Rich, later to title a book *The Will to Change,* here bitterly regrets or actively resists change; she seeks to enclose dangerous and potentially transforming experiences in set forms. By radically different routes, then, Wilbur and Rich arrive at the period's dominant idea of writing: the cult of self-insulation and closed forms as the only stays we have against the confusions of a disordered world.

Rich herself has called *A Change of World* "a book of very well-tooled poems of a sort of very bright student" who was, it appears, eager to please the literary authorities.[36] In his Foreword an avuncular and condescending W. H. Auden was happy to reassure that "the poems a reader will encounter in this book are neatly and modestly dressed, speak quietly but do not mumble, respect their elders but are not cowed by them, and do not tell fibs" (*ACW,* p. 11). Certainly the book does skillfully and respectfully restate many of what by 1951 had become the canonical views of twentieth-century verse. Like so many of her contemporaries, Rich locates herself in an "unmastered world" (*ACW,* p. 79) that seems beyond human control. "I have inhaled impossibility," she declares in a rare moment of bravado and in a voice that is more Emily Dickinson's than her own (*ACW,* p. 20); but her attention characteristically turns to the dangers we are exposed to in a violent and uncertain world. "Why are we scarred with winter's thrust today?" she asks in "Purely Local"; no answer is given because no answer *can* be given. As she suggests in "What Ghosts Can Say," the modern world is one in which "the terror" remains but "without the meaning" it possessed in earlier ages. And so without any unified framework to supply such meaning, the self becomes helpless and static, confronted with immense temporal, historical, social, and natural forces. Power is outside, potentialy invasive; experience can never really be mastered, only suffered. In this context heroic aspirations are viewed as foolish delusions, likely to be chastened by winter's thrust. Rebellious impulses are similarly dismissed as childish in a poem like "A View of the Terrace"; in fact, any action, any assertion of the self or hope for change, becomes a gesture that merely exposes us to pain in a process that inevitably leads to defeat anyway. "So from promethean

35. "Ghostlier Demarcations, Keener Sounds," reprinted in *Adrienne Rich's Poetry,* p. 161.
36. "Talking with Adrienne Rich," *Ohio Review* 13 (Fall 1971): 31.

hopes we came this far," Rich writes in "From a Chapter on Literature";
she is *not* being nostalgic. In fact, she is voicing the self-assessment of a
generation that assumed that, in literature as in life, all the larger and
more challenging possibilities were not only exhausted; they were
impossible.

So in *A Change of World,* Rich's predominant stance is to cut down
aspirations, adopt a low profile and keep a stiff upper lip—the route of
resignation and stoic endurance. "Eastport to Block Island" urges would-
be adventurers to "stay in and wait for tidings" rather than to risk a
stormy sea. In "An Unsaid Word" the later foe of the patriarchal system
advocates patient acceptance of male inaccessibility. Such stoicism helps
to explain her evident attraction to the poetry of Frost; and it permeates
the poems, an attempt to convert a feeling of powerlessness into a self-
styled mature wisdom, the unillusioned awareness of those "who know
limits" (*ACW,* p. 43).

In fact, the setting of limits, the marking of boundaries, become crucial
forms of activity in *A Change of World* as well as recurrent metaphors
for the kind of creative act that produced these "well-tooled poems." The
opening poem, "Storm Warnings," shows Rich anxiously wandering
through the house "from window to closed window," fastening shutters,
drawing curtains, lighting candles "sheathed in glass"—all to guard against
a coming storm that we are invited to interpret as a psychological as well
as a natural disturbance. Powerful forces here threaten the poet, who then
seeks safety in a tightly sealed enclosure. Throughout *A Change of World*
the making of a self or a poem is imagined as the occupying of a fragile,
self-contained space; potentially disruptive forces have been distanced
and controlled. "Storm Warnings" is thus both an expression of Rich's
yearning for the well-made autotelic poem and a revelation of the psychological needs such poetry serves. "Storm Warnings" echoes Frost's
"Storm Fear," a poem that conveys the terrifying possibility of a storm's
obliteration of all protective enclosures—the barn, the house. But this
terror and vulnerability are precisely what are missing from Rich, who
contains her dangers in timeless aphorisms and elegant images. As a result,
her poem seems *merely* a defensive gesture, merely self-protective; its
dangers never become close or specific enough to be convincingly
threatening.

"In those years," Rich recalls, "formalism was part of the strategy—
like asbestos gloves, it allowed me to handle materials I couldn't pick up
bare-handed."[37] *A Change of World* does contain two sonnets and two
poems in terza rima as well as several poems in elaborately rhymed pat-

37. Ibid.

terns; all the poems are written in meter. Yet Rich's formalism does not foreground poetic artifice and offers neither the easy virtuosity of a Wilbur nor the willed difficulties of a Lowell; in fact, the conscious modesty of her work provides one measure of the waning of ambition and energy in the poetry of the early fifties. "So from promethean hopes we came this far"—to a comfortable traditionalism. Later on Rich would conceive of writing as a process of discovery in which "the poem itself engenders new sensations, new awareness in me as it progresses." But at the beginning of her career she felt the poem to be "an arangement of ideas and feelings, pre-determined, and it said what I had already decided it should say." The poems sagaciously propound timeless truths, and their forms, similarly timeless, are external and "predetermined." Local surprises can and do occur, "but control, technical mastery and intellectual clarity were the real goals"; in the end poems are extensions of the human will.[38] It is worth pointing out that the author of *The Will to Change* has never abandoned, only complicated, this view. Beginning with *Snapshots of a Daughter-in-Law* (1963), Rich gets into more intimate touch with her disruptive impulses and she sheds set forms in order to do so. By the time of *Diving into the Wreck* (1973), the protective enclosure of the early poems has become a "prison house" (*DW*, p. 17) and a fiery language burns away "composed" (*DW*, p. 7) (preexisting, detached) social and poetic orders. But Rich does not simply counter her youthful discipline with an affirmation of impulsive abandon. "The words are purposes. / The words are maps," she writes in "Diving into the Wreck," and her symbolic descent into the unconscious differs from male versions of that archetype by insisting on human control; the poem ends in fact by proposing the integration of passion and purpose in a unified, androgynous self. *A Change of World,* however, seeks stability by tightening the barricades and trying to shut out the storm by the imposition of "composed" orders.

Poets as different as Eliot, Williams, and Stevens had all sought to evolve new kinds of literary order out of the disarray of their contemporary experience; but the early Rich, like Wilbur, assumes a tension between art and experience, form and flux. In "Life and Letters" Rich speaks of the artist as a "violent gardener," "forcing" life into "form." "Art is out of love with life," she pronounces in "At a Bach Concert," and she goes on:

> This antique discipline, tenderly severe,
> Renews belief in love yet masters feeling,
> Asking of us a grace in what we bear.

38. "Poetry and Experience: Statement at a Poetry Reading (1964)," in *Adrienne Rich's Poetry,* p. 89.

Form is the ultimate gift that love can offer—
The vital union of necessity
With all that we desire, all that we suffer.

A too-compassionate art is half an art.
Only such proud restraining purity
Restores the else-betrayed, too-human heart.

Elsewhere in *A Change of World,* Rich tritely laments the loss of spontaneous feeling in an overly analytic present; she more often feels, as she
does here, that passion is dangerous and that a personal and literary
severity is required to achieve shape or order. "At a Bach Concert" may
hypothesize "the vital union" of emotion and control, but the poem itself
decidedly tilts toward a "discipline" that "masters feeling." It is no ac-
cident, then, that Rich here employs a variant of terza rima, for those
forms that best master feeling are "antique," traditional. In her well-
known essay "When We Dead Awaken: Writing as Re-Vision," Rich
wants "not to pass on a tradition but to break its hold over us";[39] but in
"The Uncle Speaks in the Drawing Room," the young Rich sympathetically creates the admonishing voice of a custodian of culture. The "mob"
"standing sullen in the square" reminds the uncle of "certain frailties of
glass" which "lead in times like these to fear / For crystal vase and
chandelier." "Let us only bear in mind," he complacently concludes,
"How these treasures handed down / From a calmer age passed on / Are
in the keeping of our kind." The author of *A Change of World,* respectfully
preserving those delicate forms handed down from the past, has clearly
internalized such paternal admonitions.

Richard Wilbur's father was a painter, and in one of the few poems in
The Beautiful Changes that have any overt autobiographical content ("My
Father Paints the Summer") the son celebrates the imaginative power of
the father who, in the midst of a rainy summer, still "tricks into sight"
"a summer never seen, / A granted green." The father possesses exactly
that magical, visionary power which Wilbur indirectly discredits in his
lifelong "public quarrel" with Poe. By this strategy the son avoids direct
rivalry with the father and counters imaginative omnipotence with a skillful traditionalism. Rich, in her striving to meet paternal demands, seems
even less rebellious. Her father encouraged her writing, criticized her
work, and tried "to get me into more regular meters and rhymes";[40] "for
a long time" she tried "to please him, or rather, not to displease him";

39. *Adrienne Rich's Poetry,* p. 91.
40. Robert Shaw and John Plotz, "An Interview with Adrienne Rich," *The Island* 1 (May
1966): 2.

his influence, she says, expanded into the figure of the "literary master."[41] Confronted with a change of world, Rich aligned herself with powerful figures who had managed to impose their vision on the world, forcing it into form. In her first book Yeats and Auden were two of these masters; another, and in many ways more interesting one, was Robert Frost. One of Rich's strategies, even clearer in her second book, *The Diamond Cutters* (1955), was to avoid rivalry with the dominating presences of twentieth-century poetry by connecting herself with a less threatening literary tradition, the poetry of New England, which can be heard in her echoes of Dickinson, Robinson, and Frost himself. Frost can be heard in early Wilbur, too: many of his poems proceed from imaginative flight back to earth in a way that is strongly reminiscent of "Birches."[42] In fact, from Wilbur in the late forties to James Wright in the late fifties, Frost's poetic realism offered a possible route for younger poets seeking an alternative to a symbolist poetics, particularly poets, like Rich, who wished to renew, not to break, traditional verse forms.

The presence of Frost can be heard in the dramatic monologues such as "Autumn Equinox" and "The Perennial Answer" in *The Diamond Cutters* and in the rhythm and idiom of short poems ("Boundary," "Storm Warnings," and "For the Conjunction of Two Planets") included in *A Change of World*. More generally, Rich's ironic assessment of romantic idealism, her insistence on human limits, and her stoicism link her with Frost, as does her notion of poetic form as a defense against disorder, a "momentary stay against confusion." Yet the writing of the young Rich appears timid and genteel beside the tough, spare verses of her mentor, whose stoicism seems hard-won. Rich's "well-tooled poems" always know exactly where they are going; hardly "unfolded by surprize," they do not cut the figure a Frost poem makes and they end, as we have seen, by seeming *merely* defensive gestures. In fact, Rich's "By No Means Native" hints at her own awareness that, for her, adopting the New England inheritance was something of an affectation, and not just because she had been born in Baltimore. The poem describes a young man who leaves home and settles into a new locale only to find that while he carefully mimes the outward forms of his adopted culture, he cannot feel "the sense of being held and owned / By one ancestral patch of local ground." To this wanderer, a fully autonomous existence seems fearful; yet participation seems impossible. Like this character, the author of *A Change of World*, self-consciously emulating forms and attitudes that she does not

41. *Adrienne Rich's Poetry*, p. 93.
42. See Wilbur's remarks on Frost and on "Birches" as a poem of "limited aspiration" in "Poetry and Happiness," in *Responses*, pp. 110–14.

genuinely feel and excluding too much of the violent but living present, fears that she may only be going through the (dead) motions.

Traditional forms, because they are imagined as dissociated from and imposed upon contemporary experience, may kill as they protect, and they may not even protect very effectively. The "violent gardener" is not enough. In its mistrust of its own idea of order, *A Change of World* is most honest and alive. In "Aunt Jennifer's Tigers" the aunt weaves the powerful animals into her tapestry, but her art does nothing to change a life she is "mastered by." Similarly, in "Mathilde in Normandy" women weave tapestries to compensate for the absence of their voyaging husbands, but their "keen remembrance" and "anxiety" return to disturb their creative work. Rich's first book typically imagines the creative act as an effort to master feelings in an order that is about to crack precisely because it is dissociated from life. Ultimately the self *is* helpless. Our instruments can predict but they cannot prevent violent weather, Rich finally acknowledges in "Storm Warnings," where a "keyhole draught" admits "the insistent whine / Of weather through the unsealed aperture" in spite of all her efforts at self-protection. Although she enjoys the romantic atmosphere in "The Kursal at Interlacken" Rich still senses that this safe world is a mere "charade," the product of withdrawal and exclusion, while in "A View of the Terrace," she stands apart, ironically viewing those who fancy themselves "impervious" to experience. Describing a clock that has lost its hands, Rich pronounces that "time may be silenced but will not be stilled" (*ACW*, p. 36) and the poems continually evoke powerful forces (sea, wind, time) that not only thwart the violent gardener's efforts to subdue them into form but actually shatter all of mankind's strivings for order. In fact, the book's two concluding poems— "Unsounded" and "For the Conjunction of Two Planets"—both suggest that human orders, not grounded in reality, are arbitrary projections, empty impositions. Just what makes "predetermined" orders attractive— their independence from any immediate occasion—also makes them seem empty and dead. In the end these poems undermine even the guarded affirmations of "mature" wisdom that they at first seem to make, though such self-questioning made possible the subsequent growth and change of Rich's poetry.

Yet, what is most disturbing about the younger poets of the postwar period is the way their basic assumptions reflected the social and political consensus of their time. The twenties produced an aesthetic, the thirties a social dissidence; the fifties produced an accommodation which dismissed critical perspectives as "irresponsible." In the editorial statement introducing a 1952 symposium called Our Country and Our Culture, the editors of the once-Marxist *Partisan Review* observed that for better or worse, most writers no longer accept alienation as the artist's fate in America; on the contrary, they want very much to be a part of American life. More and more writers have ceased to think of themselves as rebels and exiles. They now believe that their values, if they are to be realized at all, must be realized in America and in relation to the actuality of American life.[43]

The list of contributors to this symposium, including Jacques Barzun, Richard Chase, Leslie Fiedler, Sidney Hook, Reinhold Niebhur, Philip Rahv, David Riesman, Arthur Schlesinger, Jr., and Lionel Trilling, reads like a *Who's Who* in American intellectual life of the fifties; *no* contributor questioned the accuracy of the editors' characterization, and only three—Norman Mailer, Irving Howe, and C. Wright Mills—found anything to lament in the writers' rediscovery of America. In one of the more flabbergasting remarks in a symposium that provided an abundance of them, William Barrett beamingly reported that it was good "to know that George F. Babbitt had virtues which the '20s never recognized" (p. 9).

In retrospect, the reasons for the shift from opposition to acceptance seem clear enough. America no longer seemed the cultural barrenness perceived by the expatriates of the twenties—largely because of the accomplishments of these same expatriates. More important, American democracy was no longer viewed, as the *Partisan Review* editors put it, as "merely a capitalist myth but a reality which must be defended against Russian totalitarianism" (p. 3); it was the Soviet threat that made criticism "irresponsible." Unlike Europe, the United States had prospered after the war and it was a prosperity in which artists and intellectuals, with their academic positions and their grants, shared. But the important thing about this prosperity was that it demonstrated that American capitalism, as altered by moderate New Deal reforms, had "a responsible and stable basis."[44] The system worked, and it worked so well that Daniel Bell could announce that "there is today a rough consensus among intellectuals on political issues: the acceptance of a Welfare State; the desirability of decentralized power; a system of mixed economy and of political pluralism."[45] Critical perspectives, theory of any kind, were obsolete. In poli-

43. The symposium was subsequently published as *America and the Intellectuals* (New York, 1953); my quotation is from p. 3. Much later, in "On My Own Work," Richard Wilbur observed that the American poet "shows somewhat less of the conventional romantic defiance, somewhat less of the bitterness of the wallflower; he is increasingly disposed to think of himself as a citizen." "In becoming the poet-citizen rather than an alienated artist," the writer is running certain risks, the ever-balanced Wilbur concedes; "but I myself would consider them risks well taken." See *Responses,* pp. 115–16. Subsequent references to the *PR* symposium will be made in the text.
44. Michael Paul Rogin, *The Intellectuals and McCarthy: the Radical Specter* (Worcester, Mass., 1967), p. 9.
45. "The End of Ideology," *The End of Ideology* (New York, 1962), pp. 402–3.

tics, as in literature, all the major innovations had already been accomplished; it was "the end of ideology."

In the fifties, writers were thus by no means alone in making an ideology out of the denial of ideology. In fact, a major irony of the period is that young writers and New Critics alike characterized their activities as disinterested and dogma-free, and in this way they could claim to transcend personal and historical limitations; yet it was just such claims that placed them solidly in their historical era. Philip Rahv warned that it was time "to be done with Utopian illusions and heady expectations" (p. 88), and the lesson of the Nazi and Soviet regimes was, fifties liberals tirelessly repeated, that ideologies of both left and right inevitably culminated in totalitarian orders. Bell's critique of chiliastic illusions in "The End of Ideology" sounds remarkably like New Critical "complexity of attitude" applied to politics; in both cases idealisms were attacked as abstract styles of thought that evade the complexities of actual experience. According to Bell, ideologies are always extreme; they are always passionate and thus committed to social transformation; and they are always passionate simplifications, thus their dangerous appeal to the all-too-heady expectations of the masses. Similar views of ideology informed a variety of influential texts in the fifties. In his revisionist history *The Age of Reform,* Richard Hofstadter found the Populists and Progressives animated by a regrettable "moral absolutism"; Daniel Boorstin carried this revisionist propensity several steps further by arguing that the genius of American politics had always been its apathy toward theory; and this antitheoretical theory was given pop form in the wharfside philosophizings of Eric Hoffer in *The True Believer.*[46]

All of these men speak with their generation's voice of sober disenchantment. Sternly warning against Utopian illusions, responsible, tough-minded intellectuals strove to construct a liberalism that realistically acknowledged man's mixed, imperfect nature. Writing with the affectionate exasperation of a wisely disillusioned parent, Richard Hofstadter complained that we Americans "are forever restlessly pitting ourselves against" life's evils, "demanding changes, improvements, remedies, but not often with sufficient sense of the limits that the human condition will in the end insistently impose upon us."[47] In social theory, politics, and even in theology, as in literary circles, acceptance of limits was identical with wisdom. Traditional liberalism had pictured "man as perfectible," according

46. See Richard Hofstadter, *The Age of Reform* (New York, 1955), especially the Introduction; Daniel Boorstin, *The Genius of American Politics* (Chicago, 1953), especially the first chapter: "How Belief in the Existence of an American Theory Has Made a Theory Superfluous"; and Eric Hoffer, *The True Believer* (New York, 1951).
47. *The Age of Reform,* p. 16.

to Arthur Schlesinger in *The Vital Center,* but "the Soviet experience, on top of the rise of fascism, reminded my generation rather forcibly that man was, indeed, imperfect."[48] The period's most influential theologian, Reinhold Niebuhr, similarly sought in *The Children of Light and the Children of Darkness* to provide democracy with "a more realistic vindication" than that given by a "liberal culture" that holds man to be perfectible.

> A consistent pessimism in regard to man's rational capacity for justice invariably leads to absolutistic political theories; for they prompt the conviction that only preponderant power can coerce the various vitalities of a community into a working harmony. But a too consistent optimism in regard to man's ability and inclination to grant justice to his fellows obscures the perils of chaos which perennially confront every society, including a free society.[49]

Steering his moderate course between optimism and pessimism, "secular idealisms" and "moral cynicism," Niebuhr shows how the period's disillusioned awareness of limits produced a rhetoric of balanced reasonableness.

To take this point one step further: in the fifties artists and intellectuals, while professing eclecticism and pluralism, drew rigid boundaries marking what was acceptable discourse. Skeptical of passions and absolutes, a writer like Bell promoted pragmatic compromise and the "politics of civility."[50] In *Economics and the Art of Controversy,* John Kenneth Galbraith decided, like Bell, that all the major issues that had generated the controversies of the thirties and forties had now been settled; one result was that the diminishing number of those standing outside the consensus "can be polemical, unreasonable, self-righteous, and violent," while those within it are "persuasive, well-mannered, and ingratiating, and, in the end, disposed to a reasonable compromise"—in short, like Galbraith himself.[51] The "family" of intellectuals surrounding the *Partisan Review* found in the journey many of them had made from Marx to Freud another way to locate dissent outside the proper bounds of discourse. In the symposium Our Country and Our Culture, Newton Arvin could only understand alienation as "the continuance into adult life of the negative Oedipal relations of adolescence" (p. 6); Richard Chase supposed "estrangement" to be "a merely literary pose or the product of personal neurosis" (p. 27). The

48. *The Vital Center* (Cambridge, Mass., 1949), pp. viii–ix.
49. *The Children of Light and the Children of Darkness* (New York, 1944), pp. xii–xiii.
50. See "The End of Ideology" throughout, but particularly the closing pages where we are also promised "the end of rhetoric"; Bell takes the phrase "the politics of civility" from the sociologist Edward Shils; see Bell's "The Dispossessed," in *The Radical Right,* ed. Daniel Bell (New York, 1963), p. 2.
51. *Economics and the Art of Controversy* (New York, 1955), p. 99.

fifties produced a lot of anxious hand-wringing on the part of adults who
had made a not-so-separate peace with America and who fretted over the
younger generation for doing no more than following in their mentors'
footsteps. But in a symposium in the *New Leader,* Norman Podhoretz
embraced young people for seeing that "the real adventure of existence
was to be found not in radical politics or in Bohemia but in the 'moral
life' of the individual, within the framework of his efforts to do his duty
and assume his responsibilities in a world of adults."

> They discovered that "conformity" did not necessarily mean dull-
> ness and unthinking conventionality, that, indeed, there was great
> beauty, profound significance in a man's struggle to achieve freedom
> *through* submission to conditions. . . . Very much aware of how
> complicated and difficult all problems were, very much alive to the
> dangers of ideologies and enthusiasms and passions, very much per-
> suaded that *la verité reste dans les nuances,* they struck a perfect
> attitude of the civilized adult: poised, sober, judicious, prudent.[52]

To be critical or passionate was to be "adolescent"; a kind of psychoanalytic moralism enforced bourgeois values of decorum, prudence, and
accommodation. When he confronted the beat generation writers in "The
Know-Nothing Bohemians," Podhoretz deployed the fifties' rhetoric of
dismissal: they were a "populist" and adolescent threat to culture itself.
The Bohemians of the twenties, he contended, constituted "a movement
created in the name of civilization: its ideals were intelligence, cultivation,
spiritual refinement." Having recreated the moderns in the image of the
fireside poets, Podhoretz then used this image to flail fifties bohemianism,
which he called "hostile to civilization."[53] As Michael Rogin points out
in *The Intellectuals and McCarthy,* a rhetoric based on propriety and
reasonableness subtly delegitimized all radical challenges and even assertions of difference.[54]

The fifties consensus and its "political pluralism" were, then, based
rather nervously upon careful exclusions; in fact, the period can most
accurately be characterized as one combining a complacent sense of well-
being with insecurity and anxiety. Robert Lowell's image of "the tranquilized fifties" in *Life Studies* perfectly captures the violence and uncertainty just below the bland surface. To Bell, ideologies threaten the
"politics of civility" and the "fragile consensus," both precarious orders
vulnerable to unruly disturbances from below.[55] Significant here is the

52. Quoted in James Wechsler, *Reflections of an Angry Middle-Aged Editor* (New York, 1960).
53. "The Know-Nothing Bohemians," *PR* 25 (Spring 1958): 307.
54. *The Intellectuals and McCarthy,* p. 278.
55. "The Dispossessed," p. 2.

distinction Bell draws between the "scholar" and the "intellectual." "The scholar," says Bell, "has a bounded field of knowledge, a tradition, and seems to find his place in it, adding to the accumulated, tested knowledge of the past as to a mosaic." Bell might have been describing the archetypical young poet of the fifties. The scholar, he believed, "is less involved with his 'self,' " but "the intellectual begins with *his* experience, *his* individual perceptions of the world, *his* privileges and deprivations, and judges the world by these sensibilities"; since the intellectual will feel alienated in a commercial civilization, he is apt to become "political," which is to say, ideological.[56] As this piece of mythologizing shows, even prophets of the end of ideology can fall into simplifying abstractions; yet what is most interesting about this dubious distinction is what motivated Bell to make it in the first place—the need to create in the idealized image of the scholar a disinterested figure exempt from the temptations of passion, of theory, and of self. Bell's pluralism becomes a covert elitism, our only stay against the confusions of mass democracy.

In an English department Bell's disinterested scholar would appear as the New Critic, similarly suspicious of enthusiastic idealisms and attuned to complexity. The problem is not simply with the elitism of such conceptions, but with their anxious preoccupation with a fragile order that must be conserved, as in Rich's "The Uncle Speaks in the Drawing Room." Delmore Schwartz in Our Country, Our Culture rightly accused the intellectual class of "a flight from the flux, chaos and uncertainty of the present, a forced and false affirmation of stability in the face of immense and continually mounting instability" (p. 107). The *Partisan Review* symposium itself offered plenty of evidence of such evasion. Irving Howe and Norman Mailer were the only participants seriously concerned with issues of poverty, racism, the war economy; not even that fifties obsession, the Bomb, was much talked about. What worried the contributors were not questions of political or social structure but cultural issues—specifically, the threat of mass culture. As it turned out, the going view was that it was "our culture"—not theirs. A depoliticized Dwight MacDonald became the decade's leading articulator of this fear: "a tepid, flaccid Middlebrow Culture," he warned, "threatens to engulf everything in its spreading core."[57] In defending their reconciliation with "our country," artists and intellectuals were, of course, eager to convince themselves that they had not abdicated their critical function, which they then ex-

56. "The End of Ideology," p. 2.

57. Dwight MacDonald, "A Theory of Mass Culture," in *Mass Culture: The Popular Arts in America,* ed. Bernard Rosenberg and David Manning White (Glencoe, Ill., 1957), pp. 63–64. See also "Masscult and Midcult" in MacDonald's *Against the American Grain* (New York, 1962), pp. 3–75.

ercised in expressing their fears of being engulfed or absorbed by mass
democracy. High culture was thus conceived as a defense against popular
culture, as MacDonald's insistence on separating "high culture" from
"mass-cult and mid-cult" plainly revealed. In so many spheres of thought
in the fifties, order was something to be preserved, either by Bell's scholar
or by the custodians of culture; moreover, such order was to be maintained
by a retreat, a contraction, to a fragile, self-contained space which worked
as a defense against "the flux, chaos and uncertainty of the present." In
discussing his own initiation to what he called "the age of revisionist
liberalism," Norman Podhoretz remarks that "perhaps the most exciting
thing about revisionist liberalism was its smooth compatibility with certain
of the attitudes I had absorbed through the study of literature" and he
mentions in particular "antiutopianism" and the "Niebuhrian stress on
human imperfection."[58] In poetry, this compatibility worked at an even
deeper level: the well-made autotelic poem was simply the literary version
of the fifties idea of order.

As Norman Mailer complained in the *Partisan Review* symposium,
"everywhere the American writer is being dunned to become healthy, to
grow up, to accept the American reality, to integrate himself, to eschew
disease, to re-value institutions" (p. 68). Robert Lowell, as we have seen,
thought the poetry of the fifties possessed "tremendous skill" yet to be
"divorced from culture somehow." Together, Mailer and Lowell accurately characterize the crisis which poetry had reached in the fifties: a
mode of writing which had simultaneously been absorbed by and lost
touch with its culture. According to Thomas Kuhn, "the sense of malfunction that can lead to crisis is prerequisite to revolution."[59] With the
appearance in 1957 of the anthology *New Poets of England and America,*
the poetic journey from Bohemia to suburbia was completed.[60] Outwardly,
the collection had the markings of an "important project." It came with
a Preface by Robert Frost, who affirmed the "maturity" of these young
poets and urged us to read them, though he gave no evidence of having
done so himself. Moreover, the book contained several Americans who
were to become genuinely important writers: Robert Bly, Robert Lowell,
James Merrill, W. S. Merwin, Adrienne Rich, Louis Simpson, W. D.
Snodgrass, and James Wright. Yet the final impression is that of a tame
and sedate generation of poets who are comfortable with each other, with
their predecessors, with their audience, with their wives, their children,
their professorships, their grants. No rude manifestos appeared at either

58. Norman Podhoretz, *Making It* (New York, 1967), p. 66.
59. *The Structure of Scientific Revolutions* (Chicago, 1970), p. 92.
60. *New Poets of England and America,* ed. Donald Hall, Robert Pack, and Louis Simpson
(New York, 1957).

the beginning or the end of *New Poets,* just as no bohemian attitudes or metrical experiments roughened the poems inside. "The presiding muse here is unassertive, intelligent, charming, voluble, company-conscious—the perfect guest," F. W. Dupee remarked in a reveiw; he cited Rich as prototypical: she "seems to have access to some common style, a language which she and her contemporaries all tend to speak easily, with a minimum of individual inflection."[61] James Dickey labeled the contributors the "School of Charm" and complained that "it is easy to like" the poems, but "difficult to *care* about them."[62] In fact, just three years after its publication, one of the anthology's editors, Donald Hall, conceded that the book "confronted many of us with our obvious slightness as a generation."[63] The sense of malfunction was clear.

61. "The Muse as House Guest," *PR* 25 (Summer 1958): 457–58.
62. "In the Presence of Anthologies," *SR* 66 (Spring 1958): 297–98.
63. "Ah, Love, Let Us Be True," *American Scholar* 28 (Summer 1959): 311.

THREE

The Opening of the Field

"Every order of poetry finds itself, defines itself, in strife with other orders."[1]
—Robert Duncan

The 1950s, however, was not the unified and homogeneous period that I have so far been suggesting.[2] In poetry, at least, the decade included oppositional energies along with its conservative hegemony. As David Antin remarks, "once 'modern' presents itself as closed, it becomes Modern and takes its place alongside Victorian or Baroque as a period style";[3] the fifties' domestication of modernism thus ironically recreated exactly the kind of literary predicament that had prompted modernity in the first place and so legitimatized a new opening, a new revolt. Moreover, the New Critics and the young formalist poets combined to create an orthodoxy that, weak rather than intimidating, *could* be attacked. During the fifties, then, we find clusters of adversary poets—the beats, the confessional poets, the Black Mountain, deep image, and New York groups—who were at least linked by what they were all repudiating. Their refusals generated new paradigms for poetry that made the dominant way of writing—which had seemed given, eternal—suddenly appear empty and dead. Their beginnings, in addition, established the authority for most of the activity in American poetry for the twenty years since.

Examining an historical shift like this one raises many complicated questions about its precise degree of novelty, its difference from the then-dominant artistic canons, from the earlier modernism and even from

1. "Man's Fulfillment in Order and Strife," *Caterpillar* 8/9 (October 1969): 229.
2. And as they are characterized in Morris Dickstein's *Gates of Eden*.
3. "Modernism and Postmodernism: Approaching the Present in American Poetry," p. 99.

romanticism. One problem is that the charged polemical atmosphere of
the late fifties and early sixties often encouraged both the poets and their
critics to exaggerate matters. "All past consciousness is bunk. History is
bunk," Allen Ginsberg grandly proclaimed; "there's nothing to be learned
from history any more."[4] Charles Olson identified his poetic project as
nothing less than the liberation of western consciousness from that discursive reason which had stifled and alienated it from the time of Socrates.
Robert Bly, too, was inclined to make sweeping statements about the
differences between his deep image poetry and the ego-ridden verse of
English and American modernism, and even Frank O'Hara, who was
wary of theoretical positions and manifestos, declared that his "Personism" would be "the death of literature as we know it."[5] Early critics of
these writers shared their assessment of their difference but came to more
alarmist conclusions. In his review of *Howl and Other Poems,* John Hollander denounced "the utter lack of decorum of any kind in [this] dreadful
little volume,"[6] and, as we have already seen in Norman Podhoretz's
"The Know-Nothing Bohemians," the beat writers in particular were not
lamented as inept but reviled as dangerous enemies of culture itself.[7] Even
Louise Bogan, who had remarked in the symposium Our Country, Our
Culture that "American art and thought must become awkward once more"
(p. 22) concluded her negative view of *The New American Poetry* anthology with an apocalyptic warning: "when its principal tenets and accepted formal procedures are assaulted with utter vigor, this art of language
does not merely change, it totally disappears."[8] Literature, from this point
of view, is a permanent, ahistorical category, and these brazen young
poets had clearly stepped outside its boundaries.

But *The New American Poetry* was not a perverse form of antiart; it
was, rather, an attempt to demystify the fifties' notion of "high culture,"
mock its pretensions, dissolve the boundaries it had clamped down upon
literary activity and reground art in temporal immediacy—Lowell's
"breakthrough back into life." So constricting had the period's definition
of literariness become that when Ginsberg, for instance, started to write
"Howl," he thought:

> I wouldn't write a *poem,* but just write what I wanted to without
> fear, let my imagination go, open secrecy, and scribble magic lines

4. Quoted in *Allen Ginsberg in America,* p. 86. In this passage Ginsberg cites Henry Ford
as the source of the "History is bunk" remark; by his quotation Ginsberg reveals that even
the repudiation of the past is an attitude derived from the past.

5. "Personism: A Manifesto," in *The Collected Poems of Frank O'Hara,* ed. Donald Allen
(New York, 1971), p. 499.

6. "Poetry Chronicle," *PR* 24 (Spring 1957): 296–97.

7. "The Know-Nothing Bohemians," pp. 305–18.

8. *A Poet's Alphabet,* p. 26.

from my real mind—sum up my life—something I wouldn't be able
to show anybody, write for my own soul's ear and a few other
golden ears.[9]

Only by denying that he was being *literary* and by convincing himself he
was presenting unmediated experience and feeling ("life") could Ginsberg
begin to extend the boundaries of literature. So the death of literature as
we know it became the creation of literature as we don't (or then didn't)
know it. Similarly, in their more relaxed moments these poets were willing
to define a more honest and complex relation to the literary past. In a
letter he wrote to Hollander in response to his review of *Howl and Other
Poems,* Ginsberg described the beat movement as "a new Romanticism";
he has many times expounded his debts to Blake, Whitman, Williams,
and Pound, and he has recently located himself in the ancient underground
tradition of Gnosticism.[10] Olson admitted his relations to Williams and
Pound at least as often as he denied them; Bly identified Spanish and
Latin American surrealists as a chief source of his poetics; and O'Hara
was openly receptive to a number of modern French poets. The formation
of new literary canons is integral to all revolutionary movements, and
these young poets, converting marginal into central figures, were in reality
reopening the issue of "the tradition" rather than merely repudiating it.

The issue of the historical placement of contemporary writing has been
further blurred by the widespread use—by writers and critics alike—of
the term "postmodernism" to designate our period. Of course, there is
one sense—the only sense, as it turns out—in which the term is unarguably
valid: what, after all, could the contemporary period be but *post* modern?
But in my view this term, now dignified with its own literary journal
(Boundary 2: A Journal of Postmodern Literature), accomplishes the re-
ductio ad absurdam of the critical will-to-periodize. Period terms can
provide more or less interesting critical fictions, more or less persuasive
arguments, about intervals of literary history, but their danger lies in their
tendency to degenerate into critical myths. In addition, they invite the
formulation of rather simple unities, which are then sustained by reading
out of the canon whatever does not "fit," and in this way ostensibly
historical terms become covertly evaluative. As a result, critics write
essays in which they worry the question of whether Gary Snyder, or
Robert Lowell, or Allen Ginsberg is "really" a postmodernist—when the
real question is whether the term adequately accounts for the material

9. "Notes for *Howl and Other Poems,*" in *The New American Poetry,* p. 415.
10. Part of the lengthy letter to Holland is quoted in *Allen Ginsberg in America,* pp. 163–
77; the remark about romanticism appears on p. 174. For Ginsberg's relations to literary
predecessors and Gnosticism, the fullest source is *Allen Verbatim,* ed. Gordon Hall (New
York, 1974).

within the period it designates. But these critics do have something to worry about: if their arguments fail, their poet will seem hopelessly out of it.

Postmodernism, of course, has both its proponents and its foes, whose often fierce debates reveal just how value-charged the term is. In "What Was Modernism?" a nostalgic Harry Levin calls the moderns "the Children of Humanism and the Enlightenment"—a genealogy that would have astonished Eliot and Pound, not to mention Williams, Stevens, and Crane. Levin reserves "post-modern" for the rising "anti-intellectual undercurrent" in contemporary writing.[11] But Levin's gentle humanist complaint becomes a beleaguered jeremiad in Herbert N. Schneidau's "The Age of Interpretation and the Moment of Immediacy: Contemporary Art vs. History." "Current art seeks to be apocalyptic, not just *avant-garde*," Schneidau contends. While the modernists were "accused of formlessness" in their day, "it now appears that they really wanted fixity and flux bound together in a paradoxical relationship, a new form." But contemporary art's affirmation of a "kinetic Dionysian flux" leads it to abolish all hierarchic distinctions, all separations between art and life, and even the act of interpretation itself.[12] Leslie Fiedler, on the other hand, similarly concludes that the current is apocalyptic, but he eagerly accepts the new "mutants." The new movement, Fiedler announces, has freed itself "of all vestiges of the elitism and Culture Religion" in modernism and has in fact succeeded in repudiating "Humanism itself, both in its bourgeois and Marxist forms"—along with "the cult of reason."[13] In *The Performing Self,* Richard Poirier, too, affirms "the dislocating, disturbing impulses" in contemporary modes of writing that have "come to register the dissolution of the ideas often evoked to justify [their] existence: the cultural, moral, psychological premises that for many people still define the essence of literature as a humanistic enterprise."[14]

In the sixties the academic critique of the new art did not proceed very far beyond the fifties: the issue remained that of culture or humanist values, except that some of the more swinging academics like Fiedler and Poirier were now prepared to align themselves with the foes of elitist conceptions of culture. But if this entire debate has a familiar ring, it is probably because it closely parallels the reception of modernism itself—with the ironic twist that recuperated versions of the modernists are now advanced as civilized ideals against which to judge the "anarchic" work

11. *Refractions* (New York, 1966), p. 271.
12. *ELH* 37 (June 1970): 287 and 301.
13. "The New Mutants" appears in *The Collected Essays of Leslie Fiedler,* vol. 2 (New York, 1971), pp. 379–400. My quotations are taken from pp. 403 and 383.
14. *The Performing Self* (New York, 1971), pp. xv and xii.

of the present. Moreover, assessment of the new work is undertaken by either denouncing or apotheosizing its most provocative slogans and outrageous transgressions—a little like evaluating modernism on the basis of quotations from futurist and dadaist manifestos. Yet what is most striking about this controversy is just how much agreement has been assumed even before the argument begins. All the participants characterize postmodernism in quite similar ways; they differ mainly on what judgments they want to make on the common picture. If postmodernism means the end of liberal humanism, then this observation generates a discussion which merely reveals how anxious or exhilarated such a prospect makes a given critic feel. Poirier, the only one of these critics who offers any analytic specificity, illustrates one common critical tendency, to read postmodern questionings of literary structures back into earlier writing; but for the rest there appears to be a remarkable degree of consensus on the character of the shift from modern to postmodern writing.

The distinction, it turns out, is a fairly simple one. The moderns sought to invent forms out of the flux, but the postmoderns have, as Eugene Goodheart puts it, "surrendered to the flux."[15] Such an historical account—actually not historical at all, as I'll shortly be arguing—informs such deeper and more valuable critical voices as Charles Altieri and Ihab Hassan. In his *Enlarging the Temple* Altieri derives both twentieth-century periods from their common "ancestor" in romanticism; for him, modernism remains committed to a "creative, form-giving imagination" while postmodernism emphasizes more "the discovery and the disclosure of numinous relationships within nature" than "the creation of containing the structuring forms."[16] Hassan, in his "POSTMODERNISM: A Paracritical Bibliography," concludes that "whereas Modernism created its own forms of Authority, precisely because the center no longer held, Postmodernism has tended toward Anarchy, in deeper complicity with things falling apart."[17]

Yet it is precisely where these critics most agree—in their historical picture—that I want to question them. To conceive of twentieth-century poetry as divided into two unified but distinct literary periods is to draw a very schematic map indeed; it also raises a lot of knotty theoretical and practical questions. How, for example, did the first of these stable unities change into the second? The whole sense of history as a dynamic *process* is lost by dichotomizing twentieth-century poetry into two static periods. Moreover, such periodization seems premature and moves the discussion

15. *The Failure of Criticism* (Cambridge, Mass., 1978), p. 15.

16. *Enlarging the Temple* (Lewisburg, Pa., 1979); my quotations are from the more extensive treatment of these issues in Altieri's earlier "From Symbolist Thought to Immanence: The Logic of Post-Modern Poetics," *Boundary 2*, 1 (1973): 605–41.

17. "POSTMODERNISM: A Paracritical Bibliography," in *Paracriticisms* (Urbana, Ill., 1975), p. 59.

onto a level of abstraction that is too blunt when one of these periods consists of something as diverse and open-ended as the contemporary literary scene. Contemporary poetry is not an exactly surveyable field but an ongoing process. Surely, the need to frame our own time takes on an absurd quality when the framers proclaim that what they have discovered is—the end of framing. Moreover, the specific historical characterization—modernism, form carved out of flux; and postmodernism, flux itself—has some basis, as we'll shortly see; but it also appears questionable from at least two different directions. In the first place, the distinction may have more to do with the history of reading than with the history of literature: we have now had sixty years to uncover the complex forms hidden beneath the disjunctive surfaces of modernist writings. Contemporary work, on the other hand, retains its strangeness and its capacity to dislocate us, though it is also true that a growing body of practical criticism of particular authors and works is providing ample testimony to the craft and the intellectual seriousness of contemporary poets. In many ways, the notion of a postmodern poetry that affirms "chance operations" and "the releasing of controls" is a fashionable idea whose time has already gone.[18] A very problematic idea held unquestioningly by literary critics who like to problematize, postmodernism, in the second place, amounts to a kind of critical myth—the myth of the end of mystification. That is what all the heady claims—the end of humanism, the end of interpretation, the end of form, symbol, myth, the end of logocentricity, of the Book, and of Literature itself—amount to. But the many vigorous efforts in the last century and a half to kill Literature have been the chief means of reenergizing it—which is why Roland Barthes writes that "Literature is like phosphorous: it shines with its maximum brilliance at the moment when it attempts to die."[19] Once we thought of modernism as the end of mystification; now we think it is postmodernism. Or will we have to wait for post-postmodernism? No; because for reasons I'll be talking about shortly, the end of mystification, like the end of Literature, is infinitely deferred.

My own procedure, then, has been to discard the monolithic and misleading term "postmodernism," to concentrate on the originating moment in contemporary poetry, to explore both the diversity and the shared concerns among my five poets selected from the main clusters of poets that emerged in the late fifties and early sixties, and in this way to write a literary history that acknowledges diversity yet remains specific and *literary*. At its beginnings, contemporary poetry's antiliterary rhetoric

18. Michel Benamou, "Presence and Play," in *Performance in Postmodern Culture*, ed. Michel Benamou and Charles Caramelle (Madison, Wis., 1977), p. 4.
19. *Writing Degree Zero* (Boston, 1967), p. 38.

manifested a legitimate and enlivening disruptiveness, a violent effort to dislocate the enervated but still entrenched end of the modernist line. Not all of this destructive/creative energy was, however, directed against external targets; the literary hegemony of the fifties attracted many of the beginning poets—Rich, Merwin, Wright, Plath are prime examples—so that these writers were now prompted to a kind of self-alienation, in which they stepped back from and turned on themselves, dismantling their achieved styles. According to Northrop Frye, "when a mythology crystallizes in the centre of a culture, a *temenos* or magic circle is drawn around that culture, and a literature develops historically within a limited orbit of language, reference, allusion, belief, transmitted and shared tradition."[20] But Frye's statement cannot account for what happened in both American poetry and in American culture generally in the late fifties and early sixties when a carefully drawn circle began to dissolve all along its circumference. As a result, readers of poetry, confronted with works that resisted customary ways of reading, were left without bearings. Lacking adequate models of coherence and thus left on the outside, such readers were naturally inclined to judge the new work as arbitrary, incoherent, and merely destructive.

But in reality we have, in Denise Levertov's phrase, "not a breaking down but a breaking open."[21] The antiliterary stance of the new generation became their way of recovering substance and energy for poetry; their deviation from the dominant artistic canons permitted them a rough, "unpoetic" authenticity, a return to the existential freshness of the world. At this transforming moment, then, with the shattering of the hermetically sealed autotelic poem, American poetry broke open to the physical moment—the literal, the temporal, the immediate. To characterize this change from another angle: reacting against a "decadent metaphorical" verse, poets instead pushed toward the metonymic pole of writing, its "open, tangential, and untotalized relationships" allowing the real world to retain its independence, its life, rather than being en*closed* within some metaphoric circle.[22] Ginsberg's catalogs of urban torment in "Howl," the autobiographical realism of Lowell's *Life Studies,* the quotidian detail of O'Hara's lunch hour poems, the domestic particularity of Levertov's lyrics, and the specificity of Wright's urban and natural landscapes—all these attest to a poetic imagination willing to acknowledge an immediate ex-

20. *The Critical Path* (Bloomington, Ind., 1971), p. 35.
21. *The Poet in the World* (New York, 1973), p. 240.
22. The phrase "decadent metaphoric" is taken from David Lodge's *Modes of Modern Writing* (Ithaca, N.Y., 1977), p. 118. Lodge, who offers the most lucid account of the metaphor/metonymy distinction, suggestively cites these two modes as the dynamic of literary history. The phrase "open, tangential and untotalized relationships" is taken from Herbert Schneidau's *Sacred Discontent* (Berkeley and Los Angeles, 1977), p. 292.

ternal reality that remains stubbornly other. So poetry came to ground itself in a sharply observed physical present, its dense materiality implicitly mocking the transcendent, totalizing imagination of symbolism as well as the more covertly transcendent imagination of the New Criticism and the young formalists.

Poetic authority was located not in the cultural tradition but in the literal reality of a physical moment; and it is this poetic realism that makes the shaping of a poem become, once again, a "problem"—and a challenge. A crisis of literary form develops when models of mind which have provided shared accounts of the mental operations that go into "forming" experience begin to break down; in the twentieth century we have lacked such models so that form has been in a continuing crisis—even if, as we have seen, the formalists of the postwar period acknowledged that fact by denying it. But the problem of form assumed a special character for the innovating poets of the late fifties and early sixties. For them, forms were not given from nature; nor were they desired from tradition. Literary shapes were, then, specifically human creations but ones that were, ideally, not impositional. Both their respect for a real and resistant external world and their awareness of the genteel violence of the formalists stimulated the new poets' search for ways of ordering poetry that would not stifle the very movements of consciousness and independence of objects with which they were trying to revitalize poetry. Trying to avoid what Olson called "the too strong grasping of it," they wanted to keep the world alive in a poetry of ongoing process.[23] So if these poets began by repudiating the inherited forms of their immediate predecessors (some of whom were themselves) and by attaching poetry to temporal process, their end was not to surrender to the flux; it was, rather, to find new ways of binding form and flux so that temporality will not *seem* to have been violated.

This search has generated the extraordinary surge of formal inventiveness that has characterized our poetry for the last twenty years. Since form now becomes, in theory, unique, it is best discussed in particular works by particular poets; but there are two common and basic principles I want to isolate for more general discussion. First of all, form is now understood as an unfolding process of discovery—Coleridge's "form as proceeding" replacing the predominant "form as superinduced." To justify his own work, Robert Creeley quotes the painter Franz Kline: "If I paint what I know, I bore myself; if I paint what you know, I bore you; so I paint what I don't know."[24] "As I write, the writing talks to me,"

23. "The Kingfishers," in *Selected Writings of Charles Olson,* ed. Robert Creeley (New York, 1966), p. 171.
24. "Notes Apropos 'Free Verse,' " in *Naked Poetry,* ed. Stephen Berg and Robert Mezey (New York, 1969), p. 186.

says Robert Duncan,[25] similarly conceiving of the work as the means to discover what he doesn't know rather than as an opportunity to impose what he does. One of the many poets whose careers experienced a major impasse in the mid- and late fifties, Adrienne Rich had an interval of eight years separating *The Diamond Cutters* (1955) from her third book, *Snapshots of a Daughter-in-Law* (1963). But out of this painful crisis in her career emerged a regenerated Rich who was confident enough to yield those external formal controls she had so anxiously constructed in her earlier work. "I find that I can no longer go to write a poem with a neat handful of materials and express those materials according to a prior plan," she said in 1964; now "the poem itself engenders new sensations, new awareness in me as it progresses. . . . instead of poems *about* experiences I am now getting poems that *are* experiences."[26] This stress on a poetics of discovery explains why so many of the poets write open-ended poetic sequences—like Olson's *Maximus* poems, Creeley's *Pieces,* and Duncan's *Passages*—or books that are not simply a collection of self-contained poems but themselves unfolding sequences—books like Lowell's *Life Studies,* Snyder's *Myths and Texts,* Wright's *The Branch Will Not Break,* or Rich's *Diving into the Wreck.* Both kinds of work immediately dissolve the completeness of the particular section or poem back into the incompleteness of its place in an ongoing, self-revising process.

Traditionally, poetic form creates what Murray Krieger calls an "ideal entelechy" which "admits of no errant elements" and whose parts, inevitably and purposefully, combine into a seamless whole.[27] Contemporary poems contain cracks, even fissures; they are heterogeneous. If they include disjunctions, interruptions, digressions, it is to show how they remain open, in process, rather than creating a perfectly ordered enclosure like, say, Wilbur's "Caserta Garden." Contemporary poems also remain open to contingency, colorful bits of actual matter that resist metaphorization. Olson liked to quote Heraclitus' dictum, "Man is estranged from that with which he is most familiar."[28] Just the five poets I am concentrating on deal with physical objects in very different ways. Some—Lowell, for instance—use the context of the entire book to give the literal objects in a particular poem a gentle nudge toward metaphoric resonance; but all participate in an effort to locate poetry in a world that cannot simply be swallowed up by the imagination. In short, they seek nonto-

25. "Man's Fulfillment in Order and Strife," p. 239.
26. "Poetry and Experience: Statement at a Poetry Reading (1964)," in *Adrienne Rich's Poetry,* p. 89.
27. *Theory of Criticism* (Baltimore and London, 1976), p. 102.
28. *The Special View of History,* ed. Ann Charters (Berkeley, 1970), pp. 14–15.

talizing literary forms which relate to familiar realities in a way that is not appropriating.

If the loftier formalists had sought to impose form on flux, the dissident poets wanted forms created *within* the flux—not a mere surrender to it. This change aptly illustrates Donald Wesling's point that "literary innovation is as much a matter of aversion and reverse reflection as of original invention."[29] Literary change is real even if it is something less than the absolute "fresh start" often proclaimed by the participating revolutionaries. For this reason I want to make clear that I am not claiming—as the organization of my book seems to be—that even my more limited twenty-year time span can be neatly divided into two monolithic periods. "Projective Verse," certainly one of the seminal documents for the new poetry, first appeared in 1950. During its existence between 1954 and 1957, the *Black Mountain Review* published Olson and Duncan, important early work by Creeley and Levertov, and devoted a special issue to the San Francisco poetry renaissance. "I must take pains not to *intend* anything but the work itself, to let the work take shape as it comes," Frank O'Hara wrote in a 1948 journal, anticipating his generation's poetics of discovery.[30] As it turned out, much of O'Hara's major writing would be done by 1960. During the fifties, the trend toward formalism and the countering movement toward an open poetics overlapped, and the surge of poetic innovation apparent in the late fifties and early sixties manifested the coming to the surface of underground energies, now beginning to exercise their own stimulating power and influence. Differing sets of poetic assumptions (formalist and closed versus "antiformalist" and open) gain hegemony but in neither case is their predominance exclusive and total. Any literary period will coexist with and even produce its own oppositional forces which it will deal with by neglect, assimilating reinterpretation or active repression. Yet it is from just such marginal perspectives that the limited character of the current hegemony can be recognized and alternatives— inventions, aversions, reverse reflections—began to emerge. Only by refusing the idea of a literary period as a stable unity can we account for change from one such era to the next.

This general change can, I believe, be accounted for somewhat more specifically. Russian formalism, one of the few literary theories that tries to allow for and explain discontinuities in literary history, proposes that *"new form comes about not in order to express new content but in order to replace an old form that has already lost its artistic viability."*[31] Such

29. "Thoroughly Modern Measures," p. 458.
30. *Early Writing,* ed. Donald Allen (Bolinas, Calif., 1977), p. 103.
31. According to Shklovsky in "The Connection of Devices of Plot Formation with General Devices of Style," quoted by Marjorie Perloff in " 'Literary Competence' and the Formalist Model," *Centrum* 3 (Spring 1975): 37–38.

a statement has a certain provocative charm and it is fun to imagine, for example, that Hemingway led the kind of life he did mainly to supply the appropriate content for those short, lean sentences with which he had decided to replace the lengthy periods of the late James. But the formalist principle does not deal adequately with the particular experience of the generation that I am writing about. In the summer of 1948 Allen Ginsberg had a series of hallucinatory visions which, he then believed, yielded him his poetic vision and vocation; but it took him eight years before he could develop a language and form in which to embody his revolutionary content. In the early 1950s Robert Lowell, recovering from a nervous breakdown, tried to deal with the familial origins of his pain in the thickly textured, rhymed and metered stanzas he had used in *Lord Weary's Castle;* a worksheet for a prose autobiography, "At Payne-Whitney," dramatically enacts the breaking down—and open—of Lowell's verse under the pressures exerted by personal memory and feeling.

> I sat looking out of my bedroom window at the Clinic, and once more began to type at a poem, my substitute for the regulation Occupational therapy requirement. I wrote:
>
>> I was already half-way through my life,
>> When I woke up from Mother on the back
>> Of the *Hill* in Boston, to a sky-line of Life
>
>> Insurance buildings, still in blue-print.
>
> Then the labor, cynicism, and maturity of writing in meter became horrible. I began to write rapidly in prose and in the style of a child.
>
> . . . name, Bobby Lowell. I was all of three and a half. My new formal grey shorts had been worn for all of three minutes. Autumn leaves played cops and robbers over my ankles. My perfection was that of those Olympian models in the plate-glass windows of Rodgers Peet's Man and Boy's store below the Boston State House.[32]

As Lowell's readers will recognize, the shift from a mature, detached to a more inside, but hardly childlike, perspective and the accompanying shift from poetry to prose turns up an episode and some of the specific phrasing later used in "My Last Afternoon with Uncle Devereux Winslow." Eventually, it took Lowell several years, including a massive effort at a prose autobiography, before he found a way to maneuver his new matter back into an appropriate poetic form. By dealing with visionary experience and psychological breakdown, Ginsberg and Lowell were exploring taboo subjects, ones clearly hard to manage in the predetermined

---

32. "Miscellaneous Worksheets," in the Lowell collection in the Houghton Library at Harvard. Material from the Lowell collection quoted with the kind permission of the estate of Robert Lowell and Harvard University.

forms and with the ironic self-consciousness that were the going thing. In fact, as we shall see, both "Howl" and *Life Studies* move toward a crisis in which both the self and the poem are trapped in a sealed enclosure, whose boundaries must then be shattered in a painful act of regeneration. In the work of both Ginsberg and Lowell, then, the pressures of personal feeling made formal invention both a human and a literary necessity; hitherto excluded contents made the then-canonical forms seem empty and impositional and pushed the writers to evolve literary shapes that could contain these new materials without squeezing the life out of them.

At this point, however, I want to shift attention from the possibilities opened by this new poetic to its own exclusions, limitations, contradictions, indefensible claims—in short, its practical and theoretical shortcomings. A perspective that values energy over poetic unity and finish will be accused of fomenting sloppiness and self-indulgence and it is certainly the case that a writer may become so eager to avoid "the too strong grasping of it" that he or she may not grasp it at all. Yet critical cries of "Chaos!" are almost always false alarms sounded by literary fathers dismayed to discover that the younger poets are not replicas of themselves. My own impression is that what is wrong with most of the bad poetry that appears in the literary journals and first books is not that it suffers from looseness but that the life has been sucked out of it by a poet too eager for the acceptable "literary effect." As we shall see, "open" poets are perhaps even more vulnerable to this temptation because they have already persuaded themselves of their authenticity. Moreover, the embattled circumstances of their emergence made the more prophetic and polemic-minded among the new poets—Olson, Ginsberg, Bly are good examples—apt to espouse simplified attitudes that often were a *mere* reverse reflection of what they were rebelling against. In such cases, the tendency is to think and talk about poetry in polarities—logic versus feeling, closed versus open, craft versus spontaneity—with virtue, of course, located in the second item in each of the oppositions.

Allen Ginsberg, for instance, has always insisted that the writing of each of the three main parts of "Howl" was a spontaneous act. Here is his account of Part II:

> I had an apt on Nob Hill, got high on Peyote, & saw an image of the robot skullface of Moloch in the upper stories of a big hotel glaring into my window; got high weeks later again, the Visage was still there in red smokey downtown Metropolis, I wandered down Powell Street muttering, "Moloch Moloch" all night & wrote *Howl* II nearly intact in cafeteria at foot of Drake Hotel, deep in the hellish vale.[33]

33. *The New American Poetry*, p. 416.

As even this brief prose passage suggests, Ginsberg's problem is less disorder than his luxuriating in a self-consciously elevated and literary diction ("Visage," "deep in the hellish vale") saved only by its slightly humorous effect. As an account of the composition of the Moloch section of "Howl" the statement creates an antiliterary literary fiction. The Allen Ginsberg Archives at Columbia University contain about forty pages of worksheets for Part II of "Howl," and the earliest of these sheets reveal that Ginsberg used the speed of a typewriter as a means to invent, freely, variant epithets for his repeated base word "Moloch"—"Moloch whose mind is pure machinery! Moloch whose blood is running money!"—and that at some point he went back and underlined those phrases that struck him as most effective; many, but not all, of these turn up in the completed poem. Did the bard carry his portable IBM as he journeyed deep into the hellish vale? Not very likely; but it is easy to see why Ginsberg mystified the writing of "Howl." He has often attacked literary critics for failing to perceive the real structural principles of "Howl," but the poem's polarization of the invasive, mechanical Moloch against his hysterical but saintly victims permits no middle ground, no detached, retrospective acts of ordering—as, say, in the acts of judging, selecting, pruning that actually went into the writing of the poem. As the liberator of contemporary verse and consciousness, Ginsberg was thus encouraged to adopt a theory of poetic composition which, as practicing writer, he was smart enough to ignore.

This discrepancy between Ginsberg's theory and practice has actually been created, ironically enough, by his effort to adopt a poetics of immediacy. Contemporary literary theory, particularly poststructuralism, has taught us to be suspicious of claims of immediacy or presence. According to Paul De Man, "unmediated expression is a philosophic impossibility"—as is "modernism" in another essay—and for De Man literature then becomes "the only form of language free from the fallacy of unmediated expression."[34] Defining literature by identifying its nature with a specific theme, De Man then argues an awareness of the "duplicity" of language in the romantic writers (where we least expect to find it). So, in enforcing his definition of literature, De Man mainly follows the route of assimilating reinterpretation. Starting from a similar sense of the gap between language and experience, Herbert Schneidau in *Sacred Discontent* pursues a more dismissive route, flatly declaring that "the concept of 'immediacy' is debilitating."[35] I want to respond to these critics in two ways. First of all, the goal of immediacy has been an energizing, not a debilitating, one for contemporary poets, all the more so when the poets

34. *Blindness and Insight* (New York, 1971), pp. 9 and 17.
35. *Sacred Discontent*, p. 288.

become aware of the dilemmas posed by their poetics, as Lowell and O'Hara do. Second, these problems are serious and deep, all the more so when they are not recognized by the writer, as they are generally not by Charles Olson. For illustration, I want to look at his "Projective Verse" and "The Kingfishers."

The influence of Olson as theorist, and particularly of the "Projective Verse" essay, is hard to overestimate. The essay may propound openness in a bullying tone, its ideas may or may not be deriviative, but "Projective Verse" did make available to younger writers alternative ways of measuring the line and shaping the poem. The essay's propositions were intended, as Olson keeps insisting, for "USE," and so if some of them now seem to raise serious questions, it's likely that a more finely articulated argument would have helped less to "get things started." Olson's argumentative strategies in the essay are determined by his effort to eliminate anteriority, specifically preconceived ideas and predetermined forms, both of which embody a stance toward reality which is at once distanced and projecting ("the lyrical interference of the individual as ego"). But Olson's key assumption is that a detached stance is not inevitable but the result of particular conventionalized (and thus changeable) ways of thinking and writing, ways that have been institutionalized in the tradition of "closed" verse. Olson's answer is to reground poetry in "the *kinetics* of the thing," the poem as "high-energy construct," and all of his prescriptions for verse are designed to keep this energy from being sapped, constricted, violated, and to return writing to its prelogical, physical origins. To this end Olson cracks open poetic structure and reconceives it from the inside out. He begins with the "smallest" and "least logical" poetic part, "the minimum and source of speech," the syllable, that particle of physical "sound" that exists prior to "sense." Next Olson moves outward to the poetic line, whose measure, coming "from the breathing of the man who writes, at the moment that he writes," is derived not from the accumulated practices of a literary tradition but from a physiological immediacy, the bodily presence of the poet. When he comes to consider poetic structure as a whole, Olson views it as a set of objects alive in a field of tensions. Once "breath allows *all* the speech-force of language back in," he says, "everything" in the poem can be "treated as solids, objects, things." Independent and alive, these "elements" will retain "the play of their separate energies" rather than being put into the service of some imperial formal design or "any ideas or preconceptions from outside the poem." Thinking is not banished from poetry, as Olson is often thought to believe; but it is to operate within the moment of writing: Olson's, too, is a poetics of discovery. Yet this process produces poems that are wholes: the objects are handled "in such a way that a series of tensions (which they also are) are made to *hold,* and to hold exactly inside the content and the context of the poem which has forced itself, through the poet and them, into being." Somehow, a totality has been created from the inside— a *very* problematic idea, as we shall see; it here requires Olson to attribute agency to the poem ("forced itself") lest he be imagined as stepping outside the poem and forcing its tensions to *hold.*

At this point, Olson announces the necessity to break open "the conventions which logic has forced on syntax," he suggests replacing the "word as thought" ("logos") with "word as handle" and he reconceives the sentence as a "passage of force" rather than as a statement. All these are further means for making the poetic text incarnate the energies of its original moment of coming-into-being; even more crucial, and influential, are Olson's ideas about poetic voice and the typewriter as the means of more exactly recording voice. This section of "Projective Verse" seems to have stimulated all the talk in contemporary poetry about "getting the poem off the page," the stress on poetic voice and the oral reading of poetry, experiments like Ginsberg's attempts in the late sixties to compose on a tape recorder (which he would play at poetry readings), Jerome Rothenberg's performance poetry, and David Antin's talk poetry, the last two both efforts to make the listener's experience of the poem simultaneous with its creation and so a true moment of poetic presence. For Olson, too, voice, the poem's "place of origin *and* its destination," embodies the physical presence of the poet. Now with the typewriter's "rigidity and space precisions" a poet can "indicate exactly the breath, the pauses, the suspensions even of syllables, the juxtapositions even of parts of phrase, which he intends." As a result, any reader will know how "to voice his work." Olson seems curiously reluctant to let his completed works become "separate" from him in a way that is basically at odds with his whole anti-impositional ethic, and his apotheosis of the typewriter seems to be an instance of what Renato Poggioli calls the "technologism" of the avant-garde.[36] Olson's claims for the machine are surely exaggerated: some but by no means all aspects of a poem's vocalization can be scored with the typewriter, which thus becomes a fairly dubious means for inscribing poetic presence in a printed text. But the important point is that his poetics of immediacy drives Olson to consider the text of a poem as a means, "a script to its vocalization," a way to pass back to the poem's origin (and destination) in the poet's presence.

It is when Olson asks in Part II of the essay whether projectivism "involves a stance toward reality outside a poem" that some of the latent problems in Part I begin to manifest themselves. At first Olson answers

36. *The Theory of the Avant-Garde,* pp. 131–47.

with an attitude of open-minded expectancy: "if the beginning and the end is breath, voice in its largest sense, then the material of verse shifts. It has to." New poetic procedures will inevitably produce new content; we'll just have to sit back and wait. But notice how Olson, in the very organization of the two parts of his essay, is forced to make method precede content—because the method itself claims to be free of preconceptions. But as Olson proceeds to make quite clear, the "new" content turns out to be projectivism itself—a method which, like any other, entails its own content. Olson terms his new matter "objectism." And what is objectism? It's getting away from that "peculiar presumption by which western man has interposed himself between what he is as a creature of nature (with certain instructions to carry out) and those other creations of nature which we may, without derogation, call objects"; objectism, unfortunately, is not about getting away from pomposity. Its positive side, however, is a "humilitas" which permits man to see himself as "participant in the larger force" of nature. In other words, objectism, which seems to have affinities with simpler forms of romanticism, is projectivism reinstated as a theme.

Such a logical circularity is not itself the problem; it is probably inevitable. But the difficulty for Olson is that he claims—in fact, assumes—that he can enter a moment or a poem disburdened of all preconceptions. Here we arrive at the first major problem for a poetics of immediacy, its assumption of the possibility of a kind of brutal forgetting of all that we know. But can the writing of each poem be a genuine fresh start? If Robert Creeley writes what he does not know, why is it that his poems form consistent patterns of style and theme? When Robert Duncan's writing talks back to him (as it surely will once he assumes it will), why does it sound so much like Robert Duncan? Olson does not even concede that there is a problem. Williams claimed a similar unmediated access to the moment but in *Spring and All* he represented such access as an agonizing struggle, marked by constant slipping back into personal obsession and literary cliché. But for Olson the capacity to empty his mind is a given; the only difficulty is to find a language that will "hold" the energies of the poet's pure act of creation. In "Projective Verse" Olson speaks of the "PLAY of mind" to refer to a movement of the intelligence that is free of rigidities and preconceptions; but the phrase merely names such a mental state without explaining how it might be attained.

In E. H. Gombrich's terms, Olson is trying to forget the "traditional schemata"—not just those of the current hegemony but of all western thought. As Gombrich warns, however, "there is all the difference in the world between trying to forget something and never having known it,"

and Olson often does not seem to be trying very hard.[37] Themes repeat—
from poem to poem, from prose to poetry—with obsessional insistence.
All but three lines of "There Was a Youth Whose Name Was Thomas
Granger" are quoted from William Bradford's *Of Plymouth Plantation*.
This use of an historical document, probably suggested by Williams's *In
the American Grain* and/or Pound's *Cantos,* may strike many literary
critics as too minimal a working of the material to satisfy their criteria
for art. All Olson did was to break lines of prose into verse, divide the
text into four sections and add three lines of his own. But this was done
not because Olson was lazy but because he had a certain impression he
wanted to convey—precisely the impression of a nonassertiveness in his
relation both to his material and his reader; the trouble with the poem,
however, is not that Olson has left his material alone but that he so clearly
hasn't. Quotation from an historical document makes it seem that any
truth the reader may evolve from the poem comes not from Olson but
resides, objectively, in the Bradford text. The reader is thus *presented*
with a text that Olson discovered in his reading and has now passed on.
But the poet is, in fact, everywhere nervously fussing over his material.
He has not only selected a particular incident with which to typify the
culture of New England Calvinism; he has also omitted sections of this
document that would serve to complicate the impression he clearly wants
to convey.[38] Olson's breaking of the prose into lines of verse may have
been determined by his breathing at the moment he read or transcribed
it; but the line and stanza breaks also strike emphases that have thematic
significance. In section 3, after first retreating into Latin, Bradford finally
just breaks off in mid-phrase rather than specifically naming Granger's
"grosse acts"—i.e., sodomy; section 4 begins: "Mr Bradford: I forbear
perticulers," the line/stanza break thus stressing the abstractness of Bradford's consciousness. Similarly, the three lines Olson did write—one of
them "Rest, Tom, in your pit where they put you"—explicitly align our
sympathies with Granger and against Bradford. Moreover, the polarities
the poem develops, between the "strict laws" of Calvinism and the energy
of Granger, between imposed myths and "perticulers," are the polarities

37. *Art and Illusion* (Princeton, 1969), p. 175.
38. At times Olson's omissions amount to downright distortion. Olson stresses that Bradford refuses to name Granger's crime: "I forbear perticulers." But Bradford writes, "He
was this year detected of buggery (and indicted for the same) with a mare, a cowe, two
goats, five sheep, 2. calves, and a turkey. Horrible it is to mention, but the truth of the
historie requires it." At least one Puritan historian felt bound by the truth in ways Olson
did not. Earlier Olson transcribes Bradford's "But that which is worse, even sodomie and
buggerie, (things fearfull to name,)" as "And that which is worse / (things fearfull to name)."
Apparently, the crimes were less upsetting to Puritan sensibilities than the words were to
Olson's theories. See William Bradford, *Of Plymouth Plantation,* ed. Samuel Eliot Morison
(New York, 1952), pp. 316–22, 408–13.

of "Projective Verse" historicized. Was Olson's reading of Bradford an act of discovery or an imposition?

A second major problem for a poetics of immediacy stems from the difficulty of isolating a "present" from the flow of time. A present obviously provides a very slippery and evanescent ground for living and writing, though it is precisely this ungraspable, open-ended quality that has attracted so many writers to it. Nevertheless, it remains very difficult, either in experience or in thought, to enter a present that has been utterly severed from any relation to time before and after, as my sentence itself shows: severance is a negative relation but a relation. According to Alfred North Whitehead, "what we perceive as present is the vivid fringe of memory tinged with anticipation,"[39] and William James offers a slightly less deterministic version of the same idea: "the practically cognized present is no knife-edge, but a saddle-back, with a certain breadth of its own on which we sit perched, and from which we look in two directions into time."[40] In "Projective Verse" Olson occupies the present as such a ground, from which he often looks back over his shoulder toward the past or gazes toward the horizon of some imagined future. Olson in fact reveals more ambivalence toward the past than his rhetoric of an absolute break suggests. His fulminations against "closed" verse only take on necessity if we recognize that tradition as an historical past which is still present; and Olson's own poetic projects only become intelligible when placed against this tradition as their "background." At the same time Olson does want to preserve a selective tradition: Williams and Pound among the moderns, Homer, Euripides, and Seami among the ancients. In 1950 those poets were all either sufficiently neglected or sufficiently distant in time to be nonthreatening; but their presence in the essay shows that Olson, like many another writer, accepts a past of his own invention. When Olson is demanding that "the conventions which logic has forced on syntax must be broken open," his essay reaches a crisis point: "But an analysis of how far a new poet can stretch the very conventions on which communication by language rests, is too big for these notes, which are meant, I hope it is obvious, merely to get things started." At this point Olson realizes that if he were to shatter all conventionalized forms of discourse, he would be unable to reach an audience. Yet if his rejection of those forms is less than absolute, then he is still inside the structures he's trying to destroy. Confronted with this dilemma, Olson backs off; it's "too big for these notes." At the same time "Projective Verse" also views the present as the point of origin in a linear evolution toward some desired future. A humble sense of his role as "participant in the larger force," it

39. *The Concept of Nature* (Cambridge, England, 1930), p. 73.
40. *The Principles of Psychology,* vol. 1 (New York, 1950), p. 609.

turns out, will inflate the poet with that force and give him "size, projective size." Our verse will again "carry much larger material than it has carried in our language since the Elizabethans." In fact, projectivism may eventually give us a new heroic drama and epic poetry. Here Olson imagines himself as a *pre*-cursor; it may be he is making straight the way of *The Maximus Poems,* in which case he is trying to become his own precursor. But he invents for himself an *historical* mission: to found the principles of an heroic verse to be evolved in the future. Again and again in "Projective Verse" the present folds back into history, into temporal sequence.

Moreover, the "present" which engages many contemporary poets turns out to be hidden—obscure—not present at all but a mythical construction that is buried within or beneath contemporary reality. So just as the historical past becomes an intrusive presence, the moment—the "real" present—becomes an absence which must be recovered by the poet, and this creates the third problem for a poetics of immediacy. If a writer were simply to become open to all experience, he or she would become a mere extension of contemporary values and mores. Ironically, the formalist poets of the fifties stressed the difference between high culture and popular culture as one way of convincing themselves that they were not just reflecting current views in the way that they were, while writers adopting an open poetics were actually more resistant to their culture, most notably in a social protest poem like "Howl" but, to one degree or another, in all five of the poets I will be concentrating on. But how can a poet be at once open and resistant? Again, a poetics of immediacy cannot allow for any aspect of the self that is outside, detached from, the moment; yet it is very hard *not* to allow for any such aspect of the self. What happens is that the present the poets open themselves to is, like their version of the past, a selective one, an imaginative construction which becomes the standard against which they judge the social/historical present.

Olson's "The Kingfishers" is a much stronger poem than "There Was a Youth Whose Name Was Thomas Granger" because its own movements of language are often multiple and open. "I am no Greek, hath not th'advantage. / And of course, no Roman," Olson writes in the closing section of the poem. With a somewhat pretentious modesty he abjures a smooth, richly musical, "civilized" verse idiom for one that is rugged, broken, confusing—purged of lyrical interferences to be in closer touch with reality. "Shall you uncover honey / where maggots are?" he asks. Olson liked to quote Melville's characterization of Plato as a "honeyhead," and Olson probably is criticizing here any point of view that can loosely be called "platonic"; he probably also has in mind the more "cultivated" among his poetic contemporaries. Either way, Olson wants his own work to stay close to the kind of unpleasant disintegrative realities typified by maggots. His own poem moves through a constant disintegrative/recreative process.

Avoiding either a too strong or a too sweet grasping of it, "The Kingfishers" wanders about, flying off in a variety of directions, its energies centrifugal. The poem, creating a swift, broken movement, picks up subjects then quickly drops them: from section 1 it seems that a character named Fernand will be important in the poem, but he is never mentioned again; the ostensible subject, kingfishers, is never mentioned after section 2 (about one-third of the way through the poem). Even the ordering of the sections, beginning with arabic 1–4, then changing to roman II and III, constitutes a disrupted order. When Olson urges "not accumulation but change," he is naming the creative principle of his own writing which, by continual shifts of direction, stays *in process*. In "Human Universe" Olson says that what makes "most acts—of living and of writing—unsatisfactory" is the assumption that a "form" can only be made "by selecting from the full content some face of it, or plane, some part." Instead of a "going-on,"

> it comes out a demonstration, a separating out, an act of classification, and so, a stopping, and all that I know is, it is not there, it has turned false. For any of us, at any instant, are juxtaposed to any experience, even an overwhelming single one, on several more planes than the arbitrary and discursive which we inherit can declare.[41]

Olson's writing is strongest when its texture is multidimensional in this way, as it is in section 2 of "The Kingfishers."

> I thought of the E on the stone, and of what Mao said
> la lumiere"
>   but the kingfisher
> de l'aurore"
>   but the kingfisher flew west
> est devant nous!
>   he got the color of his breast
>   from the heat of the setting sun!
> The features are, the feebleness of the feet
>   (syndactylism of the 3rd & 4th digit)
> the bill, serrated, sometimes a pronounced beak, the wings
> where the color is, short and round, the tail
> inconspicuous.

> But not these things were the factors. Not the birds.
> The legends are

41. *Selected Writings,* p. 55.

legends. Dead, hung up indoors, the kingfisher
will not indicate a favoring wind,
or avert the thunderbolt. Nor, by its nesting,
still the waters, with the new year, for seven days.
It is true, it does nest with the opening
                              year, but not on the waters.
It nests at the end of a tunnel bored by itself in a bank. There,
six or eight white and translucent eggs are laid, on fishbones
not on bare clay, on bones thrown up in pellets by the birds.

                    On these rejectmenta
(as they accumulate they form a cup-shaped
                              structure) the young are born.
And, as they are fed and grow, this
                    nest of excrement and decayed fish becomes
                    a dripping, fetid mass
Mao concluded:
                    nous devons
                         nous lever
                              et agir!

By moving from the E carved on the omphalos at Delphi to the juxtaposition of a quotation from Mao with the flight of the mythical kingfisher,
to a scientific account of the bird quoted from the *Encyclopaedia Britannica* (interrupted by the poet's comments), to another quotation from
Mao, this passage opens up multiple languages and perspectives on the
kingfisher.[42] At first Olson creates a spacious sense of wholeness in a
passage that pulls in opposite directions simultaneously—to the east and
sunrise, to the west and sunset. But Olson then questions the mythological
status of the bird by entering the dry, factual *Britannica* prose which does
not even make the bird sound beautiful, much less magical. "The legends
are"; the legends exist, but they "are / legends" and, as the beginning
of the next sentence allows us momentarily to think, they are "dead."
Rather than passively repeating old myths, we must, as Mao urges, arise
and act. So Olson again insists that the bird is—a bird, not symbolic or
magical: it "will not indicate a favoring wind, / or avert the thunderbolt"
or "still the waters." Olson, however, is not simply trying to demythologize the kingfisher; instead, he wants to make his poem enact the entire
process of remythologizing the bird. Out of the waste and rejectamenta
emerge the young birds; out of the *Britannica* data emerges a living myth;
and out of quotations, dead legends, scientific observation evolves Olson's
own multidimensional poetic text.

42. See *Encyclopaedia Britannica*, vol. 15 (Cambridge, 1911), pp. 808–9.

The neutral description of the birth of the kingfisher becomes, in poetic context, a metaphor for a creative process which is inclusive, which embraces the mess, the corruption, the rejectamenta, all the foul origins of human and poetic energy, and holds them while yet refusing to hypostatize them in a beautifully finished literary artifact. Yet the very espousal of such a dynamic wholeness contradicts itself by creating its own mythology, with its own set of hierarchical exclusions and resistances. Of this the poem makes no secret as Olson condemns the conquistadors who imposed themselves on an integral native culture, invoking the "light" of Christian civilization to justify economic exploitation. In short, the poem develops the same "closed" versus "open" polarity we have seen in the Thomas Granger poem and in "Projective Verse"; its mythology was thus conceived prior to the act of writing and what Olson discovered in the diverse materials he gathered into his poem was once again what he was prepared to find. Moreover, "The Kingfishers" is the cry of an alienated prophet, who finds that demonic, repressive forces are now in the ascendancy; contemporary society is a "dryness," an "emptiness," a "silence." Yet if we "look" and "hear" hard enough, we can penetrate these corruptions—as Olson does with the dead legends of the kingfisher— and uncover the "light," the "flower" hidden inside; wholeness and immediacy are absences which are present only to the privileged vision of the poet. In ancient times, say, before the conquistadors, no such discrepancy existed between immediacy and culture; but, as Olson laments in a passage of unabashed nostalgia, "all now is war / where so lately there was peace, / and the sweet brotherhood, the use / of tilled fields." Here Olson provides an apt illustration of Octavio Paz's point that "modern art and literature consist of continuous discovering of the very old and distant," partly because "what is very old" has been perceived as "not a past but a beginning."[43] In Olson, as in so many contemporary poets, a true present is valued because it represents a lost original wholeness. The true present thus turns out to be a lie or at least a fiction, immediacy valued because it has already been eternalized, transformed into a mythical construct.

"The Kingfishers" is a poetic text that comes to the reader laden with quotations and learned allusions. Some of these references, like the legends of the kingfisher, are evoked only to be demystified; others, like the three quotations from Heraclitus in section 4, provide authority for Olson's own views as procedures. Together, they are supposed to work to clear the ground for the beginning with which Olson ends the poem: "I hunt among stones"—where the stones could be the carved stones of

43. *Children of the Mire*, p. 4.

some ancient ruins or the rocks of some present-day landscape like
Gloucester. At the end of the poem, then, the very old and the contemporary come together in a continuous present—with no period closing the
poem. Yet the last line of "The Kingfishers" paraphrases part of a quote
from Rimbaud's "Fêtes de la Faim" that Olson has given just a few lines
before: "si j'ai du goût, ce n'est guères / que pour la terre et les pierres"
(If I have any taste, it is only / for earth and stones"). Robert von Hallberg
argues that "The Kingfishers" identifies Olson as "posthistorical man";[44]
on the contrary, even the very end of the poem, where we are asked to
see Olson transformed into a consciousness that is both pre- and posthistorical, actually identifies his beginning as a repetition or at least a
continuation of a literary past—and this predicament brings us to the
fourth of the dilemmas that are posed by a poetics of immediacy. It is
one thing to make immediacy the basis for an ethic of living; it is yet
another thing, with even more serious problems, to make it the basis for
writing. In "Literary History and Literary Modernity" Paul De Man cuts
to the heart of the problem: "The continuous appeal of modernity, the
desire to break out of literature toward the reality of the moment, prevails
and, in its turn, folding back upon itself, engenders the repetition and the
continuation of literature."[45] In writing, the fluidity and open-endedness
of the instant are incorporated into a totality and at exactly that point all
the repressed elements—all those coercive features of writing supposedly
banished in the postmodern demystification—all these repressed elements
return; the quick recorder of the moment becomes distanced, separate,
an interpreter who creates a whole in which myth, symbol, frame all
reappear. A common critical assumption has it that in contemporary or
postmodern poetry metonymic procedures have replaced metaphoric ones.
Yet a "work" that was purely metonymic would be an endless list, so
metaphor covertly returns when these critics begin to talk about links
within specific poems. Of the five poets I have selected, Ginsberg, Levertov, and Wright all approach the moment from a visionary perspective;
Lowell examines experience from a psychoanalytic frame, and O'Hara,
the one who seems freest of predispositions, is the one most willing to
admit that poetic wholes are fictive constructions. So much for the end
of mystification which, like the grasping of a true present, is endlessly
deferred in writing.

De Man's view, however, is that all writing, transforming experience
into fiction and allegory, annihilates immediacy; but this conclusion leaves
De Man no way to distinguish between Beckett, whose writings do seem
to be the disincarnated, purely linguistic acts De Man has in mind, and

44. *Charles Olson: The Scholar's Art* (Cambridge, Mass., 1978), p. 18.
45. *Blindness and Insight*, p. 162.

Williams, for whom writing works as a means of making objects like the red wheelbarrow present to a consciousness otherwise oblivious to them. Similarly, De Man could not distinguish between Richard Wilbur and Frank O'Hara or between the earlier and the more recent Adrienne Rich. All writings *are* fictional, but there are different kinds of fictions and, as I've already indicated, different kinds of totalities. Poems can't *be* immediate; but poems can (with more or less convincingness) create the illusion of immediacy and talking about such poems will require us, as we shall see, to redefine such terms as myth, symbol, frame rather than complacently observing their presence in works that set out to abolish them. Moreover, in the historical context I have described, this fiction of immediacy turned out, once again, not to be a debilitating but an enlivening one.

FOUR

Allen Ginsberg's "Howl"

"The only poetic tradition is the Voice out of the burning bush. The rest is trash & will be consumed."[1]

—Allen Ginsberg

" 'Make it new' saith Pound, 'Invention,' said W. C. Williams. That's the 'Tradition'— a complete fuck-up so you're on your own."[2]

—Allen Ginsberg

"Twenty years is more or less a literary generation," Richard Eberhart remarks, "and Ginsberg's *Howl* ushered in a new generation."[3] Many contemporary poets have testified to the liberating effect that Ginsberg's poem had on them in the late fifties, but "ushered in" is too tame a phrase to describe Ginsberg's historical impact. Ginsberg, for whom every poem begins, or ought to, with a frontal assault on established positions, thrust a battering ram against those protective enclosures, human and literary, so important to the young Wilbur and Rich. A "howl" is a prolonged animal cry and so an instinctive cry, and Ginsberg's poem still forcefully communicates the sense of a sudden, angry eruption of instincts long thwarted, of the release of excluded human and literary energies. Not irony but prophetic vision; not a created persona but "naked" confession; not the autotelic poem but wrathful social protest; not the decorums of high culture but the language and matter of the urban streets; not disciplined craftmanship but spontaneous utterance and indiscriminate inclusion—"Howl" violated all the current artistic canons and provoked a literary, social, and even legal scandal.

Yet the Ginsberg of the late fifties was an oddly contradictory figure. He was a strident revolutionary who, when not announcing his absolute

1. "When the Mode of the Music Changes the Walls of the City Shake," in *The Poetics of the New American Poetry,* ed. Donald Allen and Warren Tallman (New York, 1973), p. 327.

2. "How Kaddish Happened," ibid., p. 346.

3. *To Eberhart from Ginsberg* (Lincoln, Mass., 1976), p. 7.

newness, was busily tracing his genealogical links with underground traditions and neglected masters, especially Blake and Whitman. History was bunk, but the new consciousness Ginsberg proclaimed was empowered by a fairly familiar form of nineteenth-century Idealism, the basis for his admiration for Blake and Whitman. Ginsberg opened his poetry to sordid urban realities, and he packed "Howl" with things, with matter. Yet, as we shall see, immersion in what he calls "the total animal soup of time" was the first step in a painful ordeal which ended in the visionary's flight out of time. Ginsberg's poem reaches, nervously and ardently, after rest from urban frenzy, a resolution the poet can only find in a vertical transcendence. Ginsberg's departure from end-of-the-line modernism was a dramatic but hardly a new one; it took the form of a return to those very romantic models and attitudes that modernism had tried to shun.

Ginsberg's subversion of the prevailing artistic norms was not achieved either quickly or easily. While poets like Wilbur and Lowell early built poetic styles and earned impressive critical recognition, Ginsberg's early career consisted of a series of false starts. "Howl"—contrary to popular impression—is not the work of an angry *young* man; the poem was not written until its author was thirty, and *Howl and Other Poems* was Ginsberg's first published but third written book. Nor was "Howl"—contrary to a popular impression created by its author—a sudden, spontaneous overflow of creative energy. The poem, started, dropped, then started again a few years later, was itself the product of a series of false starts.[4] The visionary perspective of "Howl" had already been revealed to Ginsberg in a series of hallucinations he had experienced in the summer of 1948. The false starts were a part of Ginsberg's struggle to accept these visions and to find a literary form and language that would faithfully embody them. The letters, notebooks, and manuscripts in the Allen Ginsberg Archives at Columbia, along with Ginsberg's published autobiographical writings and interviews, allow us to document in ample detail the slow evolution, in the late forties and early fifties, of one dissenting poet.

In the summer of 1948 Ginsberg was living alone in a tenement apartment in Harlem. All of his closest friends—Jack Kerouac, William Burroughs, and Neal Cassady—were out of town, and he had just received a letter from Cassady ending their sexual relationship: "a great mortal blow to all of my tenderest hopes."[5] In addition, Ginsberg was soon to

4. Sections of a poem that eventually turned into "Howl" appear as early as an entry dated "Nov. 28 or 30, 1951" in the Notebook 1950–1952 in the Allen Ginsberg Archives at Columbia University. For a fuller account of the evolution of "Howl," see note 30.

5. Ginsberg discusses these visions in many places; my account relies on the version in the *Paris Review* interview, collected in *Writers at Work, Third Series,* ed. George Plimpton (New York, 1967), pp. 302–11.

graduate from Columbia, a prospect that left him with "nowhere to go and the difficulty of finding a job."

> So, in that state therefore of hopelessness, or dead end, change of phase, you know—growing up—and in an equilibrium in any case, a psychic, a mental equilibrium of a kind, like of having no New Vision and no Supreme Reality and nothing but the world in front of me and of not knowing what to do with *that* . . . there was a funny balance of tension, in every direction.

But this "balance of tension," rather than being a healthy psychic integration, actually reveals a sense of identity-diffusion, a lack of shape or direction: with "nowhere to go." Yet, along with diffusion, there is the feeling of being trapped, walled-in: "with nothing but the world in front of me, and of not knowing what to do with *that*." Abandoned by friends and rebuffed by his lover, Ginsberg feels empty and dead inside, at once lost and constricted.

When the first of his hallucinations took place, Ginsberg had just finished masturbating while reading—William Blake! And as "my eye was idling over the page of 'Ah, Sun-flower, . . . suddenly I realized that the poem was talking about *me*."

> Ah, Sun-flower! weary of time,
> Who countest the steps of the sun;
> Seeking after that sweet golden clime,
> Where the traveller's journey is done.

The vision is initiated by a kind of literary masturbation: Ginsberg, clearly no disciple of Brooks and Warren, views Blake's text not as an autonomous verbal artifact, independent of author and reader alike; instead, he gazes into the poem as into a mirror, finding a reflection of his own mood, "weary of time," pining "away with desire," and yearning for deliverance into a "sweet golden clime." Such deliverance soon came in the form of a "very deep earthen grave voice in the room, which I immediately assumed, I didn't think twice, was Blake's voice." And this voice, Ginsberg recalls,

> was so completely tender and beautifully . . . ancient. Like the voice of the Ancient of Days. But the peculiar quality of the voice was something unforgettable because it was like God had a human voice, with all the infinite tenderness and anciency and mortal gravity of a living Creator speaking to his son.

Ginsberg's emptiness is suddenly filled with an ecstatic hallucination, in which he hears the voice of an idealized spiritual and artistic father.

Ginsberg's actual father was a poet whom the son viewed as both impotent and harshly critical; the "apparitional voice" here, however, reveals the existence of a "living Creator," an awesome figure, ancient and grave and wise, who also remains capable of "infinite tenderness"—speaking as if "God had a human voice." With this vision begins Ginsberg's search for a poetic voice that would be at once powerful and tender, prophetic and personal, a search that led him to join the visionary and confessional modes in poems such as "Howl" and "Kaddish."

Just a few moments after hearing the voice of Blake, Ginsberg looked up at

> the cornices in the old tenement building in Harlem across the back-yard court [that] had been carved very finely in 1890 or 1910. And were like the solidification of a great deal of intelligence and care and love also. So that I began noticing in every corner where I looked evidences of a living hand, even in the bricks, in the arrangement of each brick. Some hand had placed them there—that some hand had placed the whole universe in front of me. That some hand had placed the sky. No, that's exaggerating—not that some hand had placed the sky but that the sky was the living blue hand itself. Or that God was in front of my eyes—existence itself was God.

His vision had transformed Ginsberg into a modern urban Blake who could see eternity in a tenement cornice. Before, there was "nothing but the world in front of me"; now, "some hand had placed the whole universe in front of me." Before, he had felt amorphous yet controlled by powerful outside forces; now, he feels unbounded yet one—released into the seem-ingly infinite span of the sky, yet lovingly enclosed in its "hand." Under this new dispensation, diffusion is replaced with direction, the sure sense of a loving guide whose presence pervades the entire universe, *is* the universe: "existence itself was God." So while Wilbur and Rich resign themselves to being secular "children of disordered days," Ginsberg iden-tifies himself as a child of the universe, a poet to whom the "living Cre-ator" speaks as "to his son."

Yet Ginsberg's contradictory feelings about both physical and spiritual realities were also apparent at this time, as a look at his second halluci-nation, occurring just several moments after the first, will show. This time the vision was inspired by a reading of Blake's "The Sick Rose."

> This time it was a slightly different sense-depth-mystic impression. Because "The Sick Rose"—you know I can't interpret the poem now, but it had a meaning—I mean I can interpret it on a verbal level, the sick rose is my self, or self, or the living body, sick be-cause the mind, which is the worm "that flies in the night, / In the

howling storm," or Urizen, reason; Blake's character might be one that's entered the body and is destroying it, or let us say death, the worm as being death, the natural process of death, some kind of mystical being of its own to come in and devour the body, the rose.

Ginsberg's two glosses on the worm in Blake's poem are significantly at odds with each other, in a way that reveals some of his conflicting feelings about life in the flesh, about *this* existence. At first, "real" selfhood is located in the body, healthy and innocent in itself, but poisoned by the invasion of abstract reason, part of what Moloch signifies in "Howl." But in the second reading the "living body" becomes the dying flesh, corrupted not by reason but by nature, the devouring powers of time and death. Moreover, death, at first a "natural process," is immediately personified into a monster, as if it had an independent and omnipotent existence. Here, then, life in the body makes the "shining," "infinite self" of the first vision become limited, time-bound, and vulnerable. Division and conflict, not eternal harmony, characterize both consciousness and cosmos—or, if there is ultimate unity, it derives from the pervasive and all-powerful (and perhaps punitive) presence of death.

Yet this devouring monster turns out to be beautiful and seductive as well as terrifying, because it offers a way out of the "divided creation."

> But anyway I experienced "The Sick Rose," with the voice of Blake reading it, as something that applied to the whole universe, like hearing the doom of the whole universe, and at the same time the inevitable beauty of doom. I can't remember now, except it was very beautiful and awesome. But a little of it slightly scary, having to do with the knowledge of death—my death and also the death of being itself, and that was the great pain. So, like a prophecy, not only in human terms but a prophecy as if Blake had penetrated the very secret core of the *entire* universe and had come forth with some little magic formula statement in rhyme and rhythm that, if properly heard in the inner inner ear, would deliver you beyond the universe.

A cosmic vision must confront the fact of death but Ginsberg goes way beyond acceptance here—to an apotheosis of death. "Existence itself was God," he said before; now the universe, all being, is doomed, but that doom is beautiful. Selfhood is attained not in the living body but in the transcendence of the physical, its inevitable limits. Seeking the certainty of an absolute, Ginsberg can only locate finality and perfection in death, an inhuman mood that will dominate much of his early poetry. "Die / If thou wouldst be with that which thou dost seek!" reads the Shelley epigraph from *Kaddish;* Ginsberg's wish for a cosmic identity turns on him and provokes thoughts of self-annihilation.

Two subsequent hallucinations, occurring about a week later, basically repeated the pattern of alternation between elated moments when the world seemed an extension of a godlike self and terrifying moments when Ginsberg felt solitary and vulnerable to vast outside forces. Either the world is an extension of me, the young Ginsberg felt, or I am an extension of it. If the visions themselves reveal ambivalences about both physicality and spirit, Ginsberg's response to the entire series of visions was similarly divided. When the voice of Blake first addressed him as "the son of the Creator," Ginsberg recalls, "my first thought was this was what I was born for, and second thought, never forget—never forget, never renege, never deny." Yet even at the time Ginsberg experienced the visions themselves as alien, intrusive forces, deluding and devouring: "suddenly I thought, also simultaneously, Ooh, I'm going *mad!*"—a panic caught in a line in "Howl": "who thought they were only mad when Baltimore gleamed in supernatural ecstasy." The most intimate source of such doubts was the poet's mother, Naomi Ginsberg, who had been hospitalized for much of Ginsberg's adolescence for having visions that, like her son's, alternately manifested benign and demonic cosmic powers. Had the son simply inherited his mother's illness?

If Ginsberg had experienced such fears in, say, the mid-sixties when the mystics were, as Holden Caulfield would say, coming in the goddam windows, it would have been one thing. But Ginsberg's hallucinations occurred at a time when "social disgrace—*dis*grace—[was] attached to certain states of soul";[6] "everybody I tried to talk to about it thought I was going crazy," Ginsberg claims, his psychiatrist. A funny but anguished poem, "The Lion for Real"—written much later in Paris in 1958—recreates Ginsberg's desperate need of ten years before.[7] "I came home and found a lion in my living room," the poem begins, crossing the matter of fact and the surreal. A terrified Ginsberg flees the apartment, runs to his father, his psychiatrist, his friends, but they all refuse to accept the lion as real. So, "confused" and "exalted," Ginsberg returns to his apartment and acknowledges the existence of the animal by feeding it. But the voracious lion—another devouring monster—takes over the poet's life. On the one hand, he can't flee or forget the animal; on the other, acceptance means self-annihilation, a fate that, by the poem's end, Ginsberg eagerly awaits: "In this life I have heard your promise I am ready to die I have served / Your starved and ancient Presence O Lord I wait in my room at your Mercy." The enveloping presence of the lion represents the beautiful and scary presences of Ginsberg's illuminations; and

6. *Allen Ginsberg in America,* p. 71.
7. *Kaddish and Other Poems* (San Francisco, 1961), pp. 53–55. In referring to Ginsberg's work, the following abbreviations will be used: *GW, Gates of Wrath* (Bolinas, 1972); *EM, Empty Mirror* (New York, 1961).

"The Lion for Real" dramatizes his frenzied uncertainties about whether these presences arose from inside him or whether they were "for real"— and whether they revealed a benign, regal power in the universe or one that was malevolent and persecutory. Ginsberg's self-doubts, moreover, were reinforced by the literary culture of the late forties. To the New Critics, visionary poets were mainly useful as foils, against which they could assess the ironic self-awareness of a "mature" poetry. "At Columbia," Ginsberg remembers, "Whitman was hardly taught and was considered like a creep. Shelley was a creep too. John Crowe Ransom and Allen Tate were like the supreme literary touchstones."[8] The young Ginsberg was also an admirer of Hart Crane, and the well-known attacks on Crane by Allen Tate and Yvor Winters showed how a Whitmanlike mysticism could subject a poet to literary as well as social disgrace. Even Blake at the time was viewed as a brilliant eccentric—attention paid to the verbal complexities of the short poems rather than the form and substance of the prophetic works.

If Ginsberg was frightened by his visions, he ultimately neither reneged on nor forgot them. Nor did he simply let them take over his psyche. Instead, he managed to make them the source of a kind of poetry which would extend the boundaries of his art. Ginsberg's father, Louis Ginsberg, wrote as a programmatic conservative and traditionalist: "When terse / Is verse, // Its zest / Is best," he writes; "so I / Shall try // To hammer / My stammer // And beat / It neat, // Exact, / Compact— // To file / My style // And pare / It bare."[9] His poems, more cerebral, clever, and ironic than passionate, serve up conventional wisdom in terse lines, a kind of kitsch formalism which denied that modernism had ever happened. In the introduction Ginsberg wrote to his father's collection, *Morning in Spring,* the son, while respectful, speaks of the older man in language that suggests obsolescence, dissociation, and death; the guiding voice of the father-poet sounds hollow, a mere echo of the past.[10] On a personal level, Ginsberg's hallucinations inspired a poetic project in which the son took up his father's medium, poetry, and, pronouncing it hollow and dead, sought to revitalize it with an infusion of the brilliance and power he associated with his mother's visions. Out of these familial pressures emerged Ginsberg's historical role—defined by a visionary perspective that violated the prevailing assumptions about the art of poetry.

On the one hand, the literary tradition, both the remote and the recent past, seems all-powerful, a pervasive presence that imposes alien stan-

---

8. *Allen Ginsberg in America,* p. 119.

9. *Morning in Spring* (New York, 1970), p. 119.

10. For a fuller account of the relations between Ginsberg and his poet-father, see my "Allen Ginsberg: The Origins of 'Howl' and 'Kaddish,' " *Iowa Review* 8 (Spring 1977): 88–95.

dards of the past onto the living present. In this respect, its power resembles that of Moloch in "Howl," a deity to whom children were sacrificed in order to perpetuate the past as mere repetition. On the other hand, this tradition, mechanically forcing conformity and coldly judging the creative efforts of the present, is itself an abstract order, dissociated from life—dead—and therefore to be abandoned. Such a perception (or, more accurately, myth) of the literary tradition as at once threatening and attenuated provides the starting point for Ginsberg's act of exorcism in "Howl," making it both necessary and possible to demolish the established order. But in his earliest poems—later published as *The Gates of Wrath*—Ginsberg, like most young poets at the time, sought the support of tradition.

At the same time, his diffidence seems partly a tactical gesture designed to placate the literary authorities, for the poems do adapt a bardic voice and visionary argument that placed Ginsberg, at best, at the margin of acceptability. For the moment at least, Ginsberg needed to keep one foot planted in the camp of conventionality while also aspiring to a promethean task that really impelled him to step boldly outside it. The results of this compromise are more interesting to the literary historian than to the lover of poetry. Most of the poems make painful reading today, as they must have even then, when, prefaced by a long, windy, partly diffident but mostly grandiose letter, several of them were submitted to William Carlos Williams. Williams, whose hostility to set forms was certainly known to Ginsberg, was a curious choice of mentor. But he responded with an act of support and a piece of advice: he acknowledged Ginsberg as literary son by including his letter in Book V of *Paterson* and returned the poems with a kindly admonition that stuck in Ginsberg's mind: "In this mode perfection is basic."[11] Perfect, *The Gates of Wrath* poems were not; prolix, awkward, pretentious, derivative, and self-consciously literary, they certainly were.

The Gates of Wrath poems creak under the weight of what seems a willed effort to lift the vulnerable, agonized human self out of space, out of time, into the more secure mansions of eternity. In their frequent references to childhood and Eden, the poems postulate an original unity, from which the self has been banished to become a "poor wandering child of time." Consequently, change is experienced as disintegration and loss, the loss of innocence ("wonder ageing into woe") and of visionary power ("Time gets thicker, light gets dim"). A gloomy consciousness of temporality and death pervades the poems, an awareness that is dramatized in the "shrouded stranger" whose mesmerizing glance haunts Ginsberg in two of the poems. As both this classic "double" figure and the similar

11. Quoted in *Morning in Spring*, p. 11; Williams's remark is also recorded in Ginsberg's Notebook May 1949–October 1950.

"shadow" image in many of the poems suggest, time imposes separation, not just from original harmony, but a division *within* the self—specifically between a corrupt (dying *and* impure) physical being and an incorruptible spirit. Conflict between the two typically takes the form of conscience flailing the body for its lusts or gnawing at it like Blake's worm at the sick rose. In fact, the shrouded stranger is an accusing, punitive presence as well as a reminder of death, and in "The Voice of the Rock" human life is imagined as an endless struggle between the physical self and a wrathful shadow that, like conscience, is felt to be at once part of the self and an alien intruder. Here the physical world, a sick rose, slowly wastes away, devoured by some mysterious force. But *The Gates of Wrath* reflects the same contradictions we have seen in the visions. In other poems, physical being becomes the alien presence, the body figured as a "shroud" or a "tomb" or, most often, as "stone"—cold, dead, and unresponsive. Describing a train ride across the Jersey marshes in November, "Ode to the Setting Sun" provides Ginsberg's version of the brief Blake poem from which the book's title is taken. But while Blake's westward journey "thro' the Gates of Wrath" ends with "the break of day," Ginsberg's closes with the disappearance of the sun and all vital life.

> My bones are carried on the train
> Westward where the sun has gone;
> Night has darkened in the rain,
> And the rainbow day is done;
> Cities age upon the plain
> And smoke rolls upward out of stone.

Movement through time enacts a journey toward darkness and death; and the physical world, seemingly turned to "stone" by the "hooded gaze" of some shrouded stranger (to be identified in "Howl" as Moloch), becomes a landscape of death and loss.

In *The Gates of Wrath* poems Ginsberg imagines two radically different ways out of the divisions, guilts, and limits of corporeal life, the two, as we shall see, to become linked in "Howl." One, deriving from the numerous images of stone, rock, and bone, is to transform the self into such a hard, enduring, and invulnerable substance: "shadow changes into bone," Ginsberg exults in a line that pleased him enough to use it in three poems. The other and the more predominant route is that of vertical transcendence, a soaring upward in which flesh changes into air, self into disembodied presence—a ghost ("visioned by the death of mind / My ghost will wander in the air") or Blakean angel ("Angels in the air / Serenade my senses in delight"). A series of eight poems deal directly with the loss of

Neal Cassady and the ensuing hallucinations; they show how the separation generated thoughts of an ideal union and how such unity immediately becomes identified with death, the cost of transformation into
either rock or air. In fact, it is the frightening dimension of the visions
that is stressed in these poems, written not long after the actual experience. In the three poems about Cassady, he is seen as a dangerous combination of killer and angel, hardness and gentleness (rock and air) as are
the presences in the visions. The deity there revealed may be a dove or
a hawk, Ginsberg suggests in "A Very Dove." "Nobody cares when a
man goes mad: / He is sorry, God is glad," a self-pitying Ginsberg laments,
as if the visions *were* a form of madness thrust upon him by a sadistic
deity. In both "Vision 1948" and "The Voice of the Rock," the visions
are experienced as a deliverance—*and* as a mutilating assault that leaves
Ginsberg illuminated but unable to function in this world.

> I shudder with the intelligence and I
> > Wake in the deep light
> And hear a vast machinery
> > Descending without sound,
> Intolerable to me, too bright,
> > And shaken in the sight
> The eye goes blind before the world goes round.

Again and again Ginsberg denounces those locked inside the temporal,
material world as "blind," without a vision; but here, in a paradox he
repeats, Ginsberg himself is blinded by an overwhelming vision, separated
from the turning world, left helpless. Yet once the visions cease, they can
be and are idealized in retrospect and their return sought. As a result,
the poet is once again left abandoned inside time, now all the more anguished with loss and yearning for a permanent deliverance via death.
"Ah! but to have seen the Dove, and then go blind," he cries in "Psalm";
all he can look forward to is the end when "I die no more / Time's many
deaths, and pass toward the last gates" to experience "pure light" once
again.
    This search for transcendent perfection informs—or, rather, deforms—
the style of *The Gates of Wrath* poems as well. In fact, literature—apotheosized as a domain where perfection and control can be attained—
attracts the young poet as a compensation for and alternative to the conflicts, impurities, and general mess of actual life. His first poems seek,
Ginsberg has said, to "perfect a rhymed, punning, silvery versification";[12]
but their language only ends by showing how inhuman (and emotionally

12. *Allen Verbatim* (New York, 1974), p. 139.

deadening) the quest for the absolute can become. Stylistically, *Gates of Wrath* combines the fashionably metaphysical with the romantic lyric, not an easy combination to effect, and Ginsberg doesn't. In many of the love poems he takes over the passionate logic and wit of Donne: "Till, as the hour chimes its tune, / Dialectic, we commune," though Donne would have struck "chimes its tune." More often, Ginsberg writes an elevated lyric that seems derived from Shelley and Crane. "The Voice of the Rock" begins:

> I cannot sleep, I cannot sleep
> until a victim is resigned;
> a shadow holds me in his keep
> and seeks the bones that he must find;
> and hovelled in a shroudy heap
> dead eyes see, and dead eyes weep,
> dead men from the coffin creep,
> nightmare of murder in the mind.

The expressed fear of the dead taking over is ironically realized in the poem, as Ginsberg's handling of accentual meter and a set stanza depletes the poem of energy and helps convert what must have been an agonizing experience in reality into a mere literary idea. An iambic tetrameter beat that, until the last line, is almost totally regular; a lack of inventiveness in the rhyming; the end-stopped lines that emphasize both the monotony of the beat and the predictability of the rhymes and reveal a lack of ease with the stanza form—all these define a versification that belongs not to a "silvery" but to an iron age. The language, too, is lifeless; a vocabulary that consists mostly of indefinite nouns that are not set into motion by the verbs creates a style that makes it easy for us to sleep even if Ginsberg can't. Indeed, the primary motive in all the poems in *The Gates of Wrath* is to eternalize experience (and the self) by converting the actual into myth and symbol, into traditional forms and often deliberately archaic language, as if the poems were spoken by the same kind of awesome and ancient disembodied presence that had spoken to him during the terrifying "sick rose" vision. "Let these dark leaves be lit with images / That strike like lightning from eternal mind," Ginsberg prays in "Psalm," and in "Howl," when he assumes that eternal mind is present in himself rather than literary authority, he does evolve a language that juxtaposes the literal and the surreal to create lightninglike flashes of eternity. But in the *Gates of Wrath* poems, which exclude the literal and the temporal, Ginsberg's poetic of the transcendent word issues in a lifeless style.

Practically all of *The Gates of Wrath* was written by 1949, when Ginsberg was twenty-three. In the spring of that year, just a few months after
his graduation from Columbia, Ginsberg solved the problem of what to
do with his life by getting himself arrested for possession of stolen prop-
erty, goods that an addict-friend Herbert Huncke, one of the best minds
of Ginsberg's generation who supported his habit by participating in a
burglary ring, had been storing in Ginsberg's apartment. Eventually, Ginsberg was allowed to plead insanity—he claims he told the psychiatric
authorities that he had heard the voice of Blake speak to him the summer
before—and so Ginsberg was committed to Columbia Psychiatric Institute
for most of the remainder of 1949.[13] Soon after his admission there, he
met Carl Solomon, to whom "Howl" is dedicated.

When he left the hospital nine months later, Ginsberg, chastened by
his arrest and hospitalization (which he then interpreted as punishment
for his visionary strivings), returned to live with his father in Paterson,
New Jersey. For several years Ginsberg had been keeping notebooks in
which he entered dreams, imaginary letters, poems, parts of poems, ideas
for poems, quotations from his reading, reflections on both immediate
and past experiences, and on the art of poetry. Some of the poems in *The
Gates of Wrath* grew out of the notebooks; the entry for 21 May 1949
reveals what were then Ginsberg's habits of composition.

> To live and deal with life as if it were a stone.
> Time like a turning stone that grinds my bones.
> Time is a dog that gnaws my bones
> and grinds my soul to sticks and stones
> It's not mere time
> that pricks my pride;
> Just let my bones
> Be satisfied.[14]

Here abstract idea becomes figure of speech, becomes rhymed, metered,
gnomic verse in a way that suggests more the will-to-poetry than its
attainment. When Ginsberg returned to Paterson, however, he renewed
his acquaintance with William Carlos Williams, visiting him several times
in the early fifties. In February 1952 Ginsberg sent Williams eleven poems
he had written about a year before by breaking the prose of his journals
into lines of verse. Williams responded enthusiastically, and by 10 March

13. See *Allen Ginsberg in America,* pp. 123–30. The Notebook May 1949–50 contains
a lengthy narrative of the events leading to Ginsberg's arrest—apparently written for his
attorney; the Notebook May 1949–October 1950 was kept during his hospitalization.
14. Entry for 21 May 1949 in Notebook May 1949–October 1950.

1952, Ginsberg had put together eighty such poems.[15] For Ginsberg, as
for many young poets, Williams offered an alternative to fifties formalism,
and his specific suggestion to Ginsberg pointed up the strengths of what
Ginsberg wrote when he was not trying to write a *poem*.

Ginsberg then reviewed at least three of his journals, converting prose
entries into the brief, flat, short-lined poems later collected in *Empty
Mirror*, trying, he says, to

> rearrange the lines according to how they might be spoken, and
> where I might take a breath, or where a breath might run counter to
> the movement of the line, or where the end of a line might make a
> little syncopation with the way the breath was moving along to the
> end of the sentence.[16]

A prose entry from the 1949 journal

> Tonite all is well . . . what a terrible future. I am 23, the year of the
> iron birthday, the gate of darkness. I am ill. I have become spiritually
> or practically impotent in my madness this last month. I suddenly re-
> alized that my head is severed from my body; I realized it a few
> weeks ago, by myself lying sleepless on the couch[17]

becomes the second (untitled) poem in *Empty Mirror:*

> Tonite all is well . . . What a
> terrible future. I am twenty-three,
> year of the iron birthday,
> gate of darkness. I am ill,
> I have become physically and
> spiritually impotent in my madness this month.
> I suddenly realized that my head
> is severed from my body;
> I realized it a few nights ago
> by myself
> lying sleepless on the couch.

As we have seen, the poems in this notebook formalize expression of
preexisting ideas, as if form were never anything more than the imposition
of form. In reworking the prose sections, Ginsberg, relieved of the burdens
of thought and literary self-consciousness, was freed to concentrate on

15. See letter from Ginsberg to Williams, 10 March 1952, in the Williams collection at
Yale. In the Notebook 1950–1952, Ginsberg has written just before the entry for 11 March
1952, "Here Williams told me poems from Journal were poetry. Henceforth everything here
has added self-consciousness."

16. *Allen Verbatim*, p. 140.

17. Entry for 17 May 1949 in Notebook May 1949–October 1950.

the problem of discovering, then marking on the page, the rhythms latent in his own *acts* of *thinking*. The result was a poetry which,

> though less pretty than the rhymed poems I was writing, actually had more humor, more life . . . , more detail, more minute particulars, less ideas, more things, . . .—*presenting* material, rather than recombining symbols that I had appropriated from Yeats or Blake or Marvell.[18]

Under Williams's guidance, Ginsberg was seeking, through the dissolution of beautiful forms, a "breakthrough back into life."

When Ginsberg showed the *Empty Mirror* poems to Williams in 1952, the older poet pronounced them "wonderful," wrote an introduction to the collection and attempted to persuade his own publisher, Random House, to accept the book.[19] They refused, and it was not hard to see why. "Wonderful," the poems definitely were not; Williams might well have returned them to Ginsberg with the further admonition that "in *this* mode, energy is basic." The poems do emulate certain of the technical features of Williams's verse, and they do so partly out of the subdued Ginsberg's desire to purge the visionary side of his personality. "That time in Paterson was, for me," he recalls, "like the renunciation of an obsessional search for the circumstances of some visionary cosmic consciousness, like the acceptance of what was real, of the world as world, absolute as it is," and he interprets the book's title as an "image for the defeat of visionary, metaphysical strivings."[20] The title also suggests a loss or dissolution of self; but in these poems such feelings of inner emptiness are countered not by visionary strivings but a turn toward physical and social experience.

Near the beginning of *Empty Mirror,* several poems establish a mood of personal and literary defeat. The book starts at a "dead / end": "I am finished."

> All spiritual facts I realize
> are true but I never escape
> the feeling of being closed in
> and the sordidness of self,
> the futility of all that I
> have seen and done and said.

18. *Allen Verbatim,* p. 141.
19. W. C. Williams to Allen Ginsberg, 27 February 1952; see also Williams's letters to Ginsberg on 7 April 1952 and 24 May 1952.
20. *Allen Ginsberg in America,* pp. 135–36.

In the second poem Ginsberg goes on to lament: "I have become physically and spiritually impotent in my madness this month. / I suddenly realized that my head / is severed from my body." The poet's "head," severed from physical life, may be "open to hallucination" but it is finally "closed in," dissociated and empty. A similar sense of failure attaches to all earlier literary efforts. Three of the *Empty Mirror* poems attempt a rescue operation by revising poems from *The Gates of Wrath,* converting ornate rhetoric into plain speech. In "Long Live the Spiderweb," Ginsberg sees his earlier poetic self as caught in the "web of ancient measure" so that his words, closed in by tight forms and severed from particular experiences, went "dead." As he writes in a poem prefaced by Thomas Hardy's advocacy of "humbly recording" life's "phenomena."

> I attempted to concentrate
> the total sun's rays in
> each poem as through a glass,
> but such magnification
> did not set the page afire.

Such grandiose ambitions issued only in the "dead / end" with which *Empty Mirror* begins. It is as though the very literary tradition that was to be the vehicle of Ginsberg's self-apotheosis had turned around and absorbed him; it is easy to see why he later thought his father's poetic voice to be dead, and why he turned to Williams, whose view of the line as breath spaced, suggested a *living* voice, located *in* the body in a given place. Williams, moreover, offered an example of a writer who, unlike Louis Ginsberg, broke with *the* tradition, immersed himself in the northern New Jersey of Ginsberg's own experience and mastered that world in verse.

For Ginsberg felt that the only way out of the sterility of his life and work was by means of a descent from Literature into immediate experience. While an undergraduate at Columbia, Ginsberg had written a story in which a character based on Jack Kerouac had attacked "Bliestein," who was based on himself:

> The trouble with you, Bliestein, is that you don't write about your
> own environment—In Galloway I'm going to throw away all this
> damned decadence. All you can write about is Rimbaud and Lautre
> mont. Look at you—a Jew from Jersey City, and you don't have a
> feeling for your own country. . . . You have no sense of the present,
> of land.[21]

21. Quoted in Ann Charters, *Kerouac* (San Francisco, 1973), p. 64.

In *Empty Mirror,* Ginsberg seeks to shed the role of the outcast, and so the poems are filled with images of yearning to return to ordinary life, a being-at-one with the world, absolute as it is. "Time then to make a / home in wilderness," the poet decides in "A Desolation," seeking to replace his restless wandering with the conventional stabilities of "wife, / family" and "neighbors" in a rustic idyll. Dreamy wanderers, dissociated and therefore empty, waste away, perishing of "lonesomeness / or want of food." In the final poem, the wasted figure of the shrouded stranger returns: now frightened by the view from a "huge tower" he climbs, he opts for safety, the earth, and enters "the house of folk" in a pastoral setting. Imagistic poems such as "The Trembling of the Veil" and "The Bricklayers' Lunch Hour" enact return to the ordinary in the careful precision of their rendering of it. Ginsberg is now, as he says, "not / declaiming" but "telling the truth." The ego-centricity behind both his social histrionics and his sexual coldness is viewed with ironic clarity in several poems, while meditative pieces such as "Metaphysics" and "The Terms in Which I Think of Reality" abjure transcendence: "The ways of *this world* / are the ways of Heaven" (my emphasis).

Yet entering the ordinary world is a process that Ginsberg talks about more than he demonstrates, and when he does talk about it, he often does so in ways that end by converting reality into pastoral or erotic fantasies anyway—both facts that suggest that Ginsberg, no comedian as the letter "g," undertakes his passage back into reality with the same mixed feelings with which he approached the gates of wrath. If in "A Desolation" he longs to build a country home, he also intends to keep a shrine by it, "an image / of my wandering" that will no doubt mark him as a saintly figure different from his neighbors. If "The Terms in Which I Think of Reality" begins by declaring that this world is "eternity," it goes on to lament that our merely physical existence fails to realize life's fullest possibilities. "The world," says Ginsberg, "is a mountain // of shit"—a disgust that is still characteristic of his encounters with any reality that is not redeemed by idealizations. Ordinary life, finally no different from the visionary quest, is a wasting away, a humiliating immersion in foul matter that ends only in death, a state, once again—in "In Death, Cannot Reach What is Most Near" and "This is about Death"—ardently wished for.

In stylistic terms, too, Ginsberg holds back from following Williams all the way into the physical moment. A stylistic shift that encouraged Ginsberg to change "Apollo's shining chariot's shadow / Shudders in the mortal bourn; / Amber shores upon the meadow / Where Phaëthon falls forlorn / Fade in somber chiaroscuro, / Phantoms of the burning morn" to "I saw the sun go down" in revising "Ode to the Setting Sun" (*The Gates of Wrath*) to "Sunset" (*Empty Mirror*)—any such change must be counted a gain. Moreover, Williams not only proposed an alternative to the formalism of the postwar period, but he also provided certain techniques (the line as breath unit) and theories (form as discovery) that Ginsberg was later able to adapt to quite different ends with "Howl." Still, in *Empty Mirror* Ginsberg employs a flat, clipped manner out of Williams more to make statements about this world than to *present* it concretely. In addition, the talk is often introspective and self-conscious ("How sick I am!" one poem begins), with the author looking into his mirror rather than at any external reality. At other points, Ginsberg invokes cosmic matters—usually by means of such weighty abstractions as time, eternity, death—a language that really requires a more expansive form than it gets here. In these poems it seems as if the poet adopts a bardic stance, puffs himself up a bit, but then speaks quietly, sensing that no one is listening but himself. The final impression created by *Empty Mirror* is that Ginsberg's adoption of Williams's manner, like his return to Paterson, was a self-consciously willed act, and one that inhibited, rather than released, his creative powers.

For about two years—from January 1950 until December 1952—Ginsberg remained living with his father in Paterson. He continued in therapy for some time after his release from the hospital, worked briefly in a ribbon factory, then for a union newspaper, wrote reviews for *Newsweek* and the *Herald Tribune,* and worked on the poems in *Empty Mirror.* Moreover, in early 1950 Ginsberg started work on a long, ambitious project based on the shrouded stranger figure who appears both in *The Gates of Wrath* and *Empty Mirror.* "Stevens, Crane, Pound, Williams, Eliot, St Perse, etc. have no human plot" in their long poems, Ginsberg observed in his working notes. Designed to "restore a plot to long poetry," "The Shrouded Stranger" was to be "a tour de force—from classic mystical shroudy psalmlike stanzas and rhymes, through the history of poetic language, to bare statement of fact objectivist speech. Begin with symbols and end with things."[22] The poem, which appears to cross the action of Williams's "The Wanderer" with the stylistic virtuosity of the Joyce of the lying-in chapter of *Ulysses,* eventually collapsed under the weight of its own ambitions. Ginsberg took the task of recreating the evolution of poetic language in English seriously: he studied Anglo-Saxon versification, for example, and he wrote some imitations of it. Yet the whole notion of moving from "rhyme" to "speech," from "symbols" to "things," is too obviously a projection of Ginsberg's own stylistic development onto the tradition to work. The failure, however, turned out to be a creative one, for the narrative poem collapsed *into* a journal which became an

22. Notebook 1950–1952.

important poetic laboratory for Ginsberg in the early fifties, a place for experiments in spontaneous writing and intimate revelation. The grandiose project of "The Shrouded Stranger," an attempt to objectify autobiography, evolved into the confessional writing of "Howl," a poem that was, in fact, discovered in the process of keeping such a journal.[23]

The early fifties were, Ginsberg has said, a time of "a gathering of forces."[24] Sometime in December 1952 or January 1953, however, he made a first step toward a new, independent life, moving back to New York City, where he held jobs as a copy boy for the *World Telegram* and in market research. A year later, in December 1953, he moved more boldly; he left family and the established literary culture in and around New York City behind him and traveled slowly, via Florida, Cuba, and the Yucatan, to California. Looking back, Ginsberg himself views the 1953 journey west as a crucial and symbolic act: "It was like a big prophecy, taking off for California. Like I had passed one season of my life and it was time to start all over again."[25] It was not quite this easy or final, as we shall see; but moving west was a dramatic attempt to break away from the threatening images of failure, disintegration, and constriction that he associated with both familial and literary authority—a gesture toward the future, toward life, an attempt to start all over again as his own man. Yet it is also true that Ginsberg made this journey half looking back over his shoulder—just as in "Howl" he would return to the experiences and emotions of his life back in New York and in Part III of the poem ("I'm with you in Rockland, Carl Solomon") deny that he had ever really left. It is certainly mistaken to imagine a re-created Ginsberg floating into San Francisco on a magic carpet, dressed in long robes, with flowing hair, hand cymbals, and a "San Francisco Poetry Renaissance" banner. The Ginsberg that emerged in "Howl"—Ginsberg the somewhat rancorous bard of mystic affection—was there but confined to the privacy of his journals; outwardly, Ginsberg was deferential and conventional. Soon after his arrival in San Francisco in the summer of 1954 he was looking for a job in market research, and he quickly found one. He had traveled several thousand miles, but ended by doing precisely the kind of work he had been doing back in New York.

Not long after he secured the job, Ginsberg became involved with a woman, with whom he eventually settled into an apartment in San Francisco's chic Nob Hill district. Life went along in this style for several months in the fall of 1954 until Ginsberg began seeing a therapist at Langley-Porter Institute, Dr. Phillip Hicks, to find out why neither the job nor

23. See note 30.
24. *Allen Ginsberg in America,* p. 137.
25. Ibid., pp. 39–40.

the woman seemed to satisfy him. According to Ginsberg, at one point in his treatment the doctor asked:

> "What would you like to do? What *is* your desire, really?" I said, "Doctor, I don't think you're going to find this very healthy and clear, but I really would like to stop working forever—never work again, never do anything like the kind of work I'm doing now—and do nothing but write poetry and have leisure to spend the day outdoors and go to museums and see friends. And I'd like to keep living with someone—maybe even a man—and explore relationships that way. And cultivate my perceptions, cultivate the visionary thing in me. Just a literary and quiet city-hermit existence." Then, *he* said, "Well, why don't you?"[26]

In several interviews Ginsberg has discussed this encounter, mythologizing it into The Great Breakthrough that allowed him to start a new life. As Ginsberg tells it, the doctor's tolerant acceptance of Ginsberg's unconventional desires encouraged self-acceptance and the end of his misguided attempt to please authority—both of which, in turn, generated "Howl." So, the story goes, Ginsberg wrote a report showing how his firm could replace him with a computer; they fired him and he went on unemployment, now free to enjoy a "quiet city-hermit existence." By this time he had already met Peter Orlofsky, and Ginsberg's increasing involvement with Orlofsky disturbed the woman he was living with. The eventual result—again not following too long after the episode with Dr. Hicks—was that Ginsberg left affluent Nob Hill for downtown San Francisco, to live with Orlofsky.[27]

Ginsberg's account of these events sounds suspiciously like a fantasy of a magical cure, and the journal he kept at the time reveals that even chronology has been transformed a bit to promote the myth of the breakthrough. Actually, Ginsberg continued to work at his market research job for three or four months *after* he moved in with Orlofsky, and the journals suggest that he felt depressed, not liberated, when he lost his job. Moreover, while Ginsberg strongly implies that his therapy and even his need for it ended with his doctor's laying-on-of-hands, the journals reveal that he continued in treatment, perhaps for as long as several months, including the time in which "Howl" was written.[28] Nevertheless, a shift in his life did begin at this point, one that led toward assertion of the "alien" visionary side of himself; and this change, in turn, led to the creation of the "angelheaded hipsters" who are at the center of "Howl." As early as August 1954, Ginsberg had urged himself in the journal: "find: con-

26. Ibid., p. 42.
27. Ibid., pp. 42–43.
28. See Notebook 1953–1956.

ception of line allowing appreciable variation allowing freedom of personal
thought-rhythms as they occur and still be in some way comparatively
measureable."[29] Beginning with "The Green Automobile" (written just
before leaving the east, and in which the journey west is imagined as a
reunion with Neal Cassady), the Notebook 1953–1956 rejects *Empty Mirror*'s myth of the physical world as absolute, returns to the imagination
("The Green Auto is rediscovery of the imagination"), and looks for a
new measure in which to transcribe the intimate movements ("personal
thought-rhythms") of the creative mind.[30] "Howl" did grow out of a
personal change in Ginsberg's life, though that change seems more gradual
when viewed through the notebooks; but it was the work he had done in
the notebooks—growing out of his sense of the deadness of the established
modes in poetry—that enabled Ginsberg, at last, to find a form and language that would embody *him*.

Ginsberg once described *Howl and Other Poems* as a series of experiments in what can be done with the long line since Whitman.[31] In "Howl"
itself Ginsberg stepped outside the formalism of the fifties, stepped away
from even the modernism of Williams, and turned back to the then-obscure
poet of *Leaves of Grass,* transforming Whitman's bardic celebrations of
the visionary yet tender self into a prophetic chant that is angry, agonized,
fearful, funny, mystic, and affectionate—the prolonged and impassioned
cry of Ginsberg's hidden self which *had* survived. "Loose ghosts wailing
for body try to invade the bodies of living men": this is how Ginsberg,

29. Ibid.
30. In November 1951 (see Notebook 1950–1952) Ginsberg returned to his shrouded
stranger project, conceiving of a section to take his hero into New York City. Then, either
as part of that project or another one, Ginsberg, stirred by the news of an old friend's death
in a New York jail a year before, conceived of a poem about the death of Joan Burroughs
and the marriage of Lucien Carr, both old friends from the late forties in New York. Several
pages of heavily revised writing follow, with Ginsberg working on a poem that catalogs (by
name) the fates of many of his old friends from New York. So far as I can tell, this writing
is the seed of "Howl." Many of these lines reappear in section VI of an undated manuscript
(in the Ginsberg Archives) for "Howl for Carl Solomon," probably worked on much later
and written in a stiff, declamatory style: "I'll sing of America and Time / for as I lay on
my bed alone / I prayed: Inspire my night / with a dream fortelling in rapt / supernatural
and natural future forms / the fate of this country wherein / I like a saint reside hidden / in
poverty," the poem begins. In his Notebook 1953–1956, this time inspired by a dream of
Joan Burroughs (see "Dream Record: June 8 1955" in *Reality Sandwiches* [San Francisco,
1963], pp. 48–49), Ginsberg begins a poem, "How to say no in America of atom bomb and
libraries full of Tears? / How to say no in front of the thunderjets on their ramps of children's
feet? / I saw the best mind angelheaded hipster damned / What consciousness in oblivion,
Joan?" With this passage, work on the poem that became "Howl" seriously began. The
notebooks, manuscripts, and letters in the Ginsberg Archives make it abundantly clear that
the writing of "Howl" was hardly the spontaneous act that Ginsberg has many times claimed
it to be: Ginsberg worked on it hard enough to make it *seem* that the poem was a spontaneous
outpouring.
31. *Allen Ginsberg in America,* p. 171.

from "Howl" onward, perceives the literary past: haunting forms eager, like Moloch, to devour the present.[32] Searching instead for a language that would incarnate the self, Ginsberg took the notion of form as discovery he had learned from Williams and pushed it in confessional and visionary directions alien to the older poet. Form was no longer self-protective, like "asbestos gloves," but a process of "compositional self-exploration," the activities of the notebooks turned into art.[33] *The Gates of Wrath* had simultaneously produced an apotheosis and an elimination of the author's personality; the elevated formality of the language, by its vagueness, confronts us with a poet who may be a grandiose figure but is also nobody, and nowhere, in particular. In *Empty Mirror,* Ginsberg had tried to shed the eternal self and descend to particulars; but his imitativeness of Williams had produced the same self-annihilating result. "Howl" links the visionary and the concrete, the language of mystical illumination and the language of the street, and the two are joined not in a static synthesis but in a dialectical movement in which an exhausting and punishing *immersion* in the most sordid of contemporary realities issues in *transcendent* vision. Ginsberg is still uneasy about life in the body, which he more often represents as causing pain (i.e., "purgatoried their torsos") than pleasure; but in this way he is, like his mother in "Kaddish," "pained" into Vision.[34] At the close of "Howl," having looked back over his life, Ginsberg can affirm a core self of "unconditioned Spirit" and sympathetic humanity that has survived an agonizing ordeal.

Of the poem's three parts (plus "Footnote"), the first is the longest and most powerful, an angry prophetic lament. Its cataloging of real and surreal images in long dithyrambic lines creates a movement that is rushed, frenzied, yet filled with sudden gaps and wild illuminations; the poem begins by immersing us in the extremities of modern urban life, overwhelming and flooding us with sensations. Generalizing personal into generational experience in Parts I and II, Ginsberg shows these "best minds" veering back and forth between extremes, with the suddenness and intensity of an electric current leaping between two poles; they adopt attitudes of defiance, longing, terror, zaniness, hysteria, prayer, anger, joy, tears, exhaustion—culminating in the absolutes of madness and suicide. Clothes and then flesh are constantly being stripped away in this ordeal; the "best minds" are exposed and tormented, then cast out into the cold and darkness. So they are at once hounded and neglected ("unknown" and "forgotten" in the poem's words). But modern civilization's indifference and hostility provoke a desperate search for something be-

32. *The New American Poetry,* p. 415.
33. "When the Mode of the Music Changes the Walls of the City Shake," p. 327.
34. *Kaddish and Other Poems,* p. 29.

yond it, for spiritual illumination. Again and again, the young men are
left "beat" and exhausted, alone in their empty rooms, trapped in time—
at which point they gain glimpses of eternity. "Howl" constantly pushes
toward exhaustion, a dead end, only to have these ends twist into moments
of shuddering ecstasy. In one of the poem's metaphors, boundaries are
set down, push in on and enclose the self—then suddenly disintegrate.
At such times terror shifts to ecstasy; the "madman bum" is discovered
to be the angelheaded hipster, and "beat" (beaten, exhausted) becomes
"beatific."

As the catalog of Part I moves through gestures of greater and greater
desperation, the hipsters finally present "themselves on the granite steps
of the madhouse with shaven heads and harlequin speech of suicide,
demanding instantaneous lobotomy"—an act that frantically mixes defiance and submission, clownishness and martyrdom. What they want is
immediate release from their heads, from suffering; what they get is prolonged incarceration, "the concrete void of insulin" shots and therapy
aimed not at liberation but "adjustment," their "bodies turned to stone
as heavy as the moon." At this point, in its longest and most despairing
line, the poem seems about to collapse, to "end":

> with mother finally ******, and the last fantastic book flung out of the tene-
> ment window, and the last door closed at 4am and the last telephone
> slammed at the wall in reply and the last furnished room emptied down to
> the last piece of mental furniture, a yellow paper rose twisted on a wire
> hanger in the closet, and even that imaginary, nothing but a hopeful little
> bit of hallucination—

With all communication broken off and all vision denied, the self is left
in a lonely, silent, empty room—the self *is* such a room—the room itself
the culmination of the poem's many images of walls, barriers, and enclosures. In having the visionary quest end in the asylum, Ginsberg is referring to his own hospitalization, that of Carl Solomon (whom he had
met in the Columbia Psychiatric Institute) and that of his mother. Moreover, madness is here perceived as encapsulating the psyche in a private
world. In a strikingly similar passage in "Kaddish" Ginsberg emphasizes
the way his mother's illness removed her into a private, hallucinatory
world ("her own universe") where, in spite of all his hysterical screaming
at her, she remained inaccessible ("no road that goes elsewhere—to my
own" world).[35] Ginsberg himself had found it impossible to communicate
his own visions, to make them real to others. At this climactic moment
of Part I, then, the condition of separation, division in time—a preoc-

35. Ibid., p. 27.

cupation of Ginsberg's poetry since *The Gates of Wrath*—has been taken all the way out: temporal reality is experienced as a series of unbridgeable gaps, a void populated with self-enclosed minds. Ordeal by immersion leaves the self feeling dead and walled-in; the body, heavy as stone, lacks affect and becomes a heavy burden, while the spirit incarcerated inside the "dead" body finds itself in no sweet golden clime but a "concrete void."

Ginsberg's state of mind at this point can be compared with his prevision mood "of hopelessness, or dead-end": with "nothing but the world in front of me" and "not knowing what to do with *that*." Here, too, at the limits of despair—with the active will yielded up—Ginsberg experiences a sudden infusion of energy; the poem's mood dramatically turns and the concluding lines of Part I affirm the self's power to love and to communicate within a living cosmos. Immediately following the poem's most despairing lines comes its most affectionate: "ah, Carl, while you are not safe I am not safe, and now you're really in the total animal soup of time." Unlike Wilbur and Rich, Ginsberg does not seek a cautious self-insularity, and he here endorses vulnerability to danger and a tender identification with the victims of time and history. "I *saw* the best minds of my generation," Ginsberg had begun, as if a prophetic and retrospective detachment exempted him from the fate he was describing; but Ginsberg now writes from *inside* the ordeal, as if the aim of writing were not to shape or contain, but sympathetically to *enter* an experience. By his own unrestrained outpouring of images and feelings Ginsberg exposes himself as writer to literary ridicule and rejection, and he does risk the annihilation of his poetic self in the released flood of raw experience and emotion. But by risking these dangers Ginsberg can achieve the kind of poetry he describes in Part I's last six lines, a poetry that bridges the gap between selves by incarnating the author's experience, making the reader, too, feel it as a "sensation."

Immediately following the poem's most intimate line comes its most exalted and grandiose, as if Ginsberg could rightfully claim a prophetic role only after acknowledging his vulnerable humanity.

> and who therefore ran through icy streets obsessed with a sudden flash of the alchemy of the use of the elipse the catalog the meter & the vibrating plane,
>
> who dreamt and made incarnate gaps in Time & Space through images juxtaposed, and trapped the archangel of the soul between 2 visual images and joined the elemental verbs and set the noun and dash of consciousness together jumping with sensation of Pater Omnipotens Aeterna Deus

to recreate the syntax and measure of poor human prose and stand before
you speechless and intelligent and shaking with shame, rejected yet confessing out the soul to conform to the rhythm of thought in his naked and
endless head,

the madman bum and angel beat in Time, unknown, yet putting down here
what might be left to say in time to come after death,

and rose reincarnate in the ghostly clothes of jazz in the goldhorn shadow of
the band and blew the suffering of America's naked mind for love into an
eli eli lamma lamma sabachthani saxaphone cry that shivered the cities
down to the last radio

with the absolute heart of the poem of life butchered out of their own bodies
good to eat a thousand years.

In biographical terms, the agonized elation of these lines may recall the
emotional lift given Ginsberg when, apparently at the end of his rope
when hospitalized, he discovered in Carl Solomon someone who shared
his "vision" of life, someone he *could* communicate with. But the mood
of these lines more obviously grows out of the writing that's preceded
them, as the poem turns on itself to consider its own nature, style, and
existence; in fact, these closing lines of Part I drop some helpful hints on
how to read "Howl," as if Ginsberg feared he had gone too far and needed
to toss a few footbridges across the gap separating him from his reader.
Later on I want to take up some of these hints and talk in detail about
the poem's idea and practice of language; for now I want to emphasize
what Ginsberg is saying here about the very act of writing his poem. In
the 1948 visions the "living Creator" had spoken to Ginsberg as "to his
son"; no secret about Ginsberg's identity here! Now, having been per-
secuted *for* his visions, Ginsberg echoes the despair of Christ on the cross:
"eli eli lamma lamma sabacthani." Yet this modern messiah incarnates
divine spirit not in his body but in his writing, which embodies the "sensation of Pater Omnipotens Aeterna Deus." So the tormented Ginsberg
arises "reincarnate" *in the apocalyptic words of his own poem.* "Howl,"
butchered out of his body, will be "good to eat a thousand years."

The movement of Part I—a building sense of being closed-in issuing in
a release of visionary energy—becomes the movement between Parts II
and III of "Howl." "What sphinx of cement and aluminum bashed open
their skulls and ate up their brains and imagination?" Ginsberg asks at
the start of Part II; his answer—Moloch!—becomes the repeated base
word for a series of exclamatory phrases ("Moloch the loveless! Mental
Moloch!") in which Ginsberg seeks to exorcise this demonic power by
naming it correctly and exposing its true nature. In Part I Ginsberg im-

merses himself and his reader in the tormented intensity and sudden illuminations of the underground world; now in Part II, strengthened by his descent and return, he can confront his persecutor angrily, his words striving for magical force as they strike, like a series of hammer blows, against the iron walls of Moloch. As we have seen, Moloch is an ancient deity to whom children were sacrificed, just as the "brains and imagination" of the present generation are devoured by a jealous and cruel social system. Moloch stands broadly for authority—familial, social, literary—and Ginsberg does not share the young Adrienne Rich's belief in an authority that is "*tenderly* severe." Manifest in skyscrapers, prisons, factories, banks, madhouses, armies, governments, technology, money, bombs, Moloch represents a vast, all-encompassing social reality that is at best unresponsive (a "concrete void"), at worst a malign presence that feeds off individuality and difference. Moloch—"whose mind is pure machinery"—is Ginsberg's version of Blake's Urizen, pure reason and abstract form. A clear contrast to the grave yet tender voice that Ginsberg heard in the first of his visions, Moloch is also "the heavy judger of men," the parent whose chilling glance can terrify the child, paralyze him with self-doubt and make him feel "crazy" and "queer." Moloch, then, is the principle of separation and conflict in life, an external force so powerful that it eats its way inside and divides the self against itself: "Moloch who entered my soul early! Moloch in whom I am a consciousness without a body! Moloch who frightened me out of my natural ecstasy!" It is Moloch who is the origin of all the poem's images of stony coldness (the *granite* steps of the madhouse, the body turned to *stone,* the sphinx of *cement* and *aluminum,* the vast *stone* of war, the *rocks* of time, etc.). Like the Medusa of classical myth, Moloch petrifies. Ginsberg's driving, heated repetition of the name, moreover, creates the feeling that Moloch is everywhere, surrounding, enclosing—a cement or iron structure inside of which the spirit, devoured, sits imprisoned and languishing; and so Moloch is also the source of all the poem's images of enclosure (head, room, asylum, jail).

"Moloch whom I abandon!" Ginsberg cries out at one point. Yet in spite of all the imprecations and even humor directed against this ubiquitous presence, the release of pent-up rage is finally not liberating; anger is not the way out. Part II begins with bristling defiance, but it ends with loss, futility, and self-contempt as Ginsberg sees all he values, "visions! omens! hallucinations! miracles! ecstasies!"—"the whole boatload of sensitive bullshit"—"gone down the American river!" And so the mood at the close of Part II, similar to the moment in Part I when the hipsters, with shaven heads and harlequin speech, present themselves for lobotomy,

the mood here is hysterically suicidal, with anger, laughter, and helplessness combining in a giddy self-destructiveness:

> Real holy laughter in the river! They saw it all! the wild eyes! the holy yells!
> They bade farewell! They jumped off the roof! to solitude! waving! carry-
> ing flowers! Down to the river! into the street!

An outpouring of anger against constricting authority may be a stage in
the process of self-liberation, but is not its end; anger, perpetuating division, perpetuates Moloch. In fact, as the last line of Part II shows, such
rage, futile in its beatings against the stony consciousness of Moloch, at
last turns back on the self in acts that are, however zany, suicidal.

But in Part III, dramatically shifting from self-consuming rage to renewal in love, a kind of self-integration, a balancing of destructive and
creative impulses, is sought. "Carl Solomon! I'm with you in Rockland,"
Ginsberg begins, turning from angry declamatory rhetoric to a simple,
colloquial line, affectionate and reassuring in its gently rocking rhythm.
Repeated, this line becomes the base phrase for Part III, its utterance
each time followed by a response that further defines both Rockland and
Solomon, and this unfolding characterization provides the dramatic movement of this section as well as the resolution of the entire poem. At first
the responses stress Rockland as prison and Solomon as victim—

> where you're madder than I am
> where you must feel very strange
> where you imitate the shade of my mother—

but these are balanced against the following three responses, which stress
the power of the "madman" to transcend his mere physical imprisonment:

> where you've murdered your twelve secretaries
> where you laugh at this invisible humor
> where we are great writers on the same dreadful typewriter

A little more than halfway through, however, beginning with—

> where you bang on the catatonic piano the soul is innocent and immortal it
> should never die ungodly in an armed madhouse—

the answers begin to get longer, faster in movement, more surrealistic in
imagery, as they, proclaiming a social/political/religious/sexual revolution,
affirm the transcendent freedom of the self. Part III's refrain thus estab-

lishes a context of emotional support and spiritual communion, and it is from this "base," taking off in increasingly more daring flights of rebellious energy, that Ginsberg finally arrives at his "real" self.

> I'm with you in Rockland
>> where we wake up electrified out of the coma by our own souls' air-
>> planes roaring over the roof they've come to drop angelic bombs the hos-
>> pital illuminates itself imaginary walls collapse O skinny legions run
>> outside O starry-spangled shock of mercy the eternal war is here O victory
>> forget your underwear we're free

> I'm with you in Rockland
>> in my dreams you walk dripping from a sea-journey on the highway across
>> America in tears to the door of my cottage in the Western night

Again, boundaries ("imaginary walls") collapse, in a soaring moment of apocalyptic release; and the self—which is "innocent and immortal"—breaks free of Moloch, of whom *Rock*land's walls are an extension. The poem, then, does not close with the suicidal deliverance of Part II; nor does it end with a comic apocalypse ("O victory forget your underwear we're free"); it closes, instead, with a Whitmanesque image of love and reunion. "Howl" moves from the ordeal of separation, through the casting out of the principle of division, toward unification, a process that happens primarily *within* the self.

According to Ginsberg, Part III of "Howl" is "a litany of affirmation of the Lamb in its glory."[36] His repetition of the colloquial "I'm with you in Rockland" turns it into an elevated liturgical chant. Words, no longer weapons as they were in Part I, build a magical incantation which delivers us into a vision of the "innocent" Lamb, the eternal Spirit locked inside Rockland, or inside the hard surfaces of a defensive personality. Carl Solomon functions partly as a surrogate for Naomi Ginsberg, still hospitalized in Pilgrim State when "Howl" was written; Ginsberg, who hints as much in the poem ("where you imitate the shade of my mother"), has recently conceded this to be the case.[37] But less important than identifying the real-life referents in the poem is to see that a literal person has been transformed into eternal archetype, the Lamb of both Christian and Blakean mythology, and that Ginsberg's loving reassurance is primarily directed to this eternally innocent aspect of himself. The refrain line in Part III articulates the human sympathy of the poet, while his responses uncover his messianic and visionary self which at first rendered him terrified and incommunicado but later yielded what Ginsberg calls in "Kaddish"

36. *The New American Poetry*, p. 416.
37. *To Eberhart from Ginsberg*, p. 11.

the "key" to unlock the door of the encapsulated self. "Howl" closes with Ginsberg's loving acceptance of—himself; the part of him that had been lost and banished in time in *The Gates of Wrath* has been reborn ("dripping from a sea-journey") and reintegrated. The mirror is no longer empty.

Yet this unity, occurring only in a dream, is attained by means of flight and return. "Howl" struggles for autonomy, but Ginsberg, as he had when he moved to the West Coast, keeps looking back over his shoulder, affirming his fidelity to Carl Solomon, to Naomi Ginsberg, to images from his past life. Similarly, he says the tradition is "a complete fuck-up so you're on your own," but Ginsberg leans for support on Blake and Whitman, both of whom he perceives as maternal, tender, and therefore non-threatening authorities. Ginsberg in fact ends by withdrawing from the social, historical present which he so powerfully creates in the poem. He stuffs the poem with *things* from modern urban life; but materiality functions in the poem as a kind of whip, flagellating Ginsberg into vision. Moloch, it seems, cannot be exorcised, only eluded through a vertical transcendence; what starts out as a poem of social protest ends by retreating into private religious/erotic vision, and Ginsberg's tacit assumption of the immutability of social reality establishes one respect in which he is a child of the fifties rather than of the universe. Ginsberg decided not to "write a *poem*" so that he could express his "real" self—which turned out to be his idealized self: the Lamb in its glory. Confessional poetry often presents not an exposure but a mythologizing of the self, as Plath's poems strive to enact her transformation into "the fine, white flying myth" of Ariel.[38] In "Howl" Ginsberg wants to recover an original wholeness that has been lost in time; he wants to preserve a self-image which he can only preserve by keeping it separate from temporal, physical reality. Compositional self-exploration turns out to be compositional self-idealization.

"Howl" originally ended with Part III, but some time after completing the three main sections, Ginsberg added the "Footnote," apparently to counter criticisms of the poem's negativity from some of its earliest readers. Not too surprisingly, Louis Ginsberg praised the poem's passion but regretted its pessimism. "Howl," he wrote his son,

> is a wild, volcanic, troubled, extravagant, turbulent, boistrous, unbridled outpouring, intermingling gems and flashes of picturesque insight with slag and debris of scoriac matter. It has violence; it has

38. "Ocean 1212W," in Sylvia Plath, *Johnny Panic and the Bible of Dreams* (London, 1977), p. 130.

life; it has *vitality*. In my opinion, it is a one-sided neurotic view of life; it has not enough glad, Whitmanian affirmations.[39]

Even Richard Eberhart, who was sympathetic enough to do an essay on the San Francisco poetry renaissance for the New York *Times,* complained of an absence of positive values in "Howl."[40] The "Footnote" tries to draw out the positive values implicit earlier and to balance the anger of Part II with affirmation, the base word "Moloch" now replaced with "holy." But the result is that the "Footnote" eschews compositional self-exploration for programmatic assertion of a particularly strident kind. Insisting after Blake that "everything is holy," the "Footnote" does contain some witty images, but its exclamatory rhetoric reverts to Part II's use of language as weapon and tries to bully the reader into agreement.

Ginsberg's strenuous insistence in the "Footnote" reveals persisting doubts about the nature of his visions and his capacity to communicate them to an audience. In a letter he wrote in response to Eberhart's criticism, Ginsberg cites the sympathy with which he represents the sufferings of the "best minds" in Part I;[41] but this point does more to damage than to justify Ginsberg's position, for it makes clear that his sympathy is limited to an underground elite and that the poem really says not that "everyone" is but that "my friends and I" are holy. Sympathy is extended only to those who, like Solomon, are mirror images of the author. Consequently, the only alternatives the poem permits are to see things as Ginsberg does, or to be aligned with Moloch. It is easy to see where the audience fits in this mythology. When Ginsberg presents himself near the end of Part I as standing before his reader—as he had stood before Dr. Hicks—"shaking with shame, rejected yet confessing out the soul," Ginsberg hopes to be answered with the tolerant voice of acceptance he had heard in the first of his visions and in the later encounter with his doctor, but he fears he is just speaking to a hostile, severe, Moloch-like consciousness, heavy judger of men and poets. Ginsberg responds to this predicament by trying to write a poem that will break down all difference between author and reader, forcing the reader to surrender all critical detachment and judgment. It does so in two ways. Like many confessional works, "Howl" floods the reader with painful, even extreme experiences so that aesthetic criteria seem trivializing and interpretation superfluous. Moreover, the fast pace and surrealistic dislocations of the poem's language work to short-circuit the analytic consciousness of the reader, who will then experience both the disjunctions and the unexpected visionary leaps of con-

39. Louis Ginsberg to Allen Ginsberg, 27 May 1956.
40. See *To Eberhart from Ginsberg* throughout.
41. Ibid., p. 18.

temporary life as *sensations,* at a level of consciousness that is prior to reflection or assessment.

The "Footnote" to "Howl" really exposes Ginsberg's doubts that his language can be as coercively immediate as he would like it to be; there he makes one last assault on the separateness of the reader. Throughout *Howl and Other Poems,* Ginsberg's writing is weak when he loses confidence in the reader and waxes exhortatory ("you too must seek the sun," p. 26) or explanatory, dispensing interpretations of symbols that are already too obvious, as he does with the sunflower in "Sunflower Sutra" or the racks in "In the Baggage Room at Greyhound":

> it was the racks and these on the racks I saw naked in electric
> light the night before I quit,
> the racks were created to hang our possessions, to keep us together,
> a temporary shift in space,
> God's only way of building the rickety structure of Time,
> to hold the bags to send on the roads, to carry our luggage from
> place to place
> looking for a bus to ride us back home to Eternity where the
> heart was left and farewell tears began.

As these lines also show, Ginsberg's vision of the ideal is one conducive to certain stock romantic attitudes and language. He often veers toward either self-pity or grandiosity, and in a phrase like "I am so lonely in my glory" he collides with both at once. In the opening line of "Sunflower Sutra"—

> I *walked on the banks* of the tincan banana dock *and sat down under the
> huge shade of a* Southern Pacific locomotive *to look at the sunset over the*
> box house *hills and cry*— [my emphasis]

the italicized phrases seem to have been assembled out of a literary cookbook specializing in romantic elegies; the urban details are supposed to instill novelty and life into this language, but they have been too obviously appropriated for literary effect, just as the sunflower of the title—covered with railroad dust yet still "a perfect beauty of a sunflower"—has been appropriated for abstract meaning: the golden soul that persists beneath the "veil" of the flesh. In "A Supermarket in California" and "America" Ginsberg's sense of humor saves him from his worst propensities. The "Supermarket" poem links Ginsberg and Whitman as "childless, lonely" dreamers and could easily have opted for self-pity; but schmerz is avoided by Ginsberg's playfulness: "What peaches and what penumbras! Whole families shopping at night! Aisles full of husbands! Wives in the avocados, babies in the tomatoes!—and you, Garcia Lorca, what were you doing down by the watermelons?" "America" is both satirical and self-ironical, with Ginsberg playfully implicating himself in what he's criticizing:

America how can I write a holy litany in your silly mood?
I will continue like Henry Ford my strophes are as individual as
    his automobiles more so they're all different sexes.
America I will sell you strophes $2500 apiece $500 down on your
    old strophe. . . .

I'd better get right down to the job.
It's true I don't want to join the Army or turn lathes in precision
    parts factories, I'm nearsighted and psychopathic anyway.
America I'm putting my queer shoulder to the wheel.

A poem like "America," then confirms the reality of an individual who, while surrounded by the deadening pressures of "mechancial consciousness," remains spontaneous, funny, and human—alive.

But Ginsberg's principal achievement in his first book was the crackling energy of the language of "Howl"—a hard-won effect of poetic craft. Like his humor, Ginsberg's craft presupposes a detachment that his polarization of mechanical and ecstatic consciousness in "Howl" does not allow for. Moreover, the way the poem seems to go outside literature to deal with brutal, sordid features of the present has led many readers to ignore its handling of form and measure. Yet Ginsberg's journals, along with his published prose and interviews, reveal a poet who is a serious, knowledgeable, and intelligent student of his craft. His journals of the early fifties are filled with meditations on the problem of poetic measure. At one point, for instance, he speculated that Williams's poems in *Spring and All* (a *very* obscure text at the time) were written in syllabics and tried to measure them in this way; not too long after he first arrived on the West Coast he compiled and read his way through a long list of books on meter.[42] So "Howl's" long line, as Ginsberg says, "came after 7 yrs work with fixed iambic rhyme, and 4 yrs work with Williams' short line free form,"[43] the culmination of his search for a line that would allow "freedom of personal-thought rhythms as they occur" and yet still be "comparatively measurable." It is easier to feel their energy and the gradual build-up of feeling in each of "Howl's" sections than it is to talk precisely about the way in which the lines are measured. They are not to

42. The booklists appear on the pages marked 6 April and 20 and 21 April 1952 in Ginsberg's predated diary book (Notebook 1953–1956). The entries were actually written in the summer of 1954, while Ginsberg was staying with Neal Cassady in San Jose just prior to coming to San Francisco.
43. *To Eberhart from Ginsberg*, p. 36.

be measured by the counting of either stresses or syllables, or by "quantity." Instead, Ginsberg, like Olson, views each line as "a single breath unit": "my breath is long—that's the Measure, one physical-mental inspiration of thought contained in the elastic of a breath."[44] Most of the poem's lines are long, some, as we have seen, extraordinarily so—the length required to catch the whole *run* of each pulse of inspiration. Moreover, the "short-line verse" of *Empty Mirror* does not "offer any kind of *base* cyclical flow for the build-up of powerful emotion."[45] Each of the three main sections of "Howl" has a different rhythm, but they all make use of a repeated base word or phrase—"who" in Part I, "Moloch" in II, "I'm with you in Rockland" in III—that creates a movement that soars outward then returns in a "cyclical flow." As in Whitman, the measure partly relies on the syntactic parallelisms established by the repeated words. In Part I his "elastic" measure permits Ginsberg to follow each rush of inspiration all the way out, without any predetermined end, but then to return to the stability of his fixed point of origin. In Part II the long line breaks down into a series of short "exclamatory units," anger generating a staccato series of outbursts,[46] while in Part III the litany pattern of refrain and reply builds as the replies become longer and freer until, in the final line, response modulates into a calm, loving tone that flows out of the base line and integrates the two voices.

"The only way to be like Whitman is to write *unlike* Whitman," Williams believed.[47] Ginsberg certainly did take over some specific technical features of Whitman's work—the long line, the catalog, the syntactic parallelisms; he was in fact rereading *Leaves of Grass* as he was working on "Howl." Is it possible, then, that in learning to write unlike Williams Ginsberg ended up writing like Whitman and thus being like neither of these independent and innovative poets? The answer, I think, is that while Ginsberg did not accomplish the absolute fresh start that he sometimes liked to imagine, he does not merely repeat the literary past. He imagines Whitman as the founder; Ginsberg wants to move forward along lines initiated by the earlier writer. "Whitman's form had rarely been further explored," Ginsberg said;[48] the character of his advance can be defined by comparing the first two lines of one of Whitman's long catalogs in "Song of Myself"—

The pure contralto sings in the organ loft,
The carpenter's plane whistles its wild, ascending lisp,

44. *The New American Poetry,* p. 416.
45. *To Eberhart from Ginsberg,* p. 36.
46. *The New American Poetry,* p. 416.
47. "America, Whitman, and the Art of Poetry," *Poetry Journal,* November 1917, p. 31.
48. *The New American Poetry,* p. 416.

with two lines near the beginning of Part I of "Howl":

> who bared their brains to Heaven under the El and saw Mohammedan angels
> staggering on tenement roofs illuminated,
> who passed through universities with radiant cool eyes hallucinating
> Arkansas and Blake-light tragedy among the scholars of war

Both poets build a catalog out of long, end-stopped lines that are syntactically parallel. Yet Whitman's lines, each recording a single observed image in a transparent style, are simple and move with an easy insouciance, while Ginsberg, an embattled visionary, packs his lines with surrealistic images and makes them move with an almost manic intensity. As he does here, Ginsberg works throughout the poem by juxtaposing the language of the street ("El," "staggering," "tenement roofs") with the language of vision ("Heaven," "Mohammedan angels," "illuminated") in electrifying ways. "Howl" thus arrives at the visionary by way of the literal, as the poems in *The Gates of Wrath* did not; and Ginsberg here creates "images / That strike like lightning from eternal mind" rather than discussing the possibility. Ginsberg's language incarnates gaps—between street and heaven, literal and visionary—then leaps across them in "a sudden flash." His use of "images juxtaposed" shows that Ginsberg came to Whitman by way of the modern poets; but the resulting line is his own. The line serves an expressive purpose in baring the tormented mystic consciousness of the poet; but it serves a rhetorical purpose as well—seeking "to break people's mind systems open" by rationally subverting ("mechanical") consciousness and replacing it with a wild associative logic which sees connections where before there were oppositions. As a final example we can look at the line

> incomparable blind streets of shuddering cloud and lightning in the mind
> leaping toward poles of Canada & Paterson, illuminating all the motionless
> world of Time between

At first the line moves toward a terrifying dead-end ("blind streets") but then the landscape is internalized ("in the mind") and a flash illuminates the temporal world and releases "the archangel of the soul" from the dead-end of time. As we have seen, the poem as a whole—immersing us in the literal and temporal, then releasing us in a moment of vision—works in just this way.

FIVE

Robert Lowell

"I think I was a professional who was forced, who forced myself, into a revolutionary style in writing *Life Studies,* the biggest change in myself perhaps I ever made or will."[1]

—Robert Lowell

In February 1977, announcing a joint reading that the two men were to give at St. Mark's-in-the-Bowery, the New York *Times* described Allen Ginsberg and Robert Lowell as "opposite ends of the poetic spectrum."[2] While "Howl" and *Life Studies* are certainly the crucial texts in any account of the transformation of American poetry in the late 1950s, it is easy to see what the *Times* had in mind, even in 1977 when the cleavage between the two men was not as sharp as it was, say, in 1957. Ginsberg, the son of Jewish immigrant parents from Newark, began his career as the poetic prophet of the bristling, zany defiance of the beat generation, while Lowell, whose ancestry extended back by way of Amy Lowell and James Russell Lowell to colonial New England, started out with the active support of those fastidious literary authorities—Eliot, Ransom, Tate— that the antics of the beats were most designed to antagonize. Ginsberg— the rhapsodic hip visionary; Lowell—the ironic and reserved aristocrat. Both poets, it is true, were eventually drawn toward confessional writing; but if Ginsberg at least begins his revelations by immersing himself in immediate feeling and thought, Lowell always preserves some personal distance and artistic control. Hence, Ginsberg gives us his prophetic *howl,* while Lowell provides life *studies.* Talking about the beat generation, Lowell sounds a bit stuffy and condescending—a cooler version of Pod-

1. Quoted in Steven Gould Axelrod, *Robert Lowell, Life and Art* (Princeton, 1978), p. 86.
2. Emily Wallace, "Lowell and Ginsberg Share Spotlight with Williams," *William Carlos Williams Newsletter* 3 (Spring 1977): 25.

horetz's critique: The beats were "useful" because "a certain amount of ice [was] broken," but, Lowell insists, "you've got to remain complicatedly civilized and organized to keep your humanity under the pressures of our various governments, not go into a bohemian wildness."[3]

The antithesis between the two poets, it seems, could hardly be sharper. Yet at the reading itself Lowell, questioning the simple polarity, announced he wanted to amend the statement in the *Times:* that he and Ginsberg were "at opposite ends of the poetry of William Carlos Williams, whom they had both known and admired."[4] Is there in fact some ground common to these writers? And can it be related to the poetry of Williams? Both Ginsberg and Lowell began as religious sensibilities writing in traditional verse forms, though there was every difference between Lowell's devotional Catholicism and Ginsberg's ecstatic mysticism. In the mid-fifties, Lowell told an interviewer, "most good American poetry was a symbol hanging on a hatrack. Many felt this," and one of them was Ginsberg.[5] Both poets, then, shared a sense of attenuation and crisis in American poetry, and they sought to renovate their art by going outside literature to a referential language and an open poetics. With weak actual fathers, both poets were especially eager to find literary mentors and in Williams they discovered a benign paternal figure who provided poetic models for the alternatives they were seeking. As he was completing *Life Studies,* Lowell wrote to Williams:

I like to think that often I have crossed the river into your world. It
meant throwing away a lot of heavy symbolic and metrical armor,
and at times I felt frightened by the journey.[6]

Like Ginsberg, Lowell did not derive image, phrase or rhythm from Williams: to be like Williams you had to write unlike Williams. Moreover, the older poet was no Virgil who guided his poetic successor through eternal realms; Williams, instead, presided over Lowell's "breakthrough back into life." From *Land of Unlikeness* (1944) to *Life Studies* (1959) Lowell's career marks a slow, painful, and sometimes frightening journey

3. A. Alvarez, "Robert Lowell in Conversation," reprinted in *Profile of Robert Lowell,* ed. Jerome Mazzaro (Columbus, Ohio, 1971), p. 39. The interview originally appeared in the *London Observer,* 21 July 1963, p. 19. Subsequent references are to the reprinted *Profile of Robert Lowell.*

4. *William Carlos Williams Newsletter,* p. 25.

5. Ian Hamilton, "A Conversation with Robert Lowell," *Modern Occasions* 2 (Winter 1972): 44.

6. Robert Lowell to William Carlos Williams, 26 September 1958, in the Williams collection at the Beinecke Library, Yale University. This and subsequent quotations from items in the Williams collection are made with the kind permission of Yale University and James Laughlin.

toward something that originally repelled him—physical actuality; *Life Studies* itself enacts such a journey.

Nevertheless, in spite of some common poetic targets and a common poetic source in Williams, the differences between Lowell and Ginsberg remain basic; and they are differences not just of poetic style but of ultimate assumption. "Howl" describes, in its crackling, rhapsodic language, a tormented passage through a sordid urban world, an ordeal that issues in revelation of the absolute: "Pater Omnipotens Aeterna Deus"; "Life Studies" reviews familial past with an outward air of casual detachment—tightening at moments into stern and terrifying insights—in order to renounce absolutes and, in "Skunk Hour," to accept the imperfections of a secular world. The autobiographical realism of *Life Studies* implicitly rebukes Ginsberg's visionary idealism.

"We [Americans] have some impatience with prosaic, everyday things of life—I think those hurt us," Lowell told an interviewer.[7] He admires a writer like Frost for his "directness and realism," his "abundance and geniality": "the virtue of a photograph but all the finish of art."[8] Ginsberg, on the other hand, might stand as exemplary for all that Lowell finds suspect and dangerous in American poetry and culture. Our culture, formed on abstract principles rather than a long tradition, is idealistic, and this is precisely what makes it dangerous, for "violence and idealism have some occult connection."[9] Hemingway claimed that all American literature began with *Huckleberry Finn;* Lowell claimed that "American literature and culture begin with *Paradise Lost.*"

> I always think there are two great symbolic figures that stand behind American ambition and culture. One is Milton's Lucifer and the other is Captain Ahab: these two sublime ambitions that are doomed and ready, for their idealism, to face any amount of violence.[10]

Lucifer and Ahab: radical individualists whose passionate ambitions made them heroic and whose fanatical idealism made them doomed and demonic. According to Lowell, American writers, similarly impatient with limits and tortured by otherness, imperiously avoid the prosaic and "leap for the sublime."[11] Poetry is then imagined to be something far grander than a mere craft; it becomes the means to transcendence and self-apotheosis. The poet is "reborn" in his art "and almost sheds his other life";[12]

7. A. Alvarez, "A Talk with Robert Lowell," reprinted in *Profile of Robert Lowell,* p. 45.
8. "The Art of Poetry: Robert Lowell," p. 34.
9. "A Talk with Robert Lowell," p. 44.
10. Ibid., p. 45.
11. Ibid.
12. Ibid., p. 48.

in *Life Studies,* as we shall see, the poet is reborn by shedding his imperial self. But in the apocalyptic mode, poetry and violence come to have a not-so-occult connection and literary history becomes "a sequence of demolitions, the bravado of perpetual revolution, breakthrough as the stereotype with nothing preserved."[13] Like Ahab's, the American poet's furious quest for heroic independence becomes emotionally exhausting and self-destructive. Dissociated from historical, social, and physical realities, which hurt by confronting them with limitations, our poets fall into what Lowell calls "the monotony of the sublime."[14]

As literary history, Lowell's account is provocatively inadequate; he may be able to explain many of the features of "Howl," but not its humor; and he cannot explain even the existence of books like *The Beautiful Changes* and *A Change of World.* Lowell can account for Crane but not Williams, much of Whitman but very little of Frost. Lowell's theory is most valuable when understood as a projection onto the American past of his own struggles as a beginning poet. The New Englander started as an angry idealist whose impatience with prosaic, ordinary things was manifest in his lofty concentration of language and his adoption of the stern certainties of a religious faith that seems more Calvinist than Catholic. Eliot's conversion to Christianity had meant a chastening of literary style (no longer "desiring this man's gift and that man's scope"); but in Lowell the promethean ambitions of the language contradict the humility entailed by the religious commitments, while the religious ideals manifest a fierce disgust with ordinary, unredeemed realities—Lowell's apocalyptic vision. In fact, the rage of the young poet is so relentless and so violent that, continually destroying the world in his fanatical efforts to save it, Lowell often seems to be of Ahab's party without knowing it.

Ginsberg's notebooks of the late forties and early fifties open a kind of boundless space for the writer—allowing for self-analysis and self-expression, transcription of dreams and fantasies as well as actual persons, places, and events, experiments in spontaneous writing. Lowell's notebooks from the mid- and late forties—in the Houghton Library at Harvard—are, in contrast, strikingly nonintrospective and narrowly literary. Into them, in a small, tense, crabbed script, Lowell copied poems he admired and worked on his own poetry. Rather than providing a chance to release the flow of creative energy, these notebooks record Lowell's scrupulous efforts to wrench turbulent feelings into compressed language and form—a stumbling, laborious, deliberate, and back-breaking struggle for perfection of style. It is an elevated, a grand style—a gnarled sublimity

---

13. "Digressions from Larkin's Twentieth-Century Verse," *American Poetry Review* 6 (January–February 1977): 33.
14. "A Talk with Robert Lowell," p. 48.

toward which Lowell does not so much leap as he carefully climbs, as if up a slippery, rocky mountain where any error would be disastrous.

Each of the poems in *Lord Weary's Castle,* for instance, evolved gradually through numerous changes of word, image, rhythm, idea, and the writing of many of the poems was carried on at the same time. Lowell's deliberation, at once cautious and ambitious, sometimes results in an overworked verbal surface that stifles emotional impact. But Lowell's disciplined procedures also created the intricate force of particular poems and the elaborate unity of the book as a whole. Indeed, Lowell's critics have, if anything, underestimated the degree to which verbal cross references, the pairing of poems, and the unfolding drama of a spiritual quest pull these poems together into a single work. As a whole, *Lord Weary's Castle* records a quest through the confusion and violence of the years just before and just after the end of World War II—a quest for personal sanctity. But if the young Lowell yearns, angrily, for the stasis of a disembodied perfection, his strongest poems are made dynamic by their tracing of the movements of the poet's consciousness as he desperately searches for spiritual illumination. "Christmas Eve under Hooker's Statue" illustrates this process.

"Tonight a blackout," the poem begins—with a harsh, clipped notation of fact which evokes the pervasive violence of the war, in brutal contrast to the traditional associations of peace and joy that are released by "Christmas Eve" in the title. Almost immediately, however, Lowell recoils from the stark reality of the present and eases into a more flowing language in which he recalls what seem to be more pleasant memories of Christmas in boyhood: "twenty years ago / I hung my stocking on the tree," but the sentence moves forward only to turn back on its speaker: "and hell's / Serpent entwined the apple in the toe / To sting the child with knowledge." In fact, Lowell is so alienated from this past that he shifts from first to third person ("the child"), and his fond reminiscence hardens into symbolic drama, as Christmas becomes a grotesque repetition of the Fall. Personal memory, uncovering only the universal knowledge of guilt, offers no way out of a darkened present. So Lowell's attention next turns to the statue of the Civil War General Joseph Hooker, the monument serving to widen the scope of the poem to include the national past. But if Lowell turns to history in search of some ideal that might offer an alternative to the desolate present, he is disappointed. There is an ironic undertone in the very introducion of Hooker, a man of tyrannical temperament who is best known for his defeat at the battle of Chancellorville; he is thus represented here through ironic images of futility, ineffectuality, and decay: "Hooker's heels / Kicking at nothing in the shifting snow, / A cannon and a cairn of cannon balls / Rusting before the blackened Statehouse." Moreover, when these subjects (at first lifelessly suspended in the cold and dark) finally do get a verb—in "*know* / How the long horn of plenty broke like glass / In Hooker's gauntlets"—they are linked with the young Lowell's painful sting of *knowledge;* the Civil War, betraying and shattering public ideals, becomes a national version of the Fall.

"Once I went to Mass": again the poet moves back into his own past, this time recalling an activity that was premised upon religious faith, a vision that could redeem time and the world's violence. But "once" establishes the hope as distant, lost, before it is even identified; and this brief, simple clause is joined in a compound sentence to a long series of weighty, elevated clauses (vast, in fact cosmic, in their view of the present) whose symbolic import extinguishes the glimmer of recalled hope.

> Now storm clouds shelter Christmas, once again
> Mars meets his fruitless star with open arms,
> His heavy saber flashes with the rime,
> The war-god's bronzed and empty forehead forms
> Anonymous machinery from raw men;
> The cannon on the Common cannot stun
> The blundering butcher as he rides on Time—
> The barrel clinks with holly.

Now snow may soften and beautify the wintry landscape, and Mars may at first seem to greet the star of Bethlehem with warm enthusiasm; but the god's passion turns out to be murderous. The god of war, not the Prince of Peace, presides over this Christmas—an awesome, all-powerful but mindless force that converts raw men to the anonymous machinery of a modern army; Mars is the young Lowell's version of Moloch. Moreover, in these lines Lowell turns to examine the present through planetary images and classical myth, but "once again" a widening of the poem's scope (here both spatial and temporal) not only fails to open a way out of the "blackout," it merely serves to extend the predicament by finding it to be universal and perennial. History, then, is repetition ("once again"); but as the clear difference between the defeated Hooker and the "blundering butcher" of contemporary warfare suggests, history is also disintegration. Violence is inevitable, and increasing; the wheels of history are winding down. So in the contemporary "blackout" the star of Christianity is "fruitless" and no one recognizes the irony of placing a Christmas decoration on the barrel of a gun.

From this panoramic and mythical vision, developed in long paralleled clauses, Lowell, in another of the poem's dramatic shifts of tone and concern, concludes the second stanza with his first directly expressive statement: "I am cold: / I ask for bread, my father gives me mould." A simple action, a search for warmth and relief, is undertaken ("I ask"), but immediately thwarted ("mould"). Moreover, the religious connotations of "bread," along with the fact that "father" can be read as heavenly father, ancestors in general, or literal father, make the line a condensed comment on familial, historical, and religious breakdown, the failure of all these traditions to nourish the present. At the same time the measured brevity and control of the line (established partly by the antithesis) makes it seem powerfully understated rather than self-pitying.

"His stocking [the father's] is full of stones" begins the poem's final stanza; the father, having little to offer and deserving less, is linked with the cold impotence of the Hooker monument. The opening of the next sentence ("Santa in red") approaches a more benign and generous figure, but then across the line break—and Lowell is as conscious of these terminations as any disciple of Olson—the cheerful dispenser of gifts takes on sinister implications: "Santa in red / Is crowned with wizened berries." "Wizened," something withered or dried up, picks up the connotations of such words as "mould" and "rusting"—all the poem's images of decay; the father of Christmas merges with, rather than offers an alternative to, the literal father. In fact, "Santa in *red*" also identifies him with Mars; and "crowned with wizened berries," recalling the crucifixion, makes Santa a blasphemous mockery of Christ. In wartime, Christmas reenacts not the incarnation of Christ but his murder. "Man of war," Lowell continues, "where is the summer's garden?" Even more directly and more poignantly than at the start of the poem, Lowell, thrust solitary out into the cold and vulnerable to the world's violence, yearns for an original innocence. But even his question, its being addressed to the "man of war" conceding him to be the ruling force in the poet's world, supplies its own negative answer; and Lowell realizes that such a return would only initiate another cycle, a repetition of the same pattern, another fall from perfection into passion and disorder: "In its bed / The ancient speckled serpent will appear, / And black-eyed susan with her frizzled head." The black-eyed susan, with its rich sensuous beauty, may suggest Eve; in any case, it is a *wild*flower excluded from orderly gardens. Both the flower and the serpent thus introduce uncontrollable energies into the easy perfection of summer's garden and adumbrate its ruin. At this point Lowell seems to draw back, as if he had arrived at the poem's conclusion and need only drive it home with an impressive historical contrast:

> When Chancellorsville mowed down the volunteer,
> "All wars are boyish," Herman Melville said;
> But we are old, our fields are running wild. . .

"All wars are boyish, and are fought by boys, / The champions and enthusiasts of the state," Melville wrote, and Lowell, as we have seen, shares his predecessor's ironic vision of the barbarity of such idealism. Yet "we," losing even the facade of innocence, seem to have carried the process even further: "we are *old,* our fields are running *wild.*" The poem seems to be building toward some final apocalyptic vision, but the closing line—"Till Christ again turn wanderer and child"—suggests at least the possibility of an *end* to this collapse. The last line neither denies nor softens the poet's perception of present chaos; rather, it balances the horror of disorder against a mode of redemption and recognizes that salvation, a matter of divine intervention, lies outside human control.

Throughout the poem, then, Lowell keeps looking for some source of order, but finding each one he comes up with inadequate; the poem, continually opening possibilities only to close them off, slowly turns downward toward a sense of imminent collapse, a vision modified only by the last line's leap of faith in a transcendent order. A Christian perspective, Lowell said, "gave me some kind of form, and I could begin a poem and build it to a climax";[15] the climaxes of his early poems, however, have often been faulted as intrusive and unconvincing. But in "Christmas Eve under Hooker's Statue" the climax *is* the arrival at a Christian perspective, a resolution that follows out of the poem's systematic exclusion of alternatives and its view of time as cyclical (emphasized in the "again turn" of the last line). In *Lord Weary's Castle,* the poet yearns for some principle of absolute order that will resolve conflicts within the poet and violence in the world; the poems, often packed almost to the breaking point with division and disorder, dramatize the *search* for resolution, something that, as in the Hooker poem, is more often anticipated than actually achieved. "Christmas Eve under Hooker's Statue" closes with a conditional statement ("till") and in this sense the ending includes an element (a frightening one) of openness: it is not certain that Christ *will* come, just that his return is the necessary precondition for order. Nevertheless, the sense of closure at the end of the poem is quite strong. In three stanzas Lowell has wrenched himself into confronting the contemporary world, located that world historically, and arrived at its (and his) only source of hope; his quest—enacted in the poem's turnings—is completed. Moreover, the sense of closure is reinforced by Lowell's use of an external, stanzaic form. The specific form (nine lines, rhymed aba-babacc) is one that, because of the final couplet, would ordinarily emphasize the stanza as a self-contained unit. At first, Lowell's syntax works to counter such artificial divisions, although not violently so; the first two

15. "The Art of Poetry: Robert Lowell," p. 29.

stanzas end in mid-sentence, with a semicolon marking both a pause and continuity: the syntax, tracing the poet's agonized search, restlessly pushes onward. Hence, at the end of the third stanza, when syntax and stanza finally coalesce, the reader feels that the poem's energies have been brought to a kind of rest—an effect reinforced by the emphatic rhyming of stressed monosyllabic words, "wild" and "child") and even by the closed "d" sound of the rhyme words. Similarly, the first line of the poem establishes a regular iambic pentameter ("Tonight a blackout. Twenty years ago"); many subsequent lines, though staying within permissible variations, speed up or slow down the rhythm with four or six stressed syllables; but at moments of stern insight the poem returns to regularity: "to sting the child with knowledge" or "The ancient speckled serpent will appear." In both human and literary ways, then, the poem enacts the struggle toward acceptance of an external order.

Strenuous, compressed, and oracular, the language of *Lord Weary's Castle* seems inspired by such poets as Hopkins, Thomas, and Crane. "Like Thomas, Crane is subjective, mystical, obscure and Elizabethan," an admiring Lowell wrote in 1947;[16] and as late as 1961 Lowell ranked Crane as "the great poet" of the generation before his own, because "all the chaos of his life missed getting sidetracked the way the other poets' did."[17] Yet from the beginning Lowell was equally "preoccupied with technique, fascinated by the past, and tempted by other languages."[18] If he wanted his poems to be "loaded and rich," he also wanted (unlike Crane) to build them on a foundation that was "perfectly logical."[19] His characterization of Hopkins in a 1945 essay reveals the young Lowell's personal and literary ideal: an "inebriating exuberance" "balanced" by a "strict fastidiousness."[20] The appeal of such fastidiousness explains Lowell's enthusiasm when he first met Allen Tate: "I became converted to formalism and changed my style from brilliant free verse, all in two months."[21] Crane might be the greater poet but Tate "was somehow more of a model and he had a lot of wildness and a lot of construction."[22] Combining wildness and construction, loaded language and formal severity, the young Lowell aimed at becoming the total poet, the culmination of the modern movement.

16. "Thomas, Bishop, and Williams," *SR* 55 (Summer 1947): 493.
17. "The Art of Poetry: Robert Lowell," p. 32.
18. Stanley Kunitz, "Talk with Robert Lowell," reprinted in *Profile of Robert Lowell*, p. 54.
19. "The Art of Poetry: Robert Lowell," p. 32.
20. "The Hopkins Centennial," *KR* 6 (Autumn 1944): 583.
21. "The Art of Poetry: Robert Lowell," pp. 28–29.
22. Ibid., p. 32.

But in his own more impatient and imperious way Lowell participated in the postwar domestication of modernism. Unlike Wilbur and Rich, Lowell saw that traditional poetic forms could not simply be inherited, that in the modern era such forms require justification *in the work*. "Shelley can just rattle off terza rima by the page, and it's very smooth, doesn't seem an obstruction to him," Lowell observed; but when "someone does that today and in modern style it looks as though he's wrestling with every line and may be pushed into confusion, as though he's having a real struggle with form and content."[23] Of course, this is just how it should look if such forms are to seem authentic. In other words, Lowell energizes—and validates—his external forms by making the poem record the resistance to such forms posed by contemporary chaos and confusion. Yet it remains the case that in both religious and poetic ways *Lord Weary's Castle* contains disruptive energies by submission to a preexisting order—precisely the kind of order modernism had tried to abolish.

Lowell's Puritan severity, his "symbolic armour" and his gnarled Miltonic splendor make a peculiar combination, but all three manifest a desire for what he later called "the attenuate ideal."[24] Reservations about this poetic project began to trouble Lowell in the late forties. As Steven Axelrod points out, "Lowell was clearly at odds with his own style of poetry for at least a decade before *Life Studies*."[25] In a 1947 review ("Thomas, Bishop, and Williams") Lowell continues to admire Thomas but he spends considerable time cataloging the excesses of his old literary hero ("self-imitation," "verbal overloading" that creates a "crowded and muscle-bound impression") in a list that sounds like a critique of Lowell's own manner. "If Thomas kept his eye on the object and depended less on his rhetoric," Lowell admonishes, "his poems would be better organized and have more to say."[26] So would Lowell's, as he was apparently coming to see. Lowell then went on to praise the two poets, Bishop and Williams, who became the leading models for *Life Studies* precisely because they did keep their eye on the object and, as Lowell later put it in a letter to Williams, "give rhetoric a nap."[27] Bishop's poems are "unrhetorical, cool, and beautifully thought out"; hers is a poetry—unlike Thomas's, but like Williams's—"absorbed in its subjects."[28] "For experience and observation," Lowell concludes, *Paterson I* "has, along with a few poems of

23. Ibid., p. 17.
24. "A Conversation with Robert Lowell," p. 37.
25. *Robert Lowell, Life and Art,* pp. 85–86.
26. "Thomas, Bishop, and Williams," p. 495.
27. Robert Lowell to William Carlos Williams, 19 June 1957, in the Williams collection at Yale.
28. "Thomas, Bishop, and Williams," pp. 496–97.

Frost, a richness that makes almost all other contemporary poetry look a little second-hand."[29]

Fears that his own writing had become overly rhetorical, narrowly literary, and more than a little secondhand prompted Lowell to explore character and plot in the dramatic monologues of *The Mills of the Kavanaughs* (1951). But Lowell's move toward narrative only made clearer the limits of his "intemperate, apocalyptic" style,[30] as the reviewers were quick to point out. Williams connected the tragic mood of the poems with their acceptance of external constraints and he, predictably, imagined "a poet of broader range of feeling" who might be released by dispensing with the poems' iambic pentameter couplets.[31] William Arrowsmith, too, accused Lowell of a narrowness of feeling and language: "a loss of delicacy, a forcing of effect, a monotony of violence in both language and subject."[32] Peter Viereck complained of self-imitation: "By now, his style is beginning to freeze in its particular 'fine excesses,' so that its surprises, though ever more skillful, are ever less surprising."[33] And in a review that Lowell said affected him deeply, Jarrell noted that Lowell's style was too cumbersome for the narrative poems he was now writing and that it was therefore merely self-imitative. "Sometimes Mr. Lowell is having great difficulties," Jarrell wrote, "and the rest of the time he is seeking refuge from them in some of the effects that he has produced so well and so often before."[34] Lowell remarked that "a true review sinks into the reviewed's mind causing change and discovery," as these reviews did— in part because they articulated the poet's own doubts.[35]

"The anguish of the most original" symbolism, Lowell once remarked, "is its tension and ungainliness in descending to the actual, the riches of days."[36] The interval of eight years between *The Mills of the Kavanaughs* (1951) and *Life Studies* (1959) felt like "a slack of eternity" until his autobiographical poems came as a "windfall" in two "spurts" of writing in 1957 and 1958.[37] The interval was a time of personal anguish and literary frustration for Lowell; but it was also a time of gathering of forces in Lowell's struggle to renounce a tense, ungainly symbolic mode and descend to the actual, the riches of days. Like Pound before him, Lowell

29. Ibid., p. 503.

30. The phrase is quoted from "Marriage," in *History* (London, 1973), p. 70.

31. "In a Mood of Tragedy: The Mills of the Kavanaughs," in *Selected Essays of William Carlos Williams* (New York, 1954), p. 325.

32. "Five Poets," *HR* 4 (Winter 1952): 624.

33. "Technique and Inspiration," *Atlantic Monthly* 189 (January 1952): 82.

34. "A View of Three Poets," *PR* 18 (November–December 1951): 697.

35. "A Conversation with Robert Lowell," p. 35.

36. Review of *The Testing Tree* by Stanley Kunitz, in the *New York Times Book Review*, 21 March 1971, p. 1.

37. "A Conversation with Robert Lowell," p. 37.

sought restoration for a decadent poetry in "the prose tradition"; but unlike Pound, he was not looking for *le mot juste* of Stendhal or Flaubert. Rather, he was after a realistic fullness of representation that he found in writers like Chekov and Tolstoy. "The ideal modern form seems to be the novel and certain short stories," Lowell said in the *Paris Review* interview.

> Maybe Tolstoi would be the perfect example—his work is imagistic, it deals with all experience, and there seems to be no conflict of the form and content. So one thing is to get into poetry that kind of human richness in rather simple descriptive language.[38]

Lowell was moving toward a poetics of reference that would diverge from an overly restrictive notion of literariness. As early as 1953, in a review of Robert Penn Warren's *Brother to Dragons,* Lowell proposed "the prose genius in verse" as counter to the symbolist tradition. Ceding the ephemeral to prose, "our traumatically self-conscious and expert modern poetry" has achieved, according to Lowell, the "scrupulous and electrical" but at the cost of exclusion. "These amazing new poems could," it seems, "absorb everything—everything, that is, except plot and characters, just those things long poems have usually relied upon." But Warren's narrative poem, "though tactless and voluminous," is "alive."

> Warren has written his best book, a big book; he has crossed the Alps and, like Napoleon's shoeless army, entered the fat, populated riverbottom of the novel.

In the crossing of Warren, "one of the bosses of the New Criticism," Lowell found support for the journey "beyond the Alps" that his own work would take in *Life Studies.*[39]

By 1953 Lowell was a poet alienated from his own achievements but without the new matter that might generate a more vigorous style. No grave Blakean voices appeared to fill the void. Rather, as he later sardonically recalled, "I thought that civilization was going to break down, and instead *I* did."[40] His mother died in early 1954 and "I began to feel tireless, madly sanguine, menaced, and menacing."[41] By the summer of that year he had been hospitalized at Payne-Whitney in New York City, the first of two serious breakdowns in the fifties. Unlike Roethke, who yearned for his psychotic bouts as "breaks with reality," Lowell never romanticized his illnesses, but he was able to make creative use of the

38. "The Art of Poetry: Robert Lowell," p. 17.
39. "Prose Genius in Verse," *KR* 15 (Autumn 1953): 620–21.
40. "Robert Lowell in Conversation," p. 35.
41. "At Payne-Whitney," n.p., MS #2227, in the Lowell collection in the Houghton Library at Harvard University.

collapse of his personal life and of the self-examination encouraged by his treatment. At the suggestion of his psychiatrist Lowell began an autobiography and we have already seen how this peculiar form which exists at the margin between the creative and the factual, the imaginative and the historical, inspired him to turn from verse to prose. The earliest version of this autobiography, "At Payne-Whitney," alternates episodes from his life at the clinic with remembered episodes from both his recent and early life. Lowell hoped, he wrote, that the autobiography would "supply me with my swaddling clothes, with a sort of immense bandage for my hurt nerves."[42] Even at this early point Lowell's aim was not to bare but restore the self. The fragments that are available in the Harvard collection suggest that Lowell expended considerable time and effort on this project. Eventually, he evolved a full-length, chronologically organized autobiography, with formal characterizations, dramatic scenes, dialogue—the story related by the adult author who is relaxed and playful at times, devastatingly ironic at others. These worksheets also reveal that as Lowell worked and reworked his material he wrapped more and more bandages around his wounds, so that the most finished section, "Ante-Bellum Boston" (the only part professionally typed), has a stiff formality. It begins, "I, too, was born under the shadow of the Boston State House, and under Pisces, the Fish, on the first of March, 1917," and on one copy Lowell has written in "like Henry Adams" lest we miss the point.[43] In 1957, however, Lowell abandoned his prose project for the more selective, more condensed, and more discontinuous representation of his life that we get in the "Life Studies" sequence—or, rather than abandoning, he renovated his prose work: he returned to "At Payne-Whitney," the earliest and most urgent version, and made its prose the source for such poems as "My Last Afternoon," "Commander Lowell," "Terminal Days at Beverly Farm," "Father's Bedroom," "For Sale," "Sailing Home from Rappallo," and "During Fever."

In "At Payne-Whitney" Lowell had crossed the Alps and entered the rich, populated riverbottom of autobiographical prose. His problem was to explore and mine this fertile ground without draining the life out of it, as he had in the successive revisions of his prose work. His solution was the "Life Studies" sequence in which a poetry that renounced such crucial markers of literariness as regular rhyme and meter kept close to its invigorating prose origins. In the mid-fifties, reading Williams's *Collected Later Poems* had made Lowell wonder (in a letter to the older poet) "if my characters and plots aren't a bit trifling and cumbersome—a bit in the way of the eye, and what one lives." But the New Englander was still

42. "At Payne-Whitney," n.p., MS #2228 in the Lowell collection at Harvard.
43. "Ante-Bellum Boston," n.p., MS #2210 in the Lowell collection at Harvard.

hesitant and concluded that "I'd feel as unhappy out of rime and meter as you would in them."[44] By September 1957, as he was in the first of the two "spurts" that produced "Life Studies," Lowell was crossing to Williams's side of the river, but still determined to bring along as much baggage as he could. He wrote to Williams:

> I've been experimenting with mixing loose and free meters with strict in order to get the accuracy, naturalness, and multiplicity of prose, yet I also want the state and surge of the old verse, the carpentry of definite meter that tells me when to stop rambling.[45]

Just a few months later—in December 1957—the journey had been completed.

> At forty, I've written my first unmeasured verse. It seems to ask for tremendous fire, if it is to come off at all. I've only tried it in a few of these poems, those that are most personal. It's great to have no hurdle of rhyme and scansion between yourself and what you want to say most forcibly. I think even the best of us have much more trouble than we like [to] admit getting our rhymed and metrical verse to even make clear sense.[46]

In November 1958 Williams read a manuscript of *Life Studies,* praised its "terrible wonderful poems," and acknowledged that "the book must have caused you some difficulty to write," for "there is no lying permitted to a man who writes that way."[47] Lowell wrote back to express his gratitude and declared that "dropping rhyme does seem to get rid of a thick soapy cloth of artificiality. The true spoken language beats any scholarly alchemist's pseudo-language."[48] But the correspondence between the two poets, along with Lowell's actual practice, makes clear that Lowell's engagement with Williams did not issue in the kind of self-annihilating conversion experience that it did for many less talented poets. The autobiographical subjects and the psychological acuity with which they are explored in *Life Studies* are both foreign to Williams. Lowell still dissents, in February 1958, from the older poet's dogmatic refusal of meter: "I wouldn't like ever to completely give up meter," he says; "it's wonderful opposition to wrench against and revise with."[49] The "Life Studies" poems do, of course, make irregular use of rhyme and "the ghost of an iambic pentameter" can often be heard in the background. Skeptical of the pro-

44. Robert Lowell to William Carlos Williams, 26 April 1957, in the Williams collection at Yale.
45. Ibid., 30 September 1957.
46. Ibid., 3 December 1957.
47. William Carlos Williams to Robert Lowell, 24 November 1958, in the Harvard collection.
48. Robert Lowell to William Carlos Williams, 29 November 1958, in the Yale collection.
49. Ibid., 19 February 1958.

fessed revolutionary violence of a Ginsberg or Williams, Lowell's preservation of these conventions is integral to his meaning in *Life Studies;* the book strives for a relation to both the personal and the literary past that is neither a mere repetition nor an absolute break.

Life Studies ultimately renounces tight, external forms and preestablished symbolism; it discards rhetorical sublimity and religious myth in a quest to enter a demystified present. Lowell touches what had hurt him most, the prosaic and everyday, and he finds that his fiery creative self can survive within the quotidian. In literary terms, the achievement of *Life Studies* is twofold. Lowell creates what he calls "the confession given rather directly with hidden artifice";[50] at the same time he makes the book as a whole a self-conscious meditation on the problem of a confessional language. In a letter to Henry James, Henry Adams described *The Education* as "a mere shield of protection in the grave." "I advise you," he went on, "to take your own life in the same way, in order to prevent biographers from taking it in theirs."[51] The difference between biography and autobiography was, for Adams, the difference between murder and suicide, and his remark articulates a fear felt by many autobiographers that by fixing the self in words, they have eternalized the self at the cost of its life. "Is the frame of a portrait a coffin?" Lowell once asked.[52] Throughout *Life Studies* Lowell remains aware of the tension between the flux of temporal experience and the stasis of literary form; he constantly calls attention to the dangers of turning "life" experiences into poetic "studies." Lowell's critics, arguing the book's coherence by naming its political, religious, and familial *themes,* have imagined a unity that is static, as if *Life Studies* were suicidal. But the four parts of *Life Studies* are stages in the process of finding a language of process, so my own reading attends to the changes and movements of Lowell's language, his effort to find a way of writing that would preserve, rather than annihilate, his life.

Like so many twentieth-century works, *Life Studies* begins with a false start. In the four poems of Part I, all originally written before his breakdown, Lowell employs the literary formulae—dense symbolic language, predetermined forms—that had worked so well for him before. The problem, however, was not just that Lowell was repeating himself, but that the justifying ground for these conventions has now been lost, as we can see by looking at "Beyond the Alps." As its many commentators have established, this poem transforms a literal train ride from Rome to Paris

50. "Robert Lowell in Conversation," p. 33.
51. In *The Education of Henry Adams,* ed. Ernest Samuels (New York, 1973), pp. 512–13.
52. "A Conversation with Robert Lowell," p. 42.

into a metaphorical journey from a traditional and mythical order to a secular and empirical one, the cruel and chaotic world of "pure prose."[53] Like "Christmas Eve under Hooker's Statue," "Beyond the Alps" dramatizes the twists and turns of the poet's mind, but now Christian supernaturalism no longer offers a possible way out of history; in fact, the drama of consciousness is now generated by the conflict between the poet's wish to idealize past forms of belief and his ironic awareness that all such forms were in reality hollow and repressive. Confronted with Mussolini's imperial designs, Lowell retreats into nostalgia.

> I envy the conspicuous
> waste of our grandparents on their grand tours—
> long-haired Victorian sages accepted the universe,
> while breezing on their trust funds through the world.

The poet's ancestors, with their leisurely, secular acceptance of the world, seem more at home in it than their anxious descendant; but the last of these lines ironically exposes their privileged status in and their real dissociation from the world they seemed so comfortable in. Nostalgic mythologizing is thwarted by ironic scrutiny.

Even more strongly than family myth, Christianity attracts Lowell in the poem's second section. But in modern Catholicism the miraculous has been codified into "dogma," and the Pope, with his shaving mirror, his electric razor, his screaming crowd of worshipers and his "costumed Switzers" sloping "their pikes to push" "through the monstrous human crush"—the Pope is revealed as narcissist, modern, imperialist. The antithesis between the Holy Father and Mussolini melts into an identification. "Our mountain-climbing train had come to earth," the final stanza begins. He has crossed the Alps and renounced "the attentuate ideal," yet the weary, "blear-eyed" poet still resists rebirth into a secular, earthbound world and he still glances backward, now toward the classical world. "There were no tickets for that altitude / once held by Hellas," Lowell mourns, but when his nostalgia becomes attached to a specific object, it dissolves: "once held by Hellas, when the Goddess stood, / prince, pope, philosopher and golden bough, / pure mind and murder at the scything prow— / Minerva, the miscarriage of the brain." This god-

---

53. My discussion of "Beyond the Alps" and of *Life Studies* generally is indebted to that of Charles Altieri in *Enlarging the Temple,* pp. 60–68, but I disagree with his apparent attribution of a necessary "solipsistic" character in confessional writing (p. 60) and his skepticism about the adequacy of Lowell's solution in "Skunk Hour" to the dilemmas posed in *Life Studies.* I am fundamentally indebted to Marjorie Perloff's discussion of realism and literary convention in *Life Studies* in her *Poetic Art of Robert Lowell* (Ithaca and London, 1973), pp. 80–99.

dess, "pure mind and murder," offers yet another of the poem's images of a brutally abstract power, and the closing couplet extends this apocalyptic vision from contemporary Paris to the very remote past: Paris is "breaking up / like killer kings on an Etruscan cup." In "Beyond the Alps" grand figures are unmasked as "killer kings" (like Melville's Ahab) and both modern and ancient orders are shown to be tyrannical and empty. The poem—projecting idealizations, then undercutting them—proceeds by a series of demythologizations. Or so it is tempting to conclude. It is more accurate to say, however, that the poem proceeds by remythologizing, simply substituting demonic for positive idealizations; the poem's circling movement can thus come to a point of rest (and closure) when Lowell, in the final couplet, *fixes* secular, Christian, and classical orders as different manifestations of a single timeless essence, as he does in the phrase "killer kings."

In his ironic probing of family, Christian, and classical mythologies, Lowell presents a vision of disintegration and chaos, civilization "breaking up." Yet it is also true that these disruptive powers are held off at a distance in the poem; they certainly have not entered the writing itself, as if the poem were closer to imperial designs than it ought to be. Consisting of three sonnets, "Beyond the Alps" comes to the reader as a carefully composed artifact whose author is perfectly capable of managing the disorder both within and without. Etruscan cups may crumble but these words, it seems, will not. Moreover, while the poem explores myth ironically, its language still works through the symbolic reverberations that are set in motion through the mythical references. The speaker in the poem is represented as a helpless spectator of the chaos enveloping him; but the author of the poem possesses the power to formalize his vision of chaos into an intricately structured and timeless work of art. In *Lord Weary's Castle,* Lowell's Roman Catholicism envisioned a transcendent reality that ultimately legitimatized the strict orderings of the poems; but the traveler from Rome to Paris has lost precisely such justification. Hence, the form of "Beyond the Alps" must be accepted as a human construction or projection—in a poem that mocks the human propensity for such projections. "I thought that civilization was going to break down, and instead *I* did." By the time we reach the end of *Life Studies,* we have come to see its opening poem as an account of cultural collapse that gives Lowell's personal breakdown an historical context; but we have also come to see that in "Beyond the Alps" the poet has projected his own disorders outward, then carefully dissociated himself from them. Inner life has been "changed to landscape." In this way Lowell exempts himself, or at least his poetic imagination, from the process of disintegration that his poem proposes as fate.

Between "Beyond the Alps" and "My Last Afternoon with Uncle Devereux Winslow"—the first of the "Life Studies" poems—the contrast in language and organization is striking, all the more so once we recognize certain continuities of theme. It is not just that external form—the sonnet, any regular use of meter or rhyme—has disappeared but that Lowell's imperial ambitions as poet have been subdued. While hardly "pure prose," "My Last Afternoon" has made the prosaic an enlivening source of poetry. Rather than reaching after "the attenuate ideal," the poem's autobiographical realism, its recollection of character, setting, and event from the poet's childhood, all create a hard materiality that implicitly mocks man's pretensions toward idealized conceptions of reality. Lowell's tone, before oracular, has now modulated toward the casual and the anecdotal. In reading the poem he once remarked that "My Last Afternoon" is "meant to seem almost like a short story—it rambles along."[54] Many of its details—place names, names of characters—remain literal; and those details that do acquire metaphoric resonance do so by associations that develop gradually within the poem, not by reaching after a preestablished metaphoric system. In this way—by rejecting predetermined forms for evolved orders and by rejecting imported symbolism for a self-generated one—Lowell sought to make this seemingly rambling narrative cohere into a form that would not, imperiously, squeeze the life out of its material.

In "My Last Afternoon" the five-and-a-half-year-old Lowell, dressed in a "sailor blouse washed white as a spinnaker" and "formal pearl gray shorts," is sitting on the stone porch of his maternal grandfather's summer house where he is, incongruously, given his style of dress, mixing piles of "cool" "black earth" and "lime." At the end of the poem, Uncle Devereux is standing behind the boy.

> He was as brushed as Bayard, our riding horse.
> His face was putty.
> His blue coat and white trousers
> grew sharper and straighter.
> His coat was a blue jay's tail,
> his trousers were solid cream from the top of the bottle.
> He was animated, hierarchical,
> like a ginger snap man in a clothes-press.
> He was dying of the incurable Hodgkin's disease. . . .
> My hands were warm, then cool, on the piles
> of earth and lime,
> a black pile and a white pile. . . .

54. Tape of poetry reading by Robert Lowell, 11 May 1966, at the University of California, Berkeley.

> Come winter,
> Uncle Devereux would blend to the one color.

Uncle Devereux is a stiff, vertical, two-dimensional figure who, in spite of his unbending attitude, is literally disintegrating. Again and again in *Life Studies,* Lowell presents a static tableau—then introduces the movements of life that dissolve it. In "Terminal Days at Beverly Farms" Lowell's father is similarly composing himself, similarly crumbling: "He smiled his oval Lowell smile, / he wore his cream gabardine dinner-jacket, / and indigo cummerbund. / His head was efficient and hairless, / his newly dieted figure was vitally trim"; but these *are* his "terminal days," and the poem ends with the father's poignant admission of the emotional reality that is behind his cheerful, bland exterior: "I feel awful." In *Life Studies* characters continually aspire toward rigid, formal attitudes that deny the very temporal processes that the poet is now striving to include in his writing.

Focusing on a seemingly fixed order that is actually breaking up, "My Last Afternoon" psychologizes the themes of "Beyond the Alps." "I cowered in terror," Lowell recalls. "I wasn't a child at all— / unseen and all-seeing, I was Agrippina / in the Golden House of Nero. . . ." Silently mixing the earth and lime, the boy, dressed as formally and uncomfortably as the uncle, outwardly appears a detached, calm figure of "Olympian poise"—another tableau; but inwardly, feeling himself to be the trapped, suffering victim of a stiffly repressive order, he feels awful. The boy is helpless; or his one power is that, "all-seeing," he penetrates obfuscating forms, no matter how royal or glamorous, and sees through to the reality of disintegration, the reality that his grandfather is a kind of Nero, a killer king whose Golden House encloses a treacherous, murderous order.

"My Last Afternoon" thus moves toward the boy's initiation into the uncontrollable realities of temporal existence: loss, decay, death. The protective forms provided by the boy's family are rigidified, dissociated from life, and for that very reason they are empty, powerless, crumbling. Throughout the poem, distinct shapes (houses, rooms) are viewed as constructed in fear of or hostility toward temporal flux. As a result, they are slowly dissolving toward sameness, "putty," "the one color"—"pure prose." The young Lowell is doubly jeopardized: he is potential victim of both the repressive order and of the disintegrative processes from which it is powerless to protect him.

"I won't go with you. I want to stay with Grandpa!" the poem begins, asserting the boy's preference for the "manly, comfortable," and even magnificent order of the grandfather over the "watery martini pipe dreams" of his parents. Yet this order is also stultifying, and the stiffly dressed young Lowell seems a mere extension of it—as if he were run by remote control. "My perfection was the Olympian / poise of my models in the imperishable autumn" but the obviously perishable autumn initiates an ironic turn from timeless perfection to the transient models of contemporary fashion: "in the imperishable autumn / display windows / of Rogers Peet's boys' store below the State House / in Boston." The clothes, suggesting an imposed identity, define the boy as a mannikin, like Henry Adams in *The Education*. In the poem's first section, Lowell had described "a pastel-pale Huckleberry Finn" who "fished with a broom straw in a basin / hollowed out of millstone," this the culminating object in a catalog of "the works of my Grandfather's hands" that revealed his penchant for turning nature into "works"—with deadening effect. In his "formal pearl gray shorts" Lowell is no more Huck Finn than Adams was, and he admires himself reflected in the water of Huck's basin. However "distorting drops of water" mar the perfection of his reflected image, as Lowell once again sets static tableau into motion; and this section closes with an epigram that links the boy with the strangled game carved on the grandfather's clock: "I was a stuffed toucan / with a bibulous, multicolored beak"—as if the boy himself were another of the dead works of the grandfather's hands.

"Up in the air"; this brief phrase, the first line of the third section's characterization of the poet's Great Aunt Sarah, aptly implies her dissociation from the realities suggested by, say, earth and lime. In her youth the aunt had been a fiery, "auburn headed" "genius" devoted to playing the piano and independent enough to jilt an Astor. She practiced all one summer in an empty symphony hall, but was too frightened to play before a live audience: "on the recital day, she failed to appear." Self-absorbed and eccentric, she displays a cold, "deathlike" perfection that the poet unmasks as a fear of life, its passions, and its risks. Moreover, her eccentricity introduces the sequence's preoccupation with breakdown and madness, the cost of such removal from life. Like Lowell's fellow patients in the mental hospital of "Waking in the Blue," Aunt Sarah "ossified young."

So, apparently, did Uncle Devereux, and not just from Hodgkin's disease. In the fourth section the uncle is "*closing* camp for the winter" at his "cabin *between the waters*," some of its windows already "boarded." The cabin becomes one of *Life Studies*' many sealed enclosures, a structure that attempts to shut out natural and temporal realities. The walls of the cabin are "as raw as a board walk," but their crudity is hidden by the uncle's poster collection which, depicting scenes from the Edwardian era, reveal him to be fixated on the past, "ossified." Both his dress and physical bearing support this impression. "As if posed for 'the engagement

photograph,' " the uncle strikes an attitude that is at once formal and
fake; it is almost as if he were one of the posters. But just as drops of
water disturb the boy's reflection in the basin's "mirror," "daylight from
the doorway" of the cabin here riddles the posters. Nature dramatically
breaks into—and breaks down—this "deathlike" and encapsulated order.
Lowell sets his tableaux into motion; his sealed enclosures are cracked,
shattered—like killer kings breaking up on an Etruscan cup.

To the young Lowell, both life and death become unmanageable forces,
so he cowers in terror behind his Olympian poise. The adult poet, however, is neither the helpless victim nor the Nero-like builder of imperial
forms. Near the end of the "91 Revere Street" part of *Life Studies*, Lowell
remembers how, during long painful Sunday afternoon dinners:

> I used to lean forward on my elbows, support each cheekbone with a
> thumb, and make my fingers meet in a clumsy Gothic arch across my
> forehead. I would stare through this arch and try to make life stop.
> Out in the alley the sun shone irreverently on our three garbage cans
> lettered: R. T. S. Lowell—U.S.N. When I shut my eyes to stop the
> sun, I saw first an orange disc, then a red disc, then the portrait of
> Major Myers apotheosized, as it were, by the sunlight lighting the
> blood smear of his scarlet waistcoat. [P. 45]

Here the young Lowell aspires "to make life stop," to frame life, and to
fix it in an apotheosized image; the author, irreverently including the
garbage cans painted by his father and seeing the heroic ancestor's waist-
coat as a "blood smear," quietly undermines the boy's wish both for
idealized images and omnipotent control. The posters in Uncle Devereux's
cabin similarly express a wish to make time stop, to freeze life in some
heightened image; but the posters—the last of which depicts the bush-
whacking of three young soldiers ("they were almost life-size," Lowell
ironically comments)—these posters are death studies, a parody of Lowell's art.

The author of *Life Studies* no longer frames experience in set forms
but seeks to preserve life in orders that are shifting, evolving, open.
"Come winter, / Uncle Devereux would blend to the one color"; these
closing lines from "My Last Afternoon" confront an end, the *end,* but
they do not formally seal the poem shut as the concluding couplet in
"Beyond the Alps" does. Now, Lowell observes fixed postures and reveals the inner motions of disintegration; he observes sealed enclosures
and reveals their fissures. Similarly, the poems themselves often enclose
their material in definitive judgments, delivered in crushing epigrams, but
soon turn on and question and complicate these "conclusions." Lowell
critiques grandiloquence with a language that is flat, understated, literal;

he unmasks rigidity in a language that is constantly shifting—in motion. The "decor" of the grandfather's farm is assessed as "manly, comfortable" in one line, as "overbearing, disproportioned" in the next. Like the boy who mixes warm earth and cool lime, the poet mixes warm feeling and cool detachment in the writing and thus provides mixed, imperfect, not apotheosized, images. Crucial characters in subsequent poems—the grandfather, the father and mother—are not fixed in either heroic or demonic roles. If "My Last Afternoon" leans toward nailing the grandfather down as "Nero," the question of his character is reopened in the next poem, "Dunbarton," which stresses a tenderness and warmth in both the old man and the young boy, who is no longer cowering in terror: "In the mornings I cuddled like a paramour / in my Grandfather's bed, / while he scouted about the chattering greenwood stove." In a reading of "Life Studies," Lowell said that "Commander Lowell" was "satirical but meant to be tender";[55] the poems about the father and mother, too, progress from simple ironic assessments to more complex and ambivalent understandings, as if the sequence were structured to recreate the deepening awareness of a therapy. By his inclusion of the literal, the contingent, and the disintegrative, through the shifting, self-revising motions both within poems and between them, Lowell confronts unmanageable forces and yet establishes a control over them that is not destructive. In its *workings,* a poem like "My Last Afternoon" offers a positive alternative to the encapsulating and murderous forms its irony unmasks.

Again, *Life Studies* does not simply present a new mode of writing; the book records, as well, the process by which this mode was arrived at. In accomplishing the formal shift from "Beyond the Alps" to "My Last Afternoon," the prose of "91 Revere Street" plays a crucial role. To define its effect more precisely, we may raise three questions about Part II of *Life Studies*. Why include *prose* in *Life Studies?* Why *autobiographical* prose? Why, if autobiography, does Lowell limit himself to one relatively *brief* period of his life? Again, the four poems of Part I describe cultural and historical disintegration in predetermined forms and all of these poems were written *before* Lowell's breakdown; in Part II Lowell begins again with the anecdotal prose of "91 Revere Street" dramatically breaking down the established boundaries of the literary—by moving toward the literal and contingent, the *data* of his own life. Lowell chooses autobiographical prose, then, because such writing is, by convention, "true" and "realistic," even though we realize, and so does Lowell, that such terms become problematic as soon as the writer begins to *compose* his life in *words*. In his effort to create the impression of historical truth,

55. Ibid.

Lowell avoids both reverie over things past and confessional outpouring; he plays down inwardness and provides instead a "relentless documentary accumulation of facts: place-names, dates, brand-names, bits of history, and objects, objects, objects, each one handled with the precision of an Agassiz."[56] Hence, one reason for concentrating upon the "91 Revere Street" period of his life is that there, Lowell says, surviving "all the distortions of fantasy, all the blank befogging of forgetfulness," "the vast number of remembered *things* remains rocklike" (pp. 12–13). Remembered things, stubbornly other yet charged with personal associations, now provide the foundation for meaning rather than the imported metaphorical systems of the early poems. "The things and their owners come back urgent with life and meaning—because finished, they are endurable and perfect" (p. 13). These objects become the rocklike ground upon which writing and the self can be rebuilt.

"I thought that civilization was going to break down, and instead *I* did." Rather than projecting private anxieties onto the public world, Lowell now seeks to track down the sources of a personal sense of disintegration. In "91 Revere Street" it is the family order that is breaking up, mainly due to the weakness of the father. Lacking either the "granite *back-countriness*" (p. 12) of his wife's ancestors or the blunter self-assertiveness of his cohorts in the navy, Lowell's father combines a precise, ascetic sense of form with practical incompetence and personal weakness. 91 Revere Street—the "epitome of those 'leveler' qualities Mother found most gruelling about the naval service" (p. 16) and where she bullied her husband into resignation from the service—is the scene of the father's displacement. After resigning from the navy, the father became "literally that old cliché, a fish out of water," a "displaced" figure moving from job to job, an image of defeat (p. 18). In his own home he is constantly humiliated, dominated at times by his shrill wife, at others by military figures. Offended by the purchase of 91 Revere Street, Admiral De Stahl orders Lowell Sr. to sleep on the base, thus effecting a sexual separation between husband and wife. An old friend from Annapolis, Billy Harkness, who acted "as though he owned us" (p. 37) and "cowed" (p. 39) the older Lowell, literally takes his place by occupying his favorite chair, from which he sits in loud and confident judgment of the Lowell family.

A man who (following his family motto) would "prefer to bend than to break," the father is, in a word, "unmasterful" (p. 18). His son, fearing a similar fate, resists manhood: "I am not a man. I am a boy," he insists (p. 24). As one aspect of his boyishness and in reaction to his father's weakness, the young Lowell fantasizes about heroic glamour and omnip-

---

56. Alan Williamson, *Pity the Monsters* (New Haven, 1974), p. 63.

otence, as in the apotheosized Major Mordecai Myers or in his preoccupation with Napoleon. Yet these men of power are always exposed as "killer kings"; they bear a taint of cruelty—just as when Lowell the boy asserts himself, he does so through a sadistic betrayal of his friend Eric or by getting into fights in the Public Garden. Admiral De Stahl and Commander Billy both use their power to inflict pain. The alternatives available to the young Lowell, then, are either the passivity of the father or the cruel ascendancy of the more successful males. Lowell's early experience offers no image of an order that is forceful yet humane, based on acceptance of the other. Forms, orders, it appears, are imposed cruelly.

After the breach with Eric, Lowell's horrified classmates "devised a solemn ritual for our reconciliation. We crossed our hearts, mixed spit, mixed blood. The reconciliation was hollow" (p. 22). In "91 Revere Street" forms are not only imposed but empty, like the Sunday afternoon dinners with the Harknesses, like the form of marriage itself. Even the relationship between the two parents is represented as a conflict of styles—navy versus Back Bay Boston; yet the parents are ultimately alike in that their differing styles both stress form over substance. The father possesses "a high sense of abstract form" but remains "dubious of personal experience" (p. 17). He tries to learn carving from a book of instructions or a class, but each Sunday "he worked with all the formal rightness and particular error of some shaky experiment in remote control." Commander Billy, on the other hand, is a "born carver" (p. 34). The father's submissive approach to correct form reveals (even as it tries to veil) an inner emptiness. But the usurping mother offers no image of true strength either: her haughty style is yet another affectation. She "did not have the self-assurance for wide human experience"; "she would start talking like a *grande dame* and then stand back rigid and faltering" (p. 32). Both parents, moreover, are too immersed in fantasy to absorb the present. Their primary attachments are to old orders: the mother yearns for the "flattering bossiness" (p. 18) of her own father, while the father, raised in a matriarchy and married into one, spends his Sunday afternoons with Commander Billy nostalgically recalling their early years in the navy. Both parents, in short, evolve fixed, narrow perspectives that are antagonistic toward and dissociated from personal experience; like Great Aunt Sarah and Uncle Devereux in "My Last Afternoon" they, too, have ossified young. But the writer of "91 Revere Street" is hardly dubious of personal experience. His autobiographical realism thus not only implies a critique of the preset forms and projecting imagination of the poems of Part I, but, cutting through the "distortions of fantasy, the blank befogging of forgetfulness," his literalistic prose itself provides a corrective to the dissociated, "abstract" orders ("rigid and faltering") that the prose describes.

Yet even here Lowell does not descend all the way to pure prose; "91 Revere Street" is no more mere documentary realism than it is confessional howl. The speaker's tone is casual; his manner is anecdotal, with the offhand brilliance of an accomplished after-dinner raconteur. But Lowell's concentration upon a single era of his life, his obviously selective presentation of events even within this period, his framing of the prose with meditations on the portraits of an ancestral father and son—all suggest that personal experience, while not squeezed into abstract form, *has* been shaped. In fact, both tone and arrangement create an authorial stance that is still largely outside his material. As a boy Lowell "felt drenched in my parents' passions" (p. 19); but as an adult Lowell writes as if he were immune to them. To put it more exactly, he permits himself only the indirect and negative involvement of irony, a stance that leads him to *fix* the members of his family with brutally simple judgments. He coolly (and simply) derives his father's character from the "easy-going, Empire State patricians" from whom his Grandmother Lowell had descended (p. 12). In speaking of his father as "literally that old cliché, a fish out of water," Lowell devastatingly reduces the old man to *dead words*. The last line from "Terminal Days at Beverly Farms" ("I feel awful") gives the father an inner dimension that is missing from the prose. In "91 Revere Street" personal experience has been selected and arranged to serve preexisting psychological ends, as Lowell himself now sits in sardonic judgment of the pretensions and illusions of his parents and of his own youthful, cruel romanticism. He writes without self-pity, but also without any sympathetic or even complicated feeling for his parents. Lowell writes, in short, like a "born carver"—as if in writing "91 Revere Street" Lowell's knifelike wit enabled him, at last, to usurp those figures who had oppressed and humiliated him as a boy.

Like Part I, Part III of *Life Studies* consists of four poems, these dealing with Ford Madox Ford, George Santayana, Delmore Schwartz, and Hart Crane. Disillusioned with the "unmasterful" father revealed in the prose of "91 Revere Street," Lowell now looks for reassurances from the lives of these literary fathers and brothers who, it turns out, offer little guidance for a poet seeking passage beyond the Alps and into the rich riverbottom of quotidian reality. Lowell concentrates on the social positions of these writers, who are shunned, displaced, and isolated. "Divorced" from the "whale-fat" corruption of postwar London, Ford "died in want," while the "old trooper," Santayana, tenacious in his "unbelieving," maintained his serenity by withdrawal into a Convent "cell." As young Harvard students, Schwartz and Lowell were comic in their "universal / *Angst,*" their room, "filled / with cigarette smoke circling the paranoid / inert gaze of Coleridge, back / from Malta"—their room another of the book's claustrophobic enclosures. As Lowell observes of Schwartz's "stuffed duck," "it was your first kill"; poetic power under modern circumstances becomes destructive, "creating" a world of reified objects—again, death studies. His vocation brings pain to the poet, who responds by becoming a "killer," as does Crane, whose rage at his humiliations makes him predatory, "wolfing the stray lambs / who hungered by the Place de la Concorde." Part I of *Life Studies* had ended with "A Mad Negro Soldier Confined at Munich"; Part III, too, ends with humiliation, entrapment, and madness. The four literary figures of this section, then, generalize Lowell's own situation; but they are not models who offer any way out of his predicament. If Part III makes one last effort at salvation through an heroic figure, that effort collapses and culminates in Crane's disintegration. At the same time, Lowell at once projects himself upon and distances himself from these four writers. The portraits, mixing admiration with irony, terror, pathos, and comedy, have complexity, but they remain static and distanced; it is only when Lowell confronts the emotional sources of these poems in his own life that he produces poems that are alive and shifting: "life studies."

The two sections of "Life Studies" contain a double narrative: a series of past losses through death are accepted and resolved through present acts of poetic and psychological ordering. These two movements coalesce in the brilliant "Skunk Hour," at the end of which Lowell enters an ambiguous present, at once decaying and vital. Earlier poems in the sequence tally dying generations, stale traditions, "fogbound solitudes" (p. 65), and marital woe; but the skunks affirm a basic instinct for survival that persists, in the self as in the world, even though forms and conventions do not. Section I of "Life Studies" records a series of psychic jolts that end in breakdown; in elegiac poems about grandparents, father, and mother, the poet's life is radically condensed, epitomized in experiences of loss and separation, which the poet, as in "My Last Afternoon," struggles to manage. The last two poems of section I—"Waking in the Blue" and "Home after Three Months Away"—describe mental collapse and recovery; they define a crisis in which the alternatives of madness and sanity both ultimately issue in helplessness, dread, "lost connections" (p. 86).

The hospital of "Waking in the Blue" culminates all of the sequence's images of deadly, sealed-off enclosures; it is the Golden House of Nero stripped of its style and comforts. The "petrified fairway" of the hospital recalls the "stone porch" of the grandfather's farm, and Lowell, who had been wearing a "sailor blouse" in "My Last Afternoon," now sports a "turtle-necked French sailor's jersey," as if he had succeeded in *not* becoming a man. Like the boy who learns his uncle is dying, the adult

Lowell is a helpless onlooker. His portraits of the inmates Stanley and Bobbie stress physical vigor (the one has "the muscle of a seal," the other is "redolent and roly-poly as a sperm whale"); both are *royal* figures (the one with "a kingly granite profile," the other "a replica of Louis XVI"). Such hints of power, however, are countered by ironic suggestions of boyishness, impotence, and fixation. They may possess an animal vitality which appeals to the desiccated end of the Lowell line; but they are "more cut off from words than a seal." Stanley's "kingly granite profile" is comically juxtaposed with his "crimson golf-cap" to reveal the boy behind the royal facade—just as Bobbie, the "replica of Louis XVI," "swash-buckles about in his birthday suit" like an infant at play. Both resist time—Stanley, for instance, still "hoarding the build of a boy in his twenties"—but with the result that they fail to change and grow; Stanley, "once a Harvard All-American fullback," and Bobbie, "Porcellian '29," remain attached to past moments of glory and thus become the victims, not the conquerors, of time. These ironic suggestions come to the surface in a crushing, definitive judgment, emphatically given its own stanza: "These victorious figures of bravado ossified young."

"Waking in the Blue" could have ended here, with Lowell triumphantly fixing the inmates with his own powerful and superior irony. Instead, he immediately moves toward complicating his judgment—first by turning his irony toward the attendants who, "slightly too little nonsensical," accept "the limits" of time but illustrate a hollow normality. But in the closing stanza Lowell, no longer located safely outside the poem, turns his ironic scrutiny upon himself and moves toward a recognition of the helplessness he shares with his fellow inmates. "Cock of the walk, / I strut in my turtle-necked French sailor's jersey"; beginning with bravado but hinting of boyishness, this sentence then turns, in ironic anticlimax, to note the "metal shaving mirrors" of the hospital and a "shaky future" closing in. "We are all old-timers, / each of us holds a locked razor," the poem concludes. "We," "all," and "each of us" establish that Lowell, far from being superior, is one of them; and all, as the "locked razor" and the metal mirrors point up, are harmless, castrated, incarcerated figures, with Lowell stripped of the razor of his wit, the weapon of his rage. They are all "old-timers," the powerless victims of the very temporal realities they try to resist.

With "Home after Three Months Away," section I of "Life Studies" concludes by coming to a dead end. Like Parts I and III of Lowell's book, this section culminates in madness. Madness for Lowell, however, does not affirm transcendent reality and vindicate the omnipotent self, as it does for Ginsberg; it merely leaves Lowell locked up, both physically and mentally. Yet "Home after Three Months Away" fears and laments recovery: "I keep no rank nor station. / Cured, I am frizzled, stale and small." As in "Beyond the Alps," rebirth is resisted; change is felt as loss, specifically the loss of distinction, heroic grandeur, tragic intensity—the poet's imperial self. Now at home, he plays with his daughter while shaving; but if he cannot, as he says, "loiter here" in domesticity and "child's play," he cannot yet function as an adult either: "Recuperating, I neither spin nor toil." As a result, like the "pedigreed" tulips in his wintry garden three stories below, Lowell has become passive victim of time's "snowballing enervation." Winter has come and Lowell himself has blended to "the one color." The loss of his distinction (rank or station), it seems, means the loss of *all* distinctions. Cured, Lowell becomes a nonentity like that old cliché, his father.

Section I of "Life Studies" closes in a mood of weary impasse. No longer child but not yet adult, Lowell ineffectually drifts toward oblivion. The first three of the four poems in section II continue the sequence's leading image of confinement: the jail of "Memories of West Street and Lepke," the prison of marriage in "Man and Wife" and " 'To Speak of Woe That Is in Marriage' "; and in more general ways, these poems stress the prison of isolation, of "lost connections," of the dissociated, projecting self. But *Life Studies* ends by arriving at its point of origin; "Skunk Hour" closes with the rigid, impatient poet's opening to the prosaic world. This poem has often and sometimes brilliantly been discussed in thematic terms; I want to examine the way the poem works, to explore its place in *Life Studies* as a whole, and to define the precise sense in which the skunks can be said to be "symbolic" objects.

With the two poems about marriage, the autobiographical narrative catches up with itself and enters the present—in which the bland, "tranquilized" surface of the fifties masks homicidal thoughts, shrill invective, sheer panic. "My only thought is how to keep alive," says the terrified wife in " 'To Speak of Woe.' " But with the first four stanzas of "Skunk Hour," tone and subject suddenly shift. From manic desperation we move to the description of a "declining Maine sea town" in a detached, ironic, and even humorous tone. The poem begins with an eccentric heiress who prefers "Queen Victoria's century" to the present but who is powerless to halt temporal and social disintegration. Her "son's a bishop," her "farmer / is first selectman in our village." She *is* a figure of rank or station, but she is "in her dotage." A "*hermit* / heiress," she yearns for "hierarchic privacy," a safely controlled existence; she tries to resist time by buying "all / the eyesores facing her shore," but then "lets them fall." She at least is "Spartan" and old-fashioned, but the town has lost even its modern, showy millionaire. The heiress has a certain integrity and character, but he "seemed to leap from an L. L. Bean / catalogue"—an

anonymous figure created by remote control. "The season's ill," Lowell
coolly pronounces; "a red fox *stain* covers Blue Hill." The final phase of
the town's decay is evoked by a decorator who converts real, functional
objects of the town's past (a cobbler's bench and awl) into art objects
(aimed at the tourist trade) by painting them orange—a way of preserving
the past that empties it of its reality.

But the next two stanzas turn on and subvert the first four, as "Skunk
Hour" abruptly shifts from ironic account of disintegrating town to the
"dark night" of a personal ordeal. The disintegration, it now appears, is
Lowell's own, the changing of self into landscape. Instead of observing
that "the season's ill," Lowell now speaks of "my ill-spirit" and admits
that "my mind's not right." In fact, by presenting himself watching lovers
in parked cars, Lowell uncovers the core self—"unseen and all-seeing"—
that pervades the earlier poems. He is an onlooker, cowering in terror
and desperately in want, but while a withdrawn and helpless spectator,
he projects himself onto the outside world—a way of preserving self and
other that empties both of their reality. The two stanzas thus culminate
with a moving and crucial act of self-recognition: "I myself am hell; /
nobody's here"—the quotation from Milton's Satan defining the projecting as the *demonic* self. All the sequence's images of sealed enclosures
are really representations of the poet's own encapsulated consciousness;
Lowell now confronts his own "air / of lost connections," his radical
isolation.

"Skunk Hour" does not, however, end with a despairing perception of
inevitable subjectivity; the poem moves from easy projection, through
inward ordeal, toward authentic connection with otherness; "nobody's
here— // only skunks, that search / in the moonlight for a bite to eat."
The skunks seem to wander into the poem, seen out of the corner of the
poet's eye and qualifying his sense of isolation, and they are viewed with
a literal realism that reveals an opening of the locked self.

> only skunks, that search
> in the moonlight for a bite to eat.
> They march on their soles up Main Street:
> white stripes, moonstruck eyes' red fire
> under the chalk-dry and spar spire
> of the Trinitarian Church.
>
> I stand on top
> of our back steps and breathe the rich air—
> a mother skunk with her column of kittens swills the garbage pail.
> She jabs her wedge-head in a cup

of sour cream, drops her ostrich tail,
and will not scare.

The pun on "soles" (for "souls") emphasizes that these are literal, physical animals. Juxtaposing them against the dry, dead aspirations of the Trinitarian Church, Lowell places the skunks in a flat, mythless, modern ("Main Street") world where things lack the vertical extensions of meaning they possess within a Christian mythology. When, in "Beyond the Alps," Lowell imagines "Mary risen" as "angel-wing'd, gorgeous as a jungle-bird," the bird is only metaphor; these more earthy animals, to begin with at least, are "only skunks."

Lowell's complex relation to the external scene in this passage requires precise definition. He avoids simple projection, but he wants to avoid anxious, sterile watching as well. He is still an onlooker, but whereas his earlier voyeurism made him feel strangled by his own "ill-spirit," he now breathes "the rich air." He relaxes and participates even though, with the presence of the skunks, "rich" includes some unpleasant possibilities. He is not "at one" with the scene; but because he "will not scare," he does not withdraw. He becomes part of it. Thus the skunks, connected with Lowell, connected by Lowell with the context of "Skunk Hour," with the whole of *Life Studies,* not only literally are but also symbolically mean. Many critics have observed the numerous references to animals in *Life Studies;* these animals either manifest energies that are actively threatening or they are the dead—stuffed, carved—victims of human predators. The skunks, placed into this context of repeated images, at once continue and break the pattern. They *are* alive, their vitality embodied in active verbs: "search," "march," "swills," "jabs," "drops," "will not scare." As just these words suggest, the skunks did not wander into Lowell's yard out of a Disney movie. The notation of their "moonstruck eyes' red fire" gives them a wild, dangerous aspect; this force is related to the poet's "homicidal eye" (p. 87), his fiery rage, his "moonstruck" madness in earlier poems. But again the pattern is broken. Before, wildness is manic, dissociated, and destructive. The skunks, swilling sour cream from a garbage pail, manifest the persistence of a fiery life in a corrupt, disintegrating, ordinary world. The poet includes, but does not tame, them.

Again and again *Life Studies* returns to the question of how to preserve life against the murderousness of language and human ambition. Schwartz's stuffed duck, like the "works" of "Grandfather's hands," offers one possibility; Lowell's skunks, another. Since they are to convey a feeling of "indomitable" life, it is crucial that the skunks remain independently other—alive.[57] In "91 Revere Street" the order of the writing, like the order described, is one of fixed attitudes, rigid views that, faltering, collapse into the complex, shifting views of the poems. The significance of the skunks is not fixed by explicit statement, the way meanings are in the prose. Moreover, the way the poem moves toward them through its self-revising turns of attitude, the way the skunks seem to enter the poem almost in spite of the poet's will rather than because of it, convinces the reader that the skunks have been discovered, not appropriated, an impression that is reinforced because the skunks, domestic and wild, beautiful and scary, living in corruption, are not given a single, fixed essence. "Skunk Hour" unfolds dramatically toward an encounter with otherness—the moment of "breakthrough back into life."

The notion that confessional poetry is solipsistic is so ingrained that the phrase "confessional solipsism" is like the phrase "communist aggression": you never see the first word without the second. Yet *Life Studies* shows Lowell's journey "beyond the Alps" into the rich riverbottom of otherness; in "Skunk Hour" his mountain-climbing imagination at last comes to earth. It is also the case, however, that Lowell's relation to the skunks is one of reciprocity, not a breakthrough into unmediated vision. *Life Studies* records the formation of an ego which can manage experience without being impositional, and this project entails a more complicated model of psychic life than does "Howl," with its polarizing of repressive and visionary consciousness. In Lowell's book physical objects—say, the items in "Father's Bedroom"—possess a matter-of-fact literalness, but they also acquire metaphoric depth from their context in a particular poem, in the whole book. This combination of literal surface with metaphoric substructure allows Lowell to compose his experience into literary shapes that do not *seem* impositional: "the confession given rather directly with hidden artifice." This technique, by no means novel in twentieth-century poetry, helps explain why *Life Studies,* though an insurgent work, did not provoke the kind of literary scandal that "Howl" did.

Unlike both Olson and Ginsberg, Lowell can, then, allow and even strive for an aspect of the self that remains outside of immediate experience or feeling. Lowell's ironic detachment, however, points up the limits and occasional weaknesses of *Life Studies.* If the book proceeds by moving closer to the emotions that are "breaking up" the poet's composure, even the "Life Studies" poems remain at some distance from their emotional sources. A line like "Grandpa! Have me, hold me, cherish me!" (p. 69) is unusual for its emotional directness, and Lowell lacks the compelling emotional drive of a Ginsberg or a Plath. The "Olympian

57. Tape of poetry reading by Robert Lowell, 11 May 1966, at the University of California, Berkeley.

poise" of the boy in "My Last Afternoon" is father to the adult poet, for whom it also functions as a defense against terror. Lowell's early poems had often seemed as if they were about to explode under the weight of their own intensity; in "Life Studies," especially in poems like "Terminal Days at Beverly Farms," "Father's Bedroom," "For Sale," "Sailing Home from Rapallo," "During Fever," the writing can become emotionally slack and all-too-deftly literary under the direction of Lowell's coolly understated irony.

A poet like Plath illustrates the dangers of a confessional poetry at the other end of the spectrum. Feelings from the past are reawakened in all their raw violence, but they then turn against her and sweep her along in a "suicidal / drive." Lowell's defenses, necessary for survival, are part of an effort to gain perspective on the personal past. Not wanting to be swallowed up by it, he does not fantasize about abolishing it either. The existence of such a perspective, however, raises a crucial question: upon what ground does Lowell base his implicit claim to be able to detach himself from himself and to break from the fixations of his past? The answer is that in *Life Studies* Lowell has silently assumed psychoanalysis as the frame through which he studies his past life. "Freud is the man who moves me most," Lowell told A. Alvarez in a 1963 interview. Recalling that he had been "brought up as a Protestant," then become "a Catholic convert," Lowell observed that

> when that goes and we look at it another way, Freud seems the only religious teacher. I have by no means a technical understanding of Freud, but he's very much part of my life. He seems unique among the non-fictional teachers of the century. He's a prophet. . . . I find nothing bores me more than someone who has all the orthodox sort of Freudian answers like the Catechism, but what I find about Freud is that *he provides the conditions that one must think in.*[58] [My italics]

I do not mean to imply that *Life Studies* should be read as a cryptic text in which primal scenes, family romances, and juicy Freudian symbols have been tucked away. Critics have already examined *Life Studies* from a psychoanalytic point of view, and while no Freudian critic has ever concluded that a writer he decided to explore turned out to be lacking in latent content, I don't disagree with the conclusions these critics have reached.[59] I want, rather, to emphasize that psychoanalysis provided Lowell with a way of thinking about his life—not a surprising conclusion given

58. "A Talk with Robert Lowell," pp. 43–44.
59. See *Pity the Monsters,* passim, and George McFadden, " 'Life Studies'—Robert Lowell's Comic Breakthrough," *PMLA* 90 (January 1975): 96–106.

the book's origin in his treatment. This point of view affected Lowell's choice of parental figures as subjects of the poems, his emphsis on loss, and the need to work through loss, his picture of his relation with his wife as repetition of his relation with his mother; even more important, the self-revising movements of the "Life Studies" poems create mixed, ambivalent images of parental authorities, as opposed to the static simplifications of the prose. Like a patient in treatment, the poet proceeds from idealizations (both positive and negative) to ambivalent perceptions— again, a step Ginsberg cannot yet take in "Howl." The psychoanalytic notion of ambivalence thus performs a crucial *literary* function in "Life Studies." My emphasis on the turnings of these poems is not intended to suggest that they offer the endless oscillations of a poetry that has abjured closure; ambivalence, rather, both creates and contains those movements, the whole sequence closing with the ambiguous image of the skunks. In his early poetry Christianity had offered Lowell a preexisting symbolism and a fiercely powerful God who validated that symbolism; psychoanalysis offered Lowell not a symbolic code but a way of thinking about his life, a way that encouraged renouncing of wrathful deities and impositional desires. If Lowell's breakdown had stimulated him to go outside literature to autobiography, psychoanalysis, curiously enough, provided a frame that was not a coffin and showed the way toward a revised definition of the literary.

SIX

Denise Levertov

"We must have poems that move away from the discursively confessional, [the] descriptive, dilutedly documentary *and* from the fancies of inauthentic surrealism to the intense, wrought, bodied-forth and magical—poems that make us cry out with Carlyle, 'Ah, but this sings!'"[1]

—Denise Levertov

The formalist poetry of the fifties, passively reflecting broader social and cultural attitudes, constituted a literary *trend*. One ironic result of such trends is that they generate *movements* that are self-consciously dissident and programmatic. Poetry once again becomes critical, poetic theory polemical. One such movement in the fifties was that identified with the "beat," underground world peopled with thieves, junkies, and other decidedly unliterary and "angelheaded hipsters" that Ginsberg mythologized in "Howl." Another group, less mystical and less demonic, more literary than social in its disaffiliations, was that centered around Charles Olson and Black Mountain College.

Black Mountain, a small experimental college founded in 1933 in the foothills of western North Carolina, was floundering when Olson was brought in to direct it in 1951; and in the following and final five years of its life, Olson, putting its antitraditional, individualistic theories of education into practice, brought the college to a kind of final flowering. Under Olson's direction, Black Mountain became, according to Martin Duberman, a place distinctive

1. "Great Possessions," *The Poet in the World* (New York, 1973), p. 95. Subsequent references are made to *PW* in the text; other abbreviations used in this chapter are *DI, The Double Image* (London, 1946); *HN, Here and Now* (San Francisco, 1956); *OI, Overland to the Islands* (Highlands, N.C., 1958); *WE, With Eyes at the Back of Our Heads* (New York, 1959); *JL, The Jacob's Ladder* (New York, 1961); *OTS, O Taste and See* (New York, 1964).

not in endowment, numbers, comfort or public acclaim, but in quality of experience, a frontier society, sometimes raucous and raw, isolated, and self-conscious, bold in its refusal to assume any reality it hadn't tested—and therefore bold in inventing forms, both in life style and art, to contain the experiential facts that supplanted tradition's agreed-upon definitions.[2]

Such an innovative spirit seems a genuine extension of Olson's insistence on viewing only the man in the "field" of the present moment as real. But however much such a spirit may have penetrated the day-to-day activities of the school, it seems to have provoked accomplishment less among its students (with Ed Dorn and Robert Rauschenberg as the main exceptions) than its faculty, with the college less important for its experimental methods of education than as a meeting ground for artists (many of them exiles from New York City) who believed in "inventing forms" as a matter of human and artistic necessity. Thus, in the early fifties the faculty included important avant-garde figures from several of the arts—in music (John Cage), painting (Franz Klein), dance (Merce Cunningham), and poetry (Robert Creeley and Robert Duncan as well as Olson). Moreover, even under severe financial pressures, the college supported the *Black Mountain Review,* which had an importance far greater than its short life (seven issues between spring 1954 and fall 1957) might suggest. Not only did it provide an outlet for the work of poets not acceptable to the established quarterlies (Allen Ginsberg and Denise Levertov were two), but it allowed the inventive spirit of the college to become a visible and stimulating one in American poetry.

In a 1961 review of books by Gilbert Sorrentino, Le Roi Jones, and Paul Blackburn, Denise Levertov places these three poets "among the inheritors of a usable tradition, [who] have as ground under their feet all that Williams and Pound have given us." The three, moreover, "have been influenced in double strength, as it were: both from their reading of the older poets and through what Charles Olson and Robert Creeley have made of it (though none of the three actually studied under Olson or Creeley at Black Mountain College)."[3] Here, Levertov is also defining her own place in modern American poetry: as a poet who (as of the early sixties at least) had descended from Williams and Pound by way of Olson and Creeley, though she herself had never attended or even appeared at Black Mountain College. What the writers of the Black Mountain group shared, according to Robert Creeley, was that

2. *Black Mountain: An Exploration in Community* (Garden City, N.Y., 1973), p. 355.
3. "Poets of the Given Ground," *The Nation* 193 (October 14, 1961): 251.

each one of us felt that the then existing critical attitudes toward verse, and that the then existing possibilities for publication for general activity in poetry particularly, were extraordinarily narrow. We were trying in effect to think of a base, a different base from which to move.[4]

Along with this common antipathy, these poets shared a view of the line as breath-spaced, emphasized use of the printed page as a means of scoring the poem for speech, and defined literary form as a dynamic unfolding or process. The new "base" these poets sought had been articulated, in short, in Olson's essay "Projective Verse."

As Levertov's identification of a line of succession clearly suggests, the Black Mountain response to the poetic crisis of the fifties was neither Ginsberg's plunge into the urban underground nor Lowell's descent into the "hell" of the private psyche; rather, poets like Olson, Creeley, and Levertov proposed to continue and advance the work of such then-marginal figures as Williams and Pound. Unlike Olson, however, Levertov remains at ease within such a line of succession and, as we shall see, she develops in *O Taste and See* an attitude toward literary predecessors (and male authority in general) that is more complex than Olson's rivalry. Not viewing the literary past as a Moloch threatening to swallow her up, Levertov never makes exaggerated claims of accomplishing an absolute break with the past; she avoids the grandiose histrionics of a Ginsberg or an Olson. At the same time, Levertov may be said to be less ambitious in proportion as she is less pretentious, and her modesty raises two key questions, to which we will return. Less inclined to take risks, does Levertov play it too safe and end up being too limited? If, as she says, she derives from Williams and Pound by way of Olson and Creeley, how different is that, say, from Wilbur's descent from Eliot by way of the New Criticism? The brief answer to the second of these two questions is that her stance was the more active one at the time and that Levertov finally alters what she inherits in a way that Wilbur does not; in fact, the notion of transforming that which is given and which has been repeated through human experience becomes a crucial one in both her theory and practice of poetry.

Among the Black Mountain poets, I select Levertov not because I think she is better (though she does merit much more attention than she has received) but because of the admirable richness and complexity of her development—moving from work in the late forties that was traditional in form and romantic in substance, to poetry in the late fifties that seemed innovative but actually derived from Williams, and finally in the mid-

4. Quoted in Duberman, *Black Mountain,* p. 414.

sixties, in *O Taste and See,* to a poetry of her own, a poetics of magical realism. Often Levertov's work is condescendingly dismissed as a poetry of intense perception, and it is true that she values "an ecstasy of attention" and that her poems break open traditional forms in order to admit the objects and energies of the immediate physical world.[5] Like many of her contemporaries, she steps outside the fifties' bounds of literariness by beginning with a poetic realism. Her stress on such externality leads to her negative critiques of both confessionalism and surrealism. Yet it is also the case that in the essay where she most fully attempts to place herself in contemporary poetry—"Great Possessions" (1970)—she spends most time attacking what she calls the style of "documentary realism" that has descended from the poetry of Williams.

> What began as a healthy reaction, a turning away with relief from sterile academic rhetorics, had proliferated in an unexampled production of *notations:* poems which tell of things seen or done, but which, lacking the focus of that energetic, compassionate, questioning spirit that infused even the most fragmentary of Williams's poems, do not impart a sense of the experience of seeing or doing, or of the *value* of such experience. [*PW,* p. 90]

To speak, as Levertov does here, of the value of such experience is, of course, to posit some external (and prior) framework from which it derives value. Increasingly, as Levertov's career has proceeded, she has come to identify that framework as "supernatural" (*PW,* p. 98). Unlike Ginsberg, she locates the visionary as immanent in the here and now, but she does seek the "form beyond forms" (*PW,* p. 7). Her colloquial, literalistic language strives to become numinous. "The substance, the means, of an art," she writes, "is an incarnation—not reference but phenomenon" (*PW,* p. 50). Such stress on the self-sufficient being of a work of art sounds modernist, as do her frequent characterizations of the poem as "disinterested" or "autonomous"; similarly, she emphasizes the work as a *verbal object* much more than beat or confessional poets usually do. Nevertheless, the poem for Levertov is not simply a self-reflexive object and the poet no mere cunning artificer. A poem, she says, is "the poet's means of summoning the divine"; as she contends, the poem is a "temple," the poet a "priest"—and the language of poetry, at once summoning and incarnating the gods, is magical (*PW,* p. 47). Such a line of thought, of

5. Levertov's notion of presence is discussed by Thomas A. Duddy, "To Celebrate: A Reading of Denise Levertov," *Criticism* 10 (Spring 1968): 138–52. See also *Enlarging the Temple,* pp. 225–44; Altieri is mainly interested in showing the limitations of an aesthetic of presence when Levertov "tries to adapt her poetic to pressing social concerns caused by the war in Vietnam" (p. 226). For a book-length study of Levertov, see Linda W. Wagner, *Denise Levertov* (New York, 1967).

course, invites substituting spiritual for literal reference, a danger Levertov seeks to avoid by insisting that the divine be discovered *in* the ordinary and that it be *embodied* in the language of the poem; she really means the incarnational metaphor, and a successful poem, for her, makes the word flesh in a language of magical realism. When her poems do fail, it is most often because a mythic dimension has been merely imposed upon the poem's material and the presence of the gods is merely asserted rather than convincingly summoned. At her best, however, Levertov gives us poems that are "intense, wrought, bodied-forth and magical—poems that make us cry with Carlyle, 'Ah, but this sings!' "

Levertov's first book, *The Double Image,* appeared in England in 1946 when she was twenty-three; the starting point for her poetry, as it was for such American contemporaries as Wilbur and Rich, was the dilemma of a centerless world, how to enter it, how to live and write in it. Participating in a symposium on myth in 1967, Levertov identified "the sense of *life as a pilgrimage"* as the myth informing "all of my work from the very beginning" (*PW,* pp. 62–63). The poems of *The Double Image,* however, constitute a kind of failed pilgrimage. Divided into two sections, "Fears" and "Promises," the book is intended to record a journey that progresses from anxiety to acceptance—specifically, acceptance of life's double image, its fears *and* its promises. But while the poems do long to break out of the self-immolated solitude, they never succeed in doing so convincingly, and so the predominant feeling is one of loss and nostalgia, a lament for the absence of both vitality ("the lost élan," p. 12) and of intelligible order in experience. The first two poems, "Childhood's End" and "They, Looking Back," set the tone with their lamentations for the poet's exile from a "miraculous" Edenic world and her entry into the ambivalent temporal world of "love *and* death." Levertov's lost world is a magical one, where dreams are actualities and life a fairy tale.

> Trees in the park were wearing coats of mail:
> the nightly fairytale lived there by day—
> flying Mary Anna,
> little crying leaves,
> the eight wonderful stones.
> To bed by daylight meant a secret journey.
>
> [*DI,* p. 10]

But, Levertov continues, "time grew hostile," and she was cast out into what she later calls "the ravaged landscape of the lost" (p. 20)—a realm of isolation, walls, "barricades" (p. 14), divisions, "duality's abyss / unspanned by desire" (p. 15). Poems in the "Fears" section stress the discrepancy between reality and the poet's idealized expectations of it. Her disappointments, however, prompt withdrawal and the conclusion that the external world is "alien and unreal" (p. 30). Hence, throughout the book, physical objects are experienced as "shades," "phantoms," "ghosts," "images"—dim presences that mirror back her own subjective states. In reverie and withdrawal, the world, no longer "hostile," can be safely solipsized. Levertov no doubt has her own encapsulated condition in mind when she describes a man who "lay entranced, and heard / the soft forgetful murmur of his flowers / lovingly bent over their mirrored doubles"—an apt image of the drowsy solipsistic self, always at least one remove from reality, feeding on images rather than actualities (p. 44).

In short, rather than accepting its loss, these poems seek to recover the lost magical world of childhood by transforming objects into manipulable images and poetry into reverie. Ideals, rather than being modified by contact with experience, are stubbornly clung to. And the poet that emerges is a self-protected and self-insulated figure, not unlike the authors of *The Beautiful Changes* and *A Change of World*. Moreover, like Rich, Levertov often criticizes the sterility of her defenses; even in the "Fears" section she sometimes tries to shake herself out of reverie and enter the present.

> Now when the night is blind with stars
> now when candles dazzle the day
> now
> turn from phantoms
>
> [*DI*, p. 21]

—the repeated "now" a reminder that her next book, *Here and Now*, will make the journey that she can here only exhort herself to. Similarly, in "Only Fear" she turns on her work, critiquing its subjects ("familiar images of mellow ruin") and its style ("pensive grace"), and hopes "to penetrate / the woolen forest and discover // an earthy path and unembroidered gate, / a credible living world of danger and joy"; and in the last of the "Fears" poems, "Meditation and Voices," she attacks her "vanity," questions why she must "hear your sorrows, count your sins, / and hope to rub a genie from your ring," that is, hope for magical absolution and deliverance.

But the poems of the second half of the book never make this transition from dream to reality; instead of "promises" kept, we get mere wishfulness. Affirming a living core hidden behind the "impassive mask" (p. 33) or the "ravaged landscape," "Return" and "For B.M." open the possibility of spanning "duality's abyss"; "Ballad," "April " (II), "Days,"

"Midnight Quatrains," and "Listen!" affirm the "flame" of passionate experience. But in what will become a problem throughout all of Levertov's career, her resolutions here are simply asserted, either by uplifting discursive language or by ready-made symbolism, and in both cases a lack of specificity in her language makes it hard for us to feel she is in touch with a "*credible* living world." At the same time, the poems reveal some ambiguity about just what kind of world the poet is willing to enter: some accept a divided world of danger and joy, but others achieve acceptance only after discovering some hidden "core" or center, so that it is not clear whether Levertov is prepared to make a pilgrimage that is not made meaningful by some final end(s). "I need a green and undulating line / the hill's long contours in my words" (p. 32), Levertov writes. Earlier she tells herself that "words must be flesh and blood, not ghosts" (p. 17), anticipating her later conception of poetic language as incarnational. But the words of *The Double Image* remain ghostly rhetorical assertions, familiar symbols, and so at the book's close Levertov is still exhorting herself to leave "the comfortable myth and drowsy mansion" to wander through real life (p. 44). As much as Levertov strains to put herself and her poems into motion, her first book remains static, fixated—with the poet's consciousness locked inside the "walls of dream" (p. 14).

Throughout *The Double Image* Levertov appears at ease with set, traditional forms in a way American contemporaries such as Lowell, Wilbur, and Merwin were not; hers is not an artifice that continually calls attention to itself. Nevertheless, her poems remain even more narrowly circumscribed within a period style than theirs do. Her dreamy melancholy and her external forms, her "pensive grace," place her poems in the predominant movement in England after the Second World War, the neoromanticism in which poets such as Alex Comfort and Herbert Read were the leading figures. Levertov had by this time read Eliot and Auden, but her first book suggests that in postwar England the main strategy for dealing with the moderns, who probably appeared much less awesome against the background of the long British tradition, was to proceed as if they had never written and to return to the premises of romanticism.[6] But with *Here and Now* (1957) her view of the tradition and her sense of her own poetic genealogy radically altered.

"Only expected echoes / merit attention // not generosities," Levertov complains in "A Story, a Play," a poem responding to critical attacks on a story by Robert Creeley and a play by Williams (*OI,* p. 5). Now Levertov shuns "expected echoes," renounces the advantages of a style that had

6. For an account of this movement and a sampling of its work, see *The New British Poets,* ed. Kenneth Rexroth (Verona, Italy, 1949), especially pp. vii–xxxviii; see also Levertov's "Herbert Read: A Memoir," *Malahat Review* 9 (January 1969): 10–13.

already gained her acceptance, and enters "new ground, new made" (*HN*, p. 22), a ground she explores with just that generosity of attention that had been missing in her first book. "Rules are broken," she says in "A Story, a Play," to let us in, both to the here and now and the poem itself, new made. Compare these lines from "Casselden Road, N.W. 10" in *The Double Image:*

> Shadows of leaves like riders hurried by
> upon the wall within. The street would fill
> with phantasy, the night become
> a river or an ocean where the tree
> and silent lamp were sailing; the wind would fail
> and sway towards the light. . . .

with these lines from "Laying the Dust" in *Here and Now:*

>   The water
> flashes
> each time you
> make it leap—
>   arching its glittering back.

In *The Double Image* the moment of poetry occurs when quotidian reality is suddenly transformed by "phantasy," as if the physical world were an emptiness without a subjective presence to fill it up. But in *Here and Now* the moment of poetry occurs when an ordinary event, like wetting down dust with buckets of water, generates a flash of sensual delight. The lines in "Laying the Dust," rather than marking off predetermined units of measure, mark off parts of a physical activity for careful attention at the same time that they dramatize the processes of the mind attending to that experience: first we get an object ("water"), then its thrust into brilliant motion with "flashes," then the generalized activity of "flashes" is separated into "each time," then the involvement and energy of the human agent ("make it leap"), and then the poet's own metaphoric leap which makes the water ("arching its glittering back") seem animal-like, alive and independent. "Laying the Dust" does not give us a world of phantasies imposed by human subjectivity but an exchange between self and world, "an / interpenetration, both ways," as Williams puts it.[7]

Ten years had passed between *The Double Image* (1946) and *Here and Now* (1956); "the early '50s were for me transitional, and not very productive of poems," recalls Levertov (*PW*, p. 67). For this English-born

7. *Paterson* (New York, 1958), p. 3.

poet, too, mid-century was a time of personal change and poetic crisis. The year after publication of *The Double Image* she married Mitchell Goodman and, after a year's travel in Europe, they settled in New York City; in 1949 Levertov's son was born. In 1953 Allen Ginsberg would move from the East to the West Coast to free himself from both family and the established literary culture; Levertov moved from England to the East Coast for similar reasons, and with similarly liberating effects. "There are no miracles but facts," she declared in a 1951 poem (*OI*, p. 3), and with her removal to America she had not become the romantic wanderer she had exhorted herself to be in the closing poems of *The Double Image* but, with marriage and motherhood, she had rooted her life in domestic experience. As we shall see, acceptance of limits—physical, temporal, domestic—becomes integral to her definition of the creative process. At the same time there were specifically literary influences in helping her find an alternative to "expected echoes" and "the fabulous / poem" (*OI*, p. 2). Not long after coming to the United States, she met Robert Creeley, whom her husband had known at Harvard, "and through our friendship with him we later came to know a number of people connected with Black Mountain College."[8] She read Olson, including the essay "Projective Verse," and she came to know Williams, who "became the most powerful influence on my poetry" in the fifties (*PW*, p. 67).

Levertov had first read Williams, both poems and *In the American Grain*, while living in Paris in 1947, just after her marriage. She had "an *immediate* feeling that here was something, something that was going to speak to me," but at first she was bewildered by Williams's versification or his apparent lack of one. "I literally didn't know how [the poems] would sound. I couldn't read them aloud. I couldn't scan them, you know. I didn't understand the rhythmic structure."[9] Levertov has since attributed her difficulties with Williams to her lack of familiarity with American speech. With her actual experience of "American speech" and "the pace" of American life, "I picked up [Williams's poems] again, and I found to my joy that I could read them—and I think it was simply that my ear had gotten used to certain cadences."[10] By 1951 she was exchanging letters with Williams, and their correspondence reveals him relating to her as both loving paternal supporter:

Take care of yourself my dear and keep on with your writing. Because we love you. And don't bother to come out to the suburbs

8. *The New American Poetry*, p. 441.
9. Walter Sutton, "A Conversation with Denise Levertov," *Minnesota Review* 5 (October–December 1965): 324.
10. Ibid.

where you can do nothing to help us find ourselves in this mystifying dilemma in which we all find ourselves.

The poet is the only one who has not lost his way, and you are a poet. We must look to you. Keep on doing what you are already doing for us.[11]

And as tough artistic conscience:

Cut and cut again whatever you write—while you leave by your art no trace of your cutting—and the final utterance will remain packed with what you have to say.[12]

In fact, "Pare down, peel away" was exactly the advice that Levertov was urging upon herself in one of the earliest (1951) poems in her new manner—excellent advice for the author of the wordy poems in *The Double Image*.[13]

Williams thus encouraged Levertov to strip down her language and to expand the range of her work, leading her to conclude that "the artist doesn't impose form upon chaos," as so many poets and critics of the fifties supposed, "but discovers hidden intrinsic form."[14] According to Levertov, "the mountain is master of the landscape in which it is a presence," but "one does not emulate such a master, except by being more oneself" (*PW*, p. 243). In the early fifties, Levertov was drawn to the Williams of the shorter poems, with his "sharp eye for the material world" and his "keen ear for the vernacular" (*PW*, p. 67), but in *Here and Now* (1956) and *Overland to the Islands* (1958) she often emulated this figure (to adopt his own distinction) by *copying* his manner rather than by imitating his essential spirit.[15] To a significant degree, she was replacing "expected echoes" with unexpected ones.

"Silence / surrounds the facts. A language / still unspoken," Levertov writes in "A Silence." It is the language of fact ("precise / as rain's first / spitting words on the pavement," *HN*, p. 32) that she now proposes to speak, rejecting the ghostly diction and "mirrored doubles" of her first book. Yet even in her new poems it is quickly apparent how little the sharply defined visual image, the poem as *"notation"* engages her; her observations are exact, her poetry highly sensuous, but her perceptions

---

11. *Stony Brook* 1/2 (Fall 1968): 168. Twelve letters from Williams to Levertov are printed in this issue. The letters are in the Williams collection at Yale.

12. Ibid., p. 164.

13. "Land's End," *Gryphon* 3 (Spring 1951): 11.

14. "A Conversation with Denise Levertov," p. 326.

15. I treat *Here and Now* and *Overland to the Islands* as a single collection; Levertov let Lawrence Ferlinghetti select which, out of a large number of poems, were to be included in *Here and Now* (see Levertov correspondence in the City Lights collection in the Bancroft Library, University of California, Berkeley), and many of the poems he rejected appeared in *Overland*, so that the two books in no way reflect a chronological order of composition.

are given value and force as manifestations of "the core / lost impulse" (*HN,* p. 31; compare "the lost élan") which she now locates in physical experience and in language itself. As we have seen with Olson, Levertov celebrates the "here and now," but she does so mainly because she finds hidden within it an absent core of energy. In her poems of the late fifties she avoids any open sacralizing or mythologizing of this force. She finds it in the vigorous "laughing" bird of "The Bird," the "intently haphazard" dog of "Overland to the Islands," the plunge of the "real rain, sensuous" in "The Way Through," the bird caught in her room who, after almost battering itself to death against the walls, finally soars "straight out" the window in "The Flight," in the "waterwoman" who "goes dancing in the misty lit-up town / in dragon-fly dresses and blue shoes," in the poet's dance "alone among the fireflies on the / dark lawn, humming and leaping" in "In Obedience."

As Levertov writes in "Beyond the End," "It's energy: a spider's thread: not to / 'go on living' but to quicken, to activate: extend"—and both the poem's argument and its title (which she at one time considered using as the title for *Here and Now*) suggest her renunciation of the weariness and detachment that characterized so much of American poetry in the fifties. Levertov now holds that it is "the will to respond," the manifestation of human energy, which allows us to do more than merely "go on living," to go "beyond the end / beyond whatever ends: to begin, to be, to defy," that allows the poet to break open those "walls of dream" which had enclosed her in *The Double Image.* Levertov's poems now mock the conventional wisdom that admonished us, "DISPOSE YOUR ENERGIES / PRACTISE ECONOMIES" (*HN,* p. 18); the "unlived life" (a phrase from Rilke, *HN,* p. 14) is, in a recurring figure, "caged," based on "civic prudence" (*HN,* p. 15) and issuing in sterile repetition, "passing / repassing, drooping, / senselessly reviving" (*HN,* p. 17), with "senselessly" a pun suggesting both "meaninglessly" and "without sensual content": for Levertov a life without sensual contacts *is* a life without meaning. Opposed to both caution and obsessive repetition is the pilgrimage, "the will to respond" extended into the world. "*It was thus and thus /* repeats the head, the fantasist"; instead of being caged in dreamy retrospectiveness Levertov now urges *"continuing variously"* (*OI,* p. 20). So, again, it is energetic motion (as in the dance) that holds her attention, not the static visual image. In "Turning," as she is describing a room full of objects—

> planes tilt, interact, objects
>   fuse, disperse,
> this chair further from that table . . .

Levertov suddenly tries to *fix* her attention: "hold it! / Focus on that: this table / closer to that shadow," but as the very necessity of locating the table in relation to the shadow reveals, holding the attention is as impossible as it is undesirable. "Turn, turn!" Levertov declares; "loyalty betrays"—a paradox based upon acceptance of change in an open and fluid universe.

The energy manifest in physical experience is also hidden within language itself; poems are therefore at least as much linguistic acts of discovery as they are discoveries of objects and forces in the "real" world. As a result, "copies of old words" will not do (*HN,* p. 9). Counter to such poetic repetition is what Levertov identifies in "Ink Drawing" as "energy, gay, terrible, rare, / a hope, man-made"; poetic energies are finally linguistic ones, man-made, and it often seems that the vital physical forces that engage Levertov are not fully accessible to human consciousness until they are embodied in language, in words that, because they are carefully chosen, are themselves alive, not mere copies. "The mirror caught in its solitude / cannot believe you as I believe," Levertov writes in "The Lovers." A mind that merely reflects the world may "go on living," but does so in solitude and silence, lacking the will to respond that makes us fully human. Similarly, poems that mirror the world—as (in Levertov's view) documentary notations and confessional poems do— are dead copies, while poems that are authentic acts of discovery give us that "rare" "man-made" energy. Such claims are, of course, vulnerable to the kinds of objections I raised in connection with Olson's "Projective Verse" in chapter 3. In particular, what Levertov "discovers" is hidden; presence, for her, turns out to be absent, and so the possibility is raised as to whether or not we are getting psychic projection or mythic imposition rather than actual discovery—a possibility that becomes all the stronger when we recognize that the energy she celebrates comes very close to a universal, mythic force, one perhaps all too man- (or woman-)made. At this point in her career Levertov is not yet ready to explore, as she will be in *O Taste and See,* some of these dilemmas of her poetic, but it is true that her stress on the poem as construction keeps her from adopting a naive conception of poetic presence. "Honesty // isn't so simple," she writes in "The Third Dimension," questioning the premises of the simpler forms of confessionalism before it had been invented: "a simple honesty is // nothing but a lie" because "the words / change it." Levertov, however, does not move from this perception into a never-ending meditation on the differences between language and its objects. Instead, she acknowledges poetic artifice, the status of the poem as a verbal illusion; poems are fictive, not actual incarnations. In "The Third Dimension" she refers to a love story she would like to write as a "fiction," reminding us that she had started reading Wallace Stevens when she found his work in the same

Paris bookstore in which she had come upon Williams.[16] Levertov derives little from the style of Stevens, but she does share his sense that a phrase I used a few pages earlier, "the language of fact," contradicts itself, expressing an end the poet may pursue but which he will always miss because the words *do* change it. What attracted her to Stevens, Levertov told an interviewer, was "a sense of magic" in his early work, and she went on to say that a combination of the "realism" of Williams and the "illusionism" of Stevens would produce an ideal poet, one whose work, as we shall see, would embody a poetics of magical realism.[17]

For Levertov, then, a poem is a made object, a construction—but, as Olson had said, "a high-energy construct." In "Merritt Parkway" Levertov describes the perpetual movement of the cars speeding "relentlessly" along "the / sealed road" (*OI*, p. 8)—another version of the "unlived life" in which nothing changes, nothing is experienced, the highway a parody of Levertov's pilgrimage, which takes her from a "sealed" and "dreamlike" consciousness into an open world, from the closed autotelic poem to the poem as a field of action. The "new ground" she is claiming ("every step an arrival," *OI*, p. 1) is a world of fact *and* movement, not lost in "copies of old words" enclosed in copies of old forms but incarnated in "lines alive, *acts* of language" (*HN*, p. 16) that produce a poem that is "a dance of the words" (*HN*, p. 20).

But while Levertov repudiated the expected modes of the fifties, the ground she enters in *Here and Now* and *Overland* was not entirely new poetic territory. It is not just that her poetics, as I have been suggesting, derives from Williams by way of Olson, but that she also takes subjects and even tone of voice from Williams. "Sunday Afternoon," "Broken Glass," and "Jackson Square"—all poems where Levertov finds instinctive vitality in a "dusty" urban world—are close to Williams's proletarian poems. "The sink is full of dishes. Oh well," she begins "The Dogwood," a poem strongly reminiscent of "Le Médicin Malgré Lui," where Williams makes light of his medical obligations. Like the Ginsberg of *Empty Mirror*, she learned from Williams how to play prose sense against the brief pauses signaled by the end of a line—how, in short, to space and break lines, "the proper space / holding existences in grave distinction" (*OI*, p. 36); but when she writes,

I want to speak to you.
To whom else should I speak?

                                                                    [*HN*, p. 27]

or

16. "A Conversation with Denise Levertov," p. 335.
17. Ibid.

We are faithful
only to the imagination. What the
imagination
        seizes
as beauty must be truth.

[*HN*, p. 23]

she is trying to emulate her "illustrious ancestor" by becoming him. Williams did open possibilities that encouraged Levertov "to begin, to be, to defy"; but the here and now she enters in these poems is one that often seems to have been invented by Williams, experienced through his eyes and ears.

"The Shifting," published in *Origin* in 1952, announced a "change of pleasure," a pleasure *in* change; the shift from *The Double Image* to books like *Here and Now* and *Overland to the Islands* took Levertov from reverie to more immediate experience, from the "sealed" to the open poem. But in her next two books, *With Eyes at the Back of Our Heads* (1960) and *The Jacob's Ladder* (1961), Levertov continues to shift, now turning even more explicitly to discovery of what lies hidden within or beyond physical reality: "the quick of mystery" (*WE*, p. 49). In her work of the late fifties she had concentrated upon the surfaces of ordinary objects, but she now identifies "the real," as she writes in "Matins," as a "new-laid / egg whose speckled shell / the poet fondles and must break / if he will be nourished" (*JL*, p. 58); the poet still handles the surfaces of things lovingly, but she is now concerned to "break" the outside open and arrive at what she calls in "A Ring of Changes" the "true form" (*WE*, p. 39). At the end of "Matins" Levertov invokes a "Marvelous Truth" which can be found in the quotidian world, and her search for it leads her to view visible objects as "guises" (*JL*, p. 60), to be cracked open, like the speckled eggshell. In several poems she represents the muse as blind but "all-seeing" (*JL*, p. 40) because intuitive sight (of the sort accomplished with the eyes at the back of our heads) or the visionary ascent (of the sort accomplished by climbing the Jacob's Ladder) is what she finally stresses in these poems. In fact, what Levertov has done is to return to that magical world where form and content, being and becoming are one, from which she had been exiled at the start of *The Double Image*.

This change in Levertov's work—movement toward a kind of visionary poetry and toward a more elevated and more richly musical language—was not a totally abrupt one; signs of a mystical consciousness can be found in both *Here and Now* and *Overland to the Islands*. In "Homage," for example, Levertov praises a poet, "solitary in your empire of magic," who can "sing / dreaming wideawake" (*HN*, p. 20). Poems such as "The

Sharks" and "Action" suggest that the way to activate, extend, is through the unconscious "depths" of the mind (associated with the sea); "The Instant," "Scenes from the Life of the Peppertrees," and "Pure Products" all seek to uncover "the old powers" manifest in the momentary. In "The Instant" (*OI*, pp. 16–17), one of the strongest poems in these two books, Levertov recalls an early morning hunt for mushrooms with her mother, recreating the scene with precise detail: "wet scrags / of wool caught in barbed wire, gorse / looming, without scent"; but suddenly the surrounding "mist rolls / quickly away" and her vision is swept up and outward:

> "Look!" she grips me, "It is
>   Eryri!
>   It's Snowdon, fifty
>   miles away!"—the voice
> a wave rising to Eryri,
> falling.
>   Snowdon, home
> of eagles, resting-place of
> Merlin, core of Wales.

Her mother's spontaneous use of "Eryri" (legendary Welsh name for Snowdon) helps make this instant a timeless one, as Levertov proceeds from the realistically observed to "the fabulous / poem" which discloses, by invoking the old powers, that remote world of magic and myth (both "home" and "resting-place," beginning and end) that she had sought in *The Double Image*. Ultimately *Here and Now* and *Overland* reflect a certain ambiguity in Levertov's assumptions about the nature of reality and of poetry. Yet it is easy to see how her focus on energy manifest in physical life could easily slide over to a sense of an underlying (and therefore eternal) principle, how the "here and now" can become the locus of "the old powers"—as happens, in fact, in the poetry of Williams himself.

The change in Levertov's work, however, did not result from a deeper reading of Williams, though in "Williams and the Duende" (1973) she claims a Williams who takes us to "the edge of the world, where all is unknown, undefined, the abyss of the gods" (*PW*, p. 265), a Williams who is consonant with her own new interests. Insofar as the origins of the change were specifically literary, they can be related to her reading of Robert Duncan and H.D. Levertov first met Duncan in the early fifties. Levertov's "The Shifting" "released my sense of a new generation in poetry," according to Duncan;[18] perhaps it did so partly because of the

18. *The New American Poetry*, p. 434.

way the poem ("the shifting, the shaded / change of pleasure," it begins) enacts shifting in its transformations of full vowels and lush consonants—a quality that makes it very like Duncan's poetry. Duncan, in any case, acknowledged the impact of her work in "Letters for Denise Levertov: An A Muse Ment," published in the *Black Mountain Review* in 1955.[19] On the other side, Duncan's work, Levertov writes in "Great Possessions" (1970), "has for twenty years been appeasing my own hunger" for a poetry that is authentically magical (*PW*, p. 101). In 1959 she named Duncan and Creeley as "the chief poets among my contemporaries"; but, as she later told an interviewer, "Duncan has been for me much more of a stylistic influence," citing principally "the greater sort of fullness in his style."[20] Most important, perhaps, is the conviction behind that fullness that language "is not a set of counters to be manipulated, but a Power" (*PW*, p. 54); poetry then becomes the summoning of a god, the invoking of the old powers, that are hidden *in* language itself. It was Duncan, finally, who introduced Levertov to H.D. in London in the early sixties (*PW*, p. 247) and who, with the early chapters of the "H.D. Book," no doubt affected the way in which Levertov read H.D.[21] The Levertov who had descended from Williams by way of Olson, now turned to H.D. by way of Duncan.

While Levertov had been "for years familiar" (*PW*, p. 244) with the early short poems of H.D., it was not until she read "Sagesse" in the *Evergreen Review* (no. 5), that she experienced H.D. as a creative source, sensing "doors, ways in, tunnels through" in her work (*PW*, p. 244). From "Sagesse" Levertov proceeded chronologically backwards to the *Trilogy—The Walls Do Not Fall* (1944), *Tribute to the Angels* (1945), and *The Flowering of the Rod* (1946)—and then back to a rereading of the early "imagist" poems in light of the later mythopoeic work (*PW*, p. 245). Levertov then recognized that "the icily passionate precision" of the short poems "had not been an *end,* a closed achievement, but a preparation," developing a poetic strength that would enable H.D. to "carry darkness and mystery" in the later poems (*PW*, p. 245). As Levertov puts it in "H.D.: An Appreciation," "she showed a way to penetrate mystery; which means, not to flood darkness with light so that darkness is destroyed, but to *enter into* darkness, mystery, so that it is experienced"

19. *Black Mountain Review* 3 (Fall 1955): 19–22.

20. William Meyen and Anthony Piccione, "A Conversation with Denise Levertov," *Ironwood,* No. 4 (n.d.), p. 26.

21. The first section of Duncan's H.D. book to be published appeared in *Coyote's Journal* 5/6 (1966): 8–31. But this and other chapters are dated as written in the very early sixties, and I am assuming that Levertov was in close enough contact with Duncan at this time to know—either by reading the unpublished chapter or by conversation—Duncan's views on H.D.

(*PW*, p. 246). "Let us substitute / enchantment for sentiment, // re-dedicate our gifts / to spiritual realism," H.D. wrote in *The Walls Do Not Fall;*[22] it was in this direction, toward a spiritual or magical realism, that Levertov now rededicated her own work. Williams had opened the sensuous world for Levertov; H.D., along with Robert Duncan, suggested ways to "tunnel through," "to penetrate mystery."

Toward such a passage—toward the poem, in Duncan's term *as* "passage"—Levertov, at first hesitantly, begins to turn in *With Eyes at the Back of Our Heads*. Yet, even if the journey has taken on a spiritual dimension, the poem continues to be process, as it is in both Williams and H.D., Olson and Duncan. A poem like "A Straw Swan under the Christmas Tree," for example, begins with a concrete object, but it is the interplay between mind and object that generates—in fact, becomes—the poem.

> Its form speaks of gliding
>   though one had never seen a swan
>
>   and strands of silver, caught
>   in the branches near it, speak
>
> of rain suspended in a beam of light,
>   one speech conjuring the other.

Here Levertov is not concerned with evolving a language that will carry the presence of objects, as she had been in *Here and Now;* rather, external things (like the shape of the straw swan) *are* a kind of language, their suggestive appearances conjuring speech in her, as in the poem itself. Moreover, this power of objects is directed toward the imagination, since we need not literally to have seen a swan in order to "see" gliding in the shape of the straw figure. Objects, again, are less important than energies, motions; but the movement is now emphatically a linguistic and mental one. "All trivial parts" of the mundane world possess this power, Levertov goes on, to speak of "themselves" and of their metaphoric "counterparts," as the tinsel now speaks of "rain suspended in a beam of light"; she continues,

> Rain glides aslant
>   swan pauses in mid-stroke,
>   stamped on the mind's light, but aloof—

22. *Trilogy* (New York, 1973), p. 48.

The real scene—straw swan, tinsel on a Christmas tree—fades as it conjures an imaginary (or perhaps remembered) one; it has been transformed by the "mind's light" or the imagination into a poetic image, an all-too-poetic image. For there is something unsatisfactory about the created scene; it may be "stamped" forever on the imagination but it remains "aloof" from the actual world that generated it in the first place. Moreover, the way Levertov switches the gliding from swan to rain, and the pause from rain to swan, reinforces the sense that she has moved too far from a world of objects, into a world of pure magic where words conjure words, instead of objects conjuring words. So the poem curves back from the "mind's light" to the physical "eye":

> and the eye that sees them refuses
> to see further, glances off the
> surfaces that
>   speak and conjure,
> rests
>   on the frail
>   strawness of straw, metal sheen of tinsel.

At first it may sound as if Levertov is simply moving back from imaginative flight to literal reality; but she does so only in a very special sense. The eye, which cannot get inside hard, opaque objects, glances (like a beam of light) off surfaces, to come to rest—the movement beautifully caught in the placement of the lines—on the "straw*ness* of straw." Levertov has now arrived at the "true form" of her object, the swan, and it is not form as external shape (as it was in the first line of the poem) but form as intrinsic being, a point supported by Levertov's allusion here to a remark by John Donne, "God is a straw in a straw," a sentence that she quotes in an essay, "Origins of a Poem" (1968), commenting that "the strawness of straw, the humanness of the human, is their divinity" (*PW,* p. 51). The poem, then, seems to come to a rest, and to an end, with the discovery of immanent form; but in fact the poem closes not with rest, but with motion, as Levertov asks herself:

> How far might one go
> treading the cleft the swan cut?

The closing line shows how Levertov can toughen what might be an idealized poetic image, that of the swan gliding across a lake or pond. Earlier, the sounds of "rain glides aslant" easily glide into each other, and the sounds of "swan pauses in mid-stroke" (a line that pauses at midpoint) are similarly soft; the smooth flow of both lines is part of what makes them beautiful but "aloof," while the hard *t*'s and *k*'s in "treading the cleft the swan cut" create a crispness of sound that assures us that the poet is carefully attending to her words: "lines alive, acts of language."

The question that Levertov raises, of course, is how far one might go in following out the suggestions of objects, the evocative powers of words themselves ("one speech conjuring the other"). In other words, how far can she go in pursuing the notion of art as magic that she found in H.D. and Robert Duncan? The danger in following such a lead all the way out is that the poet will end up in a world (and a poem) that is beautiful but remote, disembodied—one that only glances off the surfaces of things rather than perceiving form *in* matter. But it is also true that "A Straw Swan under the Christmas Tree" closes with a question, an open ending that is intended to provoke and to continue movement on the part of the reader, rather than to seal the poem off neatly. The journey continues, the interplay between mind and world persists, beyond the final lines, "beyond the end" of a poem that seeks to activate, extend.

In the mid-sixties the received critical estimate of Levertov's writing was that, while it showed superior craftsmanship, it lacked, as Robert Bly put it, "a vision."[23] A careful reading of even her earliest poems will, I think, show the superficiality of such a judgment; Bly is really complaining about the absence not of "a" but of his own kind of vision. In fact, *With Eyes at the Back of Our Heads* and *The Jacob's Ladder* both reveal an increasing commitment to a conception of art as magic, as the unveiling of the secret powers hidden inside things, and Levertov's style accordingly becomes fuller, more suggestive, a vernacular expanding to an oracular voice. At the same time, Levertov makes this change slowly, hesitantly, almost reluctantly, so intense is her attachment to concrete experience, and one of the reasons "A Straw Swan under the Christmas Tree" is so rich a poem is that it grows out of her hesitations and conflicts. Moreover, while the two books of the early sixties include many fine individual poems—"With Eyes at the Back of Our Heads," "Another Journey," "The Room," "The Communion," "The Goddess," "To the Snake," "To the Reader," "A Common Ground," "The Jacob's Ladder," "The Necessity," and "A Solitude" are among them—the overall impression created is that Levertov is moving toward a vision she has not yet fully articulated and which she cannot yet consistently embody in her style.

"I like to find / what's not found / at once, but lies // within something of another nature / in repose, distinct," Levertov writes in "Pleasures,"

23. "The Work of Denise Levertov," *Sixties* 9 (1965): 55.

one of the poems in *With Eyes at the Back of Our Heads*. She does not want to remain "composed," fully and finally formed, but to break open, to explore and discover, to leap into the world, now characteristically experienced as invigoratingly harsh, "intemperate" (*WE,* p. 23). "I'm tired / of all that is not mine"—all that is imposed upon or expected of her (*WE,* p. 22). So in "The Goddess" a demonic muse flings her out of Lie Castle, the poet landing face down in the mud where she finds, and eats, seeds, as if she were a hungry animal. The goddess brings Levertov back to her body because living in her body the poet becomes a goddess. The physical energy stressed in the two previous books is now explicitly transformed into a sacred power, the "animal god" the poet tries to summon in "The Vigil." Throughout *With Eyes,* Levertov conceives of the imagination as a dark, mysterious force, a sacred power, that lies within our physical nature, in repose, distinct.

In *The Jacob's Ladder,* Levertov has pushed even further toward the visionary, now thinking of the imagination as light, a form of spiritual illumination. "A Solitude" describes a blind man whose mind is still active, "filled / with presences," while in "The Illustration" the muse is given "closed all-seeing eyes." Together, the poems suggest the degree to which the physical world—a shell, to be fondled then cracked in "Matins"—recedes in importance for Levertov. The title poem thus defines life's pilgrimage (and the movement of "the poem" itself) as a slow, arduous ascent toward the light, a passage relieved by those moments when "wings brush past" and angelic presences are sensed. The stairway is made real in the poem; it is not a "radiant evanescence" but "of stone," "of sharp / angles, solidly built" and the climber "must scrape his knees" in ascending it; even the angels, who "spring" from one step to the next, "giving a little / lift of the wings," are made physical. Still, the process described is not that of finding the "true form" of a physical object, like a straw swan, but of making substantial a symbolic and spiritual conception, the same process that Levertov describes in "The Necessity." As she says in "The Jacob's Ladder," "the poem ascends," toward the light, and when she does confront immediate objects in this book, they typically become radiant. She speaks of "everlasting light" (p. 15), "the dense light of wakened flesh" (p. 25), "the walls of the garden, the first light" (p. 20), "the heart of fire" (p. 56).

In "The Message," one of the finest poems in her next book, *O Taste and See* (1964), the "Spirit of Poetry" appears "out of a sea fog" in a dream, writing to Levertov to ask her to gather "seeds of the forget-me-not." The spirit, which seems to arise from the depths of her own being, bids her to "remember my nature, speaking of it / as of a power," and the poem stresses that the creative power, its seed, is to be found *within* the poet, as even the name of the seed (forget-*me*-not) confirms. At the poem's close, Levertov awakens at daybreak and starts to question the "message" delivered in the dream.

> Shall I find them, then—
> here on my own land, recalled
> to my nature?
>   O, great Spirit!

But what starts out as a question ends as an exclamatory affirmation, and a syntactic ambiguity allows us to read "O, great Spirit" *both* as direct address to an external presence *and* as in apposition with "my nature," and thus referring to an indwelling spirit. The spirit of poetry lies hidden inside the poet, a seedlike power that comes to fulfillment in a poem, the *"flower of work and transition."* "Returning," she had written in "The Charge," "is a mourning or ghostwalking only" (*WE*, p. 11)—one of several poems in which she had urged a break with nostalgia or obsession, with repeating the past. But Levertov now imagines the poem as at once a return and an arrival—an old form, an ancient archetype, discovered in new experience, when the poet speaks out of her own nature, a power. Many of the poems in *O Taste and See* deal explicitly with such a return to origins, and they do so because Levertov, not so much shedding as internalizing her illustrious literary ancestors, returns to the whole of her own nature, now strengthened and deepened by the almost twenty years of living and writing since her first book. In *O Taste and See,* her poetry, integrating the dream consciousness of *The Double Image* with the realistic precision of *Here and Now,* achieves its most successful embodiment of magical realism, as her career, enacting the myth that is the seed of *O Taste and See,* becomes a "sequence / returning upon itself, branching / a new way" (p. 12).

Indeed, the notion of a return that is also an advance ("a new way") generates a coherent mythology that informs all of the poems and the single short story that are collected in this distinguished book. Again and again the poems refer to origins, beginnings, sources that are not lost, distant, inaccessible (like Mount Snowdon in "The Instant") but are present, immanent, within the poet's own nature. In "Kingdoms of Heaven" paradise is at first identified as an "endless movie" that "draws you into itself"—a field in which "the attention / never wavers," the field of the poems of *Here and Now.*

> The attention
> lives in it as a poem lives or a song
> going under the skin of memory.

The comparison between the attention and the poem or song, however, shows how Levertov's attention lives among the words of the poem; the comparison speaks back to her, reminding her that works—poems, songs, movies—only live *on* because they live *in* us; they "get under our skin." So Levertov can make a leap of faith, suggesting a different location for the kingdom of heaven:

> Or, to believe it's there
> within you
> though the key's missing
> makes it enough? As if
> golden pollen were falling
> onto your hair from dark trees.

In this poem, too, the poet is recalled to her own nature; it is not in being drawn into otherness but, as the short line emphasizes, "within you" that paradise is to be found. Paradise, then, is not a place but, like the spirit of poetry, an energy, a power of the mind; the "key" to unlock it may be missing, but its living presence can be felt in sudden moments of discovery, as when "*golden* pollen" falls from "*dark* trees." "The Film" dramatizes the relation between the work of art and its audience, and Levertov similarly suggests that we deal with the external reality of the work by taking it inside of us; the work, a seed, flowers in our new perceptions of the world. Here she watches a symbolic movie in which "young Heroes," after an encounter with a threatening "Turtle Goddess," are then initiated into a vision of life as a "corridor / of booths," containing "scenes / of bliss or / dark action." But while others in the audience reject or forget the vision of the film, it gets under the skin of the poet's memory and lives on, not just in the poem we are reading, but in the very way Levertov apprehends experience. She equates the passage in the film from the Turtle Goddess to a "confused" life, blissful and dark, with the loss of her mother; she returns home after the movie to see "Mother is gone, / only Things remain. // So be it"—an acceptance that enables her to *begin* to live.

In *O Taste and See* the process of poetic transformation is now at once more magical and sacred and yet more intimately physicalized; creative activity becomes an incorporation, a taking into the body—as the title poem makes plain.

> The world is
> not with us enough.
> *O taste and see*

> the subway Bible poster said,
> meaning *The Lord,* meaning
> if anything all that lives
> to the imagination's tongue,
>
> grief, mercy, language,
> tangerine, weather, to
> breathe them, bite,
> savor, chew, swallow, transform
>
> into our flesh our
> deaths, crossing the street, plum, quince,
> living in the orchard and being
>
> hungry, and plucking
> the fruit.

Just as Levertov herself twists the well-known line from Wordsworth ("The world is too much with us") and transforms the phrase on the subway Bible poster into her own "meaning," she urges actively taking the world into ourselves, transforming it "into our flesh our / deaths," into our very physical being; experience, in this way, is poetically *embodied,* incarnated. Moreover, it is "all that lives" and even "our deaths" that we are exhorted to assimilate, any principle of selection, moral or otherwise, necessarily distancing us from experience. In the poem's closing lines Levertov, again enacting its theme, transforms both the myth of Eden and the world of the present by identifying the two, depicting us as "living in an orchard and being // hungry" and rather than deferring to biblical prohibitions, "plucking / the fruit," as Adam had done. In Levertov's mythology, of course, plucking and eating the fruit is precisely the "new way" to energize the self and expand its field of activity. All of this poem from the third line onward consists of a single sentence, the phrase *"O taste and see"* becoming a kind of seed from which, via Levertov's active reading of its "meaning," all the subsequent poem grows. A series of static nouns ("grief, mercy, language / tangerine, weather") at first define experience; but then human activity is introduced in a series of infinitive phrases ("to breathe," "bite, / savor, chew, swallow, transform"), the infinitives characterizing an activity that, being untensed, seems eternal—as well as an activity that we are exhorted to carry on. But after "transform // into our flesh" all actions are rendered in present participles ("crossing," "living," "plucking"), the testing urged by the poster finally transformed into an activity, both concrete and mythical, that occurs in a continuous present. The self, hungrily taking in new experience, becomes a continually moving and constantly *re*formed center.

The recognition achieved at the end of "The Film," according to Levertov, is that "the house is occupied only by things, not by a psychic presence" (*PW,* p. 79). It sounds as if Levertov has purged herself of the parental images carried into adult life from childhood, along with the projections that stem from them, and managed to step, barefoot, into reality. But even her capitalization of "Things" in the poem implies an archetypal dimension to them; her poems are, in fact, pervaded with spiritual presences, clearly extensions of psychic ones. Such presences are often female and when they are, they are not simply versions of "the archetypal dominating Mother" (*PW,* p. 79) like the Turtle Goddess: they are more ambiguous figures, half demonic, half benign, as in Levertov's representation of the muse, evident in the recurrent figure of the moon, in the "Song for Ishtar" (a moon goddess), and most fully and explicitly in "To the Muse." What is striking about this poem is the way Levertov locates her muse within the domestic world, but without domesticating her. The muse in fact manifests the presence of the mysterious within the house, "within you," within a newly conceived domestic order. A "wise man" had told Levertov of the muse, assuring her that the goddess is not an external power "who comes and goes"; "having chosen," Levertov writes, "you remain in your human house," a presence that Levertov compares to "the light of the moon on flesh and hair," a presence that does not intrude upon but illuminates physical reality, as Ishtar is shown to do. At times it seems as if the muse has gone; in reality "you were not gone away / but hiding yourself in secret rooms."

> The house is no cottage, it seems,
>
> it has stairways, corridors, cellars,
> a tower perhaps,
> unknown to the host.

The domestic order within which the muse is housed is not a simple one, safely closed and sealed (a "cottage"); Levertov has already described the warmth and openness necessary to evoke the muse in the first place, and she now suggests a domestic order that has mysterious extensions downward into the dark earth and upward toward the sky. So, while the muse may seem to have vanished and the "host" may rail against her for leaving, "all the while // you are indwelling, / a gold ring lost in the house," the gold ring symbolizing both personal and marital wholeness, linking vision and body, like the image of "the light of the moon on flesh and hair." But just as it's not clear where the muse is, neither is it clear how to find her; once again, "the key's missing."

> Not even a wise man
> can say, do thus and thus, that presence
> will be restored.

The house (self, marriage, poem) *is* occupied by an obscure powerful presence, one that cannot be unlocked at will—but which does appear at those intense moments of communion when we taste and see the world, plucking its fruit.

The house is often occupied by male presences as well, usually in the form of guides whose wisdom is real but limited and which the poet must therefore incorporate and pass beyond. Sometimes, the poems merely represent simple idealizations, as in the loving, patient pastor in "A Cure of Souls." "Old Day the gardener," remembered from girlhood in "A Figure of Time," is more complex, looking like "Death himself, or Time, scythe in hand," but his scythe is really a pruning hook and his destructiveness—cutting back, clearing, weeding—is really life-enhancing; all the gardens "thrived in his care" and he becomes a figure of godlike omnipotence in whose care the poet would like to remain and whose artistic powers she would like to emulate. Such yearnings for protection *are* a form of "mourning or ghostwalking," but more often Levertov represents male guides who open up a vision for her, then depart, leaving her on her own, making the end of the poem a beginning. The "wise man" in "To the Muse" can assure her that the muse is indwelling, but he cannot give her the key to unlock the muse, just as the director in "The Film" offers her a vision in his movie, accompanies her home afterwards, but does not go in with her. When she enters the house, then, both "director" and mother are literally "gone," though aspects of them have been incorporated into her own vision. Similarly, a man and a boy in "The Novices" are drawn by "a clear-obscure summons they fear / and have no choice but to heed." When they arrive at a small clearing, they are met by a "wood-demon" who turns out to be "not bestial" or "fierce" but a "shabby," "shambling" bearlike figure, both "gentle and rough." "To leave the open fields / and enter the forest, // that was the rite," he tells them. "Knowing there was mystery, they could go." In "The Instant" it had been the mother who served as guide, to revelation of a serene, distant, godlike masculine power represented by Mount Snowdon. But in these poems the situation is reversed: a male figure presides over a revelation of dark mysterious powers that are within the poet and which she thinks of as distinctively female. In this sense, too, Levertov is, in *O Taste and See,* recalled to her own nature.

Levertov's desire to establish both continuity with and yet independence from the past applies to her relations to literary predecessors too.

In the early sixties some of those modernist poets who, as Stanley Kunitz lamented, "would never consent to die," finally did. In "September 1961" Levertov writes not exactly of the deaths but of the withdrawal into silence of Pound, Williams, and H.D., their preparation for death beautifully described as "a painful privacy // learning to live without words."

> This is the year the old ones,
> the old great ones
> leave us alone on the road.

As they withdraw "the light of their presence," darkness closes in, leaving the younger poets feeling lost, confused, anxious, leaving them with the painful obligation of learning to live with words. But "we have the words in our pockets, / obscure directions"—a sentence we can read as saying that we have both words and obscure directions and that we have words that *are* obscure directions, an ambiguity that shows one of the ways in which Levertov embodies "obscure directions" in her own words. The description of the words as "in our pockets" makes them sound like raisins brought along on a hike; along with "grief, mercy," "tangerine, weather," *"language"* is taken in, absorbed, transformed "into *our* flesh *our* / deaths." Moreover, the very obscurity of the directions and the sense of language itself as mystery allow both for continuity and for plenty of space for difference from the previous generation. The darkening landscape in which the young poets are left—a long road surrounded by "deep woods"—is one that similarly combines direction and obscurity, linearity and digression. Near the end of "September 1961" Levertov writes:

> One can't reach
>
> the sea on this endless
> road to the sea unless
> one turns aside at the end, it seems,
>
> follows
> the owl that silently glides above it
> aslant, back and forth,
>
> and away into deep woods.

"The road leads to the sea," Levertov declared earlier in the poem. What the sea represents, however, is never made clear: it may be death awaiting us at the end of the road of life; it may be eternity; it may be vigorous, primitive life, as the poem's final image ("we think the night wind carries / a smell of the sea") suggests. Throughout the poem the end of the journey remains indefinite; so does the route. We are told that the road is "end-less," yet two lines later an "end" is assumed. The only way to reach the sea, moreover, is by turning aside into the woods—"it *seems*." The endless journey toward a mysterious end is not a simple linear one; nor is the reader's movement through the poem, which often turns aside before continuing forward. The act of turning off the road is described through the image of the owl, an image that catches the poet's imagination and which, in a seeming digression, she "turns aside" to "follow"; by doing so, she comes to the image of the "deep woods," which balances and completes the image of the road. Again and again the writing allows the reader to experience "obscure directions," and the poet relates to her reader as her guides had to her—as someone who initiates into mysteries, then withdraws. "Knowing there was mystery, they could go," as do the young poets in "September 1961."

The images of the house in "To the Muse" and the road in "September 1961" reveal Levertov's manner of constantly accepting, and then dis-solving, boundaries. In "The Novel" she develops an analogy between the lives of two characters in a work of fiction and the creative life of its author. These characters "live (when they live) in fear // of blinding, of burning, of choking under a / mushroom cloud in the year of the roach." Like their author, they feel "cramped" and would like to take "a thick black / magic marker," strike out all restricting circumstances, and attain "the eternity / of today." The hemmed-in Allen Ginsberg breaks out by means of apocalyptic transcendence—pure magic; but in Levertov self-hood is earned within the limits—physical, temporal, domestic—of secular life, an acceptance that makes possible those moments when we "halt, stretch, a vision / breaks in on the cramped grimace, / inscape of trans-formation." Only within the house or along the road can we experience the magical extensions of the real: the poetics of magical realism. Levertov gives us not transcendent but immanent vision.

Her poems, in fact, are strongest when they combine linearity with mystery, definition with obscurity. When she goes wrong, it's because she doubts herself or her reader and so floods the poem with light; darkness is destroyed, not experienced. Sometimes, particularly at the ends of poems, mystery is lost in directives and/or explanations. While hosing down "The Garden Wall," Levertov suddenly uncovers "a hazy red, a / grain gold, a mauve / of small shadows, sprung / from the quiet dry brown—"; but Levertov, nervous about significance, converts her par-ticular experience into a general point about discovery: "archetype / of the world always a step / beyond the world, that can't / be looked for, only / as the eye wanders, / found." These lines also illustrate a propensity in Levertov and in Black Mountain poetry generally: to write too many poems about the writing of poetry, so that the poet spends too much time fussing over procedures, too little time deploying them. Elsewhere, Levertov uses familiar (or archetypal) symbolism without sufficient grounding, so that the tropes seem imposed. They have not, in terms of Levertov's own poetic, been taken *in* and given substance. "To the Muse," with its figures of the house, the garden, the hearth, the cave, and the tower, is such a poem; "Claritas" is another. "The All-Day Bird, the artist, / whitethroated sparrow," the poem begins, immediately appropriating the bird for one of Levertov's favorite themes, the poetic process. It is no surprise, then, that in the poem's closing section—

>Sun
>light.
>   Light
>light light light.

—all specific reality, all precise distinctions, all *"shadow of a difference,"* disappear in a celebration of pure radiance.

In "The Runes," a prose poem that closes *O Taste and See,* Levertov writes, "In city, in suburb, in forest, no way to stretch out the arms—so if you would grow, go straight up or deep down." Trees fascinate Levertov, perhaps because they go both straight up *and* deep down. Her poems are most successful when they are at least "half in darkness" (*OTS,* p. 6)— a quality that can be found in "Shalom," a poem that comes immediately after "Claritas" as if to balance its simple ascent. "A man growing old is going / down the dark stairs," Levertov begins.

>He has been speaking of the Soul
>tattooed with the Law.
>Of dreams
>burnt in the bone.

Another of those guides who appears, then withdraws, the old man has been speaking of wisdom, of yearnings, and of sufferings, so ancient they are part of his (and our) very nature, soul and body. As he passes downward he looks up "to the friends who lean / out of light and wine / over the well of stairs." Outwardly comfortable, they are inwardly uneasy, asking his "pardon / for the dark they can't help" because they, like the director's wife in "The Film" ("The darkness / should not be revealed," she insists), they themselves fear the darkness. But at this point the poem makes a series of striking temporal and metaphorical leaps, obscure jumps that transform end to beginning, darkness to light:

Starladen Babylon
buzzes in his blood, an ancient
pulse. The rivers
run out of Eden.
Before Adam
Adam blazes.

The poem seems to spiral backwards in time, from present to Babylon to Eden and "before" even that. In reality, however, time is not a linear sequence, and human experience constantly returns upon itself, branching in new ways. The moment is elusive—"what is passing // is here," she writes in "The Coming Fall"—but within it, here, are both recurrence and new experience. The moment, then, contains the Eden from which Levertov had thought she was banished in *The Double Image*, the magical world to which she now returns; *O Taste and See* takes us "back into life, back to the gods" (*OTS*, p. 65). In the figure of the aging man, seemingly a victim of time, the search for the light (as in "starladen Babylon") persists, passionate, buzzing in his blood, an ancient pulse. He carries forward an archetypal search. But as words like "tattooed" and "burnt" suggest, it is in descending the stairs, living inside the elusive and often agonizing reality of time—rather than limiting ourselves to the "light and wine" of a comfortable existence—that a full, passionate search becomes possible. Moreover, it is not in the arrival at some final end that illumination lies; rather, it is the burning intensity with which the search itself is conducted that makes the old man blaze even as he descends to the darkness. When we reach the line "Before Adam," we expect the next line to assume a simple temporal sequence and name someone, something, that came earlier than Adam; instead, "Adam blazes" asserts that Adam, being eternal, lives now, in the old man. His descent toward death can be compared with Adam's exile from Eden; both are radiant in their acceptance of, entry into, a life that includes pain and death. In the mythology of *O Taste and See*, the descent of the old man, like the "fall" of Adam, is a fortunate one, as we have already seen in the title poem. "Shalom" closes, then, with the old man's acceptance of the dark passages in human experience:

"It's alright," answers
the man going down,
"it's alright—there are many
avenues, many corridors of the soul
that are dark also.
Shalom."

Images of a light discovered in darkness, as in "Shalom," recur throughout *O Taste and See;* there is the light of the moon at night (p. 25), the bright movie screen in a dark theater (pp. 18–19), the "field / of sparks" moving "in darkness" (p. 15), "golden pollen" falling from "dark trees" (p. 13), and "dark" figures "outlined" by the setting sun in "a fur of gold," "a blur defining them" (pp. 38–39). The muse herself is a light, a "gold ring," that is hidden, obscure. Such images define a kind of wholeness, the poet's striving to take into the poem "*all* that lives." As the contrast between "Claritas" and "Shalom" suggests, however, she most often realizes this wholeness when she goes "deep down" rather than "straight up."

Sometimes, as we have seen, Levertov's endings make significance all too explicit, so that the poem becomes more an act of will than of discovery. At other times, however, her endings tactfully draw a boundary around experience at the same time that they open fresh perspectives that extend the poem "beyond the end." The last line of "The Film"—"So be it"—marks the completion of the movie's effect on the poet's mind and so the beginning of a new sense of reality. "September 1961" ends: "we don't / stop walking, we know / there is far to go, sometimes // we think the night wind carries / a smell of the sea. . . ." Images of the road and the sea circle the reader back to the beginning of the poem, but with the mood now changed from anxiety to tenacity, fortified by occasional but indefinite hints ("we *think*") that they are headed in the right direction, and the ellipsis at the very end both suspends the mystery of their quest and defines it as an ongoing one, just as the series of present participles at the end of "O Taste and See" characterizes the process of taking the world in as a continuous one. Often, Levertov's poems will end with a dark orphic utterance ("A silence / of waking at night into speech," p. 23) or, more often, with a very suggestive concrete image that, at first, seems to follow out of nothing that has come before in the poem. The end of "The Coming Fall" provides an instance: "—a wisdom, // a shiver, a delight / that what is passing // is here, as if / a snake went by, green in the / gray leaves." Earlier in the poem Levertov had resisted the change of season; at the end she moves into the flow of time, her lively awareness of its full nature expressed in the quick turns from "shiver" to "delight," from "what is passing" to "is here," in the similar balancing of green snake and gray leaves. Though at first it seems a surprising turn of thought, the image of the snake follows out from what has come before; but it also has rich suggestions that take us off in new directions. It is hard to read of snakes and not to think of the Garden of Eden, and once we do, we read the poem's title "The Coming Fall" in a new sense. We may then see the "human figures dark on the hill / outlined" by the "last sunlight" as Adam and Eve about to leave the Garden, and, in fact, we may see the whole landscape of the poem as at once literal and suggestive of a postlapsarian Eden. Yet in this landscape of "somber beauty" (p. 80) snakes are not symbols of evil; they are simply animals that make us "shiver" with fear or delight. "The Coming Fall" marks an invigorating change, one that takes us back into life, and just as autumn begins as well as ends something, the end of the poem provides an image that both achieves closure and evokes new beginnings. At its close, the Levertov poem simultaneously returns upon itself and branches a new way.

But one of Levertov's most impressive achievements in *O Taste and See* is in her questioning of her own poetic aims and achievements in "Say the Word," a short story that, beneath its simple, almost flat surface, yields complex implications. The story takes place at an old farmhouse where the main character's husband and son are clearing the land of alders—"not wholesale but with judgment—to *reveal the form of the land* and give back some of the space years of neglect had stolen" (my emphasis). When the woman spontaneously mentions that a poplar which is blocking her view of some distant mountains "needs cutting," the two men eagerly take up the task. She loves mountains, strong silent presences with "dignity" and "distance," but as soon as she has "said the word," she becomes uneasy about cutting down the tree. At the end, when the poplar has been cleared, the man and boy are triumphant, while she feels "loneliness and confusion"—until she looks up to see "the last of daylight, and against it the far mountains were ranged, a wistful blue, remote and austere."

"Say the Word" affirms Levertov's preference for a landscape that is half wild, half domesticated, for a space that is open yet enclosed by distant mountains. One day the family picnics at a nearby abandoned farm where the overgrowth has "begun to close it in, block the horizon" and create a "melancholy" feeling. In contrast, their pruning and cutting reveal "the form of the land" on their own farm, where the atmosphere is one of "lightness and calm." Yet the story focuses most on the central character's fears that she is cruelly imposing her own wishes on the landscape. Is she revealing the "true form" of the place or thrusting one upon it? Unlike Olson and Ginsberg, Levertov does not project coercion outward onto a mythic abstraction like Moloch, but instead explores such propensities, and the possibility of controlling them, within herself. As a result, she comes to the realistic recognition that being in the world involves changing and even violating it—"not wholesale but with judgment." We may respond that it is not easy to say where good judgment ends and wholesale imposition begins, but that's exactly Levertov's point: the difficulty of exercising individual judgment when we no longer have the support of some external value system. Both the title of the story and its preoccupation with pruning, with cutting away, to uncover a hidden form suggest that Levertov is also thinking about the difficulties of writing, of forming experiences into wholes that will not just manifest an anxious craving for mastery. In Levertov, making and judging are not, a priori, coercive and inauthentic activities, as they are in much contemporary writing. She affirms a possible reciprocity—"an interpenetration, both ways." So at the end of "Say the Word" she is elated when the "remote and austere" mountains are suddenly revealed; she questions, explores doubts, but does not finally reject her poetics of discovery.

As in *The Double Image,* the vision of Eden provides a unifying myth in *O Taste and See,* as we might expect in a book so preoccupied with origins; but Levertov now deals with this theme with an emotional toughness and literary inventiveness that allow her to *real*ize it in a way it had not been realized in her earlier work. Of course, the very presence of a unifying myth confirms, again, that Levertov possesses a vision that exists prior to and in fact enables her particular acts of "discovery." But Levertov's representation of the theme makes her poems seem, at best, convincing artistic illusions of such moments of discovery. For one thing, Eden enters these poems not as a mythical narrative but as a series of glimpses, as if in spontaneous moments of vision. Sometimes the allusions to Eden are explicit, as in "The Old Adam," "Another Spring," "The Stonecarver's Poem," and "Shalom." At other times, they are implied, as in the garden in "The Figure of Time," the snake in "The Coming Fall," or in the title poem. Moreover, Levertov does not repeat but actively takes in and revises the Judeo-Christian version of the myth. The poems "Sparks" and "O Taste and See" explicitly reverse biblical injunctions, which Levertov sees as fearfully preoccupied with ends rather than beginnings. "The threat / of the world's end is the old threat," she says in "Sparks," and in a playful rewriting of the medieval lyric, "Who Is at My Window," she calls the fear of both death and life "the old song." "The Old Adam" is a man who pines nostalgically over "a photo of someone else's childhood, / a garden in another country"; he wants to repeat an idealized past that was never his in the first place, a particularly ironic form of "mourning or ghostwalking." Neither outside time nor fully in it, the old Adam, like J. Alfred Prufrock but unlike the vigorous old man in "Shalom," merely grows old with a "floating / sense of loss." If fear is "the old song," mourning is "the lost way."

Against the old man's craving for repetition, Levertov posits an Eden in the here and now, the prospect of "living in the orchard and being // hungry, and plucking / the fruit." But the Eden that remains as a perpetual possibility for Levertov is no simple idealization; it coexists with pain, "the ache of marriage," a sense of "what is passing," temporality and

death itself. According to "Another Spring," "Death in us goes on //
testing the wild / chance of living / as Adam chanced it." Adam ate the
forbidden fruit in spite of the threat of death as punishment; he risked
death in order to extend his experience. His fall was fortunate, then,
because with it Adam entered time, a mortal body, in which, as we've
seen, "Adam blazes." "I could replace / God for awhile," Levertov writes,
somewhat pretentiously, in "Earth Psalm"; she could reject him "to
worship *mortal*," who is, she says, "the summoned / god who has speech,"
the muse who dwells in "our flesh our / deaths." The magical world is
immanent in the real world. "Paradise," says Levertov in "Kingdoms of
Heaven," lies "within you"; death, in "Another Spring," "goes on in
us." In the poems of *O Taste and See*, Levertov again and again says the
words that incarnate her double image of life, its fears and its promises,
that she had sought but missed in her first book.

SEVEN

James Wright

"I work like hell, clipping away perhaps one tiny pebble per day from the ten-mile-thick granite wall of formal and facile 'technique' which I myself erected, and which now stands ominously between me and whatever poetry may be in me."[1]

—James Wright

"To plumb the fall
Of silver on ripple, evening ripple on wave,
Quick celebration where she lives for light,
I let all measures die."[2]

—James Wright

Another influential alternative to the formalist poetic of the fifties was developed by the poets of the "deep image"—a group that included Robert Bly, Louis Simpson, William Stafford, and James Wright. These poets, lacking the geographical center that the beat, Black Mountain, and New York poets had, were an even looser cluster of writers. In the late fifties and early sixties, Bly lived on a farm in western Minnesota; Simpson taught first in New York City and later in Berkeley, California; Stafford taught in Portland, Oregon; and Wright in Minneapolis. In fact, to all these men inwardness and isolation were crucial to their program for poetry. Nevertheless, there was personal contact, correspondence, and familiarity with each other's published work, and their common interest in what Bly has called "the modern poetry of the deep images of the unconscious" defines this group as a self-conscious *movement* in contemporary poetry.[3]

Excerpts from this chapter appeared in *American Poetry Review* 11 (March–April 1982): 39–46.

1. James Wright to Theodore Roethke, August 5, 1958; the letter, along with 29 other letters from Wright to Roethke, is contained in the Roethke collection at the University of Washington; this and subsequent quotations from the Roethke collection are made with the kind permission of the University of Washington and Mr. Wright.

2. "The Morality of Poetry," *Collected Poems* (Middletown, Conn., 1972), pp. 60–61; all subsequent references to this book will be made in the text with the abbreviation *CP*.

3. "On English and American Poetry," *Fifties* 2 (1959): 47. Subsequent references to Bly's critical essays are made in the text with the following abbreviations: *IRB*, Kathy Otto and Cynthia Lofsness, "An Interview with Robert Bly," *Tennessee Poetry Journal* 2 (Winter 1969): 29–48; *DW*, "The Dead World and the Live World," *Sixties* 8 (1966): 2–7; *WRC*, "The Work of Robert Creeley," *Fifties* 2 (1959): 10–21; *WT*, "A Wrong Turning in American Poetry," *Choice* 3 (1963): 33–47.

The catalyst in this movement was clearly the dynamic figure of Bly, whose early theories provide the best context for reading James Wright, who was at once deeply affected by them and able to elude many of their dangers and oversimplifications. Bly's response to the poetic crisis of the fifties was not to turn to the marginal figures either of romanticism (Ginsberg's Blake and Whitman) or of American modernism (Black Mountain's Williams and Pound) but to a neglected aspect of a neglected movement—surrealism. In 1956, while on a Fulbright in Oslo, Norway, Bly discovered the work of "men like Pablo Neruda, Juan Ramón Jiménez, César Vallejo, George Trakl" and felt "avenues opening into kinds of imagination that I sort of dimly sensed somewhere off on the horizon, but I had never actually seen in words" (*IRB,* p. 30). Bly had hit upon what had become of surrealism once it left France and entered (especially) the work of Spanish and Latin American poets, in whose writing, as Paul Zweig puts it, "the explosive imagery and the torrential rhythms of automatic writing became charged with Whitmanesque emotion."[4] On his return to this country Bly decided a "good service" could be performed by starting a magazine that would print translations of the European and Latin American poets he admired and that would also, with Bly filling the role of self-appointed literary conscience, publish fairly lengthy critical estimates of young American poets that would try "to make criticisms that would be of real value to the poet himself" (*IRB,* pp. 30–31). To this end Bly founded *Fifties* (later *Sixties* and *Seventies*) as well as his own press, which published books of translations (mainly by himself and Wright) of the poetry of Trakl, Vallejo, and Neruda. Thus pointing to innovative possibilities through translations and by cracking the whip over the heads of errant contemporaries, Bly hoped to—and did—open avenues to the "new imagination."

But what, exactly, is this "new imagination"? And what, exactly, is a "deep image" and how can one be discriminated from the images of imagism? Theoretical statements turn out to be surprisingly hard to come by; this movement produced no equivalent to Olson's "Projective Verse," no full-scale articulation of its ultimate premises and characteristic procedures. Bly, the most likely source of such a statement, writes more as a polemical defender than as an expounder of his views. The closest thing to a theoretical manifesto occurs in Robert Kelly's "Notes on the Poetry of the Deep Image," in which he argues that deep images transform "the perceived world," that while the line is a "breath period" punctuated by "key silences," "centrality of image" must replace Olson's "centrality of syllable and line," that "rhythm of the images" can be counterpointed

---

4. "The New Surrealism," *Salmagundi* 22–23 (Spring–Summer 1973): 274.

against "rhythm of the breath expressed in line," and that poetic language must be based on American speech.[5] But Kelly's essay seems mainly both an assimilation of and an answer to Olson's "Projective Verse," and it remains silent on the critical issue of the nature and kind of transformations of the perceived world that deep images perform.

Occasional remarks from Bly's polemical essays and reviews do take us a bit further. In "The Dead World and the Live World" Bly calls for "a poetry that goes deep into the human being, much deeper than the ego, and at the same time is aware of many other beings" (*DW*, p. 6). Like Creeley's "form is never more than an extension of content," Bly's proposals may strike us as blandly familiar, unless we return them to their historical context, where we can appreciate their liberating force as an alternative to the literary hegemony of the fifties. Bly often derides the rapprochement between the poet and the middle class at this time, and the poems of his first book, *Silence in the Snowy Fields* (1962), are solitary, rural, contemplative, and serenely visionary—alien and critical in these fairly traditional ways. In his essays as well, Bly continually endorses inwardness and solitude, a descent to the unconscious which makes possible imaginative leaps, metaphoric transformations, images that arise from the depths of the psyche. Out of such an imaginative process will evolve poems "in which everything is said by image, and nothing by direct statement at all. The poem *is* the images, images touching all the senses, uniting the world beneath and the world above" (*WRC*, p. 14). Like Olson, Bly identifies discursiveness as the malignancy that is sapping the life from American poetry but, rather than Olson's swift movement, "instanter, from one perception to the next," Bly urges a slow descent to the deep images of the unconscious.

According to Bly, in fact, practically all twentieth-century English and American poetry has been guilty of a flight from inwardness. "A Wrong Turning in American Poetry" occurred with modernism, which placed "more trust in the objective, outer world than in the inner world," considered the poem "to be a construction independent of the poet," and drove "toward the extinction of personality" (*WT*, pp. 33, 37, 35). From this point of view Olson, for whom "the poet's inwardness is 'lyrical interference' " (*DW*, p. 36), continues rather than overturns modernism. To put American poetry back on the straight and narrow path, Bly recommends Neruda, Vallejo, Jiménez, Machado, Rilke, for whom poetry is not a self-extinction but

an extension of the substance of the man, no different from his skin or his hands. The substance of the man who wrote the poem reaches

5. "Notes on the Poetry of the Deep Image," *Trobar* 2 (1961): 14–16.

> far out into the darkness and the poem is his whole body, seeing with his ears and his fingers and his hair. Impersonal poets construct; great poets merely are sensitive. [*WT,* p. 36]

Bly's fundamental opposition between discursive and deep image writing, like that of Olson between closed and open poetry, provides yet another version of a duality persistent in literary theory since romanticism: between ordinary and literary language, between science and poetry. And again like Olson, Bly is not a dialectical thinker; he continually sets up pairs of contraries only to identify the virtuous with one side, the demonic with the other. Discursive utterances, in this account, are dissociated, existentially impoverished and manipulative, while a poem which "is images," Bly makes clear, possesses the integrity, vitality, and fullness of physical "substance" ("the poem is his whole body"); the image, in brief, makes the word flesh—with the emphasis now falling not on taking in the external world ("plucking / the fruit" from the "orchard") but on inwardness and reverie, plucking images from the depths of the mind.

Arbitrary, private associations and ultimately solipsism constitute the dangers for poems evolved in accordance with this program for poetry, but Bly actually makes the unconscious the basis for community. At the prelogical and primordial levels of his psyche the poet experiences the interdependency of all life, participating in an energy he shares with the natural world, with other human beings, and thus with readers. In this intersubjective force we have the ground of Bly's poetics; and it is a sacred ground. If Freudian psychology enabled Robert Lowell to grasp and to present his private psyche, Jungian assumptions shape Bly's concept of the unconscious. As Paul Breslin points out in "How to Read the New Contemporary Poem," Freudian interpretations try to "recover part of our self-knowledge, part of our response to the external world, which we had disowned and feared," but in the Jungian view "we must give ourselves over to the unconscious as to a god whose scripture is the dream"—or in Bly, the image.[6] Freudian understanding of the historical self generates Lowell's version of confessional poetry; Jungian notions of the unconscious as "a well-spring of religious revelation" issue in Bly's deep image poetry.

As Bly's denunciation of the modernist faith in objects and in the poem *as* object suggests, his images are not mimetic ones. Imagism he dismisses as "Picturism" in order to affirm "a poem in which the image is released from imprisonment among objects" (*WT,* pp. 40, 47). Rather than imitating, deep images transform the perceived world in ways that startle the

6. "How to Read the New Contemporary Poem," *American Scholar* 77 (Summer 1978): 363.

conscious mind into awareness of our hidden connections with the perceived world. On the one hand, there is the "poetry that is locked inside
the ego" (*DW,* p. 2), a man-centered verse written by just about everyone
who has ever written except for Bly, his associates, and his mentors; this
category especially includes confessional poets like Lowell, even though
we have already seen that *Life Studies* provides a critique *not* an instance
of the "locked ego." On the other hand, there is the "poetry that reaches
out in waves over everything that is alive." Like Ginsberg proclaiming
that "Everything is holy!" or Levertov taking in "all that lives," Bly
claims inclusiveness. Yet Bly's espousal of a poetry that acknowledges
man's interdependence with nature (and his attacks on man-centered poetry that does not acknowledge it) reveals that his poetics of the deep
image is not, à la Olson, a purportedly value-free *method* for writing but
a specific *content,* an ideology, with its own hierarchies and exclusions.
One consequence is that Bly's journeys into the unconscious turn up
images for a unity that Bly knew was there before he even started; the
wild imaginative leaps that he advocates are enabled and finally con-
strained by doctrine. Unlike Lowell, Levertov, and O'Hara, all of whom
in their different ways at least raise the possibility that they may be
creating and imposing what they claim to be discovering, Bly never en-
tertains such self-doubts, all the more surprising since his word "image"
suggests an illusory creation rather than substantial being. Hence, as
Charles Altieri points out, Bly's "metaphors frequently ask to be taken
as literally true relationships," as literally true disclosures, we may add,
of sacred truths.[7]

Yet the model of mind entailed by his account of the poetic process
creates at least two crucial problems for Bly. Once Bly has turned his
back on the ego and begun his dive into the psychic depths, he has left
behind him all the mental gear that would allow him to judge particular
images as good or bad, true or false—just as he has repudiated that part
of his mind that would permit him to become self-conscious about his
creations. The result is that, in theory at least, Bly has no alternative but
to accept all images granted by the unconscious as sacred truths. This
dilemma helps explain, in turn, Bly's wrathful impatience with writers
who profess any interest in craft; he often makes fun of the Black Mountain group, for example, for talking as if the breaking of the lines were
more important than what they had to say. But Bly's own theory cannot
account or even allow for all those acts of selecting, weighing, revising
that go into the actual making of a poem. He really *does* mean it—he *has*
to mean it—when he says that "great poets merely are sensitive." Like

7. *Enlarging the Temple,* p. 90.

both Olson and Ginsberg, Bly can only imagine a will that is coercive and inauthentic; and having done *that,* he has no choice but to cut away this corrupt faculty—leaving him with a simplified model of the poetic process.

Bly's theories are oppositional and salvationist, at once impassioned and rigid. Yet, whatever their inadequacies as theory, they *were* generative—nowhere more than in the case of James Wright. We can get a still more concrete sense of this poetic and of its key term, "deep image," by looking at a poem from Wright's third book, *The Branch Will Not Break* (1963).

Spring Images

Two athletes
Are dancing in the cathedral
Of the wind.

A butterfly lights on the branch
Of your green voice.

Small antelopes
Fall asleep in the ashes
Of the moon.

What strikes us first about this poem is the use of such phrases as "the cathedral / Of the wind," "the branch / of your green voice," "the ashes / Of the moon"; each of them involves a kind of magical transformation of the perceived world. Or, to put it more precisely, each of the poem's stanzas enacts the process of such a transformation: a word that we at first take literally ("cathedral," "branch," "ashes") becomes metaphorical by way of an imaginative leap that coincides with the breaking of the line. The metamorphosis in the second stanza involves a radical kind of metaphor—synesthesia (in "green voice")—and all three metaphors have a similar quality in their linking of impossible-to-join nouns: cathedral, wind; branch, voice; ashes, moon. It is this distance between the two terms of his metaphors that has prompted many critics to describe Wright as surrealist; yet this label disguises the crucial fact that Wright's images (like Bly's) embody a vision that is closer to that of Walt Whitman than that of André Breton. Each of these "spring images" (perhaps suggesting "leaping images" as well as "images of spring") evokes a natural harmony, a feeling that becomes stronger as the poem goes on. The joyous vigor of the athletes merges them with the motion of the wind, its swirling movements felt as a lofty, sacred yet light and soothing presence; the butterfly seems to trust the "green" (alive and sturdy and supportive) voice enough to light on it in a double sense—just as the young antelopes trust the nighttime world enough to fall asleep in spite of the cold, dead "ashes." This confidence is well placed, since the "ashes" turn out to be spots of moonlight. Each of the three stanzas suggests a benign, protective presence, a supportive context for life's rhythms: vigor, lightness, repose. Again, it is precisely the confidence in such a ground of support that permits Wright's imaginative leaps; the poem defines a vision that is dramatized in its bold language.

How do Wright's spring images differ from the images of imagism? Because a term like "imagism" clamps together some fairly divergent ways of writing, it would be easy to exaggerate the difference by comparing Wright's poem with, say, Williams's "The Red Wheelbarrow." Williams effaces his personality before the bare object, while Wright magically transforms the object. When Bly denounced imagism as "Picturism," he probably had a poem like "The Red Wheelbarrow"—actually written several years after imagism had collapsed—in mind. But take a more troublesome example—Pound's "Metro" poem: "The apparition of these faces in the crowd; / Petals on a wet, black bough." Both the Wright and the Pound poems participate in a recurrent poetic project of the last hundred and fifty years; to *present* images, without comment. Both poems also generate poetic energy by the startling juxtaposition of images, and they seem even closer when we recall Pound's account of his poem as recording that instant when something "outward and objective" "darts to a thing inward and subjective."[8] Yet, even though they abjure explicit comment, the Wright and Pound poems say very different things by the *way* they present images. Wright blends where Pound keeps distinct. Pound offers the superpositioning of two images that remain separate; Wright offers the process of transforming the literal into the metaphoric: his images are fused. Pound gives us a self-reflexive artifact, the autotelic poem; Wright gives us the poem as a passage—into an awareness of the secret forces linking man and the natural world.

Wright had met Bly by the late summer of 1958. Upon reading the first issue of *Fifties,* Wright wrote Bly a letter, sixteen single-spaced pages long, and Bly responded by inviting Wright (then living in Minneapolis) to visit at his farm in Rochester, Minnesota.[9] The two men quickly became close, at a time of both personal and literary crisis in Wright's life. "I felt that, for myself, a certain kind of poetry had come to an end," Wright later told an interviewer, "and I thought that I would stop writing poetry completely."

8. *Memoir of Gaudier-Brzeska* (London and New York, 1916), p. 103.
9. See letter from Wright to Roethke, 18 August 1958, and "The Art of Poetry XIX: James Wright," *Paris Review* 62 (Summer 1965): 48.

Robert Bly suggested to me that there is a kind of poetry that can be written. People have written it in some other languages. He said it might be possible to come back to our own language through reading them and translating them, and I think that in one sense this has been the value of translation. It led me into some areas of thought, and of rhythm also, that I hadn't tried to work out before.[10]

Three of Wright's poems appeared in the second issue of *Fifties* (1959), along with the grandiose (and misleading) announcement that, with them, Wright had abandoned "nineteenth century poetry";[11] and during the early sixties, as they collaborated on their translations of Neruda, Vallejo, and Trakl, Wright and Bly remained in close contact. A much less theoretical poet than Bly, Wright had found an ideal friend and literary mentor: he seems to have ignored the irritating oversimplifications of Bly's polemics while making rich use of the imaginative avenues his friend opened for him.

At first, however, in *The Green Wall* and *St. Judas,* Wright emerged as a young poet with a dark vision and a poetic voice that were clearly his own, but which stayed discretely within the accepted boundaries for poetry in the late fifties.[12] His early poems reveal Wright to be a participant in the fifties' revival of traditional forms, though the poems now seem more carefully than skillfully constructed. Wright had derived his faith in disciplined craftsmanship from eminent authorities. As an undergraduate at Kenyon (1948–52), he was a student of John Crowe Ransom's, and later, while a graduate student at the University of Washington, Wright studied creative writing with Theodore Roethke. In short, Wright began his career at the end of a powerful line of succession—a position he seemed at first able to turn to his advantage. He steered away from any major derivation of style from either of these two mentors, though glimpses of

10. Michael André, "An Interview with James Wright," *Unmuzzled Ox* 1 (February 1972): 3.

11. "In the Hard Sun," "In Fear of Harvests," and "They Dream of the American Frontier," *Fifties* 2 (1959): 38, 39, 2. "In the Hard Sun," is an early version of "Goodbye to the Poetry of Calcium," collected in *The Branch Will Not Break* (Middletown, Conn.: Wesleyan University Press, 1963). I should mention here the usefulness of Belle M. McMaster's "James Arlington Wright: A Checklist," *Bulletin of Bibliography* 31 (April–June 1974): 71–88. Such a checklist is particularly helpful for studying Wright, who published many poems in periodicals that he did not collect in books. The bibliography, however, contains one erroneous or at least misleading statement: Ms. McMaster says that the poem "At the Executed Murderer's Grave" (her item #143) "is completely different from the poem collected in [*St. Judas*] under the same title." Nevertheless, it is an early version of that poem; in fact, a close study of this poem, a later version printed in *Poetry,* August 1958 (item #126 in the bibliography) and the final version in *St. Judas* would reveal a good deal about Wright's attempts to break with the style of his early work.

12. On Wright's evolution as a poet, see William Matthews, "The Continuity of James Wright's Poems," *Ohio Review* 18 (Spring–Summer 1977): 44–57. I am indebted throughout this chapter to Robert Hass's brilliant "James Wright," *Ironwood* 10 (1977): 74–96.

the manner of Roethke can be found in *The Green Wall*. What Wright did learn from the two older writers was something deeper—a sense of poetry as an acquired craft. Kenyon offered, he remembered, "a very classical and disciplined kind of education";[13] Roethke "taught mainly the craft, and he, like Berryman and like Lowell, was an entirely conscious craftsman"—a view of Roethke's poetry writing course that is supported by other former students as well as by Roethke himself.[14] "There is a constant effort to remind students that poetry is a classic art and requires that its exponents read intensively in all literatures," Roethke states in "The Teaching Poet."

> Each student is expected to revise pieces when necessary and to preserve successive versions in a workbook handed in at the end of the course. He also includes the results of his reading in a selective anthology of his own making—somewhat on the order of Edith Sitwell's *Notebooks*—consisting of remarks on craft, good lines, poems, anything that has been genuinely pertinent to his development.[15]

Wright took the poetry class from Roethke in the spring of 1954, and most of the workbook he submitted for the course can now be read among the Roethke papers at the University of Washington. Much of the project was devoted to single line exercises; Wright was asked, for example, to write a series of three beat lines with the caesura after the first syllable, then with the pause after the second syllable, and so on. Subsequent exercises vary both the length of the line and its syntax—lines with triads of nouns, pairs of nouns, parallel constructions, and the like. In addition, many of Wright's lines are accompanied by model lines, quoted from the whole range of English literature from Wyatt to Yeats. The exercises may in part have been contrived out of Roethke's own habit of composing in single lines, and Wright was sometimes annoyed by them: at one point he complained that the assignments had undercut his capacity to write any whole poems. Still, as Richard Hugo points out, recalling similar exercises in "Stray Thoughts on Roethke and Teaching," the exercises say, "give up what you think you have to say, and you'll find something better," and for Wright they *were* productive.[16] At least two of the poems later collected in *The Green Wall*, "To a Troubled Friend" and "Poem: For Kathleen Ferrier," were originally written for this course.

13. Joseph R. McElrath, Jr., "Something to Be Said for the Light: A Conversation with James Wright," *Southern Humanities Review* 6 (Spring 1972): 137.
14. "The Art of Poetry XIX: James Wright," p. 42. For two accounts of Roethke as a teacher of creative writing, see Richard Hugo, "Stray Thoughts on Roethke and Teaching," *American Poetry Review* 3 (January–February 1974): 50–51, and John Haislip, "The Example of Theodore Roethke," *Northwest Review* 14 (Spring 1975): 14–20.
15. *On the Poet and His Craft*, ed. Ralph J. Mills, Jr. (Seattle and London, 1965), p. 47.
16. "Stray Thoughts on Roethke and Teaching," p. 51.

As a result of both temperament and training, then, the young Wright's response to early modernism was, like that of many of his contemporaries, to participate in the revival of traditional forms, to look away from the now exhausted line of descent from Eliot as well as from the more immediate and possibly even more threatening presence of Ransom and Roethke—and to identify his work with somewhat more obscure and more "classical" poetic origins. "I've tried hard to write in the mode of Robert Frost and Edwin Arlington Robinson," Wright declared on the dust jacket of *The Green Wall*. "I've wanted to make my poems say something humanly important instead of just showing off with language." This statement is perhaps nowhere more characteristic of its time than in its bold assertion of an unarguable truth as the basis for a poetic program. Who, after all, is in favor of "showing off with language"? Nevertheless, in his cautious way, Wright is tossing a spear in the direction of the self-referential and "well-wrought" language of the symbolist poem, and he clearly announces his attempt to find in the New England tradition a vital alternative to the dominant mode.

"The trouble with your poems, Frost, is that they have subjects," Stevens patronizingly informed his fellow New Englander. In many respects, the poetry of Robinson and Frost offered a rich and unique set of possibilities for a young poet in the 1950s, not just because their work was then relatively unexplored but precisely because their poems do have "subjects," and realistic ones, not "bric brac," as Frost had (in return) accused Stevens. Robinson and Frost are neither system builders nor myth makers; they reject both radical innovation and *poesie pure*. Both attempted what Frost, describing Robinson, called "the old-fashioned way to be new," and so their work, while adhering to traditional forms, represents ordinary characters, located in identifiable places, speaking actual speech.[17] And it was precisely this realism that made the New England poets potentially so useful to poets, like Wright, seeking an alternative to symbolist poetics.

Yet Wright's actual use of these well-chosen predecessors constitutes an attenuation, not an extension, of the possibilities in their verse, for what could have been most generative in their work—their poetic realism—is just what Wright misses. The many dramatic poems in *The Green Wall* and *St. Judas* (focused on the defeated and the dispossessed) offer one piece of evidence for Wright's attempt to draw upon the poetry of the New Englanders; but the poems lack the specificity of character, locale, and language to be convincing. In fact, their language remains

17. The phrase is from Frost's "Introduction to Robinson's *King Jasper*," in *Robert Frost: Poetry and Prose*, ed. Edward C. Lathem and Lawrence Thompson (New York, 1972), pp. 346–53.

misty partly because the characters are so obviously projections of the poet's own emotional concerns; the poems are finally lyric rather than dramatic. In one interview Wright praised the "tragic" vision of Frost;[18] and in another he placed Robinson as "one of the great poets of the dark side of American experience; and his language is very strict and clear."[19] In his first two books, then, Wright sought tragic feeling, spare language, and the discipline of traditional forms—the "plain language and stubborn skill" we value in a poet like Robinson. But what Wright actually achieved was nostalgic feeling, imprecise diction, and a formal ineptitude that pushed him toward a vagueness of style and emotion.

The poems do make a noble effort toward realistic acknowledgment of the dark side of *personal* experience. "All the beloved lie / In the perpetual savagery of graves," Wright mourns in "The Refusal"; the presiding deities in his early work are what he calls the "cold divinities of death and change" (*CP,* p. 66). It may be the loss of a childhood paradise, as in "A Fit against the Country," or the loss of an idealized self-image, as in "Elegy in a Firelit Room"; it may be the loss of primitive, magical power, as in "The Horse," "The Fishermen," or "On the Skeleton of a Hound"; it may be the loss of a lover ("Complaint," "Paul," "The Accusation," "The Assignation," "The Ghost"), a friend ("Arrangements with Earth for Three Dead Friends"), a brother ("Lament for My Brother on a Hayrake"), or father ("Three Steps to the Graveyard," "Devotions"); but the experience of loss persistently provides the starting point for the poems of Wright's first two books. In their world, external orders have dissolved and the self, ño sovereign power capable of creating its own orders, is continually faced with extinction—nothingness. "I hear the last sea in the Ohio grass, / Heaving a tide of gray disastrousness," Wright declaims near the end of "At the Executed Murderer's Grave"—invoking the gray tide of social and natural forces that threaten to pull the self down to the anonymity of a savage grave.

Wright responds to the world's "brutal formlessness" (*CP,* p. 58) with a variety of mutually conflicting attitudes. At times he endorses the stoic acceptance he found in Robinson and Frost—a personal hardness he extols in "Sappho." At other times he identifies with life's victims—the disaffiliated, the defeated, even (in the poems about George Doty and Caryl Chessman) the criminal, though his compassion for these outsiders, observed as early as Auden's "Foreword" to *The Green Wall,* often seems

18. "The Art of Poetry XIX: James Wright," p. 46.
19. "Something to Be Said for the Light," p. 137. In "The Art of Poetry XIX: James Wright," p. 45, Wright says that when he wrote "St. Judas," he was trying "to write a sonnet that would be a genuine petrarchan sonnet, and at the same time be a dramatic monologue. I got that idea from Robinson."

merely a form of self-pity. In "The Angel," Wright speaks of "the perfect pleasure of the eyes," and in many poems he seeks the *perfect* pleasures of the carefully distanced observer, often, as in the poems about ghosts, a disembodied observer. Many of the poems thus yearn for an austere transcendence—a flight out of the body. Yet just as many poems offer an opposed theme—a preoccupation with the "underground" of human passion, with the wild and demonic, with instinctual energy that can be found in "The Horse," "On the Skeleton of a Hound," "Sappho," and "A Poem about George Doty in the Death House." So what begins as tough-minded acceptance soon drifts toward evasive maneuvers—yearnings for transcendence or for instinctual release.

In poems such as "At the Executed Murderer's Grave" and "St. Judas," Wright attained the stripped intensity of language he found in Robinson; more often, his style, verbose, inexact, and etherealized, leads him to evade the unpleasant realities he is ostensibly struggling to confront. Here are some examples:

A child among the frozen bushes lost,
Breaking the white and rigid twigs between
Fingers more heavenly than hands of dust,
And fingernails more clean.

["Elegy in a Firelit Room"]

And, when it [a quail] sang, you left my hand
To voyage how softly down the even grass.

["The Quail"]

One arm beneath your neck, your legs uprisen,
You blow dark thighs back, back into the dark.

["Morning Hymn to a Dark Girl"]

More likely, though, the laboring feet
Of fieldmouse, hedgehog, moth and hawk.

["At Thomas Hardy's Birthplace, 1953"]

When, as in the last passage, Wright does labor toward specificity, he ends up by giving the moth feet. The poems are filled with fuzzy idealizations, even when they take up harsher subjects, as in "A Poem about George Doty in the Death House." Doty emerges as one of those "underground heroes of hell" that Wright speaks of in the poem to Caryl Chessman, and Doty is mythologized (which is to say, idealized) by way of a terse, oracular style that eliminates any concrete sense of the man, a murderer-rapist. "At the Executed Murderer's Grave" in *St. Judas*

revises this poem from *The Green Wall,* and Wright now speaks of his
"leaning for language on a dead man's voice" in the earlier poem, which
does take its cadence and oracular tone from a man named Yeats. "At
the Executed Murderer's Grave" begins dramatically in a blunt, angry,
literalistic style that is radically different from the passages we have been
looking at:

> My name is James A. Wright, and I was born
> Twenty-five miles from this infected grave,
> In Martins Ferry, Ohio, where one slave
> To Hazel-Atlas Glass became my father.

The new poem moves toward a frank exposure of Wright's identification
with Doty, "dirt of my flesh, defeated, underground." In the earlier poem,
however, Wright had written:

> Caught between sky and earth,
> Poor stupid animal,
> Stripped naked to the wall,
> He saw the blundered birth
> Of daemons beyond sound.
> Sick of the dark, he rose
> For love, and now he goes
> Back to the broken ground.

Not only does Wright speak in a borrowed voice, he also elevates his
subject through the cosmic reverberations of the language as well as
through periodic sentences and balanced constructions in a stanza that
builds neatly toward "he rose" then falls toward its end (and Doty's) in
the "broken ground." In this way Wright simultaneously heroizes the
demonic and maintains his own (and our) final separation from it, a distance necessary to sustain belief in the demon as hero. In the first poem
of his first book ("A Fit against the Country") Wright claims that he has
climbed over "the green wall" and left a now "vacant paradise" behind
him, but in fact he seldom really enters, with his *language,* the hard,
imperfect world outside in the way that Robinson and Frost so often do.

"I advocate a semi-revolution," Frost declared.[20] Such a stance of
balance and moderation—maturely acknowledging human limits while still
pushing the art forward—had a widespread appeal to poets in the fifties,
many of whom felt that modernism was not only exhausted but that its
experimental imperatives had made it wrong from the start. Both Robin-

20. "A Semi-Revolution," *The Poetry of Robert Frost,* ed. Edward Lathem (New York,
1964), p. 363.

son and Frost had experienced critical neglect and even hostility because of the genuine ways in which they did remake the poetic conventions of their day. Even more cautionary than his semirevolutionary models, Wright stayed within the literary conventions of his period, and, as we saw in chapter 2, he was by no means the first young poet in the postwar era to take up Frost as a major model. The literary results of his project were, at best, mixed; but his literary career flourished. At Kenyon he had won the Robert Frost prize for poetry; while a graduate student he published extensively in such journals as *Kenyon, Sewanee, Hudson, Poetry,* and the *New Yorker;* he won the Eunice Tietjens Memorial Award from *Poetry* in 1955 and was made a *Kenyon Review* Fellow for 1958/59; *The Green Wall* was selected by W. H. Auden for the Yale Younger Poets series. Robinson and Frost evolved an old-fashioned way to be new; Wright participated in the new way of being old-fashioned.

Yet in spite of this success, Wright felt at the completion of *St. Judas* that his work had reached a "dead end." "After I finished that book I had finished with poetry forever. I truly believed that I had said what I had to say as clearly and directly as I could, and that I had no more to do with this art."[21] Yet Wright elsewhere suggests that the problem was not so much the exhaustion of material for poetry as the limitations of his means, no longer adequate for what he did have to say. *St. Judas,* Wright told an interviewer, was "very strict and careful in its form," but in retrospect "it seemed to leave out so much of life."[22] This assessment of his dilemma is supported by the harsh self-estimate written in a letter to Roethke in the summer of 1958. "My stuff stinks," Wright declared, "because it is *competent.*" He had begun "with nothing but absolutely unbearable clumsiness," Wright went on, and so "I deliberately set out to learn the craft"; but now, ironically, he has been "trapped by the very thing—the traditional technique—which I labored so hard to attain." His efforts, of the sort recorded in the workbook, merely left him imprisoned in a "ten-mile-thick granite wall of formal and facile 'technique.' " As a result, he told Roethke, "I've been cracking my own facility, my competence, my dead and dull iambs, to pieces."[23] Wright's problem, as we have seen, was actually more one of *in*competence, but what he is suggesting is that he could not employ traditional forms without adopting an unreal diction and rather severe limitations of mood and subject. Like so many of his contemporaries, then, Wright moved toward the dismantling of traditional technique, the cracking apart of a wall of formal control, a

21. "The Art of Poetry XIX: James Wright," p. 48.
22. "Something to Be Said for the Light," p. 142.
23. James Wright to Theodore Roethke, 5 August 1958.

"breakthrough back into life" which would permit evolution of a new language for poetry.

The character of the shift in Wright's poetry can be defined more precisely by looking at one of the best poems in *St. Judas,* "The Morality of Poetry," a poem in which Wright self-consciously contemplates the change in his work and begins the process of enacting it stylistically. Like such poems as Whitman's "Out of the Cradle" and Stevens's "The Idea of Order at Key West," "The Morality of Poetry" offers a seaside meditation on the relations between mind and world, language and reality. At the start, as Wright muses about the "words" of a young poet (Gerald Enscoe, to whom the poem is dedicated), he sees the "human images" and "human voice" of poetry as our means of achieving clarity and definition in the midst of natural chaos; order, as in Stevens and other moderns, is a purely human construct. So the sea, though "sown and generous" in the opening line, soon becomes associated with whatever is con*fused,* undifferentiated and thus, ultimately, with death; "intricate, cold," "complicated," the sea is a brute force into which all life seems to be passing, like the "hundreds of gulls descending to the froth, / Their bodies clumped and fallen, lost to me." But at just this point of unrelieved despondency, the poem makes the first of its self-revising turns:

> Counting those images, I meant to say
> A hundred gulls decline to nothingness;
> But, high in a cloud, a single naked gull
> Shadows a depth in heaven for the eye.

—just as "under the wail and snarl" of sea sounds "a single human word for love of air / Gathers the tangled discords up to song." At first, all aspiring movement (as in the flight of the gulls) appears to be sinking down to oblivion, but a more discriminating view, associated with the precise activity of "counting," reveals the "single" detail that redeems the desolate seascape, gives it depth and life, and reassures the poet that not all is "lost to me." Significantly, it is "counting" (and later "measure" shows that Wright partly has versification in mind here) that makes possible human clarity and order, definition as opposed to the intricate din of the sea. Poetry, like the lonely, heroic motion of the gull, becomes a form of flight, a measured movement away from the threatening flood of immediate experience—a gathering of "tangled discords *up* to song," expressing "a love of *air*" (or spirit). The flight that Wright imagines here, however, is not an ecstatic release, but a disciplined act. "Summon the rare word for the rare desire," he admonishes Enscoe; language will rise "above the blindness and the noise / Only as long as bones are clean and spare, / The spine exactly set, the muscles lean." Clearly no advocate of either easygoing sensuality or spontaneous inspiration, Wright warns against any relaxing into the body or even into the "body" of language and instead urges a lean, hard, austere style, the product of conscious craftsmanship. Poetic language thus accomplishes a kind of willed transcendence of a "tangled" reality that relentlessly pushes us toward "nothingness"; the poem, achieving such transcendence, manifests a "rare" spirit.

"So through my cold lucidity of heart / I thought to send you careful rules of song," Wright begins the poem's final verse paragraph.

> But gulls ensnare me here; the sun fades; thought
> By thought the tide heaves, bobbing my words' damp wings;
> Mind is the moon-wave roiling on ripples now.

The turn here is even more radical than before. Wright now moves from contemplation to identification with the ocean, from a poetry of detached meditation to one of ecstatic reverie. Accordingly, the will—along with its "careful rules of song"—dissolves, as the poet, wishing "to plumb" the mysteries of moon and sea, lets "all measures die." Poetic language, now enacting immersion rather than willed transcendence, must be renovated, a process that begins in this final paragraph where many of the poem's stylistic features change in a way that suggests surrender rather than control, imagistic reverie rather than discursive thought. In the first two sections verb forms had either revealed Wright's detached, speculative stance ("I stood," "to muse," "I wondered") or they expressed commands ("summon," "starve," "lash")—in either case emphasizing purpose and control. Now both the poet ("gulls ensnare me") and his language ("bobbing my words' damp wings") appear as predicates, and the tense is no longer the past of reflective thought but the present of immediate experience. Moreover, in contrast to the "cold lucidity" of describing the sea with words like "intricate" and "complicated," we get the bold metaphorical leap and richness of sound in "Mind is a moon-wave roiling on ripples now"; and whereas earlier the image of the spare, lean body had been used to illustrate an idea (of discipline), the poem now offers the kind of metaphorical transformations that occur when the boundaries between man and nature—which Wright had been so eager to establish—break down, as in the "mind" as "moon-wave," the equation of "thought" and "tide," of language and bird (in "words' damp wings"), or in the vision of the moon as "woman or bird." The poet has now entered the world, and it is flowing, animalistic, alive with magical transformations.

One result is loss: the words with which he had begun to answer Enscoe fail: "my voice is gone, / My words to you unfinished"; the "human voice" celebrated as a "rare" achievement at the poem's start now collapses, to be replaced by the "echoes of my voice" that Wright provides in the poem's beautiful closing lines:

I send you shoreward echoes of my voice:
The dithyrambic gestures of the moon,
Sun-lost, the mind plumed, Dionysian,
A blue sea-poem, joy, moon-ripple on wave.

As the word "shoreward" indicates, Wright is no longer speaking as he muses on but as he is merged *with* the sea; not neatly and clearly articulated, his language more closely resembles "echoes," reverberations of his fusion with the sea—here a series of images in which poet and outer world coalesce. Thus, at the end of the poem Wright begins to let syntax "die"—into a series of floating parallel phrases that combine and recombine in multiple ways but are not untangled and gathered either into tight lyric song or into discursive statement. The "dithyrambic" verses, joyous and "Dionysian," along with a phrase like "sea-poem," remind us of Whitman, source of the poem's epigraph. The references establish that in "The Morality of Poetry" Wright was rejecting the predetermined forms of his early work and moving toward the idea of form as discovery that we find in a poet like Whitman.[24]

Of course, in "The Morality of Poetry" Wright does not yet "let all measures die": even at its close the poem stays within the iambic pentameter measure with which it began. No public signs of Wright's struggle to crack his "dead and dull iambs" "to pieces" occurred until 1959 in the three poems that were published in the second issue of *Fifties*. Moreover, the Whitmanesque dithyramb was not to provide the mode for

24. See Wright's "The Delicacy of Walt Whitman," in *The Presence of Walt Whitman*, ed. R. W. B. Lewis (New York, 1962), pp. 164–88. Wright stresses Whitman's ability to confront the violence of American social reality and yet to retain his delicacy and precision, in just the way Wright was then trying to do in the poems of *The Branch Will Not Break*. Wright also observes how Whitman's "parallelism" "lets his images grow, one out of another," so that "finally, we discover the form of the poem *as we read it,* and we know what it is only after we have finished" (p. 180; my italics). In addition, Wright concludes that Whitman is "an immediate presence" (p. 182) made available to contemporary poets partly through Malcolm Cowley's reissue of the first edition of *Leaves of Grass* and partly through the work of Spanish and South American poets where "the spirit of Whitman is everywhere present" (p. 184), as it is, according to Wright, in the poetry of such contemporaries as Bly, Simpson, and Levertov. The essay makes abundantly clear that Wright conceived of his poetry (and that of the poets of his generation he regarded as closest to his own) as deriving from Whitman by way of the Spanish-speaking poets he had been translating with Bly.

Wright's new verse. But "The Morality of Poetry," does point toward the new direction, and it brings to the surface and seeks to resolve a conflict between release and restraint that pervades Wright's first two books.

By early 1958 Wright had written all of the poems in *St. Judas,* was teaching in the English Department at the University of Minnesota, and was working on his doctoral dissertation on the early novels of Charles Dickens. The choice of Dickens, which may seem curious at first, probably stemmed from Wright's desire to maintain some distance between his scholarly and his creative work; Wright's main teaching field remained the English novel. Yet the dissertation, written during 1958, reveals many of Wright's preoccupations at the time, mainly his preoccupation with a theme he calls "the insolence of office," Dickens's unmasking of the sadistic cruelty of official authority and his concern with ways of subverting it (sometimes criminal ways) in order to preserve the integrity of the individual self. Most interesting, however, is Wright's early contention that "the possession of a 'wandering' intelligence" made Dickens a great writer because it made him "capable of 'wandering' until he *discovered* the point, rather than evaded it."[25] The four years between *St. Judas* and *The Branch Will Not Break* were a time of reassessment, experiment, and struggle for Wright—the search (begun in "The Morality of Poetry") for a poetic language and form that would allow his imagination to "wander," allow his poems to record the *process of discovery.*

"Goodbye to the Poetry of Calcium," the second poem in *The Branch Will Not Break,* offers Wright's farewell to the lean, hard, carefully hewn style that he had at least sought in his first two books. His new sense of poetic language and form can best be illustrated by looking at a later poem in the new volume, "Beginning."

The moon drops one or two feathers into the field.
The dark wheat listens.
Be still.
Now.
There they are, the moon's young trying
Their wings.
Between trees, a slender woman lifts up the lovely shadow
Of her face, and now she steps into the air, now she is gone
Wholly, into the air.

25. "The Comic Imagination of the Young Dickens" (Ph.D. diss., University of Washington, 1959), p. 6. See "The Art of Poetry XIX: James Wright," pp. 43–44, for Wright's thoughts about his interest in the "poetry" of the English novel; he has also written an "Afterword" for the Signet edition of Thomas Hardy's *Far from the Madding Crowd* (New York, 1960), pp. 315–82.

> I stand alone by an elder tree, I do not dare breathe
> Or move.
> I listen.
> The wheat leans back toward its own darkness,
> And I lean toward mine.

Compared with Wright's previous work, this poem displays a dramatic immediacy. Instead of the reflective, we get the imagistic lyric—a series of images presented without rational connectives in a slow, deliberate movement that is filled with suggestive silences. The images themselves, while they partly refer to a literal scene, also enact metaphoric transformations (moon as bird, wheat listening, etc.) that blend human consciousness with that scene, as if the speaker were, in Levertov's beautiful phrase, "dreaming wideawake." Wright does not present the clean, hard-edged perception of the physical surface that we get in much of imagism; instead, his images, carrying suggestions of invisible, magical realities beyond the literal world, seem to float up out of the unconscious at the moment when the boundaries between self and world are crossed. They are *deep* images. "Each moment of time is a mountain," says Wright (*CP*, p. 133), who had earlier experienced time as a slow process of dissolution ending in nothingness. In *The Branch Will Not Break,* however, each poem opens an expanded moment, in which the physical and social worlds are perceived, along with their vertical extensions of spiritual meaning. In his third book, then, Wright writes from a mood of imagistic reverie like that we have seen in "The Morality of Poetry."

As the mystical image of the woman who "steps into the air" attests, Wright is now even more avowedly a visionary poet, though one whose sense of the visionary as immanent in *this world, this moment,* leads him to make the poem into a recording of the *act* (or *process*) of vision. This conception of the poem as process provides yet another source of the feeling of immediacy conveyed by a poem like "Beginning." Not only is the poem written in the present tense; its repetition of the word "now" emphasizes that an experience is being recorded as it happens, while both syntax and lineation maintain the feeling (which we've already seen embodied in the images) of a mind in the *act* of submitting to an experience. Just as syntax collapses into a series of floating phrases at the end of "The Morality of Poetry," Wright here avoids the lengthy sentences and elaborate subordination of the poetry of calcium and instead writes in a series of simple declarative sentences (or compounds joined by "and") that are suspended in parallel structure. Lines, too, are shaped not by metrical requirements but by the movements of the poet's mind. After the long (12-syllable) opening line, the brevity of "the dark wheat listens" creates an expectant pause, a silence in which the poet begins to listen. The increasing brevity of the next two lines—"Be still. / Now"—takes the poem to the edge of complete silence, at the same time that the gradual tightening of the lines suggests the effort of concentration, a silence not of withdrawal but of rapt attention. The poet descends into his body, into the moment, and his silent receptivity is then filled as the poem, describing first the flight of the young birds, then of the woman, moves out into its longest, most flowing lines. When Wright observes that "now she is gone," it seems at first as though the vision will merely end in loss and frustration, but the turn of the line—"gone / Wholly, into the air"—corresponds to a turn in the poet's mind: his discovery that she has not been lost but diffused into surrounding air as an invisible pervasive presence. For the first time in the poem the speaker, "alone," becomes an "I"; yet he feels awe and wonder, rather than sorrow, and at the close he is still quietly listening, turned toward the external world, feeling affinity with it, accepting its darkness and mystery. Endings in Wright's first two books often took the form of discursive comment, part of a general tendency on Wright's part to do practically all of the reader's work for him. The syntax of the final two lines in "Beginning" place the poet in a parallel relation to the natural world, as if he were separate from but leaning toward it; the final image—of leaning *toward* the *darkness*—reports an activity that is continuing rather than completed, and the end of that activity (the dark) is something in itself obscure, mysterious. The open ending, like the silences within the poem, embodies in the language Wright's claim that he is at ease with darkness, mystery, otherness. As do many of the poems in *The Green Wall* and *St. Judas,* "Beginning" represents vision and the fading of vision. But Wright no longer tries to *possess* that fleeting moment by setting it within a fixed verse form; he now seeks to enter that moment, to make the poem retain the quality of an actual event unfolding in time. As a result, the reader experiences the poem itself as a "beginning" rather than as a finished artifact.

Like "Beginning," many of the poems in *The Branch Will Not Break* have a tone of hushed orphic solemnity that decidedly limits the range of feeling Wright can deal with. At the same time, however, Wright mostly avoids the practical dangers of a deep image poetics. If, as Bly says, the image is "released from its imprisonment among the objects," the risk is that the poet will merely substitute imagistic dissociation for discursive dissociation. The risk will be that much greater if, as is the case with Wright, the poet's enrapt moments reveal indistinct presences in a "dark," flowing world; his language may become soft and precious while his visions may seem too easily projected. But by cracking his dead and dull iambs, Wright was seeking a tougher and tighter language. Perhaps one reason he always objected to calling his poems surrealist is that their clipped brevity and restraint mark them as crafted, not the products of automatic writing.[26] In fact, the power of the poems derives from their combination of a plain, matter-of-fact language with their bold imaginative leaps. So Wright "freed" his language only to make it more concentrated, at once more realistic and more visionary. *The Branch Will Not Break* represents the midwestern landscape with abundant particularity, and we get a sense of its freight yards, factories, mines, workers, ravished countryside along with its moments of ecstatic beauty. In poems like "Eisenhower's Visit to Franco, 1959" and the two poems on President Harding, Wright has extended his range to include political subjects. So physical and social realities enter these poems in ways they hardly ever did in *The Green Wall* and *St. Judas*. Such actualities do not accumulate, as they do in Ginsberg, to pain the poet into vision; rather than imprisoning, they become the supportive ground which makes possible and makes convincing Wright's glimpses of the magical world just beyond the visible one.

Wright, then, had newly conceived the lyric poem as a "passage" or "corridor" (two recurring images in *The Branch Will Not Break*) and in doing so he was breaking down, and breaking open, the modernist notion of the self-enclosed autotelic poem. His poems now become passageways into and beyond the physical world. More than this, *The Branch Will Not Break* as a whole enacts a psychological and spiritual passage, Wright's personal ordeal of the early sixties. Asked by an interviewer if, in putting together his books he had any "idea of coherence in mind," Wright replied by citing Robert Frost's remark that "if you have a book of twenty-four poems, the book itself should be the twenty-fifth"; and, he added, "I have tried that every time, every time."[27] Wright's third book *is* a single poem, a sequence punctuated by the silences between the poems, that records his painful passage from emotional constriction to openness. Yet this very unity points toward another danger of the deep image poetic. Robert Pinsky and Paul Breslin have pointed out that the difficulty of much contemporary surrealist writing is not the unintelligibility of its private associations but its drawing upon a "lexicon" of stock words and phrases. "The point is not only the predictability of the diction," Breslin writes, "but also the way in which the key words are used, as if they came to the individual poem already charged with significance." Wright

26. "I think of myself as being a very traditional writer; all of the formal devices in my later work are pretty plain," Wright says in "Something to Be Said for the Light," p. 141, and he says "I regard myself primarily as a craftsman, as a Horatian" in "The Art of Poetry XIX: James Wright," p. 38.
27. "The Art of Poetry XIX: James Wright," p. 52.

certainly uses "darkness" in such a mechanical way, trying to pump the poem up with portentous mystery by means of this verbal tic. My own judgment, however, is that in *The Branch Will Not Break* Wright gives us enough repetition to provide coherence but not so much that he merely seems to be drawing on a "shared rhetoric"; in 1963 no such rhetoric existed to be drawn upon, because Wright was in the process of inventing it.[28]

Like many of the poems in the book, its first and last poems are paired in a way that suggests the development of the whole. In the opening poem ("As I Step over a Puddle at the End of Winter, I Think of an Ancient Chinese Governor") Wright compares the journey of Po Chu-i "entering the gorges of the Yang-Tze" to his own "black twilight" among "the tall rocks of Minneapolis" and wonders, not too optimistically, whether Po Chu-i ever completed his journey or has been "holding the end of a frayed rope / For a thousand years." "Where is the sea, that once solved the whole loneliness / Of the Midwest?" Wright asks. In "A Dream of Burial" (the final poem) Wright dreams of his body in the grave, slowly decomposing to "nothing." Old women mourn but he himself, peacefully accepting death, hears them as "faint mosquitoes near still water." "So I waited, in my corridor," Wright says, listening for "the sea / To call me."

> I knew that, somewhere outside, the horse
> Stood saddled, browsing in grass,
> Waiting for me.

Both poems represent the poet as alone, enclosed in a narrow space, slowly disintegrating; both invoke the sea as the "end" of life's journey, its bleak suffering, its painful divisions. But while in the first poem Wright desperately calls upon the sea to "solve" the problem of loneliness, in the second he waits for it to call him. The book begins in a tone of anxious futility ("What's the use?") but it ends in a tone of patient assurance: not "you made it, I *guess,* / By dark" but "I *knew.*" At its start the book describes a journey that goes nowhere; at its end the book describes an expectant stillness, a waiting for a journey that the poet *knows* will take place. The endless black gorge of the first poem is transformed into the "corridor"—an *open* passageway—of the last. *The Branch Will Not Break,* then, records an evolution from fear to acceptance, from enclosure to openness, from self-absorption to self-transcendence—a movement that is paralleled by the seasonal progression from autumn and winter to spring. Such growth, moreover, is achieved not by a linear but by a cyclical

28. "How to Read the New Contemporary Poem," pp. 363 and 359. See also Robert Pinsky's *The Situation of Poetry* (Princeton, N.J., 1976), pp. 111–18.

movement, beginning with a descent into the poet's most primitive fears.
Like Roethke, Wright now holds "that to go forward as a spriritual man
it is necessary first to go back" through dream and memory.[29] Before he
can proclaim that "each moment of time is a mountain," Wright must
explore the underground, what he calls "the dark green crevices / Of my
childhood" (*CP*, p. 124). Unlike Plath, however, Wright's regression begins a cycle that ends in reintegration, the kind of spiritual vision we have
seen in "Beginning." "Black snow, / Like a strange sea creature, / Draws
back into itself, / Restoring grass to earth" (*CP*, p. 129); Wright, too,
draws back into himself in order to accomplish a metamorphosis, finding
fresh life instead of wintry barrenness.

As part of its inclusiveness of vision, *The Branch Will Not Break* has
an historical and a political dimension that is best embodied in "Eisenhower's Visit to Franco, 1959." A comment on contemporary public life
is made—Wright unmasks "the insolence of office" in America and Spain—
but it is done quietly, not through the invective of "Howl" but through
a series of opposed images that create a complex irony. Throughout the
poem the two political leaders are associated with light: Eisenhower "has
flown through the very light of heaven"; Franco "stands in a shining
circle of police"; the two embrace "in a glare of photographers" while
the wings of the American bombers "shine in the searchlights." With
these images Wright exposes the cold glitter of a political order bent on
reducing all life to its own sterile terms: "The American hero must triumph
over / The forces of darkness," and Franco "promises all dark things /
Will be hunted down." Yet the poem's central section, describing yawning
state police, the exiled poet Antonio Machado following "the moon /
Down a road of white dust," caves of "silent children," wine darkening
"in stone jars," wine sleeping "in the mouths of old men"—this section
affirms a slow, dark, ancient, and silent life that is enclosed and hidden,
protected from the ruthless glare of modern civilization; the poem's irony
is finally directed not just against the repressiveness of the political order,
but against its deeper impotence. The oppositions that we find in "Eisenhower's Visit to Franco, 1959" are, moreover, characteristic of the
sequence as a whole, for what is presented here as social conflict appears,
internalized, as the poet's own conflict in many of the poems, and it is
the same division between a cold ordering and lively instinct that can be
found in Wright's earlier poems. The difference is that in *The Branch Will
Not Break* Wright consciously explores this inner conflict and moves
toward resolving it. Considered as a single poem, this book moves toward
acceptance of otherness as mystery and, as we have seen in "Beginning,"

29. *On the Poet and His Craft*, p. 39.

Wright embodies that acceptance in a poetic medium that is willing to embrace, rather than to triumph over, "the forces of darkness."

"The self-seeker finds nothing," Wright declares in "Three Stanzas from Goethe." In the early poems of *The Branch Will Not Break,* the attitude is one of panicked and sterile self-regard. Wright is typically alone in a cold, dark, or barren field, feeling frightened, empty, and worthless. "I can see nothing," he laments in the opening poem; "I am nothing," he says in "Goodbye to the Poetry of Calcium." In a similar series of images, "the waste devours" the self-seeker of the Goethe translation, while Wright himself feels, in the controversial last line of "Lying in a Hammock at William Duffy's Farm in Pine Island, Minnesota," that "I have wasted my life." At times (as in "The Jewel") he imagines a secret and inviolate part of himself (a "cave / In the air behind by body") that not only offers immunity to the frightening processes of decay, but provides an enclosed space in which he can transform his life, or himself, into hard, eternal objects: "When I stand upright in the wind, / My bones turn to dark emeralds."[30] But as titles such as "In Fear of Harvests," "Fear Is What Quickens Me," and "In the Face of Hatred" attest, Wright is primarily interested in exploring his fears, most often the terror felt by someone to whom, as to an abandoned child, all outer forces are perceived as mysterious, powerful, and threatening. In poems like "Autumn Begins in Martins Ferry, Ohio" and "Miners" the figure of the father, alternately "dreaming of heroes" and wishing for his own death, is resented for his impotence, which leaves the son exposed to a variety of dangerous forces. Ironically, these forces, too, are perceived as paternal, and they are represented—like Eisenhower—as heroic, glittering ("father of diamonds," *CP,* p. 112) with a power that the son sometimes wishes for himself (as in "The Jewel") but which he more often fears as murderously cruel. In "Fear Is What Quickens Me" Wright, alone and threatened, is not hard, "upright," but like a terror-stricken animal.

> Many animals that our fathers killed in America
> Had quick eyes.
> They stared about wildly,
> When the moon went dark,

---

30. Compare the text of "The Jewel": "There is this cave / In the air behind my body / That nobody is going to touch: / A cloister, a silence / Closing around a blossom of fire. / When I stand upright in the wind, / My bones turn to dark emeralds" with Wright's translation of the second stanza of Vallejo's "Espergesia": "There is an empty place / in my metaphysical shape / that no one can reach: / a cloister of silence / that spoke with the fire of its voice muffled." The translation appears in *Twenty Poems of Cesar Vallejo,* trans. Robert Bly, John Knoeple, and James Wright (Madison, Minn., 1962).

the poem begins. Now, though "the loss of the moon to the dark hands" in the "freight yards" of Chicago may not disturb the deer "in this northern field," it does frighten the poet. "What is that tall woman doing / There, in the trees?" he asks in part two of the poem. "I can hear rabbits and mourning doves whispering together / In the dark grass, there / Under the trees." The poet's senses are alerted—not in calm attentiveness but in wary self-protection; the "tall woman," who anticipates the "slender woman" of "Beginning," is felt to be ominous, as are the "whispering" animals. The word "there," repeated emphatically at the beginnings and ends of lines, reveals the frightened speaker's desire to assign a definite location to (and so distance himself from) these mysterious presences. But the third part of the poem—consisting of a single line: "I look about wildly"—dramatizes Wright's transformation into one of the hunted animals who stare "about wildly" in the first part.

As the identification of the hunters as "our fathers" makes plain, the predatory forces with which Wright is contending are historical, deriving from both his family and the national past. At the start of *The Branch Will Not Break,* as in Wright's first two books, the present is experienced as an emptiness, devoid of shape and meaning; at the same time the past, in the form of ghostly presences, hovers over the present, imposing its rigid orders. The present, in short, is not really *experienced*. "How My Fever Left" ends with futility: "It's no use, she won't listen, / She's gone" (the last word later taken up and beautifully transformed in the "gone / Wholly, into the air" of "Beginning"), but the first line of this poem asserts that "I can *still* hear her"; it is also futile to try to break free of the witchlike maternal presence the poem describes. The public past, too, hangs on, bequeathing a destructive order that seeks to hunt down all dark things. Images of the spoliation of nature, particularly through strip-mining, appear again and again in the poems. "How many honey locusts have fallen, / Pitched root long into the open graves of strip mines, / Since the First World War ended / And Wilson the gaunt deacon jogged sullenly / Into silence?" Wright asks in the first of the "Two Poems about President Harding." The defeated miner or factory worker may be "dreaming of heroes" (*CP,* p. 113), but political and economic institutions are in fact activated by "the cancerous ghosts of old con men" (*CP,* p. 120), the reality inside the "father of diamonds." History itself has become a slow, ever-widening process of corruption: "The unwashed shadows / Of blast furnaces from Moundsville, West Virginia, / Are sneaking across the pits of strip mines / To steal grapes / In heaven" (*CP,* p. 116). The result, as in "Miners," is that all vital life is pushed underground, buried, enclosed. The men work "deep in a coal hill behind Hanna's name," while the women, miners too, "mount long stairs / In the *shafts* of houses."

Each of the sexes, exhausted and isolated from the other, yearns for a way out: the men long for death; the women "fall asleep, and emerge suddenly into tottering palaces," but even their dreams, like the suicidal fantasies of the males, are imaginings of disaster. In "Stages on a Journey Westward" Wright parallels the movement of his own early life, from Ohio to Washington, with America's westward expansion, both journeys viewed as rapacious and self-destructive. For the first time in *The Branch Will Not Break* home is associated with security and the father with affection (in a dream "the old man limps to my bed, / Leading a blind horse / Of gentleness"); in this book it is not the cold perfection of the poetry of calcium that Wright finally seeks but what he calls a "wild, gentle thing" (*CP,* p. 135), a mixture of power and kindness that he frequently associates with horses. But early in the book, such gentleness has been lost: "I cannot find him," Wright says of the father; the rest of the poem bares the consequences. In its second section, Wright, alone in "western Minnesota," dreams of "old Indians, who wanted to kill me"; and in the third section, he is again haunted, this time hearing a snowstorm on an "abandoned" prairie as "the voices of bums and gamblers, / Rattling through the bare nineteenth-century whorehouses / In Nevada." In the final section of the poem Wright is drunk in a Washington cemetery where miners, on their way to Alaska, "spaded their broken women's bodies / Into ditches of crab grass." In a graveyard at the edge of the continent Wright comes to a vision of the end, a collapse back to the beginning that casts an aura of futility over the entire journey: "America is over and done with. / America, / Plunged into the dark furrows / Of the sea again." America, seeking to triumph over the forces of darkness, dissolves into the dark chaos of the sea; a cold, self-seeking civilization finds nothing.

The predatory drives of "our fathers" may be ultimately self-destructive and ineffectual and hollow, but the ghosts of these old con men *are* cancerous, so much so that their ambitions are internalized by the poet himself. Wright's sense of external reality as corrupt and void partly derives from his own feelings of guilt and emptiness; he, too, fears the dark, perceiving mysteries as sinister, as he does with the "tall woman" in "Fear Is What Quickens Me." One side of the poet would like to view himself, pityingly, as a helpless victim; a more acute side comes to recognize that, self-engrossed, he is "lost in myself" (*CP,* p. 135). But exploring his fears, he learns their origins and sees that he is "dying of thirst / In his own desert" (*CP,* p. 113). Yet the possibility of self-transcendence is sometimes suggested in the early poems of *The Branch Will Not Break.* In "Lying in a Hammock"—the poem immediately before "The Jewel," where "I stand upright in the wind"—he has sufficiently relaxed his defenses to concentrate upon the immediate natural world which, carefully observed, contains both physical beauty and hints of timelessness in such images as "*bronze* butterfly" and "*golden* stones." It is the fullness of this moment that allows him to leap to the realization that "I have wasted my life." "In the Face of Hatred" points out that there is more than one way to respond to fears of attack; the poem shows two boys, both pursued by the police, but while one "cries for his father's death," the other, "the silent one, / Listens into the hallway / Of a dark leaf." *The Branch Will Not Break* traces the reemergence of the silent and gentle boy in the man, who then, in spite of the surrounding violence, attends both to the physical world and its hints (the leaf as "hallway") of a secret world beyond. This change in Wright is a gradual one and cannot be assigned to any single poem, but its character is clearly revealed in the differences—in tone, attitude, image—between the "Two Hangovers," which appear just about halfway through the book.

In the first of these two poems, the numerous and elaborately developed images merely reflect the depressed state of the speaker; they do not open a "hallway" to physical or spiritual realities but mirror the bleak distortions of a hangover. This is the poetry of self-regard. "I slouch in bed," Wright begins, reminding us of the transcendent moment "lying in a hammock," but this poem offers an instance of wasted rather than apprehended life. Outside "all groves are bare." But the language subtly points up the fact that the poet's perceptions merely distort literal reality— "locusts and poplars *change* to unmarried women / Sorting slate from anthracite / Between railroad ties"—and that the transformations are themselves shaped by childhood memories: "the yellow-bearded winter of the depression / Is *still alive* somewhere," specifically in the figure of an "old man" counting bottle caps "in a tarpaper shack under the cold trees / Of my grave." It is as if the speaker, hung over and "still" "half drunk," is "dreaming wideawake" in a quite different sense from that which we find in "Beginning." Like the first, the second stanza, where Wright imagines that old women outside his window "are hunching toward the graveyard," closes with thoughts of death. The rising sun, bringing suggestions of warmth, vigor, and new life, enters the poem in the third section—

Drunk, mumbling Hungarian,
The sun staggers in,
And his big stupid face pitches
Into the stove.

—but the sun, as the comic distortions of the language make clear, is only the drunken poet himself. While asleep, Wright had dreamed of discovering "green butterflies" while "searching for diamonds / In coal seams" and of watching "children chasing each other for a game / Through the hills of fresh graves." The dreams suggest the possibility of finding delicate beauty in a dark, ugly underground world or of finding joyful vigor in a landscape of death; the dream images open a corridor to parts of the childhood past that has been lost to conscious memory, preoccupied with "the winter of the depression" and thoughts of deprivation and death. Moreover, as the poem goes on to show, Wright also uncovers aspects of present life that are lost to the self-immolated poet. For the waking world, with its images of a reinvigorated sun, a sparrow that sings "of the Hanna Coal Co. and the dead moon," and "cold light bulbs" that "tremble / In music like delicate birds"—this waking world hints at transcendence, as did the dream. But the still hung over poet abruptly ends the poem with a disgusted "Ah, turn it off."

The "it" seems to refer to the sun, the bird's song, the music of the light bulbs, but it may also refer to the projecting consciousness of the poet himself. The second poem, in dramatic contrast to the first, begins with a single, clear image of otherness:

> In a pine tree,
> A few yards away from my window sill,
> A brilliant blue jay is springing up and down, up and down,
> On a branch.

But whereas an imagist poet might have stopped here, Wright goes on to implicate himself with the image, which then (in spite of its concrete specificity) becomes, like the images in the dreams, a "corridor" to both emotional response and spiritual insight.

> I laugh, as I see him abandon himself
> To entire delight, for he knows as well as I do
> That the branch will not break.

Wright does not fuse with the image, he does not become the bird the way Whitman would; instead, maintaining the integrity of both self and object, he establishes a ground of resemblance between them. He leans *toward* the other, but he does not dissolve into it. The bird joyfully "abandons himself," as does Wright when he laughs or when he carefully delineates the movements of the blue jay in the first four lines. What makes such an act of self-transcendence possible is the poet's confident knowledge (as in "I *knew* that, somewhere outside" of the book's final poem) that the external world offers not a merciless threat but a supportive context: "the branch will *not* break." Wright, who had before sought diamonds in coal seams, now discovers vigorous life, and entire delight, in the "*brilliant* blue jay."

Many of the poems in the latter half of *The Branch Will Not Break* deal with the discovery of a vital life that does persist through winter ("In the Cold House," "Snowstorm in the Midwest"), with the struggle to survive winter into spring ("American Wedding," "Two Spring Charms," "Mary Bly"), or with the burgeoning life of spring itself ("Depressed by a Book of Bad Poetry," "Spring Images"). "Black snow, / Like a strange sea creature, / Draws back into itself, / Restoring grass to earth." But, as we have seen in "Two Hangovers," when Wright now draws back into himself he is not moving into self-absorption but away from it; he is drawing back in order to let external reality alone—to let it be, independent of him. Self and object, grounded in being but remaining separate, can then be joined—without projection. Along with the autobiographical, the social and historical concerns of the first half of the book recede; the poet *has* withdrawn into a rural landscape, and his verse becomes a mode of visionary pastoralism, as in "Beginning." Insofar as Wright still hopes for "The Undermining of the Defense Economy" (and he does), it is through subversive presence rather than ironic critique. "Once, / I was afraid of dying," says Wright. "But now [I try] to keep still, listening / To insects that move patiently."

Perhaps they are sampling the fresh dew that gathers slowly
In empty snail shells
And in the secret shelters of sparrow feathers fallen on the earth.
[*CP*, p. 134]

Like Roethke, Wright focuses on "the minimal," and he uncovers the fresh life that is hidden in small, obscure places in a way that gives him new life. In "Fear Is What Quickens Me," "I look about wildly"; but in "To the Evening Star: Central Minnesota," expressing an assurance that pervades these poems, Wright compares himself to wild animals who "know / The open meadows are safe." At the end of "By a Lake in Minnesota," the poem that comes just before "Beginning," he stands, "waiting / For dark." In "Depressed by a Book of Bad Poetry," "I close my eyes for a moment, and listen." Accepting its cycles of dark and light, winter and spring, the poet (in "March" and "American Wedding") now willingly submits to nature's slow rhythms, to accept that it will change "in its own good time" (*CP*, p. 128). The restless self-seeker finds nothing, and journeys westward, away from the self's origins, are futile. Instead of impatient searching, we get quiet attention, a drawing back and opening of the self that restores vital energy to what had seemed a sterile existence.

Wright's spiritual evolution in *The Branch Will Not Break* is not represented through narrative, but through the repetition and transformation of an elaborate set of images. Narrative organization would imply the validity of a search, a journey, and thus of a kind of controlled ordering of events, but a narrative, Wright knows, would find nothing. His own use of recurrent images to order a work of length draws on a technique common enough in both modern and contemporary poetry. His contribution, however, comes from the way many of the images are transformed during the sequence. Moreover, one of the dangers of deep image poetry is that the images will strike the reader as either contrived or obscure or both. But through the experience of associations that accumulate as the book proceeds, the reader can gradually enter and unfold its world and come to each poem with the knowledge of the whole. Many of the details of "Beginning," for instance, become richer in meaning when they are read with the entire sequence in mind. The literal situation of the poem (Wright alone in a dark field) is reminiscent of such earlier poems as "Fear Is What Quickens Me," the dramatic similarity stressing the difference in attitude: now it is wonder that quickens him when the "slender woman" appears. Here, as elsewhere, the moon is associated with a benign maternal presence, before "lost" to the "dark hands" of the Chicago "freight yards" but now restored to the poet. Even specific words such as "still," "now," "listen," and "lean"—repeated from surrounding poems—gain force in their creation of a silent and confident expectancy, and we have already seen how Wright transforms the sense of "gone" from "How My Fever Left." Darkness, central in "Beginning," is probably the leading motif in the book. In addition to the dark and the moon, important images include diamonds, horses, silence, the sea, mines, graves, and caves. Early in the book, what is present (e.g., the moon, the sea) is mourned, but later, absences (such as silence) can be creative, magically filling up with presences that were thought to be lost (the moon, horses, the sea) and which are now experienced as powerful but tender. Most interesting of all are the interconnected images of grave, mine, cave, corridor. At the beginning, the numerous graves and mines reveal the poet's concern that predatory forces will hunt him down and kill him *and* the way his fear of such a death ironically consigns him to a sealed-in and deathlike existence. At times, as in "The Jewel," caves are associated with self-protection, the creation of a private fantasy world where control can be exercised, but they are also associated with the acceptance and preservation of "dark life," as they are in "Eisenhower's Visit to Franco." And as the sequence proceeds, graves and mines are transformed into hallways and corridors;

the emphasis shifts from enclosures to passageways, spaces that are shaped but not sealed shut. In this shift, of course, we find Wright's redefinition of the self *and* the poem.

In Wright's work, then, the poem—no longer imagined as a cold, glittering artifact—becomes a corridor, a domesticated and human space that opens a passageway between self and world. In both the book as a whole and in individual poems, passage is a complex and difficult process which requires at once a loosening of conscious controls and disciplined acts of silent attention and waiting. The self must slowly enter and become immersed in the world, as Wright does in "Snowstorm in the Midwest":

> I step into the water
> Of two flakes.
> The crowns of white birds rise
> To my ankles,
> To my knees,
> To my face.

Wright no longer fears the drowning he had seen as the ordained fate of children in "Miners." Still, such passages in his work are always ordeals; they are often dark, narrow, hard to enter and cross but, unlike the "black gorge" of the first poem, they can be crossed and when they are, the poet feels a sense of expansion—just as the process of contraction ("Be still. / Now") leads to the expanded vision in "Beginning." Such moments, mountains of time, are poems. Such poems, being visionary, open access to "the other world" (*CP*, p. 136); the poet, no longer isolated and bereaved, discovers hidden presences that do not haunt (or hunt) him.

> Whatever it was I lost, whatever I wept for
> Was a wild, gentle thing, the small dark eyes
> Loving me in secret.
> It is here.
>
> [*CP*, pp. 135–36]

Another of the book's repeated images, the sea, suggests timelessness and primal unity. At first the sea, which had once solved all the loneliness of the midwest, was lamented as absent; in "Stages on a Journey Westward" its "dark furrows" seemed ominous, though the plunge he imagines there (like the drunkenness in "Two Hangovers") can also be viewed as the start of a process of re-creation. Certainly, in the later poems of *The Branch Will Not Break,* the sea is perceived as a wild, gentle thing, Wright's figurative language continually making it a presence on the vast midwestern plain. He speaks of "the slow whale of country twilight" and a "spume of light" in "By a Lake in Minnesota"; the "black snow" of "Two Spring Charms" is compared to a "strange sea creature" and in "To the Evening Star: Central Minnesota," the wind creates a "ripple / In the grass fields." "Snowstorm in the Midwest," perceiving drifts as "haunches of whales," transforms snowy landscape into seascape. Air and water, holding mysterious but benign presences, become elements of magical transformation.[31] The Bly baby "is braiding the waters of air into the plaited manes / Of happy colts" (*CP*, pp. 133–34), and in "Milkweed" the poet himself becomes the agent of such transformation: "At a touch of my hand, / The air fills with delicate creatures / From the other world" (*CP*, p. 136). The passage, an arduous ordeal that issues in self-metamorphosis, is a drawing back, a return; what the poet thought he had "lost" is actually "here"—in the magical and timeless space of an expanded instant.

This sense of the surrounding environment as separate yet benign and even nurturing leads to the stunning metaphorical leap that is made at the end of Wright's brilliant poem, "A Blessing."

> Just off the highway to Rochester, Minnesota,
> Twilight bounds softly forth on the grass.
> And the eyes of those two Indian ponies
> Darken with kindness.
> They have come gladly out of the willows
> To welcome my friend and me.
> We step over the barbed wire into the pasture
> Where they have been grazing all day, alone.
> They ripple tensely, they can hardly contain their happiness
> That we have come.
> They bow shyly as wet swans. They love each other.
> There is no loneliness like theirs.
> At home once more,
> They begin munching the young tufts of spring in the darkness.
> I would like to hold the slenderer one in my arms,
> For she has walked over to me
> And nuzzled my left hand.

31. This transformation of air into ocean can also be found in many of the poems in Bly's *Silence in the Snowy Fields* and is one of many fairly specific resemblances between the two poets. Solitude, the journey to the sea, darkness, silence, dream states—all are as important and important in the same ways in Bly as in Wright. "We want to go back, to return to the sea, / The sea of solitary corridors, / And halls of wild nights, / Explosions of grief, / Diving into the sea of death, / Like the stars of the wheeling Bear," Bly writes ("Return to Solitude") in a tone and imagery that are remarkably close to that of Wright. Which poet influenced the other is, however, hard to say.

She is black and white,
Her mane falls wild on her forehead,
And the light breeze moves me to caress her long ear
That is delicate as the skin over a girl's wrist.
Suddenly I realize
That if I stepped out of my body I would break
Into blossom.

After beginning with literal simplicity—"Just off the highway to Rochester, Minnesota"—the poem immediately begins to metaphorize experience and to subvert distinctions, by identifying the movement of the
light with that of the horses in the second line. This interplay between
fact and metaphor continues throughout the poem, allowing Wright to
present a precisely rendered, realistic scene, a process which ultimately
becomes the means to a leap of visionary insight, a "corridor" to "the
other world." Similarly, Wright at first remains realistically aware of separation and self-boundaries, though he feels an increasingly powerful wish
to transcend them as the poem proceeds. The horses have been "alone"
all day; they have been enclosed in a "barbed wire" fence; "there is no
loneliness like theirs." Yet the poet and his friend can enter their pasture
without intruding (so, "at home" again, the horses begin eating); the
animals have come "gladly" to "welcome" the humans and in an image
that anticipates the breaking of self-boundaries at the end of the poem,
"they ripple tensely, they can hardly contain their happiness / That we
have come." "Two Horses Playing in the Orchard" directed irony toward
the man who claimed to "*own*"—to possess—"a horse, an apple tree, a
stone." But in "A Blessing" Wright feels a kind of mystical union with
the horses; literal contact becomes more intimate as one of the horses
nuzzles his hand and he caresses its ear so lightly that his hand seems no
different from the breeze. In many respects the poem resembles one of
Robert Frost's meditations, partly romantic, partly skeptical, on the
boundaries between human and natural worlds, boundaries that Frost is
characteristically concerned to maintain. But when Wright touches the
horse and feels the thin delicacy of its skin, he can hardly *contain* himself:
"Suddenly I realize / That if I stepped out of my body I would break /
Into blossom." When we reach the phrase "I would break," we expect
to find something like "apart" in the next line; instead, in an image
reminiscent of the moment in "Beginning" when the "slender woman"
"steps into the air," we get a blossoming, a flowering of the spirit. The
startling power of the poem's conclusion thus derives from the way the
breaking of the next-to-last line coincides with an unexpected turn of
thought (an act of discovery) which tightens into the abrupt brevity of the

final line. Wright does not actually make the "step" he hypothesizes, however; "A Blessing" does not move toward a moment of transcendence but toward an intuited confidence in the surrounding environment, both visible and invisible, as a supportive context. Slow in movement, precise in detail, the poem builds a passageway into the external world and then beyond it—but without annihilating the physical in its moment of visionary insight. Earlier, in "The Jewel," Wright had anxiously sought to preserve his separateness, his inaccessibility, in a "cave / In the air behind my body," but in "A Blessing" he boldly enacts a blossoming, an opening, of the self.

"We endure a bloated body of verse which drops a shroud between the true feelings of the reader and the true character of the poet," Wright lamented in a 1962 review. "It is only after the most devoted labor that a poet can strip his language of everything except what he sees and feels."[32] In *The Branch Will Not Break* Wright by no means completed the labor of purifying his language, a project he carried forward in subsequent volumes; but his revision of his poetic premises enabled him to begin the process. By repudiating predetermined forms Wright was able simultaneously to expand his range and to concentrate his language. His new verse was thus able to include autobiographical, social, and political realities that were missing from his own earlier work as well as from American poetry generally in the fifties. But at the same time that his poems were more firmly grounded in external experience, they became more openly, more joyfully—and more convincingly—visionary. *The Branch Will Not Break* marked not only a "breakthrough" but a major achievement both for Wright and for contemporary American poetry.

32. "A Plain Brave Music," *Chelsea,* 12 (September 1962), pp. 136–37.

EIGHT

Frank O'Hara

"Grace / to be born and live as variously as possible."[1]

—Frank O'Hara

"He had none of the polemical anxiety which must establish itself for a movement or style and against any or all others."[2]

—Frank O'Hara

In the twentieth century poetry has become such a problematic activity that it has often had to become a programmatic activity—particularly at moments of crisis and renovation. Of all the clusters of poets that emerged during the 1950s, the writers of the New York school remained the least polemical, the least interested in committing themselves to a theory of poetry. The closest thing they produced to a manifesto, O'Hara's "Personism," partly parodies such manifestos.[3] Like their contemporaries, writers like O'Hara, Ashbery, and Koch broke from the canonical orthodoxies of the fifties. Eliot had had a "deadening and obscuring and precious effect" on American poetry, according to O'Hara,[4] who also complained against the New Criticism's restrictions on "the comportment in diction that you adopt" (*SS*, p. 12). More generally, Ashbery has recalled that when he was a student at Harvard in the forties, "there was

Excerpts from this chapter appeared in *American Poetry Review* 12 (November–December 1983): 7–16.

1. *The Collected Poems of Frank O'Hara*, ed. Donald Allen (New York, 1971), p. 256. Hereafter cited in the text as *CP*.

2. *Art Chronicles, 1954–1966* (New York, 1975), p. 45. Abbreviations used in the text are *AC* for *Art Chronicles* and *SS* for *Standing Still and Walking in New York*, ed. Donald Allen (Bolinas, Calif., 1975).

3. O'Hara later described the manifesto as "a little diary of my thoughts, after lunch with LeRoi [Jones] walking back to work" (*SS*, p. 114). "Personism," in other words, does not define anything like a permanent position. In fact its flip tone and its many contradictions make it not a solution to but an instance of the kinds of problems found in the poems.

4. O'Hara's remark on Eliot's effect is quoted by Marjorie Perloff, *Frank O'Hara: Poet among Painters* (New York, 1977), p. 9.

in fact almost no experimental poetry being written in this country." Of course, to be a beginning poet in such circumstances is not all bad, as Ashbery goes on to suggest: "to experiment" in those days "was to have the feeling that one was poised on some outermost brink."[5] More than any other writer of his generation (with the possible exception of Ashbery), O'Hara wrote at the outermost brink. Less the orotund and grandiose revolutionary than Olson or Ginsberg, he yet offers the deepest questioning of traditional ways of ordering both poetry and the self.

O'Hara's indifference to collecting, publishing, and even preserving his poems is well known. "I think he was rather careless with his work," Ashbery writes; "he had a tremendous energy and zest for it while he was working on it, and then seemed to rather lose interest once it was done."[6] In fact, the achievement of O'Hara derives from his renunciation of poetic achievement. O'Hara did not seek to build a poetic career or to form a poetic style. In an interview he tells of an exchange between Max Ernst and Picasso, who asked Ernst to come out for a walk. Ernst refused "because I'm in search of a style": Picasso calmly walked on, declaring that "there is no style" (SS, p. 13). O'Hara, then, does not follow the generational pattern of adopting a period style which he then dismantles. O'Hara was never seduced by style in the first place; instead, he gives us a multiplicity of styles.[7] More concerned with the *activity* of creation than with fetishizing its *products,* O'Hara eluded the stability of any theoretical position, any style. "To move is to love," he wrote (CP, p. 256), reversing the usual sense of love as a permanent commitment. His imagination remains uncommitted—mobile, protean, contradictory, and alive.

O'Hara hated "all things that don't change"—like "photographs" and "monuments" (CP, p. 275). "The Critic," from this point of view, emerges as "the assassin // of my orchards"; "you lurk there / in the shadows, meting out // conversation like Eve's first / confusion between penises and // snakes." The language of criticism, meting out weighty judgments and fixing the meaning of the Edenic snake as phallic symbol, is potentially a murderous language. Writing about O'Hara thus poses special critical challenges. In reading the *Collected Poems* the critic is alternately con-

5. "The Invisible Avant-Garde," in *Avant-Garde Art,* ed. Thomas Hess and John Ashbery (New York, 1968), pp. 182–83.

6. *Homage to Frank O'Hara,* ed. Bill Berkson and Joseph LeSueur (Berkeley, 1978), p. 21. The correspondence between O'Hara and Lawrence Ferlinghetti in the City Lights collection in the Bancroft Library (University of California, Berkeley) suggests more than carelessness: that O'Hara, who took more than four years to put together the book-length manuscript Ferlinghetti had invited him to submit, had an active resistance to collecting his poems.

7. Barthes, *Writing Degree Zero,* pp. 50–52.

fronted with poems that embarrass him out of interpretation by their simplicity and with poems that proliferate interpretations by their opacity and multivalence. In thinking about the one the critic does not quite know how to start, and in thinking about the other he does not quite know how to stop. Moreover, once he stops reading and starts to write or even think about O'Hara, the critic will inevitably select out a poetic canon from the works of a poet who shied away from establishing his own. The critic, in short, will transform O'Hara's creative acts into monuments, and his selection will, of course, hardly be innocent. My own characterization of O'Hara as an experimental poet, for instance, might seem harmless enough, but it immediately reads out of the O'Hara canon the numerous perfectly traditional poems that he wrote. Or do these poems actually support my broader contention about O'Hara's elusiveness: he cannot be caught in the closed versus the open poetry opposition that informed the literary polemics of the late fifties. In any case, I have focused on the mobility and contradictions of O'Hara in order to unfold rather than to contain his poetic energies.

So far, literary critics have come at O'Hara by relating his poetry to movements in painting during the fifties, and Marjorie Perloff in particular has assembled abundant evidence for such a case. "Poetry was declining / Painting advancing / we were complaining / it was '50," O'Hara recalled.[8] At a moment of crisis in his own verbal medium O'Hara turned not, say, to the "prose tradition" but to the visual arts, as Williams and Stein had done earlier in the century. Painters, O'Hara testified, were important to him as exemplary experimental artists; they provided "the only generous audience for our poetry" in the early fifties. Some of them collaborated with O'Hara on multimedia projects. Their works sometimes inspired particular O'Hara poems, and their inventions and theories, particularly those of the "action painters," stimulated O'Hara to push his own medium in new and adventuresome directions. Yet it is not as if the visual arts offered a simple, fixed reference point to which we can relate—and by means of which we can unlock—O'Hara's work. His taste in painting and sculpture was eclectic. He heroized the abstract expressionists, especially Pollock, but he also admired Larry Rivers, whose "Washington Crossing the Delaware" scandalized the abstract expressionists with its use of figuration and deliberately corny subject. In fact, if we try to place O'Hara, contexts begin to proliferate maddeningly: he was familiar with and affected by film, dance, music, Russian writing (especially Pasternak and Mayakovsky), French poetry (especially dada and surrealism), American poetry (especially Whitman and Williams), and his taste in all media was

---

8. Quoted in Perloff, *Frank O'Hara: Poet among Painters*, p. 9. The lines are taken from one of the lithograph stones that O'Hara collaborated on with Larry Rivers.

open-minded and eclectic. O'Hara illustrates a receptivity to, rather than
an anxiety about, a variety of influences, literary and otherwise.[9]

One reason that he could be so open to the influence of the painters
was that he possessed a very subtle awareness of the difference between
their medium and his own, as we can see by looking at "Why I Am Not
a Painter."

> I am not a painter, I am a poet.
> Why? I think I would rather be
> a painter, but I am not. Well,
>
> for instance, Mike Goldberg
> is starting a painting. I drop in.
> "Sit down and have a drink" he
> says. I drink; we drink. I look
> up. "You have SARDINES in it."
> "Yes, it needed something there."
> "Oh." I go and the days go by
> and I drop in again. The painting
> is going on, and I go, and the days
> go by. I drop in. The painting is
> finished. "Where's SARDINES?"
> All that's left is just
> letters, "It was too much," Mike says.
>
> But me? One day I am thinking of
> a color: orange. I write a line
> about orange. Pretty soon it is a
> whole page of words, not lines.
> Then another page. There should be
> so much more, not of orange, of
> words, of how terrible orange is
> and life. Days go by. It is even in
> prose, I am a real poet. My poem
> is finished and I haven't mentioned
> orange yet. It's twelve poems, I call
> it ORANGES. And one day in a gallery
> I see Mike's painting, called SARDINES.

Ironically the painter begins with a word, "sardines," and the poet begins
with a color, orange; each starts by working with the other's means in
his own medium, and in certain respects their creative processes are

9. One of the strengths of Perloff's book is that, while emphasizing O'Hara's relation to
the painters, she also demonstrates the breadth and variousness of O'Hara's interests,
especially his connections with modern French poetry.

similar. They both begin with an identifiable subject that seems whimsical but that subject, though it supplies the title for the finished work, disappears during the actual process of creation. Moreover, the activities of both artists are stressed as processes happening in time although they are processes that O'Hara is careful not to elevate into agonizing, heroic struggles.

But the differences between painter and poet are basic. The atmosphere in Goldberg's studio is relaxed and congenial ("Sit down and have a drink") and O'Hara casually drops in, goes, drops in again. The short, simple sentences give the evolution of the painting a flat, almost bland character. Goldberg himself expresses a detached, casual attitude toward his work: "it needed something there" or "it was too much." Working on a bounded canvas, the painter can step back and make judgments so that painting becomes a process that is at least somewhat controllable and one that can be completed. At the end of the poem, "Sardines" has been hung in a gallery. O'Hara begins casually enough: "One day I am thinking of / a color: orange." The color orange hardly sounds like a deep, tormenting, or even very significant subject, but the words come pouring out. What little sense of order O'Hara starts out with by writing "a line" quickly dissolves as he fills up a "whole page of words, not lines." He goes on and on; he can hardly stop because he cannot grasp his subject: "there should be / so much more." Writing is described in a tone that is characteristically suspended between flippancy and seriousness; the urgency of "there should be / so much more" is lightened by "of how terrible orange is / and life." A painter could simply *present* orange but O'Hara cannot even fully re-present it and this absence makes writing an endless activity, both self-mocking and desperate—in which closure is always arbitrary. "My poem / is finished," O'Hara announces, only to admit first that it's incomplete ("I haven't mentioned / orange yet") and second that it's actually twelve poems. Goldberg can detach himself from and so complete his work; O'Hara always remains inside language and so he cannot reach any external perspective that would allow him to view either his work or its putative subject as a whole. The poet remains close to a subject from which he is also finally alienated; his words cannot grasp his objects. O'Hara thus locates writing inside temporal process and, as we shall see, he does so with radical literary results.

At a poetry reading held on Staten Island in the early sixties, O'Hara read a poem which he had less trouble with than "Oranges": he said he had written it on the way over on the ferry. Robert Lowell, following O'Hara, sardonically apologized for *not* reading a poem he had written

on the ferry.[10] Lowell was no doubt annoyed by O'Hara's arrogant assurance that he could write a good poem so quickly and easily, but the
anecdote also reveals a basic difference of poetic principle between the
two men. Lowell had relinquished many of the traditional resources of
poetry in *Life Studies*, but his poems remained serious acts designed both
to include and to contain the movements of time and consciousness.[11]
Writing for O'Hara was a much more casual activity, taking place inside
the flow of daily activities (like riding the ferry), many of the poems—the
"lunch hour" poems, for instance—enacting sheer process: agile, shifting,
unpredictable *movement*.

A Step Away from Them

It's my lunch hour, so I go
for a walk among the hum-colored
cabs. First, down the sidewalk
where laborers feed their dirty
glistening torsos sandwiches
and Coca-Cola, with yellow helmets
on. They protect them from falling
bricks, I guess. Then onto the
avenue where skirts are flipping
above heels and blow up over
grates. The sun is hot, but the
cabs stir up the air. I look
at bargains in wristwatches. There
are cats playing in sawdust.
On
to Times Square, where the sign
blows smoke over my head, and higher
the waterfall pours lightly. A
Negro stands in a doorway with a
toothpick, languorously agitating.
A blonde chorus girl clicks: he
smiles and rubs his chin. Everything
suddenly honks: it is 12:40 of
a Thursday.
Neon in daylight is a

10. The poem O'Hara wrote was "Poem [Lana Turner has collapsed]"; the anecdote is
told by Joe LeSueur in "Four Apartments: A Memoir of Frank O'Hara," in *Homage to
Frank O'Hara*, p. 48.
11. Lowell told a Harvard class that a lyric poem is "a monument to immediacy"; quoted
by Helen Vendler, "Lowell in the Classroom," *Harvard Advocate* 113 (November 1979):
24.

> great pleasure, as Edwin Denby would
> write, as are light bulbs in daylight.
> I stop for a cheeseburger at JULIET'S
> CORNER. Giulietta Masina, wife of
> Federico Fellini, *è bell' attrice*.
> And chocolate malted. A lady in
> foxes on such a day puts her poodle
> in a cab.
>   There are several Puerto
> Ricans on the avenue today, which
> makes it beautiful and warm. First
> Bunny died, then John Latouche,
> the Jackson Pollock. But is then
> earth as full as life was full, of them?
> And one has eaten and one walks,
> past the magazines with nudes
> and the posters for BULLFIGHT and
> the Manhattan Storage Warehouse,
> which they'll soon tear down. I
> used to think they had the Armory
> Show there.
>   A glass of papaya juice
> and back to work. My heart is in my
> pocket, it is Poems by Pierre Reverdy.

"A Step Away from Them" possesses a charming immediacy and spontaneous energy. These very qualities, however, may tempt any critical assassins lurking in the shadows to conclude that "A Step" is something worse than a bad poem—no poem. So this critic once concluded.

Yet, O'Hara titled so many of his works "Poem" precisely because he was aware that many of his readers would deny them the status of poetry. But rather than closing the issue prematurely, we should explore the ways in which O'Hara has redefined the specifically poetic quality. "Picasso made me tough and quick," O'Hara writes in "Memorial Day 1950," and he locates the poetic in a tough realism and an elusive mobility. Whereas normally in reading poetry we experience a tension between the urge to go on and the desire to linger over the parts and prolong our pleasure, in O'Hara the poem is *all* forward push. "A Step Away from Them" sits at the opposite end of the literary spectrum from the self-reflexive autonomous works of the modernists. If the modernists tried to spatialize lyric form, O'Hara radically temporalizes it.

"A Step Away from Them" represents time as an ongoing experience, purely physical and purely transitory. During his lunch hour, O'Hara steps away from his fellow workers at the Museum of Modern Art and strolls out into the animate, shifting life of the city at noontime. He keeps moving, taking things in with the speed and precision of a movie camera; the poetic self seems a transparency—again, like a movie film—and experience is absorbed with a kind of evenly suspended attention that does not permit discrimination, emphasis, or even interpretation. O'Hara thus moves through a demystified and secular world of immediacy, from which all vertical, transcendent extensions of meaning have disappeared. Sensations are not "corridors" toward transcendent vision, as they are in Wright; materiality is not given only in order to be chanted out of existence, as it is in Ginsberg; the poem is no "temple," the poet no "priest," as they are in Levertov. An O'Hara poem—unlike Oakland—is a there that is simply *there*. "After all / who does own any thing?" he wryly asks in "The Three-Penny Opera." Physical objects in O'Hara do not invite, much less justify, any search for hidden meanings; they cannot be possessed (owned) by means of any frame of reference, sacred or secular. Objects in O'Hara lack depth and duration; they lack depth *because* they lack duration: they go by too quickly to yield meanings.

Of course, even in the relatively small body of criticism that has been written about O'Hara, the interpretive assassins, unwilling to revise their reading habits, have entered the orchards. In *Poems in Persons,* Norman Holland cites another of the lunch hour poems, "The Day Lady Died," and confesses that he found the poem "irritating" because its details seemed "so random and inconsequential." "As for me," Holland writes, "I can only make sense of such a poem by trying to bring all its puzzling elements into some fairly tight relation." And so, rather than trying to discover the poetic motives behind the casual flow of detail in the poem, Holland instead chooses to allay his professional nervousness and reconfirm his belief in organic form "by bringing a psychoanalytic concept to bear," specifically, the concept of orality.[12] Where there was surface, Holland implies, let their be depths, preferably familiar depths. Once Holland or any other critic gets on a track like this, he is not likely to be derailed and his critical engine runs smoothly across O'Hara's poetic orchards, if not converting snakes into penises, then converting the purchase of a pack of cigarettes into an oral fantasy.

Yet O'Hara's poems are filled with signals that such interpretative procedures are inappropriate to them. In his quick, forward-moving medium, observations are not held, weighed, ruminated over, fetishized. O'Hara does not even seem very involved with his objects—but a step away from them. As a result, both persons and objects, and ideas and feelings, become momentary events, experience consumed almost in the instant it is

12. *Poems in Persons* (New York, 1973), pp. 119–20.

given. Sometimes the experience can be an unexpected sense of unity: "Everything / suddenly honks, it is 12:40 of / a Thursday," but the very precision with which O'Hara locates this moment of unity (12:40, in digits) reminds us of its ephemerality. Williams is one of the few American poets who meant a lot to O'Hara, but if we contrast O'Hara with Williams, we see how steadfastly O'Hara refused to eternalize his objects. Williams slows us down and concentrates our attention on both the object and the words representing it; his poems present isolated images arrested in an empty space. The object has been lifted out of the temporal flux and preserved in "eternal moment."[13] But O'Hara's observations are not grasped and eternalized in this way; as he writes in "Meditations in an Emergency," "my eyes are vague blue, like the sky, and change all the time; they are indiscriminate but fleeting." What is preserved in O'Hara is precisely this fleeting, ever changing experience of temporal process itself.

To say all of this is to say that it is not entirely true to argue, as Marjorie Perloff does, that O'Hara replaces an aesthetic of "transcendence" with one of "presence."[14] His lunch hour poems do create a wonderful sense of immediate experience, but they also represent immediacy as evanescent, fleeting, transitory. Sensations disappear almost as soon as they are presented. Objects and people thus remain alien to a poet who can never fully possess them. O'Hara, in other words, remains "a step away from them"; the poem's title in fact offers a double-edged statement that precisely defines the poet's relation toward experience. He's separate, different—the *observer* of all the others—yet his observations are detailed, close, and his own energy parallels the vital life he sees all around him: he's *just* a step away from them. He's both at home and alien, comfortable and anxious, in the city, and, as "A Step Away from Them" shows, both of these contradictory feelings are necessary to O'Hara's sense of self. When he remarks that the "several Puerto / Ricans" make the street seem "beautiful and warm," he experiences the city as a pleasurable fullness, a feeling that passes almost instantly as O'Hara recalls loss and death: "First / Bunny died, then John Latouche, / then Jackson Pollock." With the next sentence, "But is the / earth as full as life was full, of them?" the flow of observations comes to a sudden halt. O'Hara pauses for self-conscious, reflective questioning; the reader is halted by the peculiar word order and by the need to spell out the ways in which the sentence plays

13. *Spring and All,* in *Imaginations,* ed. Webster Schott (New York, 1971), p. 89.
14. My account of O'Hara thus differs from those two of his critics that I am most indebted to, Perloff and Altieri in *Enlarging the Temple,* pp. 108–22. Perloff stresses presence, while Altieri puts much more emphasis on the anxiety in O'Hara's work; see his review of Perloff's book in *JEGP* 77 (April 1978): 299–301.

with a cliché. Ordinarily we think of certain people as "full of life," but O'Hara turns the phrase around so that life was full with those now absent. Is the earth (where they are buried and decomposing) now full as life was once full with them? Is the earth, human life, now full as it used to be when they were alive or is temporal experience one of loss and decline? The reader is brought to a heavy stop with the emphatically placed word "them," which, in the poem's only self-reflexive gesture, takes us back to the title for another set of referents for its "them." Like everybody else, O'Hara is always just a step away from his lost friends, from his own mortality.

Conventionally, such thoughts of time and loss prompt the poet to adopt some eternal perspective from which they can be reconciled; in O'Hara, these weighty issues are simply dropped. O'Hara's mood does change; the ebullient, separate "I" becomes a melancholy, anonymous "one" who keeps moving but who seems merely to be going through the motions in a depressed, mechanical way, passing tawdry magazines and posters and a warehouse, once thought to be the scene of the heroic Armory Show, now about to be torn down. Temporality is felt to be destructive, not a fullness, and the poet seems passive and sad and empty. It's as if the thought of the mortality shared by all makes him just another anonymous figure in the city; he's lost his animating sense of difference.

But O'Hara's depression simply passes. The poem presents a rapid series of unconnected moments and any vestigial desire we may feel to spatialize the poem by viewing it as a conflict between feelings of presence and loss is thwarted by the way these issues are just dropped and by O'Hara's steadfast refusal to provide anything like a resolution at the end. In the final paragraph he drinks some papaya juice and cheerfully returns to work, with a book of poems he loves tucked away in his pocket. Next to this, even an anticlimactic closure like "Come winter, / Uncle Devereux would blend to the one color" sounds heavy-handed and literary. O'Hara's casualness, however, makes the poem not less but more moving, giving it an *emotional* verisimilitude. O'Hara, then, is not the kind of writer who presses down on or even gently prods a subject until it yields its essence. Another reason he called so many of his works "Poem" is that he didn't want them to have identifiable subjects like a photograph or a monument. Instead, "A Step Away from Them" presents shifting, contradictory moods, tones, perspectives, selves without either gathering them together into a center or nailing them down with a resolution. As O'Hara says in "Personism," "you just go on your nerve." The poetry that results offers plurality rather than unity, energy and movement rather than the comforts of a stabilizing form.

From Eliot to Ginsberg the modern city poem has been structured as a mythical purgatorial journey that strips away illusions and yields at least the possibility of transcendence. The differences between Eliot's aloof irony and Ginsberg's angry howl or between Eliot's sibylline Sanskrit revelations and Ginsberg's Blakean mysticism are profound, but both "The Waste Land" and "Howl" offer panoramic views of the modern city only in order to annihilate social and physical realities in a moment of hallucinatory vision. Frank O'Hara's lunch hour poems demythologize the poetry of the modern city—as we can see by looking at "Personal Poem."

Now when I walk around at lunchtime
I have only two charms in my pocket
an old Roman coin Mike Kanemitsu gave me
and a bolt-head that broke off a packing case
when I was in Madrid the others never
brought me too much luck though they did
help keep me in New York against coercion
but now I'm happy for a time and interested

I walk through the luminous humidity
passing the House of Seagram with its wet
and its loungers and the construction to
the left that closed the sidewalk if
I ever get to be a construction worker
I'd like to have a silver hat please
and get to Moriarty's where I wait for
LeRoi and hear who wants to be a mover and
shaker the last five years my batting average
is .016 that's that, and LeRoi comes in
and tells me Miles Davis was clubbed 12
times last night outside BIRDLAND by a cop
a lady asks us for a nickel for a terrible
disease but we don't give her one we
don't like terrible diseases, then

we go eat some fish and some ale it's
cool but crowded we don't like Lionel Trilling
we decide, we like Don Allen we don't like
Henry James so much we like Herman Melville
we don't want to be in the poets' walk in
San Francisco even we just want to be rich
and walk on girders in our silver hats
I wonder if one person out of the 8,000,000 is
thinking of me as I shake hands with LeRoi

and buy a strap for my wristwatch and go
back to work happy at the thought possibly so

Like "A Step Away from Them," "Personal Poem" creates an interplay
of playful and serious tones in a quick, light movement. The poem begins
with a paragraph of recollection in which the reader may be tempted to
stop and to metaphorize the "old Roman coin" and the "bolt-head," the
one rare and the other plain, but he is not given enough clues to justify
such a procedure. The charms simply affirm O'Hara's faith in chance and
randomness rather than in control or coercion, and it would be a serious
error to place them in "some fairly tight relation" with each other or with
other details in the poem.

O'Hara is no poetic "mover and / shaker"; he just goes on his nerve
and so does the poem. O'Hara did not like "elaborately sounded structures," he tells us in "Personism"; in fact, he did not like elaborately
articulated structures of any kind. "Pain always produces logic, which is
very bad for you," he declares. Instead of intricate form or subtle argument, "Personal Poem" gives us a rapid catalog of reflection, observation,
conversation, fantasy. A catalog presents material apparently without
selection or hierarchy; it eliminates logical connections, and it *moves*—
without containing any principle that would determine the end (goal or
termination) of that movement. "Do you think we can ever / strike *as*
and *but,* too, out of the language," O'Hara asks in "Essay on Style";
"then we can attack *well* since it has no / application whatsoever neither
as a state / of being or a rest for the mind no such / things available." In
O'Hara's world of ongoing process *states* of being and rests for the mind
are not available; that is why his speculation on the possibility of eliminating logical connectives from poetic language is at least half serious.
That is why no periods (rests) are to be found in "Personal Poem," which
comes very close to a language of pure parataxis, of ongoingness. Nor is
it the case that behind its discontinuous surface we can discover a hidden
system of connections, the way we can in reading works as different as
"The Waste Land" and *Spring and All*. O'Hara remains *inside* the flow
of experience, not reaching nervously after some external perspective
from which, safely, to view the modern city.

According to O'Hara, the trouble with Olson was his weakness for
the "important utterance" (*SS,* p. 13). The last thing that O'Hara wants
to do with experience is to transmute it into conclusive statement: "no
such / things available." Abstract statements can be found in his poetry,
but ideas are to O'Hara what balls are to a juggler: the last thing you want
to do is to hang on to one. "We don't like Lionel Trilling"; "we don't
like / Henry James so much"; "we don't want to be in the poets' walk

in / San Francisco," but the childish insistence with which these attitudes are expressed makes them seem playful and theatrical rather than positions the speaker is deeply committed to—just as the fantasies in the poem ("we just want to be rich / and walk on girders in our silver hats") are mock fantasies rather than ones that O'Hara cherishes or is obsessed by. If the tone does become serious, he lightens it by making "terrible diseases" into a grammatical joke or by flippantly dismissing his concern about isolation ("possibly so"). At the same time "Personal Poem" is not merely flippant; it contains a continuous and realistic recognition of the pains and limits of urban life. There is an unspecified "coercion" that might have forced him out of New York (or did his charms keep him in New York up against coercion?), the low batting average in his love life, the beating of Miles Davis, the "terrible diseases," the "crowded" restaurant, the isolation and animosity of a large city and the feeling all through the poem of the pressure of time, the ephemerality of both pleasurable and painful experiences ("now I'm happy *for a time* and interested"). "Personal Poem" thus includes an awareness of the coercive and even violent realities of the city, but O'Hara does not respond with Ginsberg's outraged howl of protest. Ginsberg's dilemma is that he deifies coercion into "Moloch," a force so powerful and ubiquitous that it can only be eluded by soaring upward toward transcendence, permanence, and rest.

One of O'Hara's special qualities, then, is that while he does not long to control events, he is not controlled by them either. He dwells on his frustrations no more than he dwells on his satisfactions. If his "batting average / is .016," well, "that's that," and he goes on. The beating of Miles Davis—which Ginsberg would have made into an entire poem in lamentation for the martyred "bop saint"—outrages O'Hara no more than did the rich lady putting her poodle into a cab in "A Step Away from Them." Social realities are not transformed into social issues; instead, they are simply presented, given equal weight and emphasis along with all the other items in the quick play of the poet's attention. At the end of the poem O'Hara wonders "if one person out of the 8,000,000 is / thinking of me." It's an ironic speculation since he *is* shaking LeRoi Jones's hand at the time and he might assume that Jones has him in mind, but then of course O'Hara is not thinking of Jones so there's no reason to suppose that Jones is thinking of him. Isolation *is* a serious matter in the poem. It may be the cost of living (and writing) without connections, and concern about it stays with O'Hara for a fairly long time, from shaking hands with Jones until he buys a strap for his watch. But in the *poem* the experience speeds by and O'Hara thus avoids self-pity; the tone, moreover, is lightened by the strap, a mundane and neutral object. "Personal

Poem" thus does not close with epiphany, some moment of self-recognition; the serious mood merely dissolves as O'Hara playfully leaves the question to chance: "possibly so."

"I was crowded with / windows," O'Hara exclaims in "A Rant"; or near the beginning of "In Memory of My Feelings," he similarly writes, "my quietness has a number of naked selves." With their realistic precision and their swift, free, uncommitted movement, the lunch hour poems create the poetic self as a rapid, filmlike series of transparencies, open to experience, neutrally and indiscriminately taking it in, the self an "appropriate sense of space" in which things can remain themselves and poems become themselves (*CP*, p. 307). Such receptivity poses the dilemma of ending and entails real dangers. The self may be so open and sensitive to sensation that it may feel engulfed and glutted. "I know so much / about things, I accept / so much, it's like / vomiting," O'Hara complains in "Spleen." In fact, so fragile and unstable are the boundaries of the self that O'Hara lives just a step away from self-extinction. That is why the dangers of death and anonymity enter "A Step Away from Them" and "Personal Poem." But by running these risks O'Hara created a poetic medium that seems delivered from the violence of a formed style or personality. "Personism," he says, "does not have to do with personality or intimacy, far from it!" No confessional poet, O'Hara does not explore the unconscious depths in order slowly to construct a managing ego, the way Lowell does in *Life Studies,* nor does he plumb the unconscious looking for "deep images," the way Wright does in *The Branch Will Not Break.* Objects in the lunch hour poems lack metaphoric depth; the poems' speaker lacks psychic depth—as if he sensed the unconscious to be clogged with weighty obsessions, maddeningly repeated scenarios and themes, and so to descend to those depths would be to fix rather than to free the self. For the last hundred and eighty years poets have been pumping the well of the unconscious in order to explore new interior states and yet to claim a universal or shareable status for those private feelings. The only trouble with the unconscious, for O'Hara, is that it's a bore, a structure of repetition.

After all, who does own or even wants to own anything, including a self? Rather than the self as the organized and organizing center, O'Hara works from a self that is mobile, shifting, multiple ("crowded with / windows"), contradictory, elusive, and incomplete. Always present and always open and exposed ("naked"), O'Hara is nevertheless continually disappearing over the next hill or, more accurately, around the corner of the next skyscraper. His protean movement reminds us of Whitman, whom O'Hara rated, along with Williams and Crane, as one of the three American poets who is "better than the movies" (*CP*, p. 498). But Whitman's fluidity has the assurance of both an origin and an end in his transcendent "Me myself," an identity that persists outside of time and change. O'Hara has no such permanent center to start from or return to. Like many poets of the fifties, he repudiated the "impersonal ideal" or what he called in "Personism" the "abstract removal" of the poet. Instead, he gives us *person*ism, or a "personal poem" that is spoken in a casual, intimate tone and filled with the quotidian details of his day. But although O'Hara went further than practically any of his contemporaries in stripping down the poem, he did not fall into the generational trap of simply reversing an impersonal into a "naked" poetics. Personism, remember, does not have to do with personality or intimacy; the lunch hour poems offer no stable self for us to become intimate with.

The self in O'Hara is, then, at once transparent *and* opaque—perhaps his deepest contradiction. Like the color orange in "Oranges," O'Hara exists both everywhere and nowhere in his poems. We see things through his eyes, but we can never step back, surround, and frame him—he is "always bursting forth" (*CP,* p. 197). If O'Hara is not the withdrawn artist of modernism, he is not wholly present to himself or to us either. Many of the same features that make the poems seem so direct and immediate (absence of connections and depth) also estrange and conceal the speaker from us, just as his use of the names of his friends, as if they were just as familiar to us as to him ("First / Bunny died, then John Latouche"), creates a *tone* of intimacy while pressing upon us the *reality* of O'Hara's difference and distance from us.[15] It is this sense of estrangement that makes these light, casual poems quietly unnerving and adds another voice to their rich, contradictory play of tones.

"The only way to be quiet / is to be quick," says O'Hara in "Poetry," "so I scare / you clumsily, or surprise / you with a stab." Renouncing the prophetic voice of Olson or Ginsberg, O'Hara approaches us in a quieter, conversational tone. Yet this familiarity is assumed rather than actual, as his equation of intimacy with awkwardness and hostility reveals. O'Hara does wish he could exist on easy terms with his reader—"as if / I were used to you." In fact, even this wish is exposed at the end of the poem as egoistic—"as if," O'Hara concludes, "you would never leave me / and were the inexorable / product of my own time." The clichéd language mocks this desire for a permanent fusion as a narcissistic fantasy, as if he wanted to get close only in order to take over. Yet poet and reader remain separate and O'Hara's efforts "to / deepen you by my quickness / and delight" only mobilize resistance in readers who cling to what's "logical and proven." Just as "Poetry" itself proceeds through quick turns

15. Altieri, *Enlarging the Temple,* p. 112.

of thought and witty reversals of "proven" truths, so O'Hara destabilizes
and complicates the relation between poet and reader. The gap between
the two becomes a space in which familiarity, awkwardness, estrangement, delight, and hostility all coexist.

A similar gap divides the world from the poet, who can never fully
possess ("own") his objects. Continually aware of this disparity between
actuality and its representations, O'Hara offers both the most vivid instance *and* the most powerful critique of his generation's poetics of immediacy. In O'Hara, as in the poetry of Ashbery, an elusive immediacy
always remains other, and if O'Hara's lunch hour poems strain toward a
literal realism, their rapidity (they do move much faster than time actually
does) suggests an uneasiness with reality, as if O'Hara kept moving because he was afraid to stop and get involved. To put it another way,
O'Hara proposes no reality beyond and above time, but he is not comfortably at one with it either. He takes one short step back and away—
then he starts moving. His separateness sometimes makes O'Hara anxious, sometimes it makes him playful, and sometimes it makes him both,
as it does in "On Seeing Larry Rivers' *Washington Crossing the Delaware*
at the Museum of Modern Art."

Now that our hero has come back to us
in his white pants and we know his nose
trembling like a flag under fire,
we see the calm cold river is supporting
our forces, the beautiful history.

To be more revolutionary than a nun
is our desire, to be secular and intimate
as, when sighting a redcoat, you smile
and pull the trigger. Anxieties
and animosities, flaming and feeding

on theoretical considerations and
the jealous spiritualities of the abstract,
the robot? they're smoke, billows above
the physical event. They have burned up.
See how free we are! as a nation of persons.

Dear father of our country, so alive
you must have lied incessantly to be
immediate, here are your bones crossed
on my breast like a rusty flintlock,
a pirate's flag, bravely specific

and ever so light in the misty glare
of a crossing by water in winter to a shore
other than that the bridge reaches for.
Don't shoot until, the white of freedom glinting
on your gun barrel, you see the general fear.

Based on Emmanuel Leutze's "Washington Crossing the Delaware," Rivers's work manages simultaneously to mock the academicism of his source and to outrage the contemporary New York avant-garde.[16] What make his painting a scandal was not his use of figuration (both DeKooning and Pollock had already moved in that direction) but his subject matter; it was not only recognizable, it was historical, patriotic, nostalgic, corny, pop—calendar art. As he later told O'Hara in an interview,

> I was energetic and egomaniacal and what is even more important, cocky, and angry enough to want to do something no one in the New York art world could doubt was *disgusting, dead,* and *absurd.* So, what could be dopier than a painting dedicated to a national cliché—Washington Crossing the Delaware. [*AC,* pp. 111–12]

Moreover, the research and the many sketches Rivers drew to prepare for the painting constituted an almost pedantic repudiation of abstract expressionist faith in spontaneity. His thin application of paint departed from their thick, painterly surface, just as his irony mocked their intense earnestness. Worst of all, Rivers rejected his predecessors' heroic conception, their sacralization, of the act of painting.

Rivers's work makes its double-edged comment by being, in O'Hara's phrase, "bravely specific." As Rivers goes on to say in the O'Hara interview, Leutze

> thought crossing a river on a late December afternoon was just another excuse for a general to assume a heroic, slightly tragic pose. . . . What *I* saw in the crossing was quite different. I saw the moment as nerve-racking and uncomfortable. I couldn't picture anyone getting into a chilly river around Christmas time with anything resembling hand-on-chest heroics. [*AC,* p. 112]

In Leutze's painting, the front side of the boat, the oar at the left, and the line established at the right by the heads of other occupants of the boat create a triangle with the head of Washington at its apex. At the same time, the icy river, the stormy sky, and the winter glare create a blurred natural background, against which the heroic mastery of Wash-

16. There is a color reproduction of the Rivers painting in Sam Hunter's *Larry Rivers* (New York, n.d.). For Rivers's own account of this painting, see Larry Rivers, *Drawings and Digressions,* with Carol Brightman (New York, 1979), pp. 59–60.

Larry Rivers, *Washington Crossing the Delaware* (1953). Oil on canvas, 6' 11⅝" × 9' 3⅝". Collection, The Museum of Modern Art, New York.

ington is dramatically asserted. All of the painting's other elements are subordinated to Washington, its idealized heroic center. Less illusionistic than Leutze's, Rivers's work is nevertheless more realistic, treating the father of our country with a mixture of mockery and tribute. This crossing *is* "nerve-racking and uncomfortable"; it is cold, as our hero's pink nose testifies, and it is disorderly, as the dispersion of the viewer's gaze out from the center to independent areas of interest (e.g., top and bottom left) testifies. Moreover, the cold white river, no mere background in Rivers's painting, becomes a threatening, invasive force, breaking out of its boundaries to the left of Washington, its white reappearing first in the horse, then in the landscape at the upper left. More ominously, parts of Washington—his right arm and leg—have dissolved into this cold white. Yet Washington, framed by the boat, aligned with the sun, larger than the other figures, and straight across from the viewer, remains the center, not the idealized but still the calm heroic center. In this painting, abstraction (via the color white) threatens to obliterate human presence, and human powers (of generals, of painters) are no longer sufficient to pull the parts of an army or of a painting into stable unity. Yet emerging out of the surrounding cold, disarray, blur (what O'Hara calls "the general fear"), Washington struggles to achieve, and does achieve, presence, distinction, heroism. So Rivers does not merely parody Leutze and debunk heroism; he redefines it, locating the mythic in the real.

Like Rivers's painting, O'Hara's poem mixes mockery and tribute to create the complex image of a "revolutionary" hero. His fun with "pop" phrases from the "Star-Spangled Banner" ("and ever so light in the misty glare") or from grade school histories ("Don't shoot until you see . . .") were probably suggested by Rivers's play with Leutze's visual cliché and Rivers's use, while working on the painting, of illustrations from grade school history books. But in this poem at least O'Hara is less interested in adapting specific techniques from painting than he is in making his meditation on the Washington the occasion for formulating an aesthetic he shared with Rivers.

At first O'Hara's poem seems to pose a simplified antithesis between realistic and mythical versions of Washington, as if Rivers and O'Hara were somehow powerful enough to burn away all "theoretical consider-ations and / the jealous spiritualities of the abstract" to arrive at the authentic "physical event." Instead of the mythical "robot" of national folklore, noble, courageous, totally honest, they present an actual *person* who is cold, afraid ("his nose / trembling like a flag under fire"), a calm, cool, intimate killer, a secular but still abstracted idealist ("the white of freedom glinting / on your gun barrel"), and an incessant liar. Mythol-ogizing, which abstracts from and rigidifies what's "alive," O'Hara im-plies, is prompted by "anxieties and animosities"—"the general fear." The alternative, he suggests, can be found in the "bravely specific" (and totally honest) works of Rivers and O'Hara, whose demythologizings create rather than allay anxiety, since intimacy and specificity become forms of violence when the audience clings to what's familiar, abstract, logical, and proven.

Rivers repudiates abstract expressionism; O'Hara repudiates the fifties' amalgam of symbolist and New Critical principles. Both painter and poet move toward realism, the "bravely specific." Yet this oppositional stance did not force O'Hara into a simplified notion of poetic immediacy, and his poem on Rivers's Washington poses the antithesis between the real and the mythic, the immediate and the fictive, only in order to dissolve it by showing how the opposed terms are implicated with each other.[17] In fact, neither poem nor painting is all that specific or realistic in manner.

17. As I have pointed out earlier, the contraries in poets like Olson, Ginsberg, and Bly are hierarchically structured and ultimately static; in the more dialectical O'Hara, they are in perpetual motion.

Their textures are aptly described by O'Hara's phrase "misty glare," indefinite and beautiful, clear and harsh. The "dear father of our country" is thus presented as both a frightened real person and as the mythical hero in "white pants," not the idealized "robot" of Leutze's work; "our hero has come back to us" as absurd, menacing, dear, duplicitous, scared, and heroic. So O'Hara (like Rivers) does not so much *de*- as *re*-mythologize Washington; in fact, the poem playfully rejects the idea that we can shed all myths and abstractions to become, at last, free persons. "See how free we are! as a nation of persons," O'Hara sardonically exclaims. Hence, if O'Hara mocks the flight from "the physical event," he also criticizes the fantasy that we can be emancipated from "theoretical considerations" and "the abstract." Washington boldly repudiated the religious idealism and subservience of a "nun," but "to be more revolutionary than a nun" is not to be all *that* revolutionary, and Washington's desire to be secular and intimate is also quickly unmasked. He gets close in order, smiling, to kill, and he slays, ironically, to impose a new secular abstraction, "the white of freedom." Animosities and theoretical considerations persist, because of the "general fear" that stirs them.

But O'Hara is not a detached observer who is describing a condition from which he has exempted himself. He mocks his own revolutionary pretensions, and he concedes his own experience (like that of Rivers's Washington) of the "general fear" in a way that makes the end of his ironic, sometimes flippant poem emotionally powerful. The poem's closing sentence begins with the reassurance of a "proven" heroic and verbal formula: "Don't shoot until. . . ." But O'Hara then interrupts the cliché with "the white of freedom glinting / on your gun barrel." The potential violence is ennobled by high purpose in "freedom," though "white" may suggest an unsullied beginning or a freedom that is all too abstract and pure, like Washington's impossibly white pants in the painting, and "glinting" makes ominous suggestions that are realized as O'Hara, turning the thought across the line break, uses the plain specificity of "gun barrel" to expose the realities behind the lofty abstraction, "freedom." At this point, ending the sentence with the expected cliché—"until you see the whites of their eyes"—would reassure the reader with its comforting familiarity and by providing a specific, locatable, and intimate target for animosities. But like Rivers's, O'Hara's work is *dis*comforting, and so he does not resolve the poem's tensions by opting either for the dead formula or its mere debunking. Instead, at the end, poet and reader are left, like Washington himself, within a "general fear" which threatens but fails to engulf and overwhelm us.

O'Hara and Rivers both combine improvisational energy, realism of detail, and a continual awareness of loss. O'Hara once remarked that

Rivers's "fluctuation between figurative absence and abstract presence" played out "the drama of our lack" (*SS,* p. 96). Rivers's paintings (like the Washington) are filled with human figures who are missing an eye, an arm, a leg, and "Washington Crossing the Delaware" is partly *about* the danger of being flooded by abstraction—losing distinct shape, color, substance. In his poem on the painting O'Hara, too, feels the threat of "theoretical considerations and / the jealous spiritualities of the abstract" obliterating "the physical event." The dispersed, transparent, mobile self of poems like "A Step Away from Them" exists at the edge of extinction and anonymity, while the people and things perceived, like ideas and feelings, vanish as quickly as they appear. Like Rivers's, O'Hara's works assert a human presence always on the *verge* of disappearance; they play out the drama of our lack—and our substance.

Like Washington, O'Hara was "so alive" he "must have lied incessantly to be / immediate." One implication of the Washington poem is that a brave specificity is an assumed posture, that immediacy is a lie, an illusion, a poetic construction. "I really dislike dishonesty [more] than bad lines," O'Hara told an interviewer, but, having ranked sincerity over literary values, O'Hara then reversed his ground by declaring that dishonesty occurs when "someone is making themselves more elegant, more stupid, more appealing, more affectionate or more sincere than *the words will allow them to be*" (*SS,* pp. 13–14; my emphasis). In short, honesty is a literary *effect,* a more or less persuasive illusion. Moreover, the very linguistic nature of poems marks them as constructs. Objects, persons, events all have a dynamic, elusive quality for O'Hara that converts writing into an activity which, as we have seen in "Why I Am Not a Painter," can never finally enclose its objects. Poetic language is thus not magically incarnational for O'Hara, as it is for Levertov. Poetic works, even ones as close to ongoing process as O'Hara's lunch hour poems, are creations that are ultimately provisional, arbitrary, and artificial—literary.[18]

As a result, the self in O'Hara's poetry—honest and duplicitous, transparent and opaque—becomes a fictional construct as well, even though it is not easy to pin down exactly *what* has been constructed. Confessional poetry often works by stripping away externally imposed, "false" selves in order to uncover an original, core self which, in a poet like Plath, turns out to be not her real but her idealized self: Ariel, the "fine, white flying

18. A point that is subtly suggested at the end of "A Step Away from Them." The last sentence—"My heart is in my / pocket, it is Poems by Pierre Reverdy"—can mean that the poet is going back to work cheerfully with a book of poems he loves tucked away in his pocket, but O'Hara's play with the cliché—"my heart is on my sleeve"—also stresses that here, as in "My Heart," O'Hara's heart is hidden and literary, identified with a book of poems. At the end of this seemingly artless poem, then, O'Hara lightly concedes its fictiveness.

myth." Such poetry, then, exploits a rhetoric of honesty and self-exposure in order to permit the writer to mythologize him or herself in ways that the ostensibly self-exploring poet remains blind to. O'Hara denounced the "emotional spilling over" he found in confessional verse (*SS,* p. 35); he attacked its excesses because he repudiated the model of consciousness that justified them. Rather than struggling to recover a lost core of identity, O'Hara creates a theatricalized self that is never completely disclosed in any of its "scenes." A title like "My Heart" leads us to expect revelation of the poet's inmost feelings. But O'Hara begins a little flippantly (and self-congratulatorily): "I'm not going to cry all the time / nor shall I laugh all the time, / I don't prefer one 'strain' to another." The poem continues to stress his elusive contradictoriness and concludes with what seems a simple affirmation of O'Hara's unguarded receptivity: "and my heart— / you can't plan on the heart, but / the better part of it, my poetry, is open." The heart is spontaneous, open to change, unpredictably alive, but this heart is not located in the flesh and blood Frank O'Hara but in his creations, "my poetry," where we encounter "the better part of it." That slippery phrase may suggest that his poems contain the more acceptable part of himself or that they contain most but not all of him. Either way, a part of O'Hara remains outside of poems in which openness is an admitted act of contrivance and duplicity. "My final merit I refuse you," Whitman warned in "Song of Myself"; like him, O'Hara cannot be contained even within the relatively gentle boundaries of his "open" literary creations, and in this self-absence we have O'Hara's final gesture of elusiveness. Perhaps more than any poet, O'Hara minimizes the difference between a poetic and an actual, interpersonal act of communication; "the poem is at last between two persons instead of two pages," he says in "Personism." O'Hara's conversational voice, along with his whole way of assuming our familiarity with his small circle of friends in New York, creates a very strong sense that the poems are spoken by an empirical individual, not the persona of New Criticism. Yet the poet can no more present or even represent the real Frank O'Hara than he can the real George Washington; O'Hara, too, had to lie incessantly to be immediate.

"It is more important to affirm the least sincere," claimed the author of the seemingly artless and spontaneous lunch hour poems, suggesting that at least one of the two persons involved in a poetic transaction might be hard to locate. In fact, the oppositions between nature and artifice, authenticity and duplicity, provide O'Hara's most pervasive contradictions, and many of his poems construct a world of display, disguise, and theatricality in which O'Hara exists with the same mixture of delight and uneasiness with which he speeds along the noontime sidewalks of New York. One place to locate O'Hara's fascination with illusion and appear-

ance is in his film poems: "The Three-Penny Opera," "An Image of Leda,"
"In the Movies," "To the Film Industry in Crisis," "Ave Maria," and the
three elegies for James Dean. Unlike writing, movies present images directly, and this immediacy makes the cinema "cruel / like a miracle"—
like the swan's rape of Leda ("An Image of Leda"). Whereas we can step
back and separate ourselves from a painting, this gap dissolves once the
lights go out and the screen lights up at the movies: the medium floods
the mind with images, giving film the invasive character of a sexual assault.
As O'Hara portrays it in "An Image of Leda," this violation is both
resisted and desired, cruel and miraculous. Yet for all their sensual immediacy, films are finally no more (and no less) a "physical event" than
a poem is. The cinema envelops us in the ravishing and miraculous presence of an illusion, though the final paradox in "An Image of Leda" is
that such an insubstantial "shadow" or "disguise" can give "real /
pleasure."

In fact, a realm of illusion and disguise conveys the same instability
and mobility that we found in the lunch hour poems, as we can see from
O'Hara's poem on the movie of "The Three-Penny Opera." Polly Pea-
chum and her friends are "free and fair," Mack the Knife is a "splendid
hero," because they refuse to become passive sufferers in "the general
fear." "After all / who does own any thing?": the question, as we've seen,
alludes to the absence of human mastery and control in O'Hara's world.
In its specific poetic context, however, the question also gently mocks
the self-justification of the lower-class thief: "I'm not imposing my will
on others because nobody really owns anything anyway." But O'Hara
shows how this defense circles back on its proponent; in "The Three-
Penny Opera" objects possess an almost magical power to elude any
would-be possessor, liberating thieves included. Polly's jewels "have price
tags in case / they want to change / hands, and her pets" are not domesticated but "carnivorous. Even / the birds." Similarly, "Mackie's knife
has a false / handle so it can express / its meaning as well as / his." It is
not as if these objects took on the actively threatening powers of Sylvia
Plath's tulips; rather, our inability to make objects into mere extensions
of our wills becomes at once scary and funny.

But what about Polly and Mackie themselves? Aren't these intriguing
figures cinematic illusions rather than substantial presences? Or, to put
the question a little differently, if O'Hara had been in Berlin in 1930,
would he have found Polly and Mackie "ambling the streets like / Krazy
Kat"? Of course, Krazy Kat, who may have been ambling the comic
pages but hardly the streets of Berlin, collapses the distinction between
reality and fiction that the question had begun by assuming. "You'd have
seen all of us / masquerading." Rather than offering a fixed reference point

that would permit us to discriminate between what's real and what's imaginary, reality itself is enigmatic, fictive, and theatrical. The actors in this play are all "chipper; but / not so well arranged"—like an O'Hara poem; they create a lively surface that is easy to recognize as a contrivance, a role. Yet these charming surfaces and lighthearted disguises cannot finally be penetrated; as in the lunch hour poems, the self ("masquerading") becomes a construction with its depths concealed. Now we can understand more fully why Washington "must have lied incessantly to be / immediate": only by being tricky, slippery—by living variously—can anyone be *alive*.

"The Three-Penny Opera," moreover, makes it particularly clear that it is the very fact that people, objects are various and "free"—and thus, unconnected—that creates "the general fear," a feeling that O'Hara shares but is not dominated by. In the lunch hour poems this lack of connection permits a rapid, shifting mobility that has undertones of anxiety and even moments of melancholy. If the more ominous consequences of such gaps and discontinuities are stressed in "The Three-Penny Opera," O'Hara still crosses the sinister with the playful. "Those / were intricate days," he concludes of the Berlin of 1930; the precisely chosen "intricate" conveys his realistic awareness, and his enjoyment, of the labyrinthine difficulties of an elusive reality.

"The Three-Penny Opera" also explicitly engages the issue of meaning. "Why, / when Mackie speaks we / only know what he means / occasionally"—in part because he speaks German in the movie but, more important, because Mackie is such a liar that we can seldom be sure we know what he *really* means. "His sentence / is an image of the times"; both—sentence and times—are deceptive. Earlier in the poem O'Hara writes that "whenever our / splendid hero Mackie / Messer, what an honest / man! steals or kills, there / is meaning for you!" O'Hara here identifies fixed meaning with violence, as he does in "The Critic," and, by conflating "splendid hero" and "honest / man" with "steals or kills," O'Hara cracks open the fixed senses of these words: *his* sentence becomes an image of the times. O'Hara's "Essay on Style" ponders, illustrates, and mocks his own desire for a mobility of meaning.

> Someone else's Leica sitting on the table
> the black kitchen table I am painting
> the floor yellow, Bill is painting it
> wouldn't you know my mother would call
> up
>   and complain?
>   my sister's pregnant and

went to the country for the weekend without
telling her
                    in point of fact why don't I
go out to have dinner with her or "let her"
come in? well if Mayor Wagner won't allow private
cars on Manhattan because of the snow, I
will probably never see her again
                                        considering
my growingly more perpetual state and how
can one say that angel in the Frick's wings
are "attached" if it's a real angel? now

I was reflecting the other night meaning
I was being reflected upon that Sheridan Square
is remarkably beautiful, sitting in JACK
DELANEY's looking out the big race-track window
on the wet
                    drinking a cognac while Edwin
read my new poem it occurred to me how impossible
it is to fool Edwin not that I don't know as
much as the next about obscurity in modern verse
but he
            always knows what it's about as well
as what it is do you think we can ever
strike *as* and *but,* too, out of the language
then we can attack *well* since it has no
application whatsoever neither as a state
of being or a rest for the mind no such
things available
                            where do you think I've
got to? the spectacle of a grown man
decorating
                    a Christmas tree disgusts me that's
where
            that's one of the places yetbutaswell
I'm glad I went to that party for Ed Dorn
last night though he didn't show up do you think
,Bill, we can get rid of *though* also, and *also*?
maybe your
                    lettrism is the only answer treating
the typewriter as an intimate organ why not?
nothing else is (intimate)
                                no I am not going
to have you "in" for dinner nor am I going "out"
I am going to eat alone for the rest of my life

The "Essay on Style" advocates both familial and literary revolt. Just as he tries to resist maternal impositions, O'Hara seeks to repudiate the coerciveness of a traditional syntax by eliminating all end punctuation and striving for the elimination of logical connectives: "as," "but," "though," etc. The aim is a quick, light, improvisatory style that is intimate with ongoing process; "you just go on your nerve" (*CP*, p. 498). But to free words from fixed, stated relations creates a linguistic field of play in which the words combine and recombine in multiple ways, thus generating a self-reflexive movement that runs counter to the poem's rushed forward impetus. In fact, following "I was reflecting the other night meaning / I was being reflected upon," the poem becomes increasingly self-reflexive. Yet even in the opening lines of the poem—

> Someone else's Leica sitting on the table
> the black kitchen table I am painting
> the floor yellow, Bill is painting it

—we can see that the reader first understands the second line to be saying that O'Hara is painting the table; but as the reader proceeds through the third line, he revises his sense of the second by deciding that "black kitchen table" is not the object of "painting" but an adjectival phrase that goes with "table" in the first line and that the object of "painting" is actually "the floor" in line three. So O'Hara is painting the floor, not the table—or so it seems. The trouble with this conclusion is that the ambiguity of "it" in "Bill is painting it" allows for three different possibilities: O'Hara is painting the table, Bill the floor; O'Hara is painting the floor, Bill the table; they are both painting the floor. Similarly, in the line "can one say that angel in the Frick's wings," "wings" at first seems to refer to a part of the museum, but the following line ("are 'attached' if it's a real angel?") makes "wings" refer to a part of an angel. And how can one speak of a "*real* angel"? Throughout the "Essay on Style" ambiguous words, floating phrases and pronouns with multiple referents create a language in which grammatical functions (and meaning) are not stable. Words become fluid, shifting nodes of energy, like the thieves and stolen goods in "The Three-Penny Opera," and language takes on the same playful intricacy that O'Hara found in the Berlin of 1930. Ironically, then, the very strategies that are developed to permit language to get close to the flow of experience here also work to make the words of the poem opaque, to slow down the reading process, and to acknowledge the poem as a self-reflexive verbal construct that is separate from the reality it seeks to grasp.

The poem's title leads us to expect a work in which O'Hara's stylistic commitments will be defined. Instead, the "Essay" enacts contradictory ideas of style—language as a transparent medium of ongoing process, language as an opaque and self-reflexive construct—and these opposed notions are conveyed in a manner that is at least as parodistic as it is serious. Certainly, the foot-stamping theatricality of filial revolt is mocked in "I am going to eat alone for the rest of my life"; in O'Hara's fluid world, no such things as fixed resolves are available. Throughout the poem O'Hara uses the typewriter—spacing, quotation marks, parentheses—to provide his writing with some of the pauses and emphases that are possible in a spoken act of communication, and yet these very techniques mark the poem as a piece of writing on the page. As a result, "treating / the typewriter as an intimate organ" is both a serious proposal for making writing present in the way a speech act is and a parody of the Olson of "Projective Verse." The project of liberating language from logical connectives—by no means original with O'Hara—is similarly made fun of with the mock connective "yetbutaswell" and with the comic predicament that produces the twisting sentence, "do you think / ,Bill, we can get rid of *though* also, and *also*?" Here, the act of thinking about eliminating such connectives generates more of them and so O'Hara is forced to turn back on his own statements in a way that is ludicrously self-reflexive. Other critics have already discussed the shiftings and ambiguities of language in this poem;[19] but they have not pointed out that O'Hara's proliferation of meanings is self-conscious, playful, and parodistic. It's "not that I don't know as / much as the next about obscurity in modern verse," says O'Hara, winking as he takes a bow. In the "Essay on Style," obscurity envelops matters that are strikingly trivial, as if obscurity were merely a game of mystification. Knowing (or not being able to know) who painted what in the kitchen is not the kind of nut which, when cracked open, yields a kernel of weighty thematic significance. Besides, the awful color scheme for the kitchen (floor yellow, table black) makes it hard to view this scene in a serious way. By elaborating slight issues, O'Hara's multivalence of language parodies the serious use of this technique in writers as different as Eliot, Williams, and Olson.

Yet the "Essay on Style" is at least as serious as it is parodistic. If obscurity can be a trick, it can also be genuinely expressive, as O'Hara implies in his characterization of "Edwin" Denby, whom it is "impossible" "to fool," who "always knows what it's about as well / as what

19. For an excellent analysis of "Essay on Style," see Marjorie Perloff's "New Thresholds, Old Anatomies: Contemporary Poetry and the Limits of English," *Iowa Review* 5 (Winter 1974): 83–99.

it is." Self-reflexiveness, not all game, marks the "Essay on Style" for what it *is*—a verbal construction which is *about* the tricky, self-reflexiveness of even those verbal constructions that strain toward immediacy. So slippery is language that we are hard pressed, say at the beginning of the poem, even to identify the literal circumstances that are being represented. In a poem like "Gerontion" Eliot shows the terrifying consequences of a decentered language: without any Logos to ground and energize it, language becomes a "wilderness of mirrors," a labyrinth in which literal realities have dissolved into sterile images and artificial reflections. But language for O'Hara is not a "prison-house," nor is it a mere fun house. To put it another way, his awareness of the discrepancy between words and experience does not lead O'Hara to conclude that writing is an empty cipher. A clean, hard, fast surface presents us with the ongoing mental activities of the poet in a way that seems unmediated—digressive, interrupted, disconnected. O'Hara's sentences are an *image*—but an image *of* the times and of himself; his poems lack metaphoric and psychological but not emotional depth. Like the last line of the Washington poem, the last line of "Essay on Style" is both funny and moving. It's funny because O'Hara is so clearly posturing; but if the feeling is admittedly a childish and transient one, it is still genuinely felt and conveyed to the reader—like O'Hara's desire to sever all syntactic connections. He is both contained and free, trapped and alive, within both language and family. O'Hara can take a step away but he can never step outside these enveloping realities. When he does try to adopt a detached perspective ("I was reflecting the other night"), his sentence folds back on itself ("meaning / I was being reflected upon") and O'Hara becomes both the subject and the object of his thought—just as he does when he sees his own reflection in the bar window he's looking through. O'Hara is crowded with such windows. Just as O'Hara must use language in order to struggle against language, he has only himself with which to reflect upon himself. The result is that O'Hara can never get fully inside—or outside—either himself or language. In the "Essay on Style" this predicament creates humor and anger, parodic play and genuine feeling. Through his incessant verbal duplicity and his emotional posturing, O'Hara becomes immediate—alive.

In fact, among the many love poems that O'Hara wrote, the best are not those that are simple and direct—and sappy; the strongest are those that combine theatricality, self-mockery, and genuine expression of feeling and the best of these are the poems, like "Mayakovsky" and "Meditations in an Emergency," that deal with the end of a relationship.

Meditations in an Emergency

Am I to become profligate as if I were a blonde? Or religious as if I were French?

Each time my heart is broken it makes me feel more adventurous (and how the same names keep recurring on that interminable list!), but one of these days there'll be nothing left with which to venture forth.

Why should I share you? Why don't you get rid of someone else for a change?

I am the least difficult of men. All I want is boundless love.

Even trees understand me! Good heavens, I lie under them, too, don't I? I'm just like a pile of leaves.

However, I have never clogged myself with the praises of pastoral life, nor with nostalgia for an innocent past of perverted acts in pastures. No. One need never leave the confines of New York to get all the greenery one wishes—I can't even enjoy a blade of grass unless I know there's a subway handy, or a record store or some other sign that people do not totally *regret* life. It is more important to affirm the least sincere; the clouds get enough attention as it is and even they continue to pass. Do they know what they're missing? Uh huh.

My eyes are vague blue, like the sky, and change all the time; they are indiscriminate but fleeting, entirely specific and disloyal, so that no one trusts me. I am always looking away. Or again at something after it has given me up. It makes me restless and that makes me unhappy, but I cannot keep them still. If only I had grey, green, black, brown, yellow eyes; I would stay at home and do something. It's not that I'm curious. On the contrary, I am bored but it's my duty to be attentive, I am needed by things as the sky must be above the earth. And lately, so great has *their* anxiety become, I can spare myself little sleep.

Now there is only one man I love to kiss when he is unshaven. Heterosexuality! you are inexorably approaching. (How discourage her?)

St. Serapion, I wrap myself in the robes of your whiteness which is like midnight in Dostoevsky. How am I to become a legend, my dear? I've tried love, but that hides you in the bosom of another and I am always springing forth from it like the lotus—the ecstasy of always bursting forth! (but one must not be distracted by it!) or like a hyacinth, "to keep the filth of life away," yes, there, even in the heart, where the filth is pumped in and slanders and pollutes and determines. I will my will, though I may become famous for a mysterious vacancy in that department, that greenhouse.

Destroy yourself, if you don't know!

It is easy to be beautiful; it is difficult to appear so. I admire you, beloved, for the trap you've set. It's like a final chapter no one reads because the plot is over.

"Fanny Brown is run away—scampered off with a Cornet of Horse; I do love that little Minx, & hope She may be happy, 'tho She has vexed me by this Exploit a little too.—Poor silly Cecchina! or F:B: as we used to call her. —I wish She had a good Whipping and 10,000 pounds." —Mrs. Thrale.

I've got to get out of here. I choose a piece of shawl and my dirtiest suntans. I'll be back, I'll re-emerge, defeated, from the valley; you don't want me to go where you go, so I go where you don't want me to. It's only afternoon, there's a lot ahead. There won't be any mail downstairs. Turning, I spit in the lock and the knob turns.

Different from both the headlong forward impetus of the lunch hour poems and the playful self-reflexivity of the "Essay on Style," this prose poem offers a series of shifting, contradictory responses to the end of a love affair. The title "Meditation on an Emergency" would imply that the poet has gained some detached, contemplative perspective, from which he has reconciled himself to his loss and unified his reactions into some coherent pattern. But O'Hara's "Meditations *in* an Emergency" presents a *plurality* of response, as felt *inside* the moment of crisis and instability. According to O'Hara, as we have already seen, "pain produces logic, which is very bad for you." In this poem pain produces anger, fear, self-disgust, self-mockery, grandiosity, helplessness, determination, comedy—disparate feelings that have not been structured by any meditative logic.

By letting these contradictory feelings coexist O'Hara achieves emotional complexity. One aspect of this complexity arises from O'Hara's doubts about the kind of self which can produce this kind of poem—i.e., one without any organizing center. So far I have been discussing O'Hara's elusiveness as if it were an entirely admirable human quality, but that's not how it always felt to O'Hara. At times in "Meditations in an Emergency" centerlessness is experienced as emptiness, mobility as treachery. "One of these days there'll be nothing left with which to venture forth," O'Hara fears; in fact, rather than being "adventurous," he may be anxiously repetitive, sticking to the "same names." "To *move*," we remember, "is to love." By thus refusing commitments and "always bursting forth," O'Hara may seek to become a "legend" of perpetual change, but it may be that his lack of will, his "vacancy in that department," will become legendary. "Indiscriminate but fleeting, entirely specific and disloyal," O'Hara's restless vision becomes so wholly engaged with the specific and the momentary that "no one trusts me"—including, we should add, his readers, who are seldom sure how seriously he is to be taken, especially so in a poem where he tells us that "it is more important to affirm the least sincere." And how sincerely are we to understand this profession of insincerity? "Meditations in an Emergency" poses in dramatic form a disturbing question that keeps occurring to a reader of his *Collected Poems* and to O'Hara himself: does this shifting, unanchored self possess *any* real substance or is it all, like the images on a movie screen, shadow and disguise?

The paradox of the cinema, we remember, is that its duplicities can create "real" emotion; the same can be said for O'Hara's poetry. Film works by flooding the viewer's mind with illusory images, but, according to O'Hara, self-dissociation and self-consciousness are inevitable and continual—and energizing—in the act of writing. Ironically, then, writing can achieve emotional substance and complexity by means of that same self-consciousness which keeps questioning all stances, all feelings, as theatrical and artificial, as images and reflections. In "Mayakovsky," another poem in which O'Hara shows himself to be at once posturing yet truly distraught, he turns to poetry for solace: "Words! be / sick as I am sick, swoon, / roll back your eyes, a pool // and I'll stare down / at my wounded beauty / which at best is only a talent / for poetry." He wants words and mood to be one, and the two do merge—ironically: emotional posturing rendered in trite language. Yet O'Hara's self-irony reveals how the act of expression separates him from himself, splitting him into the "wounded beauty" inscribed in the writing and the Narcissuslike admirer who stares down at his own reflected image in the words. But O'Hara then turns on both the enchanted starer and his idealized self-projection, now seen as a poetic construction of a "better part" of himself. In this passage, then, O'Hara really does feel that he is a beautiful tragic victim but, not surrendering entirely to this image of himself, he acknowledges that it is a construction, in part because the pose is conventional and literary and in part because it is an abstraction of one out of O'Hara's many selves. Words thus both express and construct a self. It's as if as soon as O'Hara expresses a feeling, he is already a step away from it and it has become transparent: he sees through it as a ruse, a disguise—not hollow but not fully or finally him either. It is easy in this context to understand why one of O'Hara's major poems should be called "In Memory of My Feelings."

In "Meditations in an Emergency" O'Hara, conscious of himself but still inside the crisis, stays acutely and mockingly aware that any of his responses will push him toward some familiar role: "Am I to become profligate as if I were a blonde? Or religious as if I were French?" As in this section, the poem's predominant figure of speech is the simile: "I'm just like a pile of leaves" or "My eyes are vague blue, like the sky" or "I am always springing forth from it like the lotus." In each case, the poet's self is compared to some object in the external world, from which the simile also marks him as separate. As we shall see even more clearly in "In Memory of My Feelings," O'Hara's poetry operates in a world of proliferating likenesses, but not identities; the "as if" character of his figures concedes difference. O'Hara is never fully identical with any of those guises that he so quickly adopts and sheds.

Indiscriminate and fleeting, O'Hara bursts forth from any and all attitudes since they are all as artificial as they are real, including whatever attitude he then goes on to "will to will." Self-consciousness is not the kind of trap for O'Hara that it is for a character like Prufrock; self-consciousness, instead, generates the fluid energy that gives life to O'Hara's multiple guises. "I'm the least difficult of men," he pleads, only to turn on himself: "All I want is boundless love." At times he feels himself to be a character trapped in a predictable, plotted fiction written by his lover. At other times he imagines himself to be the author of his own legend. Yet he fears he can't control his legend: others may appropriate it for their own fictions and make him famous for a lack of will. Perhaps, as we have seen, he really *is* hollow; it may be that his adventuresomeness is a myth and he is endlessly repeating old scenarios—fictions invented by others. Self-representation in O'Hara immediately turns into self-questioning; through such agile movements the poem proceeds, but not toward any resolution that would arrest them. No such things available. Like the "Essay on Style," "Meditations" concludes with a mock resolution. In the final section O'Hara feels desperate ("I've got to get out of here"), then in charge ("I choose"), but the objects he selects ("a piece of shawl and my dirtiest suntans") sound like a costume aimed to elicit pity. He sounds vindictively triumphant: "I'll be back, I'll re-emerge," but then "defeated." "You don't want me to go where you go, so I go where you don't want me to"; the ambiguity of the second half of this sentence— where you don't want me to go could be where the lover is going—makes it uncertain whether O'Hara is being submissive or defiant. "There's a lot ahead," he declaims, but it won't include any mail. "Turning, I spit in the lock and the knob turns"; playfully turning back on itself, this last sentence creates several possibilities. Is O'Hara making a grand exit, magically opening the door with his spit and springing forth to new adventures? Or is he stalking out in bitterness and disgust? Is he in fact leaving at all? The connection that the reader is likely to supply between the two halves of this sentence—O'Hara spits in the lock, then turns the knob—may not be a valid one. Is the returning lover opening the door from the other side? By suspending these contradictory possibilities, the poem still leaves us *inside* the emergency.

"I don't prefer one 'strain' to another," says O'Hara, in a piece of self-congratulation that is justified in his multiplicity of styles. One of the important strains in O'Hara's writing is the surrealist, which he turned toward as one alternative to the mandarin orthodoxies of the postwar period. Rather than the Spanish and Latin American surrealists who intrigued Wright and Bly, O'Hara was stimulated by the earlier French group: Breton, Tzara, Péret, Desnos. No doubt he was fascinated by their annihilation of logic, their rapid, startling transformations, their blending of the ordinary and the hallucinatory, their clashing oppositions and wild disjunctions of image and tone. O'Hara's early experiments with surrealism, in "Oranges," "Easter," and "Second Avenue," juxtapose the beautiful and the obscene, the natural and the mechanical, in ways that are more contrived than revelatory, as if bombastic French language games were a sufficient substitute for the current "academic parlor game."[20] The linguistic difficulties posed by "In Memory of My Feelings," however, are generated by a complex emotional substance and a dazzling stylistic variety. Surrealism, no longer for O'Hara merely the means to surprising effects, provides the adequate language for the dynamics of feeling and the problems of writing as they are experienced by a perpetually dislocated self. "In Memory of My Feelings" offers O'Hara's fullest exploration of the self, its relations to the world of material objects, its relations to a personal and cultural past, its love-hate relation to poetry. As such, the poem marks one of the major accomplishments of contemporary poetry.

At the start of its fifth and last section, O'Hara writes:

And now it is the serpent's turn.
I am not quite you, but almost, the opposite of visionary.
You are coiled around the central figure,
                              the heart
that bubbles with red ghosts, since to move is to love
and the scrutiny of all things is syllogistic,
the startled eyes of the dikdik, the bush full of white flags
fleeing a hunter,
                    which is our democracy
                              but the prey
is always fragile and like something, as a seashell can be
a great Courbet, if it wishes. To bend the ear of the outer world.

                                                              [*CP*, p. 256]

Writing about a poem like this is like trying to write on water. Perhaps the best way to deal with this passage is not so much by trying to extract

20. John Ashbery, "Introduction" to *CP*, p. ix.

meaning from it—all too easy, as it turns out—but by trying to articulate the processes we follow as we read it. Our best position is thus a step away from it and from there we can see how reading the poem engages the reader with precisely those difficulties that the poet is writing "about." At the other end of the literary spectrum from the lunch hour poems, "In Memory of My Feelings" lacks any literal level, carrying to an extreme a tendency already apparent in "Meditations in an Emergency" where all kinds of information that we would ordinarily get in such a poem— about the speaker, the lover, the breakup—have been omitted. Here, as we shall see, the absence of a literal level derives from O'Hara's inability, made clear at the end of the poem, to reach any originating cause or source for his feelings, his "selves." But the effect throughout the poem is to force the reader to understand all the poem's images as metaphoric, even those that are as realistic as objects in a painting by Courbet. More-over, metaphoric levels multiply: the poem deals with the personal history of the poet, with western history (from the Arabs to the Greeks and Romans to the European aristocracy to the French Revolution, American democracy and World War II), with the history of poetry, with the nature of poetry (especially its relations to number, logic, resemblance), and with the activity of writing this poem. Presumably, there are other levels.

So the poem's images are centrifugal, metaphoric forces, proliferating meanings. But it's not as if these images were themselves stable points of departure; rather, they are constantly shifting in the poem's circling, self-revising movement where, it seems, anything can turn into anything else—"as a seashell can be / a great Courbet, if it wishes." One thing a reader tries to do is to isolate parts out of this slippery, moving mass, only to discover that the parts keep blending in with each other. When I originally turned to this passage, I wanted merely to talk about the phrase "red ghosts," but I quickly saw that to give its "full" sense I had to quote the entire sentence in which it appeared, and the following sentence, and the two preceding sentences; even stopping at that point is distorting and artificial, since "red ghosts" refers back to the closing lines of section 4, where O'Hara becomes an Indian standing on the beach watching the approach of Columbus, an Indian who quickly metamorphoses into an ancient Hittite (mentioned earlier in section 4) who loves a horse in a "frieze." To love a horse on a frieze is, of course, the opposite of believing that "to move is to love." In a similar way, the last sentence in my quotation ("to bend the ear of the outer world")—along with the image of the serpent—receives a further twist of meaning from the next sentence: "when you turn your head / can you feel your heels, undulating? that's what it is / to be a serpent." In short, I discovered that units of the poem can only be distinguished by bringing to an artificial close the turning, transforming movement of the poem in process. So, in order to read at all we "construct" parts, just as O'Hara has done in writing the poem, in order to write at all. But even this will not take us very far in domesticating the poem, again because of the way these "parts" generate multiple, sometimes contradictory meanings. The relatively simple phrase, "which is our democracy," momentarily isolated in a separate line, is syntactically ambiguous: "which" can refer either to "hunter" or "fleeing," so "democracy" becomes both hunter and hunted, like George Washington in the poem about the Larry Rivers painting. The serpent coiled around the heart may be embracing, it may be protective, it may be threatening to choke the heart; and the heart itself, proposed as "the central figure" in this poem about the poet's feelings, turns out to be multiple, consisting of many "red ghosts." And the "red ghosts" themselves? Like so many things in the poem, they contain many, opposing suggestions. They are wild, primitive, red, Indianlike, alive; they are ghosts, elusive memories from a dead personal/national past. "Red ghosts" both possess and lack substance, like feelings; they are quick and ephemeral yet haunting and timeless—like feelings.

One question that concerns O'Hara in this passage is whether by trying to "capture" his fleeting emotions in language he is eternalizing or killing them. As soon as he imagines the heart as a kind of boiling cauldron bubbling with feelings, he turns to the language of logic and epigram to fix a truth about the mobility of love: "since to move is to love." But in the following line O'Hara, always a step ahead of us, turns around on his own propensity for freezing feelings into logical statements: "and the scrutiny of all things is syllogistic." As the passage goes on to suggest, the poet/logician may be a hunter with his feelings as his "prey." Earlier in the poem O'Hara had mocked the Greeks who "could speak / of time as a river and step across it into Persia, leaving the pain / at home to be converted into statuary" (*CP,* p. 254), as he had mocked the Hittite in love with a horse in a "frieze." If "The Critic" had externalized the desire to fix objects with stable meanings, "In Memory of My Feelings" reveals the wish to control and master to be the poet's own, in fact to be integral with the activity of writing, the "trying desperately to *count* them [his feelings] as they die" (*CP,* p. 254). Writing about his feelings makes O'Hara both the hunter and the hunted, but his self-conscious awareness of this dilemma creates the circling, metamorphic movement of his poem which, in turn, makes his poem the opposite of "statuary" or a "frieze."

A reader might feel more comfortable if he could grasp this dynamic, frustrating work and hold it still, if he could develop some distance and perspective that would allow him to create a text with stable parts in fixed relations. No such thing available. Instead, the reader is asked to "open" himself and let the poem invade him in the way the world constantly violates O'Hara's transparent self. Or, more accurately, the reader, too, becomes both hunter and hunted, alternately making O'Hara's "fragile" words and feelings his "prey" and becoming *their* "prey." The gratifications are those of process rather than product, movement rather than goal. In this poem, which combines self-reflexiveness and ongoing process in an even more radical way than did the "Essay on Style," there is no terminus, no stable unity that we finally arrive at. The refusal of ending in this poem can be characterized from yet another angle of approach. All of the poem's images are extensions of O'Hara; they reflect his feelings. Yet, his relation to these images is like his relation to the serpent: "I am not quite you, but almost." His images reflect O'Hara, but not quite, and this predicament has two important consequences. Objects and words cannot fully incarnate O'Hara any more than O'Hara can completely master words and objects and make them mere "prey." All three terms in this equation—world, poet, medium—remain independent from each other and in this way O'Hara acknowledges a realm of existential reality that remains resistant to himself and his poem. Yet all three terms remain intricately implicated with each other. Along with the kind of syllogistic scrutiny which strives to separate experience into fixed categories and relations, "In Memory of My Feelings" also offers resemblance, which reveals all the leaks in those fixed categories. At the very beginning of the poem, O'Hara writes that "my quietness has a man in it, he is transparent / and he carries me quietly, like a gondola, through the streets. / He has several likenesses, like stars and years, like numerals" (*CP*, p. 252). With its third line, the poem's proliferation of resemblances begins: the man is like many things, not just gondolas; he is like stars, years, numerals; and he is also like them in having many—in fact, infinite—likenesses. Surrealism characteristically works by startling imagistic transformations; Wright's version of surrealism, as we have seen, offers the metamorphosis of the literal into the magical "deep" image. But O'Hara is the "opposite" of such a "visionary." "In Memory of My Feelings" offers not metaphoric transformations but likenesses—not identifications but resemblances. The poem, then, creates a dynamic field of proliferating resemblances among parts which, in turn, remain independent of each other; they are not pulled together into some full, spherelike form.

"Grace / to be born and live as variously as possible," O'Hara writes in section 4 (*CP*, p. 256). The absence of any totalizing form allows him to explore the self fully, its insecurities, transparencies, defenses, evasions, yearnings, obsessions. He adopts, variously, a dazzling range of roles, styles, tones, "selves," in what becomes the most freewheeling and open-ended expression of his protean self. The mood of "quietness" with which the poem begins is abruptly shattered when O'Hara disperses himself into all the aspects of a scene at a race track:

> An elephant takes up his trumpet,
> money flutters from the windows of cries, silk stretching its mirror
> across shoulder blades. A gun is "fired."
> One of me rushes
> to window #13 and one of me raises his whip and one of me
> flutters up from the center of the track amidst the pink flamingoes,
> and underneath their hooves as they round the last turn my lips
> are scarred and brown, brushed by tails, masked in dirt's lust,
> definition, open mouths gasping for the cries of the bettors for the lungs
> of earth.
> So many of my transparencies could not resist the race!
> [*CP*, p. 253]

Serpentlike, O'Hara keeps shedding and taking on new transparencies, new guises. "The conception / of the masque barely suggests the sordid identifications," he declares in section 4 (*CP*, p. 256); neither the idealized, aristocratic masque nor the New Critical idea of the poem as mask can define the proliferations in the catalog that follows:

> I am a Hittite in love with a horse. I don't know what blood's
> in me I feel like an African prince I am a girl walking downstairs
> in a red pleated dress with heels I am a champion taking a fall
> I am a jockey with a sprained ass-hole I am the light mist
> in which a face appears
> and it is another face of blonde I am a baboon eating a banana
> I am a dictator looking at his wife I am a doctor eating a child
> and the child's mother smiling I am a Chinaman climbing a mountain
> I am a child smelling his father's underwear I am an Indian
> sleeping on a scalp.
> [*CP*, p. 256]

Yet, as these two passages suggest, O'Hara's ebullient mobility and his brave transparency make him feel vulnerable and helpless; they leave him either immersed in a frantic series of "sordid identifications" or close to a painful self-extinction. Other parts of O'Hara thus yearn for the stability of some "simple identification" (*CP*, p. 253); "one feels nostalgic / for mere ideas," he says, "and one of me has a sentimental longing for number" and the graceful assurances of the old order (*CP*, pp. 254–55).

In section 2 he tries to deal with familial losses and the threat of his own death in "an atmosphere of supreme lucidity" and philosophic detachment (*CP*, p. 254); in what becomes both an anticipation and a questioning of Lowell's poetic project in *Life Studies*, O'Hara wants to resolve feelings of loss by converting them into poetic "numbers." Elsewhere, O'Hara would like the protection of the "war hero" (*CP*, p. 255) or the coercive power of the hunter (*CP*, p. 253), but these images of power and stability always dissolve and multiply in just the way the single man in O'Hara's "quietness" at the beginning of the poem almost immediately begins to proliferate. The cool "facade" in section 2 collapses into a rocketlike explosion of feeling and the desire to reify emotions collapses into "the trying desperately to count them as they die" (*CP*, p. 254). The "war hero," no dependable model of a forceful, unified identity, has "many selves," as does the "meek subaltern" who replaces him (*CP*, p. 255); and the hunter in section 1 discovers that the serpent he wishes to kill turns into a Medusa, reversing the roles of victim and victimizer (*CP*, p. 253). Parts of O'Hara thus struggle for an ascendancy which always eludes them. O'Hara cannot conquer himself any more than we can conquer his poem; and for the same reasons.

Given its dynamic, shifting, open character, how can O'Hara bring "In Memory of My Feelings" to an end? Here, offered with a self-conscious awareness of the arbitrariness in deciding where a poem's ending begins, are its closing lines:

> And yet
> I have forgotten my loves, and chiefly that one, the cancerous
> statue which my body could no longer contain,
>
> > against my will
> > against my love
>
> become art,
> > I could not change it into history
> and so remember it,
> > and I have lost what is always and everywhere
> present, the scene of my selves, the occasion of these ruses,
> which I myself and singly must now kill
> > and save the serpent in their midst.
> > > [*CP*, p. 257]

Intimacy is experienced as invasive; a lover gets inside O'Hara like a "cancerous / statue"—a dead weight that has a poisonous life of its own. The poet struggles to exorcise his lover by turning him into "art," but he can't convert his experience into "history," the way Lowell does in *Life*

Studies, and O'Hara's inability to detach himself from the past produces the poem's wild temporal dislocations, the past continually invading the present. "In Memory of My Feelings" contains a number of parodic journeys: ascending the mountains in section 1, crossing the desert in section 3, voyaging to the New World in section 4. Unlike Olson, however, O'Hara always remains aware of the way the discoverer of a new "land," "so free," immediately changes into the conquistador, who tries to "stay" and "count" riches that elude him anyway. Throughout the poem, old orders are constantly crumbling—and *any* order instantaneously becomes an *old* order—but the rich new "land" of the present cannot be entirely separated from old patterns of thought and feeling. For this reason the poem abounds with old fictions—selves, images, plots—which, as we have seen in "Meditations in an Emergency," were not invented by the poet yet have invaded him and his poem. This presentness of the past explains why, in "In Memory of My Feelings," ongoing process coexists with self-reflexiveness; O'Hara both moves on and repeats.

Feelings die quickly, yet they hang on like ghosts. As a result, O'Hara, in one of the many self-contradictory sentences in this passage, has "lost what *is* always and everywhere"; he has lost what he can no more grasp or lose than the past—namely, the present. The "real" literal present is thus a source or origin, "always and everywhere," which he can neither reach nor evade; it is like the poet's self which, as we have seen, is everywhere and nowhere "present" in his poems. Like the new "land" that turns out to be slippery territory, the present is experienced by O'Hara as a theatrical "scene" for the poet's many "selves," yet something substantial enough to be the occasion, the instigation, for his "ruses."

"In Memory of My Feelings" shows what happens to the autobiographical poem when the writer can no longer find any vantage point from which to construct a sequential narrative or stable identity out of his experience. The myth of psychoanalysis provided Lowell with an external perspective by means of which he could detach himself from himself, resolve the series of losses he records in "Life Studies," disengage himself from the past, strip away projections, and, in "Skunk Hour," enter the disintegrating but substantial ground of the present. No such things available for O'Hara, who always remains both inside and outside himself, his past, his feelings, his present, his poem. At the very end of "In Memory of My Feelings" O'Hara rises up in what looks like an heroic gesture aimed at striking through all the masks, penetrating to authenticity and pulling himself together at last. But the phrase "I myself and singly" splits the self in the very act of unifying it and the final line declares O'Hara's intent to "save" that slippery, invasive, poisonous, beautiful energy that keeps proliferating new transparencies, selves, guises—the energy that allows O'Hara to work inside all these old fictions and disguises and make them *live* again. "In Memory of My Feelings" ends by refusing closure. In its final turn, the poem affirms that turning, shifting power that is always and everywhere present in O'Hara's poetry.

NINE

Our Town:
Poetry and Criticism in the Early Eighties

If American poetry in the middle fifties resembled a peaceful public park on a pleasant summer Sunday afternoon, and if by the early sixties it had been transformed into a war zone, the air heavy with manifestos, then by the early 1980s the atmosphere has lightened and the scene more resembles a small affluent town in Northern California. Anxiety about the economy or nuclear war occasionally darkens the mood, but the citizens are generally healthy, fit, stable, and productive. No one seems moved by overweening ambition or any desire to unsettle the way things are. Yet if there is a lack of risk-taking, there is plenty of life. The town's politics are liberal—which means that while there is some gossip, some backbiting, and a few ancient and bitter feuds, there are no ideological disputes. Instead, the tolerance (or indifference) of those primarily concerned with their own work is mixed with those doses of support and rivalry that characterize all human communities. Even the town hippie, once a fiery vagabond, now aging, bearded, wearing suits, is listened to seriously and, just a few years ago, won a good citizenship award. Within the town no central authority exerts strong control. The leading citizens include some reformed dissidents from the 1960s as well as some old families, and the youth, neither slavishly deferential nor bristling with rebellion, admires and respects the older generation.

The rebels of 1960, in short, have now achieved prestige and authority. Their present status can be described as "pre-canonical": while no one of them has sufficiently impressed a large number of readers over a long enough period of time to emerge as an obvious master—Lowell and Ash-

bery are probably the main contenders—nevertheless the dissidents of
the early sixties are now widely anthologized, respectfully interviewed
by editors of influential journals, awarded lucrative grants (they even
appear on the committees distributing the grants), and they win major
literary prizes, with Ammons, Ashbery, Ginsberg, Lowell, Merrill, Snyder, Rich, and Wright all getting either a Pulitzer Prize or National Book
Award. Many of them hold academic positions, and one, Allen Ginsberg,
has founded his own alternate "academy," the Naropa Institute of Poetry
and Poetics. As teachers, these poets conduct poetry workshops which,
in the absence of any contemporary handbook or manual of poetics, have
become powerful institutions in the last twenty years, with older poets
here possessing the power to admit to writing programs and particular
classes, to define quality, to provide literary and practical help, and, in
the awarding of degrees, to certify those members of the next generation
who will teach writing. At the same time that they have risen in the
academic world, these poets have become the subjects of numerous essays
and books, while their private papers and unpublished works are being
collected in libraries and archives. Our contemporary poets are being
preserved—perhaps to a degree unrivaled by any earlier generation—and
they have also reached that point in their careers when they are experi-
encing anxiety about *how* they will be preserved.

"How shall I become a legend, my dear?" O'Hara asks self-mockingly
in "Meditations in an Emergency." O'Hara knows he can't control the
ways in which future generations will mythologize him, and perhaps all
poets sense this, but that doesn't stop a lot of them from trying. A few
examples will suffice. All of Allen Ginsberg's papers down to the early
sixties—letters, manuscripts, notebooks—are now contained in the Allen
Ginsberg Archives at Columbia. Ginsberg no doubt made some money
from his contribution, but in many respects it was a generous act—all the
more so since the papers contain material that plainly contradicts some
of Ginsberg's own most cherished myths about his work and career.[1] Still,
no one can quote from the papers without Ginsberg's permission, and in
my own experience using this collection, he demanded to see and to
approve the entire essay in which the quotations appeared—a strange
stance for a man whose first book was involved in a censorship trial. At
the same time Ginsberg himself has presided over the publication of selections from his material, selections that do nothing to upset Ginsberg's
own mythologizing of himself.[2] A few years ago I was a member of a
panel discussing prosody in contemporary American poetry at the MLA

1. See my "Allen Ginsberg: The Origins of 'Howl' and 'Kaddish,' " pp. 85–87.
2. See Allen Ginsberg, *The Visions of the Great Rememberer* (Amherst, Mass., 1974) and
Allen Ginsberg, *Journals,* ed. Gordon Ball (New York, 1977).

convention. Just as we were about to start, Ginsberg walked in and sat down. He was not there to throw potato salad. Instead, he made a few corrective contributions to the discussion afterward. He was there because he knows the academic world will have considerable influence in determining how he will be preserved and he wants to set its members straight. Similarly, at a conference entitled "The San Francisco Poetry Renaissance," held in La Jolla, California, Robert Duncan and Michael McClure strongly asserted definitive accounts of the origins, character, and history of the San Francisco poetry renaissance. Both of them were extremely antagonistic toward any of the academic participants who saw things differently. In each of these cases, the issue became: how will *my* revolution be preserved?

To adopt some terms from Pound's *ABC of Reading:* around 1960 a generation of diluters was displaced by a generation of inventors, with many particular poets working both sides of the street.[3] The groundbreaking poets of two decades ago, however, have now settled in; they preside over a literary scene that shows plenty of life but few signs of avant-garde activity, except for the "language poets" and isolated figures like David Antin and John Cage. Donald Allen's *New American Poetry* is now almost twenty-five years old; it has been supplemented by *The Poetics of the New American Poetry* and revised into *The Postmoderns*—but no revolutionary anthology has risen to challenge, much less to supersede it.[4] In a new atmosphere of tolerance and permission, the sniping that often characterized relations among the clusters of insurgents and even the artillery fire aimed at the entrenched writers of "closed" verse have ceased. As Donald Hall remarked several years ago,

> In the United States, there is a spirit of *détente,* and people speak to each other who refused to know each other's names a decade ago.
> For the most part people meet and gossip and argue, and even translate together, who are supposed to oppose each other.[5]

As a result, issues once charged with moral and political values—accentual versus free verse, for instance—have been neutralized. A recent symposium, "Free Verse," published in *The Ohio Review*—in which all the participants agree that free verse is a perfectly legitimate option but so, of course, is metered verse—illustrates the way polemical edge has dissolved into bland good sense.[6] One result as well as one sign of this

3. *ABC of Reading* (New York, 1960), p. 39.
4. *The Poetics of the New American Poetry,* ed. Donald Allen and Warren Tallman (New York, 1973), and *The Postmoderns,* ed. Donald Allen and George F. Butterick (New York, 1982).
5. "The State of Poetry—A Symposium," *Review* 29–30 (Spring–Summer 1972): 39.
6. *Ohio Review* 28 (1982).

sagging of the literary battle lines is the appearance of Charles Hartman's *Free Verse*. Compare Hartman's contention that "using free verse does not simply mean discarding metrical principles but substituting new ones" with the Brooks-Warren position that free verse constitutes a "looser" poetic organization, and you have the difference between a perspective designed to begin and one designed to limit substantive discussion.[7] A major achievement of contemporary poetry has been to settle (or at least depoliticize) the issue of free verse for what should be a long time, but, ironically, the poets' very success in creating a readership sensitive to the effects of this complex medium has relocated them from the "outermost brink" to a reconceived, and much widened, mainstream.

Among younger poets a few have questioned the excesses of their experimental predecessors from a conservative position. In *The Situation of Poetry,* for example, Robert Pinsky provocatively argues that "contemporary poetry is by and large traditional," thus debunking the revolutionary claims of his elders (and disagreeing, in advance, with the thesis of this book).[8] By focusing on the conflict between the flux and particularity of experience on the one hand and the abstractness and conventionality of the linguistic medium on the other, he connects contemporary poetry with modernism and beyond that with romanticism.[9] His acute sensitivity to poetic voice and language allows Pinsky to show how the pursuit of immediacy often generates verbal mannerism in contemporary poetry, particularly when poets are unaware of their antecedents. His reassessment, however, quietly polemicizes for the legitimacy of one traditional mode that practically all contemporary factions agree, in theory, should be banished—namely, discursiveness. Thus, questioning a boundary line that contemporary poetics took as a given, *The Situation of Poetry*—along with the poetry of Pinsky, Ammons, Bidart, and others— has successfully extended critical tolerance and poetic practice. But Pinsky's is a traditionalist, not an avant-garde, gesture, and it has not overtoppled the reigning authorities.

On the whole, poets of the now-emerging fourth generation—born after 1940 and beginning to write around 1960—seem to have grown up as fascinated readers of the generation of innovators who preceded them. One reason for their admiration, aside from the quality of the work, was the dispersion of authority in the older generation; power was never concentrated in a single figure (like Eliot) or a single faction (like the New Critics) as it had been in the fifties. Ironically, permissiveness and dispersed authority have made it harder for younger poets to rebel—denying

7. *Free Verse* (Princeton, 1980), p. 81.
8. *The Situation of Poetry* (Princeton, 1976), p. 6.
9. Ibid., pp. 4–5.

them a repressive and therefore easily hated and locatable foe. On the other hand, one might reply that it is precisely such liberal conditions that make rebellion unnecessary. Beginning poets nowadays have a seductive variety of modes to choose from, as if in my imaginary small California town there were so many jobs, shops, restaurants, and recreation areas that one never had to leave it. In a recent essay in the *American Poetry Review,* Eric Torgersen recalls his own formative experiences, which I suspect are prototypical for his generation:

> I started to read and write poetry in the early sixties, a fine and exciting time for poets. Time was moving fast; Frost, Williams, Roethke, Eliot died, and the generation of poets born in the twenties that dominates American poetry today was just emerging. . . . I carried around the Allen anthology and *For Love* and *Reality Sandwiches, The Opening of the Field* and Koch's *Thank You* and *Lunch Poems.* . . . But I also carried around *All My Pretty Ones, Silence in the Snowy Fields, The Branch Will Not Break, Heart's Needle,* X. J. Kennedy's *Nude Descending a Staircase, The Spring of a Thief.*[10]

Torgersen remembers two camps, roughly corresponding to the Simpson-Hall-Pack group and the Allen anthology crowd; he conflates, I think, two quite different antagonisms: those among the separate dissident clusters and those between the dissidents and the writers in "closed" forms. But Torgersen himself feels pressure from the older poets to make a choice in polemical battles that are long since over and which would artificially force him to deny significant parts of himself.

> The issues that divided the generation of my poetic parents externally are inside me, and they work themselves out in my writing. There are poles of, say, willed and discovered form in my work, and it seems to be true that after ten years in which "Some Notes on Organic Form" was the text I depended on most heavily to keep my head clear, the pole of willed form seems to have a certain new insistence.[11]

At the close of his essay, then, Torgersen makes a rather ambivalent declaration of independence: "to the extent that members of the generation of our poetic parents, whom we must in the nature of things displace, push us forward to fight their battles as their proxies, this seems the right time to tell them the final *no.*"[12] Torgersen imagines displacement of the poetic parent as a fated natural process ("in the nature of things"), not

10. "Cold War in Poetry: Notes of a Conscientious Objector," *American Poetry Review* 2 (July–August 1982): 34.
11. Ibid.
12. Ibid.

as a willed, aggressive act, and so his refusal to yield to the authority of any *one* of these parents actually constitutes his submission to the authority of a parental *generation,* whose options and terms (e.g., discovered versus willed form) he cannot think his way outside of.

My characterization of the contemporary scene so far may suggest that poetry has come full circle and returned to the timidity of the early fifties. Certainly, the scarcity of risky innovation and demolition work, the preference for consolidation and generational continuity, plus the development of these trends within a reactionary political climate—all these establish striking parallels. Yet, without a strong central authority, the current period possesses a kind of heterogeneous unity whose diversity supports vitality; poetry is now less defensive and constricted than it was in the fifties. An even more crucial difference concerns the altered relations between poetry and criticism in the last thirty years. The New Criticism was essentially a *literary* movement, founded and promulgated by poet-critics. During the 1950s, however, the program turned into a Frankenstein monster, which, instead of turning on its inventors, terrorized their children. To put it another way, criticism dictated to poetry, as if in a patriarchal marriage. In the sixties, however, they were divorced and the patriarch now seems to have lost all interest in the opposite sex. Like contemporary poetry, contemporary criticism tolerates diverse perspectives, but as among, say, Freudian psychoanalysis, Lacanian psychoanalysis, Marxism, reader response, structuralism, feminism, deconstruction, Marxist deconstruction, Marxist feminist deconstruction, none of them is specifically literary in origin. They typically use extraliterary sources to return to criticism the concepts of author, reader, world banished from discussion by the New Critical fallacies (intentional, affective, mimetic). Moreover, in literary criticism deconstruction occupies a dominant position so that the alternatives must place themselves in relation to it, and it has achieved its prominence in the late seventies and early eighties, like the New Criticism, by once again separating poetry from history.

In the 1950s, as we saw in chapter 2, all fundamental social, political, and literary problems were declared solved. Theory (or "ideology") was politely escorted to the borders of the republic and exiled as a dangerous subversive. What *was* on the agenda, however, was the practice of disinterested experts who could be counted on to implement received views without raising troublesome questions. In literary criticism, this entailed the exacting verbal scrutiny of canonical texts, themselves conceived as embodying and therefore eliciting in the reader a disinterested (or aesthetic) consciousness severed from pragmatic concerns and in fact transcendent of the social, historical, and even psychological dimensions of the self. Nevertheless, in spite of its elitist premises and its often explicitly

conservative politics, the New Criticism contained a creeping egalitari-
anism in its definition of expertise as "sensitivity to the literary medium"
rather than as the acquisition of that body of knowledge required, say,
for a Ph.D. in English literature. The method, though self-evidently in the
hands of the few, could be taught to anyone—and was. Moreover, in
freeing the reader from such traditional constraints as author, history,
society, the New Criticism contained a potential anarchism, a propensity
it sought to control through the impersonalization of consciousness before
the fetishized—or even sacralized—text and through its constant evocation of "the tradition."

   In the seventies and eighties, however, the prodigal theory has returned
and, now proclaiming its subversiveness, mounted to a position of regal
sway, so much so that practical critics (i.e., those engaged in making more
or less plausible statements about literary works) have descended to the
status of automobile mechanics in a community in which everyone owns
a BMW and/or Mercedes. Yet the character of this theoretical activity
cannot be separated from its specific historical moment. If the fifties
decided that all problems had been solved (a premature closure if there
ever was one), we now experience, as Christopher Lasch writes, "a
pervasive despair of understanding the course of modern history or of
subjecting it to rational direction."

> Liberalism, the political theory of the ascendent bourgeoisie, long
> ago lost the capacity to explain events in the world of the welfare
> state and the multinational corporation; nothing has taken its place.[13]

Whereas the fifties mixed its complacency with an underlying anxiety, we
combine our despair with a cheerful narcissism. The breakup of the New
Critical hegemony resulted in part from the critique of disinterestedness
put forward by the political consciousness of the sixties; blacks and women,
in particular, exposed obvious racist and sexist values silently assumed
not just in particular interpretations but in the formation of "the canon."
Increasingly, criticism became self-critical, aware of its own inevitable
biases and ideologies, the ways in which any critical method becomes
self-verifying by constituting its own objects for investigation. Episte-
mological doubt, which might have been paralyzing, instead generated
the dismantling of established procedures, the demystification of "givens"
as historically shaped attitudes, the problematizing of the text, the death
of the author, the return of the reader, destabilization, deconstruction. As
Geoffrey Hartman observes in "Criticism and Its Discontents," "on looking into the intellectual heavens we see a chaos: a plurality, perhaps

13. *The Culture of Narcissism* (New York, 1980), p. xxiii.

infinity, of competing hypotheses and mind-wearing speculations."
"Here," he goes on,

> we might discover a motive, even a justified role, for theory. For the-
> ory is (in theory) supposed to do away with itself, and lead to more
> exact, concrete, focused insight. . . . But every new theory adds it-
> self to the heap and increases the burden it was supposed to remove.
> Every theory, in short, is but another text.[14]

From a school of disinterestedness we have moved to schools of suspicion,
from a dominant ideology to a proliferation of mutually conflicting and
self-regarding theories, and both the proliferation of theories and the predominance of one that removes literature from life and history confirm
Lasch's account of our time: no longer convinced we can control or even
understand history, we retreat from it.

After such knowledge, what forgiveness? "So once again I have made
the text disappear," Stanley Fish announces, with a pleased bow and a
wave of his polemical wand, at the end of "Interpreting the *Variorum*."[15]
The New Critical object, its ontological ground snatched from under it,
has vanished, and the critic no longer speaks of "subordinating himself
to the text"—because the text has disappeared. If interpretation attempts
to "fix" the meaning of a text, then the contemporary critic is a hunter
who owns several very expensive rifles but whose game vanishes as soon
as he catches it in his sights. For Fish, "there are no fixed texts, but only
interpretive strategies making them";[16] for Harold Bloom, there are no
fixed texts but only psychological strategies for misreading them; and for
deconstructionists, there are, simply, no fixed texts. According to Derrida,
writing, filled with shifting signifiers, limitless ambiguities, infinite echo-
ings, is always on the move, and any effort on the part of the "subject"
(writer, reader) to close down linguistic freeplay is forced to posit a center
or origin which is both "*within* the structure and *outside* it"—a logical
impossibility created by "the force of a desire," a wish for closure, mastery, rest.[17] Moreover, since "everything is discourse," the search for a
center outside language will produce a fiction just where one needs to
produce a stable reality (or presence). From this point of view, it's not
just that individual texts resist interpretive centers or even that they collapse into the sea of intertextuality—but that the very concepts of a work
or an author become recuperative fictions, unifying ideas that deny the
radical heterogeneity of language.

14. *Criticism in the Wilderness* (New Haven, 1980), pp. 238–39.
15. *Is There a Text in This Class?* (Cambridge, Mass., 1980), p. 173.
16. Ibid., p. 172.
17. *Writing and Difference* (Chicago, 1978), p. 279.

Literature, then, dissolves into Language, as language itself, figurative from the start, becomes fictive and "literary." The Yale Derrideans have, however, attempted to preserve a privileged ground for literature by defining its specificity as a language that has always already deconstructed itself.[18] "Deconstruction," says J. Hillis Miller, "is not a dismantling of the structure of a text but a demonstration that it has already dismantled itself."[19] Within the radical critique of western metaphysics lurks a vestigial New Haven formalism, perhaps already manifest in the deconstructionists' tendency to write close analyses of texts as if they *were* there. But this critical holding action is hard to justify. If literary works deconstruct themselves and if critics can know *that,* then they possess an objective, literal knowledge of the work—precisely what the system began by questioning. The Yale position has prompted Gayatri Spivak to charge that "deconstruction in the narrow sense domesticates deconstruction in the general sense."

Deconstruction in the general sense, seeing in the self perhaps only a (dis)figuring effect of a radical heterogeneity, puts into question the grounds of the critic's power. Deconstruction in the narrow sense, no more than a chosen literary-critical methodology, locates this signifying or figuring effect in the "text's" performance and allows the critic authority to disclose the economy of figure and performance.[20]

Authority and even knowledge are saved for the critic, but at the cost of an impoverished idea of literature. From this wrong-end-of-the-telescope perspective, all literary works are the same; "differance" annihilates difference.

Along with the specific literary work, such old-fashioned enabling concepts as author, world, reader are questioned out of defensible existence. Since language can never be literal, any reader-interpreter will necessarily be creative; thus, as Eugenio Donato points out, no "essential line between literature and criticism" can be marked.

Each sign is in itself not the thing that offers itself to intepretation but interpretation of other signs. There is never an *interpretandum* which is not already an *interpretans,* so that a relationship of both violence and elucidation establishes itself with interpretation.[21]

18. See Paul De Man, "The Rhetoric of Blindness: Jacques Derrida's Reading of Rousseau," in *Blindness and Insight,* pp. 102–41.

19. "Stevens' Rock and Criticism as Cure, II," *Georgia Review* 30 (Summer 1976): 341.

20. "Finding Feminist Readings: Dante-Yeats," *Social Text* 3 (Fall 1980): 75. See also Michael Ryan, *Marxism and Deconstruction* (Baltimore, 1982).

21. "The Two Languages of Criticism," *The Structuralist Controversy: The Languages of Criticism and the Sciences of Man,* ed. Richard Macksey and Eugenio Donato (Baltimore, 1972), p. 95.

Flamboyant assertions of this state of affairs by Bloom, Fish, Hartman, and others have alarmed traditionalists, who grimly predict license, self-indulgence, and general critical bedlam. They need not worry; in actuality, the idea of the reader has been hollowed out: the text is created by readers who are in turn created by interpretive strategies. Relation between critic and text has been demystified as a power relation, but one in which the reader turns out to be powerless. Interpretation becomes an act of violence without either victim or criminal. To argue that readers, authors, works are all constituted *by* rather than themselves constitutive might be to push deconstruction toward an historicism, to try to account for the manifest changes in reading strategies and writing styles that occur through time. But history offers no key to the "prison-house of language." An historian cannot, say, isolate originating causes in relation to a written text, because his external reference points are themselves elusive, shadowy, labyrinthine sign systems. Historicism, itself a fictive interpretive center, only provides another instance of the problem and not a solution to it. J. Hillis Miller declares that

> the tradition is not determined by coercive "sources" which have imposed themselves century after century, but is a matter of concepts, metaphors, and myths, each generating the others, which are latently there in the lexicon, the grammar, and the syntax of our languages.[22]

As Miller's remarks make dramatically clear, history, politics, social reality, economics, psychology are all swallowed up by that leviathan, Language—outside of which nothing real, nothing not already supplemented by language, can be found. Texts are unstable, but everything is textual, and it is precisely in their refusal of "extrinsic" modes of critical discourse that the deconstructionists most resemble the fathers they never tire of slaying—the New Critics.

In spite of its insurrectionist talk, deconstruction's critique of western metaphysics entails a political and even literary conservatism. Deconstruction offers grandiosity but without a transforming vision, a quality that differentiates it from the generation of poets I have been writing about. For the followers of Derrida, changes in social or political ideologies (or institutions) constitute mere re-forms within a structure of thought that is inevitably repressive, an extension of the "totalitarian" language of western philosophy.[23] Any radical project to dismantle the system, step outside it and found a new language will either produce nonsense or

---

22. "Stevens' Rock and Criticism as Cure, II," p. 334.
23. See Frank Lentricchia, "Derrida, History, and Intellectuals," *Salmagundi* 50–51 (Fall 1980–Winter 1981): 288 ff.

replicate the system. Repetition absorbs revolution; and Emerson ought
to have written: "*words* are in the saddle and ride mankind." As J. Hillis
Miller asserts, "The human condition is to be caught in a web of words
which weaves and reweaves for man through the centuries the same tapestry of myths, concepts, and metaphorical analogies, in short, the whole
system of Occidental metaphysics."[24] Miller's (recurrent) figure of the
"web"—spatializing, dehistorizing human experience—leaves man help-
lessly ensnared in an alien and reified system whose constantly shifting
strands are made of steel. Like commodities in late capitalism, Miller's
"words" are substanceless objects moving in an autonomous realm, activated not by their usefulness but by their exchange value (substitution),
with the human speaker at once caught inside and yet a detached spectator
(as the "web" becomes a "tapestry") of a world he can no longer remember that he made.[25] To put it another way, deconstructionists are
mesmerized by a "prison-house" they themselves have built—and whose
walls they have decorated with beautiful tapestries to make incarceration
a pleasurable aesthetic experience. As a metaphor for the language of art,
the well-wrought urn has been displaced by the infinite labyrinth—an
opening that only leaves us more firmly enclosed.

Derrida himself, asserting that he has no desire to alter practice in the
sciences or humanities, has emphasized that deconstruction is "not de-
struction."[26] In fact, his strategies admittedly operate in a fated "complicity" with that which they critique.

> There is no sense in doing without the concepts of metaphysics in
> order to shake metaphysics. We have no language—no syntax and no
> lexicon—which is foreign to this history; we can pronounce not a
> single destructive proposition which has not already had to slip into
> the form, the logic, and the implicit postulations of precisely what it
> seeks to contest.[27]

Drinking from the heady waters of the Derridean critique, a literary critic,
now empowered with the means of revealing the limits not just of the
languages of competing critical schools but of the language of western
thought itself, might well feel elated—until he remembers that his method,
breeding suspicions of all systems, leaves him disillusioned, impotent, and
empty within the present form of a structure he himself has characterized
as totalitarian.

24. "Tradition and Difference," *Diacritics* 2 (Winter 1972): 11.
25. See Carolyn Porter, *Seeing and Being* (Middleton, Conn., 1981), esp. pp. 23–56.
26. "Discussion" to "Structure, Sign, and Play in the Discourse of the Human Sciences,"
in *The Structuralist Controversy*, p. 271.
27. *Writing and Difference*, pp. 280–81.

Traditionally the task of the academic scholar-critic has been more modestly defined as that of preserving and extending the literary culture. In America, especially since the Second World War, that basically conservative enterprise has been obscured and even contaminated not by the famous "pressure to publish" but by the pressure to *innovate* in publication. The ideal of a community of scholars has been transformed by institutional pressures and entrepreneurial realities. As a critical method, American deconstruction strikingly fills both needs—to conserve and to innovate, a fact that helps explain its quick ascent to prestige but one which also points up its serious problems of logical consistency. As I have already suggested, a strict Derridean analysis would abolish literature as a "privileged" category. Instead, the notion that literary works have always already deconstructed themselves has been appropriated to preserve the authority of both literature and criticism. In addition, the force of deconstructive logic would surely push toward dismantling an avowedly hierarchical term like "canon," with its suggestions of ecclesiastical law, general rule, and sacred text; and any avant-garde movement, in criticism as well as literature, normally promulgates a major canon revision, as we have seen with the poetic generation of 1960. American Derrideans do advance a new genealogical line of masters who deny mastery: Nietzsche, Derrida, Foucault. But the English-American literary canon, despite much revisionist rhetoric, has remained remarkably stable. Indeed, J. Hillis Miller has assured his professional colleagues that "I believe in the established canon of English and American literature and in the validity of the concept of privileged texts."[28] The irony is that literary canons, neither eternal nor sacred but historical, are remarkably *un*stable, but deconstructionists, given their refusal of history, are stuck with the canonical status quo—a literary version of their political quietism. Even more compellingly, deconstructing works will only really have impact if those works are written by authors revered as geniuses who were able to impose their wills on language. It will hardly do, say, to propose that Edgar Lee Masters's *Spoon River Anthology* makes a self-defeating turn to pull the ground out from under itself, and then to assert that, *for that reason,* Masters should be elevated to major canonical status.

In American deconstruction, then, we have a formalism that is (in theory) without objects, and in the literary scene of the early 1980s we have a predominant school of criticism whose considerable speculative flair has been centrally concerned with the problems of criticism itself or with producing deconstructive readings of particular authors that have the curious effect of preserving and even enhancing their authority. But if there

28. "The Function of Rhetorical Study at the Present Time," *ADE Bulletin*, No. 62 (September–November 1979): 12.

are deep continuities between the new New Criticism and the old, that does not mean we have replicated the hegemony of the fifties, for whatever deconstruction (and the many other theoretical movements of the last decade) may be interested in ruling, one of those things is not contemporary poetry, and from the point of view of the poets—given the experience of the fifties—that is probably a decided advantage. Of course, in practice, contemporary criticism, like the poetry, has been pluralistic, and it has provided a large body of writing about recent poetry, much of it dogged and mediocre, some of it enlivening and substantive.[29] In fact, some of the best of this work has been done at the margin of the theoretical activity, by critics like Charles Altieri, Cary Nelson, Marjorie Perloff, Helen Vendler, all of whom have been stimulated and challenged by contemporary theory but who, rather than simply being swallowed up by it, have evolved independent positions from which to practice—i.e., to adopt the role of mediator between an unfamiliar poetry and its readers by assessing reputations, interpreting opaque texts, and mapping a new territory.[30] Nevertheless, the criticism of our recent poetry, like the poetry itself, has produced no masters—no Eliot, not even a Tate—with the power of dictating a generation's values, its canon, its poetics. As we have seen, the result is that contemporary poetry resembles a flourishing liberal community in which power is dispersed, production lively and abundant, coercions invisible, boundaries hard to locate, and resistance hard to mount or even to imagine.

Perhaps the disjunction between critical theory and poetic practice has been a loss more for criticism than poetry. Like the New Criticism, deconstruction, with its recurrent figures of the web, the tapestry, and the labyrinth, spatializes literature, enclosing and sealing it off from material and temporal reality. When the poetic generation of 1960 spoke of "opening" poetry, they meant more than the breaking of external, predetermined forms; they were talking about extending their medium toward a world of *independent* objects in *temporal* flux. An open poetics is thus inevitably an historical poetics and, as Cary Nelson has shown, such a poetics both made possible and limited this generation's response when confronted with an historical crisis—the war in Vietnam.[31] Their poetic project, from the first, was to avoid the danger of either self-imposition or self-surrender. Both of those possible traps are connected with long-standing philosophical dilemmas. How, for example, can a poet know when projecting has

29. I base these remarks on my two years' experience writing the chapter "Poetry: The 1930s to the Present" for *American Literary Scholarship*.

30. Charles Altieri, *Enlarging the Temple;* Cary Nelson, *Our Last First Poets* (Urbana, 1981); Marjorie Perloff, *The Poetics of Indeterminacy* (Princeton, 1981); Helen Vendler, *Part of Nature, Part of Us* (Cambridge, Mass., 1980).

31. *Our Last First Poets,* passim.

ceased and perception of objects has begun—assuming that it can begin? Or, if the poet can enter the temporal flux, how can he or she avoid being swallowed up by it—without claiming for himself an ego or center that is outside time? Among the poets I have dealt with O'Hara explored these problems most fully and deeply, mainly because he never kidded himself into thinking he had solved them. Objects in O'Hara possess an independence and particularity—or presence—while they enter an imaginative space that is admittedly illusory, fictive, and theatrical. O'Hara thus combines maximum self-consciousness with maximum immediacy. Similarly, John Ashbery mixes a severe self-consciousness about the act of writing with an emotional immediacy, as in a poem like "A Man of Words."

> His case inspires interest
> But little sympathy; it is smaller
> Than at first appeared. Does the first nettle
> Make any difference as what grows
> Becomes a skit? Three sides enclosed,
> The fourth open to a wash of the weather,
> Exits and entrances, gestures theatrically meant
> To punctuate like doubled-over weeds as
> The garden fills up with snow?
> Ah, but this would have been another, quite other
> Entertainment, not the metallic taste
> In my mouth as I look away, density black as gunpowder
> In the angles where the grass writing goes on,
> Rose-red in unexpected places like the pressure
> Of fingers on a book suddenly snapped shut.
>
> Those tangled versions of the truth are
> Combed out, the snarls ripped out
> And spread around. Behind the mask
> Is still a continental appreciation
> Of what is fine, rarely appears and when it does is already
> Dying on the breeze that brought it to the threshold
> Of speech. The story worn out from telling.
> All diaries are alike, clear and cold, with
> The outlook for continued cold. They are placed
> Horizontal, parallel to the earth,
> Like the unencumbering dead. Just time to reread this
> And the past slips through your fingers, wishing you were there.[32]

Perhaps Ashbery has just finished reading a diary, snapped it shut and is ruminating over the author who has put his life into words; perhaps Ash-

---

32. *Self-Portrait in a Convex Mirror* (New York, 1976), p. 8.

bery is examining his own life as "a man of words." In his poems literal situations are occasionally glimpsed only to slip through our fingers—a quality that makes Ashbery's poems superficially unlike but deeply like those of O'Hara. What *is* clear is that the poem begins with a cold, definitive judgment that possibly echoes Pound's harsh self-estimate in "Mauberly": "the case presents / No adjunct to the Muses' diadem." Motivating his opening dismissal is Ashbery's sense that the painful sting that originally provoked the writer to words *may* be lost as it "grows" into a "skit"; nature becomes artifice, experience becomes theatricalized, in the act of verbal expression, particularly since the writer makes "gestures" rhetorically "meant" to elicit a poignant sense of loss from his audience. With a sidelong ironic critique of Williams's effort in *Paterson* to "comb" language out of experience, Ashbery suggests that combing out the tangles achieves clarity and mastery but entails loss or reduction of "the truth." Both the detachment and absence of writing make "diaries," ordinarily thought to be the most spontaneous and least theatrical of works, all "alike": "clear and cold, with / The outlook for continued cold." They are flat, "horizontal," because they lack difference and distinction. In this way Ashbery comes close to affirming J. Hillis Miller's notion of language as a web of familiar figures.

But Ashbery actually affirms that writing can achieve life and substance, and he makes good that claim in his own poem. He speaks of a natural, Whitman-like "grass writing" that "goes on," appearing "rose-red in *unexpected* places," a writing marked with human presence the way the cover of a book is marked by "the pressure / Of fingers" when "suddenly snapped shut." Behind the inevitable "mask" we discover a human presence, a fine sensibility that sounds effete ("continental") but also possesses a rare distinction which may be "dying" but not dead on the "breeze" that inspires "speech." At the end of "A Man of Words" Ashbery makes a gesture that may either be self-reflexive or an entirely new turn; "reread *this*" can refer to the poem he has been writing or to an old postcard with "wishing you were here" written on it. In any case, the poem closes with two clichés which emphasize the gap between lived experience and the dead words we're fated to repeat. But the last line is not cold, detached, and final like the opening sentence; instead, it is funny and moving, the very familiarity of the phrases makes them human, and they thus establish a connection while recognizing the reality of absence. Unlike the conception of the poem offered by either the old or the new New Critics, Ashbery's work is not a self-reflexive verbal system, nor, for all of its allusions, does it merely add a new wing to the labyrinth of intertextuality. Writing for Ashbery is not simply sterile artifice, and art is not a "prison-house"; with "three sides enclosed, / the fourth open to a wash of the weather," the literary work is both stable and unstable, spatial and temporal, formed yet open to time, change, life.

From this point of view, literature has no permanent essence any more than it has a permanent canon; literature is an open concept, an activity always in process, though its activities may be more dynamic at some times than others. At any given historical moment, however, literature will be understood as stabilized—bounded in a way that produces a hierarchy of kinds of writing, a canon, and certain kinds of literary activity will accordingly be relegated to the margin or even outside of it. The fifties offer a particularly vivid instance of such stabilization ossifying, partly because based on such a rigid set of exclusions. Even with its wider pluralism, the early eighties has its own boundaries, though they will probably not be clear to us until they are challenged by some strongly innovative poets. All "definitions" of literature are, then, necessarily incomplete, provisional, "open to the weather," subject to negation, renewal, modification, extension, or resistance. The same may be said for interpretations of literature; in writing this book, my own view has been that criticism is an imaginative activity, located in time (and history), and inspired by object love. Both sides in the recent theoretical debate about determinacy versus indeterminacy in reading have assumed that any uncertainty or instability necessarily means either total free play or total chaos, depending upon whether one happens to be celebrating or lamenting the results. With such logical absolutism, the text disappears, and without the text as limiting otherness, the literary critic becomes a solipsist—Ahab in a three-piece suit. My own attempt at reading has been to treat works as if they were stable—just as (to return to Ashbery's metaphor) the actors and audience in a theater conventionally behave as if the fourth wall *were* there. My point is not just that texts are in some sense there, but that it's even possible to care about them enough to read them intensively without deluding one's self into thinking that one has forever fixed their meanings or interpreted them exhaustively. After all, who does own any thing?

Index